The South and the Politics
of Slavery, 1828–1856

The South and the Politics of Slavery 1828–1856

WILLIAM J. COOPER, JR.

LOUISIANA STATE UNIVERSITY PRESS
Baton Rouge and London

Manufactured in the United States of America
1990 printing
Designer: Albert Crochet
Type Face: VIP Caledonia
Typesetter: The Composing Room of Michigan, Inc.
Printer: Thomson-Shore, Inc.

LIBRARY OF CONGRESS CATALOGING IN PUBLICATION DATA

Cooper, William James, 1940–
   The South and the politics of slavery, 1828–1856.

   Bibliography: p.
   Includes index.
1.   Southern States—Politics and government—1775–1865.
2.   Slavery in the United States—History.   I.   Title.
F213.C69   320.9′75′03   78–751
ISBN 0–8071–0775–1

For Mamie Mayes Cooper and Patricia Holmes Cooper

Contents

Acknowledgments

THIS BOOK has been a long time in the making. During the eight years that I worked on it many individuals and institutions gave me invaluable assistance. I am especially indebted to the numerous keepers of manuscripts who guided my way through their collections. To name each of them individually would require an additional chapter. Thus I thank collectively all those who aided me; the libraries they serve are listed in the bibliography.

In addition I am grateful to those who provided the financial assistance that greatly expedited my research and writing. My own Louisiana State University has been important: a series of summer grants from the Council on Research assisted in various stages of my work; a sabbatical award was instrumental in the completion of the book. The year I spent at the Institute of Southern History at The Johns Hopkins University in 1971–1972 was invaluable. The Institute provided a base for extended work in the Library of Congress and an excellent opportunity for the early testing of ideas. At the Charles Warren Center for Studies in American History at Harvard University, where I had a rewarding year in 1975–1976, I found a superb environment for discussion and writing. In fact I wrote the bulk of the book there.

I am also delighted to express my gratitude to my publisher. Working with the Louisiana State University Press has been a signal pleasure. Leslie Phillabaum, Beverly Jarrett, and Martha Hall all made every effort to strengthen the manuscript and ease the transformation of manuscript to book.

Without the unswerving support of friends and colleagues I would never have come to write these acknowledgments. William W.

Freehling encouraged me at the beginning and remained a steadfast supporter. T. Harry Williams and John L. Loos always responded to my calls for assistance. My former teacher David Herbert Donald has continued to be both a demanding critic and a generous friend. Karl A. Roider and R. Jackson Wilson provided indispensable aid at critical moments. Peter Kolchin listened patiently, read thoroughly, and criticized intelligently. From the beginning of this project to its conclusion Michael F. Holt listened endlessly, read repeatedly, and criticized piercingly. In the time he gave to my manuscript and me he could almost have written his own book.

Still, of course, none of the institutions or individuals noted is responsible for what is between these covers. They have contributed mightily to whatever value this book has, but it is mine. And I accept full responsibility for it.

Preface

EIGHT YEARS AGO I started out to write a history of the Democratic party in the antebellum South. But soon after I began my research, I realized that my focus of interest had changed. It changed because I became intrigued by a theme that kept appearing in the Democratic newspapers and manuscripts. I expected to find southern Democrats consumed with the slavery issue in the 1850s, but I did not expect to find that they were wrapped up in it twenty years earlier. When southern Whig sources revealed an identical concern covering the same years, I turned my attention to the rhetoric that appeared to be at the heart of southern political discussion. A closer look at the political rhetoric confirmed my initial impression. From the 1830s on into the 1850s—during the lifespan of what historians call the second American party system, the competition between the Democratic and Whig parties—southern politicians constantly talked about slavery and slavery-related issues. I was particularly struck by the sectional one-upsmanship practiced by the two parties; Whigs and Democrats strove to best each other as protectors of slavery and champions of the South. So I turned from the history of a party to what I call the politics of slavery, a term designating the world created by the interaction of the four major forces in antebellum southern politics: the institution of slavery, southern parties and politicians, the southern political structure, and the values of southern white society.

My focus on slavery as the fulcrum of southern politics represents, in part, a return to an older view. I am certainly not the first historian to insist that slavery dominated the southern political landscape, but unlike others who have discussed the connection, I have brought to this theme a massive documentation that emphasizes southern newspapers and manuscripts of southern politicians. My book is also the first full account of southern political history (excluding studies of individual states) that links the Jacksonian era with the 1850s. In addition I have not considered slavery as an influential institution that remained apart from politics. Instead I have tried to show that slavery, the political system, and the values of southern white society interacted to create the politics of slavery, which prevailed in the South from the time of Andrew Jackson to the eve of secession.

My book is a study of the counterpoint between continuity and change. Because slavery remained constantly at the center of the political debate in the South, continuity forms a powerful theme in southern politics. I was especially impressed that the controlling issues of the Jacksonian South remained the controlling issues of southern politics down to the demise of the second party system in the 1850s. I disagree fundamentally with historians who make the politics of the Jacksonian South a politics defined by economics and finance. I do not think the evidence supports such an interpretation, and in Chapter Three I present my case for the relative unimportance of such questions and the primary importance of slavery-related ones.

Although slavery remained the central axis of political debate in the South, the specific issues changed over time. As a political issue slavery assumed many forms, from abolition petitions to territorial expansion. This pattern of change involved more than mere cosmetic alterations. It affected not only the accent of political rhetoric, but also two vastly more important areas: the relations between the northern and southern wings of the major parties and the South's image of itself in the nation.

The South was not exempted from national social and economic changes that were taking place—changes such as geographical expansion with its concomitant migration of people, population increase, growth of towns and cities, and economic fluctuation. While my book does not detail such changes, it does insist that they had little impact on southern politics. Through all, the politics of slavery dominated the South. As the southern social and economic worlds changed, so did the political world of the South. The great southern parties, Democratic and Whig, knew both victory and defeat; their political fortunes rose and fell. Operating in this atmosphere of political flux, politicians searched for political certainty. In their quest they returned again and again to slavery-related issues. Their perception of where their party stood with the southern electorate, and vis-à-vis the opposition party, clearly influenced their attitude toward the politics of slavery that above all else dominated the South.

The relative standing between parties in the South was matched and ultimately overshadowed by the relations between those parties and their northern counterparts. This North-South relationship definitely did not remain the same from the 1820s to the 1850s, though the conception of the party compact held by the southern politicians never changed. The South enjoyed notable influence in the early Jackson or Democratic party and in early Whiggery. From their special place southern politicians demanded special privileges and considerations from their northern comrades. Chiefly they insisted that party policy on slavery-related questions conform to their needs. In the beginning the southerners largely had their way, and when northern Democrats and Whigs became increasingly reluctant to grant them most-favored-partner status, the southerners never relented in their demands. Finally, northern refusal to adhere to the southern conception of the party compact contributed significantly to the death of the second party system. The causes of this northern shift remain largely unexplored; few topics in antebellum history beg more insistently for a historian.

The politics of slavery built a politics of unity that blunted class differences and helped prevent any political clash between slaveowners and nonslaveowners which could threaten the security of the slave system. On the vexing question of unity and disunity in the white South, I stand with those who emphasize unity. In the political arena southern politicians did not speak simply for the few who actually owned slaves. In its political form slavery became the cherished, visible symbol of independence, honor, and equality precisely because it embraced the most fundamental values of southern white society held in common by slaveowner and nonslaveowner alike.

The potency of slavery also affected the way southerners looked at parties and politics. And my findings suggest that southerners certainly viewed them differently from northerners. Most recent students of northern politics have argued that local issues predominated, that national questions were secondary and distant. These historians have also asserted that sectional issues were not nearly so important as economic, ethnic, and religious ones, even in the 1850s. On both counts the southern experience was strikingly different. In the first place slavery-related issues always occupied center stage in southern politics (with one brief exception, which I discuss in Chapter Five), and this omnipresent concern sparked a deep and abiding interest in national politics, which always remained at the center of the southern political vision. For southerners, then, parties served chiefly as the advocates and guardians of their rights in the nation. Although local issues certainly influenced local contests, the issues discussed and the elections held all came under the canopy of the politics of slavery, and though local issues often stemming from intrastate rivalries were important in defining local politics, they paled in comparison with the politics of slavery, which overrode differences between as well as within states from the Potomac to the Rio Grande.

Having briefly described what my book is about, I want to add a few words on what it is not about. In focusing on the South as a whole I have not discussed in detail the specifics of state politics, and I have made no extensive analysis of local voting strengths, either quantitative or nonquantitative. Because all southerners were caught up in the politics of slavery, I have not tried to establish the economic or social or cultural basis for who became Whigs and Democrats. Confronting the politics of slavery southern Whigs and Democrats acted similarly. Although important in themselves, questions involving the social origins of Democrats or the economic structure of Whig counties were, for my purposes, largely irrelevant, as were problems of local party membership and the sources of local voting strength.

When writing about the antebellum South one can choose between the fifteen slave states and the eleven Confederate states. I chose the latter because the act of secession affirmed a powerful southernism. In contrast the refusal of the border states to secede revealed, in part, that different forces guided their destinies. Accordingly, when I use *southern*, I am usually referring to the eleven states that joined the Confederacy; this definition especially applies to election results and congressional votes. Chronologically I begin with the formation of the Jackson, or Democratic, party in the late 1820s. Because the central thrust of my story deals with the impact of the Democratic and Whig parties on each other and on the South, I close my narrative in 1856 when the elimination of an anti-Democratic party dramatically changed the party situation. But equally as important for my closing date—by then no new party could arise in the South under the rules governing the politics of slavery.

The South and the Politics
of Slavery, 1828–1856

Prologue
An Election

DURING THE SUMMER of 1849, Democrats in the Fourth District of Mississippi eagerly anticipated the upcoming congressional election. The district had been traditionally Democratic, and in 1849 an extremely popular incumbent, Albert G. Brown, carried the party banner. Twice governor of the state, he had won his first congressional race in 1847 without any Whig opposition and was considered an orthodox Democrat on such economic issues as opposition to banks and a protective tariff.

But the issue in 1849 was not economics; the issue was slavery. In that year Mississippians were preoccupied with the Wilmot Proviso, the effort to have Congress exclude slavery from the territories newly acquired from Mexico. On this issue Brown was the Democratic spokesman. The proviso, he had cried, was an unmitigated evil, a "black injustice" which called on southerners to abandon their birthright as Americans and their pride in themselves. "Never will [the South] submit to a wrong like this; no, sir; never, never, never!" Neither he nor his constituents would ever surrender "principle and honor."[1]

To defeat Brown, the Whigs in the district had to have an equally vigorous southern champion. In Zachary Taylor's race for the presidency the year before, they had pulled to within 120 votes of the Democrats, and with a strong candidate they believed they could build on Taylor's performance and reverse the loyalty of the district. They found one: William Winans, a slaveowning Methodist minis-

---

1. M. W. Cluskey (ed.), *Speeches, Messages, and Other Writings of the Hon. Albert G. Brown, a Senator in Congress from the State of Mississippi* (Philadelphia: Jas. B. Smith, 1859), 140–41, 149–50; Natchez *Free Trader*, July 25, 1849.

ter, a pioneer settler in southwest Mississippi, and a good Whig. Although his religious background and political affiliation might win a few votes, the Whigs knew that his success or failure depended on the ardency of his support for slavery.

To the voters of the Fourth District, they presented Winans as a man "identified with us in interest and in feeling." When Methodists in their national conferences had debated the morality of slavery, Whig newspapers revealed, Winans had supported the institution eloquently. "In an assembly of men hostile to Southern rights," one editor wrote, "He, single-handed, boldly defended our rights." When the Methodists persisted in condemning slaveholding, he refused to repudiate his section or its values. He even gave up an opportunity to become bishop rather than betray his loyalty to the South or release his slaves. In 1844, when the Methodists had divided into northern and southern churches, Winans worked with his southern brothers to establish the Methodist Episcopal Church, South. A man of such stalwart southern credentials, the Whigs proclaimed, would not rest in defense of southern rights. A victory for Winans was a victory for the South.[2]

But this Whig charge did not stampede the Democrats. Brown and his followers predictably condemned Winans' stand on the tariff and swiped at the injudiciousness of a man "throw[ing] aside the Bible and tak[ing] up the tomahawk and war club of Federal Whiggery." On the critical issue, slavery, they concentrated, and they knew they had the Whigs defeated. They revealed to the voters that in an address to the American Colonization Society in New York City in 1846, Winans had termed slavery a social evil and called for colonization as a remedy. No more needed to be said. Brandishing that speech like a flaming torch, the Democrats cried

2. Natchez *Courier*, August 28, September 7, 14, 21, October 14, 16, 1849; Vicksburg *Tri-Weekly Whig*, September 18, 1849; Jackson *Mississippian*, October 5, November 30, 1849; *Biographical and Historical Memoirs of Mississippi* . . . (2 vols.; Chicago: Goodspeed, 1891), II, 1059–63.

that Winans had defamed the South, that he had besmirched southerners as "destitute of morality."

Across the Fourth District went the Democratic cry, "Treason
stalks in our midst." They accused Winans of preaching an "heretical
doctrine" that endangered the South. A vote for Winans, shrieked
the Democrats, meant a vote for dishonor, for submission to the
North, and for surrender of southern equality. To elect Winans
would "put a song in the mouth of our enemies," that would become
the dirge for southern honor and independence.

The only alternative, the Democrats argued, was to elect Brown,
"whose whole life has been devoted to Southern rights." They
praised him for "his bold and manly defence of the South and her
institutions, and the firm and unyielding stand he assumed upon the
Southern question." They even called to the Whigs to "overleap the
party walls" and protect their honor and southern rights by voting
for Brown.[3]

Stunned by this hole in their paladin's armor, the Whigs rushed to
repair it. Editorials and letters attested to Winans' devotion to
southern rights and his commitment to protect southern honor and
equality. Winans himself admitted that he had called slavery a social
evil, but he argued that there was a distinction between social and
moral evils. To Winans the latter was the fundamental concern, and
on it he was as sound as Brown or anyone else. Pointing to his own
slaves, Winans reminded the voters that he had lived as a
slaveowner and expected to die as one; moreover his children were
also slaveholders. In short, Winans claimed that he cherished the
same values honored by his fellow Mississippians.[4]

In the end Winans' fine arguments and sincere assurances did no
good. The Whig dreams of summer shattered under a Brown landslide. Piling up a two-to-one majority, Brown even ran ahead of the

3. Natchez *Free Trader*, September 15, 22, October 13, 17, 20, November 10, 1849;
Jackson *Mississippian*, October 5, 1849.
4. Natchez *Courier*, September 21, October 12, 23, 1849.

Democratic gubernatorial candidate, who also lived in the Fourth District. Congratulating themselves on their triumph, the Democrats had no doubt that their position on slavery had made the difference. Even "battalions of patriotic whigs," they chortled, had refused to follow their party down "a truckling submissive path." To the Democrats, Brown's victory demonstrated conclusively that southerners would never surrender their equality or compromise their honor.[5]

Neither the style nor the substance of this campaign was confined to the Fourth District of Mississippi or to the year 1849. This contest of the parties and their candidates to champion the South and slavery, symbol of the South's most cherished values, dominated antebellum southern politics. And it all began with Andrew Jackson.

---

5. Natchez *Free Trader*, November 10, 28, 1849.

1 The South and the Early Jackson Party

ANDREW JACKSON STRODE across southern politics like an Olympian among mortals. Men flocked to his banner simply because he carried it. Professing devotion to Jackson personally, Virginia's Henry Wise announced, "I would have voted for him against all odds." One of Jackson's young followers in Mississippi recalled that he "found [him]self a democrat without being able to explain why [he] was of that party." "I began," he exclaimed, "as a follower of Jackson knowing nothing of the Force Bill, regarding 'nullification' as a heresy without knowing what it meant." Jackson's electoral triumphs in the South sometimes challenge credulity. In 1828 he received 81.4 percent of all popular votes cast; four years later, though he lost ground in the nation as a whole, he swept the southern states with an astonishing average of 88 percent of the popular vote.[1]

Even though Jackson stood as a hero for the entire country his southern image was special. After all, the Battle of New Orleans catapulted him to national fame. The political power of the Democrats in Louisiana stemmed not from "issue or principle" but directly from "the strength of Andrew Jackson"—a strength founded on the great victory and personal ties formed by Jackson at that time. A public rally in New Orleans in 1832 underscored the direct link between military victory and political success: "Resolved, that as

---

1. Wise to James Hambleton, October 13, 1855, in Garnett-Wise Papers, Southern Historical Collection, University of North Carolina; Wiley P. Harris, "Autobiography of Wiley P. Harris," in Dunbar Rowland (ed.), *Courts, Judges, and Lawyers in Mississippi, 1789–1835* (Jackson: Hederman Bros., 1935), 287; Edward Stanwood, *A History of the Presidency from 1788–1897* (New ed. rev. by Charles Knowles Bolton; 2 vols.; Boston and New York: Houghton Mifflin, 1926), I, 146, 163.

citizens of Louisiana, we owe a special debt of gratitude to the leader of the band of citizen soldiers, who on the 8th of January, 1815, repulsed the invader from our shores." White men in the old Southwest remembered that Jackson had destroyed Indian braves as well as British soldiers; he had made their hearths safe and to him they owed fealty. A visitor in Alabama reported that Jackson and his chief military aides were "worshipped as Deities." The chairman of the Mississippi State Democratic Convention of 1834 described Jackson as the one man who during the time of Indian danger "gallantly flew to our relief." For white Mississippians, Jackson "ha[d] fought every foe; ha[d] conquered in every field." George Gilmer, a governor and a congressman, remembered that "All in Georgia were Jackson men whilst General Jackson was in office."[2]

Besides saving the South from redcoat and redskin, Jackson was a southerner. That he was born in South Carolina, reached maturity in Tennessee, and early began to accumulate two possessions dear to white southerners—land and black slaves—clearly identified him as one of them. That personal identity, easily spilling over into politics, assumed striking importance. Announcing the election of Willie P. Mangum as the new United States senator from North Carolina, Marshall Polk told his brother James that Mangum was "a most thorough and uncompromising friend of General Jackson" and "a genuine and unblushing *Southron* in feeling and principle." To Marshall Polk the two went hand in hand. Carrying the Jacksonian message to Louisiana sugar planters, a group inclined toward the administration of John Quincy Adams and its tariff views, the energetic Democratic organizer John Slidell emphasized the intimacy between sugar and slavery and then pointed out that Jackson was a

2. Joseph George Tregle, Jr., "Louisiana in the Age of Jackson: A Study in Ego-Politics" (Ph.D. dissertation, University of Pennsylvania, 1954), 213–20, 415; New Orleans *Louisiana Courier*, October 8, 1832; Anne Newport Royall, *Letters from Alabama, 1817–1822*, ed. Lucille Griffith (University, Ala.: University of Alabama Press, 1969), 123; Jackson *Mississippian*, June 13, 1834; George R. Gilmer, *Sketches of Some of the First Settlers of Upper Georgia, of the Cherokees, and the Author* (Americus, Ga.: Americus Book, 1926), 438.

slaveowning southerner. In Alabama, Jackson was idolized as the "hero of the South."[3]

Jackson's southern identity underlay not only his popular appeal in the South but also the strategy used by the builders of the Jackson or Democratic party in the South between 1825 and 1828. Jackson himself made no overt use of that identity; in fact his role in party building was largely passive. But his southern organizers and supporters invoked his name as the new apostle of the South, the new Jefferson, the new sentinel of southern power and prerogative in the nation. These southern Jacksonians, believers in the Old Republican faith, were concerned with getting back to their conception of first principles—a small federal government that had severely limited powers, strict construction of the Constitution, states' rights, the doctrines professed in the Virginia and Kentucky resolutions. Belief in this faith identified "a Democrat of the Jackson School." Such a Democrat, as the youthful William Gilmore Simms described himself, was "a States rights man, opposed to Tariffs, Banks, Internal Improvements, American Systems, Fancy Railroads, Floats, Land Companies, and every Humbug East or West, whether of cant or cunning."[4]

Most southern political leaders believed that their creed had been endangered in the whirlwind of nationalism following the War of 1812 that culminated in the grand national vision of John Quincy Adams. Faced with Adams' administration, southerners had to embrace Jackson, in John C. Calhoun's view, to forestall the total triumph of an Adams-type nationalism inimical to the South. Likewise the Old Republicans of Virginia and the seaboard South

3. Marshall Polk to James K. Polk, December 19, 1830, in Herbert Weaver, *et al.* (eds.), *The Correspondence of James K. Polk* (3 vols.; Nashville: Vanderbilt University Press, 1969–), I, 363; Tregle, "Louisiana in the Age of Jackson," 312; Royall, *Letters from Alabama*, 146.

4. See especially Richard H. Brown, "Southern Planters and Plain Republicans of the North: Martin Van Buren's Formula for National Politics" (Ph.D. dissertation, Yale University, 1955), Chaps. 2–3; Simms to James Lawson, December 29, 1831, in Mary C. Simms Oliphant, *et al.* (eds.), *The Letters of William Gilmore Simms* (5 vols.; Columbia: University of South Carolina Press, 1952–56), I, 167.

viewed Jackson as a bulwark against the nationalism that threatened their political and social world. Virginians especially acted on this premise. The controlling force in Virginia politics, the Richmond Junto dominated by Thomas Ritchie and his Richmond *Enquirer*, considered itself the guardian of ideological purity. For Ritchie and the junto the Jackson party promised redemption. These seaboard men often thought of the national government as their private preserve. From the birth of the nation they had contributed most of the men and the ideas that governed the new republic. If the purity of the faith had been diluted after 1812, and many thought it had, still the men in charge were seaboard men totally identified with the South and with Jeffersonian politics. Symbolically as well as realistically the passing of the Virginia dynasty signaled that the seaboard men could no longer think of the national government as their particular province. Fearful of the nationalism that seemed to herald their declining importance, they canonized the Republican dogma of the 1790s systematized in the Virginia and Kentucky resolutions, which declaimed against national power. To them any transgression against that dogma denied the sanctity of their exegesis of the Jeffersonian gospel. Alexis de Tocqueville caught their mood exactly when he spoke of the "melancholy uneasiness" affecting southerners facing this nationalism.[5]

Southerners felt no aspect of this nationalism more keenly than what they called its tampering with slavery. Between the ratification of the Constitution and the War of 1812, outside hands had made no serious effort to touch slavery. But after 1815 came the American Colonization Society and its efforts to gain congressional funding, the Missouri crisis, and John Quincy Adams' proposed mission to the Panama Conference, each, in the minds of southerners, an unwarranted and dangerous attempt to involve the national government in slavery. When John Quincy Adams became president, cer-

5. Calhoun to Bolling Hall, January 12, 1833, in Bolling Hall Papers, Alabama Department of Archives and History; Lynwood M. Dent, "The Virginia Democratic Party, 1824–1847" (Ph.D. dissertation, Louisiana State University, 1974), 23–24; Alexis de Tocqueville, *Democracy in America*, ed. Phillips Bradley (2 vols.; New York: Vintage, 1954), I, 418–19.

tain southerners believed that in order to maintain his office he would attempt to array the nonslave states against the slave states; a few excitable souls even saw his encouraging slave rebellions to put down southern power.[6] Thus the Jackson party would protect not only Republican ideology but also southern guardianship of slavery, because by shackling the central government the ideology guaranteed local or southern control of all local questions, including slavery.

The organization of the early Jackson party certainly allowed, and even encouraged, southerners to think of it as their special party. Andrew Jackson headed a loosely knit and decentralized party, one which local leaders could define as a bastion defending their own interests and views. Even though Jackson's hero image and personal appeal dominated the party, he did not build it up in an organizational sense. Leading organizers of the Jackson party such as Martin Van Buren of New York in the North along with Old Republicans and Calhoun in the South used Jackson's name and popularity but they did the building, not he. In fact, when Jackson tried to work with the details of organization, he failed disastrously even in his own Tennessee.[7] Because southerners were so prominent in the creation of the party, they had every reason to think of it as a vehicle designed to carry them to their goals. Van Buren's firm belief in the Virginia doctrine and ready acknowledgment of southern political and ideological domination in the new party reinforced the southern conception of the party's identity and purpose.

Nothing in Jackson's own view of the party contradicted this assumption. For Jackson, party and politics, like everything else, became intensely personal. Loyalty was the key. Jackson simply transferred to politics his military requirement of loyalty to himself as

---

6. Dent, "Virginia Democratic Party," 75.

7. For an incisive discussion of this general point, consult Maurice Duverger, *Political Parties: Their Organization and Activity in the Modern State* (New York: John Wiley, 1963), 53, 63–67; Powell Moore, "The Revolt Against Jackson in Tennessee, 1835–1836," *Journal of Southern History,* II (1936), 335–59; James Edward Murphy, "Jackson and the Tennessee Opposition," *Tennessee Historical Quarterly,* XXX (1971), 50–69.

commander—his party became his new army. He did not view
politics through the eyes of the rising professional politicians. In
Jackson's time politics became a profession, one in which numerous
southerners excelled. And as Richard Hofstadter has noted, the new
professional separated political and personal relationships. But not
Jackson; he always referred to political enemies with such phrases as
"infamous, dastardly and vilainouss [sic]," "demagogues and apostates," "apostates and traitors," "jesuitical hypocrites and apostates," "odious and unnatural." When his old Tennessee associate
Hugh Lawson White turned against his insistence on Van Buren as
successor, Jackson assailed White as a man who "ha[d] been acting
the hypocrite all his life and individually to me." Jackson simply
tolerated no disagreements; to him personal and political loyalty
could not be divided. Jackson's longtime and valued friend, John
Coffee, advised Jackson's nephew and personal secretary, young
Andrew Jackson Donelson, "to make it a point not to mingle or
associate with anyone who the General believed, was either personally or politically unfriendly to him, although he may have un-
founded jealousies against individuals on that subject."[8]

Prior to Jackson's first administration, adherence to the Jackson
party demanded no specific creedal loyalty other than a general
support of original Jeffersonian principles and an opposition to the
Adams regime. Thus, for southerners, belonging to the Jackson
party meant loyalty to a venerated and self-protecting ideology and

8. Richard Hofstadter, *The Idea of a Party System: The Rise of Legitimate Opposition in the United States* (Berkeley and Los Angeles: University of California Press, 1969), 124–26, 215–26; Jackson to E. G. W. Butler, December 22, 1826, in Charles Gayarré Papers, Howard-Tilton Memorial Library, Tulane University; Jackson to William B. Lewis, March 4, 1839, in Andrew Jackson–William B. Lewis Correspondence, New York Public Library; Jackson to David Campbell, September 7, 1835, in David Campbell Papers, William R. Perkins Library, Duke University; Jackson to James K. Polk, August 13, 1839, in James K. Polk Papers, Division of Manuscripts, Library of Congress (all other Polk citations will be to this collection unless otherwise noted); Jackson to Andrew Jackson Donelson, May 12, 1835, in Andrew Jackson Donelson Papers, Division of Manuscripts, Library of Congress (all other Donelson citations will be to this collection unless otherwise noted); Jackson to Harvey M. Cryer, November 13, 1836, quoted in Moore, "Revolt Against Jackson," 358; Coffee to Donelson, August 8, 1831, quoted in Gordon T. Chappell, "The Life and Activities of General John Coffee," *Tennessee Historical Quarterly*, I (1942), 143.

to a fellow southerner and slaveowner who was a recognized wor-
shipper at the Jeffersonian church altar. Loyalty to party, then,
became crucial to three basic loyalties—to section, to social system,
to nation. [9] As southerners viewed national politics in the late 1820s,
only the success of the Jackson party insured sectional safety, social
security, as well as a proper direction and attitude in the national
government. All loyalties focused on and stemmed from the political
loyalty. For the South, political paradise seemed to have returned.

II

The southern unity forged by the Jackson party shone brilliantly in
1828. Adams made a respectable showing only in Louisiana, where
he gained 47 percent of the vote. Elsewhere southerners expressed
their preference for their candidate with dramatic unanimity—
Georgia led with 100 percent of its vote for Jackson; Tennessee gave
him 95 percent; Alabama and Mississippi over 80 percent; North
Carolina 73 percent; Virginia 69 percent; and though South Carolina
had no popular vote, its eleven electoral votes went for Jackson.[10]
Only Jackson himself possessed the power to break the front of his
southern phalanx, for only by his action or inaction could southerners see him as other than their political savior. The possibility of
disappointment did exist precisely because southerners expected so
much from their new redeemer. And in fact during his first term,
tremors of dissatisfaction rumbled within the South.

The most doctrinaire ideologues of the Old Republican group first
found Jackson wanting. These purists identified the tariff of 1828,
the hated Tariff of Abominations, as the most heinous manifestation
of the nationalist policy they abhorred. That protective tariff violated
their constitutional theory, for, as they interpreted the document, it
gave no permission for a protective tariff. Moreover, they saw pro-

9. For a brilliant discussion of the relationship among institutional loyalties see David
Potter, "The Historian's Use of Nationalism and Vice Versa," *American Historical Review*,
LXVIII (1962), 924–50.
10. Stanwood, *History of the Presidency*, I, 148.

tection as benefiting the North and hurting the South. When Jackson failed to strike a smashing blow at the tariff during his first two annual messages, these ideologues, mostly Virginians, began to wonder whether or not they had misplaced their trust.[11]

Additionally these Virginians looked to John C. Calhoun as the ideological preceptor of the new administration. Wary of Jackson's military background and impressed both with Calhoun's experience in statecraft and his intellectual power now turned with vehemence toward Old Republican doctrines, they expected Calhoun to provide guidance and character in Washington. His loss of favor and final break with Jackson caused great anguish among this group of Virginians. Now they saw Jackson repudiating virtue and ability as well as Old Republican tenets. Their spokesmen, Governor John Floyd and United States senators Littleton Waller Tazewell and John Tyler, turned to the South Carolinian.[12]

The term Old Republican is an inclusive one for Virginia Democrats of this period. Both leaders like Floyd and Tazewell who looked to Calhoun and those like Ritchie and his fellows in the Richmond Junto who opposed Calhoun identified themselves as Old Republicans. Although both groups professed loyalty to their conception of the doctrine of 1798, they differed on political matters both before and after the creation of the Democratic party. The Junto men were much more concerned about party in general and about loyalty to the Democratic party in particular than the men who went with Calhoun, none of whom belonged to the Richmond Junto.

Both politics and personalities doomed Calhoun.[13] Because of

11. Charles H. Ambler (ed.), "Diary of John Floyd," *John P. Branch Historical Papers of Randolph-Macon College,* V (1918), 119–21, 129–30, 132, 165; Dent, "Virginia Democratic Party," 85–87.

12. John Floyd to Duff Green, August 21, 1831, in Duff Green Papers, Division of Manuscripts, Library of Congress; John Tyler to Littleton W. Tazewell, May 3, 1831, in John Tyler Papers, Division of Manuscripts, Library of Congress; Dent, "Virginia Democratic Party," 91–93.

13. For the Jackson-Calhoun-Van Buren story see Charles M. Wiltse, *John C. Calhoun* (3 vols.; Indianapolis and New York: Bobbs-Merrill, 1944–51), II, Chaps. 5–6, and Brown, "Southern Planters," Chaps. 4–5; my account is based on those two sources.

political pressures from his native South Carolina and his own personal conviction, Calhoun had moved to an intransigent position on the tariff; protection must be abandoned and promptly. If not, then extreme measures—nullification or as Calhoun preferred, state interposition—were in order. Jackson, aware that he had more than doctrinaire South Carolinians and Virginians in his party, retained greater flexibility. Moreover, he denounced any remedies that seemed to threaten the Union as did the much discussed doctrine of nullification. Although Calhoun kept secret his intimate association with nullification until the summer of 1831, Jackson did not trust his vice-president. The confrontation at the Jefferson Day dinner in April, 1830, when Jackson pronounced his famous toast, "Our Federal Union—it must be preserved," served as public notice that the alliance between president and vice-president was indeed tenuous.

By the spring of 1830 Jackson had also come to believe that Calhoun had misled him in a personal matter, and that decision dictated a full and final break with Calhoun. Back in 1818 Jackson's activities in Florida had caused difficulties for him with some members of James Monroe's administration. Jackson thought that Calhoun, then secretary of war, had supported him in cabinet debates when in fact Calhoun had not. Since 1827 the two men had carried on an intermittent correspondence devoted to clarifying Calhoun's role in the events of 1818. By 1830 with the assistance of several close associates and an 1818 letter purloined from Calhoun's files Jackson convinced himself that Calhoun had been disingenuous and, even worse, personally disloyal—in Jackson's code the ultimate sin. The president reacted in typical Jackson fashion; Calhoun immediately became not simply an opponent but an apostate.

Calhoun's demise led to the ascendancy of Martin Van Buren. Van Buren had brought the southern Old Republicans to the Jackson standard and more than anyone else he had built the Jackson party. From the beginning of the coalition he and Calhoun hoped to succeed Jackson. With the Jackson-Calhoun break the way seemed open for Van Buren. Still both he and Jackson wanted to eliminate all Calhoun influence from the administration. To Van Buren's acute political eye such a purge ought to include cabinet reorganization. Accordingly he suggested a plan that included his own resignation as secretary of state followed by Jackson's requesting the other members to follow suit. By this method the cabinet was reorganized.

In the reshuffle, southerners John M. Berrien of Georgia and John Branch of North Carolina found themselves among the politically outcast.[14] Although neither had been, strictly speaking, a Calhoun man, each fell as a casualty in the Jackson-Calhoun feud. Not unexpectedly, their banishment engendered anger at Jackson and at Van Buren, whom they recognized as the villain in their piece. Angry, both Berrien and Branch went home to stir up opposition to the administration. Thus they joined the small but growing number of southerners who found Jackson and the Jackson party a bit less than saintly.

These dissidents found themselves in the political wilderness. The National Republicans comprised the only organized anti-Jackson group. That party had demonstrated its political impotence back in 1828, and nothing since that date indicated any upsurge in strength for the party of Adams and Henry Clay. Aside from its chronic political weakness the National Republican party offered no ideological warmth to the banished Jacksonians. Generally these exiles prided themselves on their Old Republican purity and orthodoxy. The nationalism of National Republicanism repelled and frightened them. In fact it had spurred their support for the Jackson party during the Adams presidency. The National Republican party simply did not provide an acceptable political alternative to the Jackson Democrat party.

But any move toward a new party both southern oriented and ideologically safe ran head-on into the powerful force of Andrew

14. Thomas P. Govan, "John M. Berrien and the Administration of Andrew Jackson," *Journal of Southern History*, V (1939), 447–67; William S. Hoffman, "John Branch and the Origins of the Whig Party in North Carolina," *North Carolina Historical Review*, XXXV (1958), 299–315.

Jackson. A party had to have followers as well as leaders. And these former Jacksonian leaders recognized that if they challenged Jackson directly, they would have few to lead. Jackson's personal popularity, according to one of his North Carolina opponents, probably exceeded that of the Constitution. Even the usually sanguine Calhoun admitted that few in the South would find fault with "the General Government" so long as Jackson directed it. John Tyler, who considered political popularity immoral, if not sinful, bemoaned that the South "shout[ed] hozannas with lusty lungs" for Andrew Jackson. Jackson's invincibility caused another Virginian to look beyond this world. "I fear we have no chance in Virginia," wrote John H. Pleasants, editor of the Richmond *Whig*, but "Jackson may die—God grant it, amen—if it be his will."[15]

Aware that they could not move directly against Jackson, these angry southerners vented their displeasure by attacking the man they considered their chief antagonist, Martin Van Buren. While the angriest and most eager of Calhoun's advocates strove to stop Jackson with one weird scheme after another—one even had the anti-Jackson men uniting behind William Wirt and the Anti-Mason party—most aimed at Van Buren. In 1832 Jackson formally designated Van Buren as the heir apparent by having him named as the vice-presidential nominee by the first Democratic national convention. By directing their assault specifically against Van Buren the southerners enabled themselves to continue professing loyalty to Jackson. Thus their professed goal became guaranteeing that the Jackson party stayed on its original, southern route.[16]

15. Daniel L. Barringer to Daniel M. Barringer, March 12, 1834, in Daniel M. Barringer Papers, Southern Historical Collection, University of North Carolina; Calhoun to James H. Hammond, January 15, 1831, in J. Franklin Jameson (ed.), *Correspondence of John C. Calhoun* (Washington: Government Printing Office, 1900), 281; Tyler to Littleton W. Tazewell, February 2, 1833, quoted in Lyon G. Tyler, *The Letters and the Times of the Tylers* (3 vols.; Richmond and Williamsburg: Whittet & Shepperson, 1884–85, 1896), Pleasants to James Barbour, March 23, 1832, in James Barbour Papers, New York Public Library.

16. Duff Green to Thomas Gilmer, September 24, 1832, in Duff Green Papers, Southern Historical Collection, University of North Carolina; Duff Green to William Wirt, August 9, 1832, Wirt to Dabney Carr, August 22, 1832, in William Wirt Papers, Maryland Historical Society; Robert Y. Hayne to Richard K. Crallé, May 26, 1832, in Richard K. Crallé Papers, Robert Muldrow Cooper Library, Clemson University; *Niles' Register*, XLII (July 7, 1832), 339; Milledgeville *Federal Union*, June 7, 21, 1832.

The news that Jackson intended to pass his mantle to Van Buren had occasioned a strong reaction among southern Jacksonians. James Iredell of North Carolina, in a letter to United States Senator Willie P. Mangum, put it bluntly: "Is it not of the utmost importance to the South that we should have a Vice-President of our principles?" The question of principles also concerned one of James K. Polk's Tennessee associates who feared that Van Buren, "a time serving schemer," would "embrace any doctrine and support any measure which would secure him the good will of the majority." Governor John Floyd found the prospect of Van Buren's accession appalling; to Floyd it augured the introduction of "Northern principles" which would "lead with a rapidity of lightening [*sic*] to the sudden and immediate emancipation of slavery." Many who described Van Buren in the friendliest of terms still found him "a little too far North for us Southern folks." Even Thomas Ritchie, Van Buren's partner in party building, looked upon the elevation of the New Yorker as a potential danger to the party in the South.[17]

To southerners, who saw the Jackson party as a vehicle for southern political power, handing its future leadership to a northerner seemed to undermine the rationale behind the party. The most doctrinaire and sectionally conscious felt the greatest danger, and expressed the fiercest outrage. Although anti-Van Buren sentiment surfaced across the South, Virginians took the lead in trying to stop his advance. Virginians still thought of their commonwealth almost as a nation within a nation; the chief political end was to reestablish Virginia's supremacy by naming a Virginian to head the party and the government. The Jackson party was an essential prerequisite, for the first step required the destruction of the nationalist doctrine of John Quincy Adams and Henry Clay. To attain that goal they

17. Iredell to Mangum, February 4, 1832, in Henry Thomas Shanks (ed.), *The Papers of Willie Person Mangum* (5 vols.; Raleigh: State Department of Archives and History, 1950–56), I, 472. Terry H. Cahal to Polk, May 4, 1832, in Weaver, *et al.* (eds.), *Polk Correspondence*, I, 472; Floyd to Thomas W. Gilmer, April 26, 1832, in Tyler Papers; George Blair to William S. Hamilton, May 23, 1832, in William S. Hamilton Papers (George M. Lester Collection), Department of Archives, Louisiana State University; Ritchie to Martin Van Buren, April 30, 1831, in Martin Van Buren Papers, Division of Manuscripts, Library of Congress.

accepted Andrew Jackson and worked to build a party that would
elevate the general to the nation's highest office. Then, however,
they expected a Virginian to become the champion of the new Jeffersonian party. To men of this bent Van Buren's new status as heir
apparent seemed to signal Virginia's permanent decline.

Virginians in opposition presented Philip P. Barbour as Virginia's
new gift to the party and the nation. Barbour had impeccable Old
Republican and Jacksonian credentials; President Jackson had even
offered him the post of attorney general in the aftermath of the great
cabinet reorganization. The Barbour crusaders raised anew the banner of 1798 and Old Republican principles. Judged against this hallowed text they found Van Buren lacking. In the spring of 1832
county Democratic meetings throughout Virginia urged the Democratic national convention to place Barbour with Jackson.[18]

Stalwart behind the Barbour movement stood men like Governor
Floyd and Thomas W. Gilmer, particular friends of Calhoun but
who had not yet publicly broken with Jackson. Calhoun's forthright
stand against the tariff had endeared him to many Virginian purists.
Forgiving him his early errors of nationalism they looked to him as
the national statesman most committed to their doctrines. For the
Calhounites in Virginia, replacing Van Buren with Barbour would
achieve two desired goals: eliminate the man they designated as the
great enemy both of Calhoun and of the Virginia doctrine as well as
symbolize the political resurgence of Virginia.

The Barbour movement perplexed the Richmond Junto, the organizational leadership of the Virginia party. In 1827 the junto had
commited itself not only to Jackson but to a conviction that only his
party united and strong could protect the doctrine and the institutions of Virginia and the South. Party loyalty became a necessary and
noble end, for only the unity based on loyalty insured victory over
nationalism and danger. Besides, if Virginia turned against Jackson's

18. Dent, "Virginia Democratic Party," 96–99, 106–15, has the fullest account of the
Barbour episode in Virginia; I borrowed heavily from it. *Niles' Register*, XLII (October 20,
1832), 124–25; Peter V. Daniel to Martin Van Buren, July 12, 1832, in Van Buren Papers;
Richmond *Enquirer*, spring, 1832, *passim*.

wishes, the general might turn against Virginia. Emphasizing these points Andrew Stevenson, junto member, speaker of the national House of Representatives, and Van Buren confidant, told Thomas Ritchie that Barbour must be kept off the ticket in Virginia. Virginia must support Van Buren; doing so, according to Stevenson, would give Virginia renewed leadership in the party by indebting Van Buren to Virginia. However, in late 1831 and very early 1832 the junto seemed to join the Barbour chorus. Jackson's firm decision to go with Van Buren plus Stevenson's admonitions braked that inclination. Ritchie opened the *Enquirer* to Van Buren's candidacy and spoke favorably of him. The junto also influenced the Virginia Democratic legislative convention to refrain from nominating Barbour for the vice-presidential position.[19] For Ritchie and the junto, the party meant more than Barbour.

Although the junto stopped the drive to put Virginia on record behind Barbour, it could not stifle all pro-Barbour sentiment. In fact most Virginia Democrats found it impossible to give up one of their own for Van Buren. At the Democratic national convention, held in Baltimore in May, the Virginia delegation, acting under the unit rule, cast its twenty-three votes for Barbour, almost one-half of his total of forty-nine votes. The convention, however, did Jackson's bidding and awarded the second spot to Van Buren, who won 208 votes and the nomination on the first ballot. Thereupon a call for unanimity received the approval of most Virginia delegates. A minority, Calhounites all, refused and walked out.[20]

That minority determined not to give up the fight for Barbour. Still they held back from criticizing Jackson. Rather they continued aiming at Van Buren, while promoting Barbour both as Old Republican and southerner. As Robert Y. Hayne suggested to a pro-Calhoun journalist in Virginia, "The Baltimore nomination will make a new issue, and one I think favorable to the Southern case."

19. Stevenson to Ritchie, February 4, 1832, in Van Buren Papers; Richmond *Enquirer*, February 2, March 1, 17, 1832.
20. Richmond *Enquirer*, May 25, 1832.

The fight for Barbour, Hayne declared, must be made on southern grounds. Denouncing Van Buren's northernness, the Barbour men presented their man as a fellow southerner. While they focused on Old Republican ideology, they also emphasized Barbour's southern identity. Of course these two appeals or arguments merged quite easily. The Barbour forces managed to organize a state convention and proclaimed a Jackson-Barbour ticket the true one for all southerners. [21]

Directed by the junto the regular Virginia Democrats struck back furiously. Ritchie's *Enquirer* praised Van Buren's opposition to internal improvements and his support for the lowered tariff of 1832 as well as Jackson's veto of the second Bank of the United States. Thus Van Buren stood arm-in-arm with Jackson and Virginia on all key measures in the Old Republican pantheon. Ritchie defined the Barbour movement as a front for Henry Clay and the National Republicans. Division in the Democratic ranks could only lead to the disaster of a nationalist triumph. The principles of the Virginia doctrine were too precious to risk. Under Ritchie's lash even Barbour's friends began to fall away just as Virginia's trees began to shed their leaves. Finally in October, declaring that he feared a split in the Virginia Democratic party could endanger Jackson's reelection, Barbour withdrew his candidacy and endorsed the Jackson–Van Buren ticket. On election day the dead-letter Jackson-Barbour ticket polled only 244 votes. [22]

In addition to Virginia a consequential Barbour movement appeared in four other states. A disgruntled John Branch pushed Barbour in North Carolina. Angry at being forced out of Jackson's cabinet, Branch and his followers wanted to topple their enemy Van Buren. Barbour became their agent. Pointing to the activity in

21. Hayne to Richard K. Crallé, May 26, 1832, and resolutions adopted by a Barbour meeting in Williamsburg, Va., on June 2, 1832, both in Crallé Papers, Robert Muldrow Cooper Library, Clemson University; Richmond *Enquirer*, June 19, 1832.

22. Richmond *Enquirer*, February 28, March 17, April 27, May 4, 25, June 8, October 10, 1832; Andrew Jackson to Felix Grundy, August 20, 1832, in Whitefoord Cole Collection, Manuscript Division, Tennessee State Library and Archives.

Virginia and questioning Van Buren's soundness on the tariff, the Branch forces declared that southerners could only trust one of their own. Barbour as southerner, cried the Branch men! In 1832 Branch and his supporters envisioned no new party; they did not challenge Jackson. Rather, as in Virginia, a Jackson-Barbour ticket was put forward as the true Democratic way.[23]

The same strategy evolved in Alabama and Georgia. In Alabama the extreme states' rights men, disgusted with Jackson's caution on the tariff, joined the Barbour march. Both factions of the Jackson party in Georgia remained totally loyal to the general. But one of them refused to accept Van Buren as his running mate. Because Van Buren had not stood by the South on the tariff, these Jacksonians asserted that the South could not trust him. Barbour, for them, became the man who would insure the ultimate triumph for principle and section. The Barbour rhetoric in Alabama and Georgia matched that in Virginia and North Carolina.[24]

In Mississippi the Barbour backers among the Jacksonians made the same points their eastern brethren had. First they affirmed their devotion and loyalty to Andrew Jackson. Then they announced their opposition to Van Buren's candidacy *"because* while a Senator in Congress, he proved himself unfriendly to the great interests of the Southern states." The Mississippi Barbour men did not advocate a new party; they wanted merely a vice-president "located in the south and of southern feeling." Philip P. Barbour was their choice. As a Madison County Jackson-Barbour meeting asserted: "The South is now moving in his behalf. Let our voice, too cheer them on."[25]

But as in Virginia, the Barbour affair in these four states proved abortive. The Jackson-Barbour ticket garnered but 3,855 votes out

23. Hoffman, "Branch and the Whig Party," 304–306; *Niles' Register,* XLII (July 7, 1832), 339.

24. Jonathan Mills Thornton III, "Politics and Power in a Slave Society: Alabama, 1806–1860" (Ph.D. dissertation, Yale University, 1974), 34; Milledgeville *Federal Union,* June 6, 21, July 5, October 11, 1832. Cf. Milledgeville *Southern Recorder,* October 18, November 1, 1832.

25. Vicksburg *Advocate & Register,* July 5, September 13, 20, 1832.

of more than 29,000 cast in North Carolina while the Jackson–Van
Buren slate received 21,009. In Alabama only 14 percent of the
voters backed the hopeless ticket. The ticket performed better in
Georgia and Mississippi, but because of particular circumstances in
those two states rather than a popular rush to Jackson and Barbour.
In Georgia, where the Jackson–Barbour ticket made its best showing, receiving roughly one-third of the vote, the vice-presidential
contest had become involved in a factional dispute among Georgia
Jacksonians. Even so the ticket ran far behind the vote normally
given for state candidates of the faction backing Barbour.[26]

The National Republicans in Mississippi probably accounted for a
substantial portion of the vote won by the Jackson-Barbour ticket in
that state. With no National Republican ballot in Mississippi, certain
National Republican newspapers urged their followers to back the
Jackson-Barbour ticket as the lesser of two evils. That plea was made
even though the National Republican party had played no role in
pushing Barbour. That the ticket ran strongest in the southwestern
plantation counties bordering the Mississippi River suggests that at
least some National Republicans took the advice, for their strength
in the state centered in those counties. Even so the Jackson-Barbour
ticket carried but one county and won only 1,571 votes, 27 percent of
the total vote cast.[27]

The Barbour movement simply never had any real authority and
punch. Everywhere either knowing and fearing the power of
Jackson's name or praising that name the dissidents tried to sidestep
it, but to no avail. They could not undo the general's choice of Van
Buren, and Andrew Jackson's name headed the ticket. Aside from
that difficulty no overriding issue appeared that could arouse the

26. Raleigh *Register*, November 23, 1832; Clanton W. Williams (ed.), "Presidential Elec-
tion Returns and Related Data from Ante-Bellum Alabama," *Alabama Review*, I (1948), 288;
Jack Nelson Averitt, "The Democratic Party in Georgia, 1824–1837" (Ph.D. dissertation,
University of North Carolina, 1956), 340–44, 373–75; Milledgeville *Georgia Journal*, December 10, 1832, and Stephen F. Miller, *The Bench and Bar of Georgia: Memoirs and
Sketches. With an Appendix Containing a Court Roll from 1790 to 1857, Etc.* (2 vols.;
Philadelphia: J. B. Lippincott, 1858), I, 267.
27. Natchez *Natchez*, October 12, 19, 1832; Vicksburg *Advocate & Register*, December
12, 1832.

voters to perceive the dangers enunciated by the Barbour campaign. The overwhelming majority of southern voters still placed their trust in Jackson, who still enunciated strict-construction sentiments; after all the hated Tariff of Abominations had been replaced in 1832 by a new tariff with lower rates and the Bank of the United States had been smashed. Also his Indian removal policy had made available thousands of new acres for southern farmers and planters. Moreover Jackson pronounced Van Buren trustworthy and safe. Although the Barbour supporters tried to make a sectional issue of the vice-presidency, they made little headway. The president was the key and from him the South had nothing to fear. By remaining in the Jackson camp the Barbour men undercut their own efforts. In sum, the Barbour movement was a leader movement. Southern leaders banished by Jackson or acutely sensitive to self-identified threats to states' rights claimed that the Van Buren candidacy prefaced a turning away from true Republicanism. They convinced few chiefly because Jackson still carried the party's banner and because they had no dramatic issue that galvanized a following.

2 The Arena of Southern Politics

I

NO LEADER MOVEMENT could triumph in southern politics, because from Andrew Jackson's time to the Civil War, southern politics was democratic politics. The democratization that swept across the nation during the first half of the nineteenth century definitely reached into the South.[1] Although nondemocratic features lingered in certain states until 1860, democratic reforms underscored a political system that glorified the sovereign people.

A broad suffrage forms the basis of any democratic political structure. In the pre–Civil War United States, broad and democratic suffrage meant the inclusion of all adult white males with no property or financial qualifications. Emphasizing this definition the historian of the suffrage during the prewar years subtitled his book, "From Property to Democracy."[2] Certainly the South fit this category, for by the mid-1850s every white male twenty-one years of age and over possessed the right to vote in every southern state.

Different states adopted this provision at different times, though most had come to it by the mid-1830s.[3] Practically speaking adult white male suffrage prevailed in Tennessee, Georgia, and, in part,

1. Fletcher M. Green, "Democracy in the Old South," *Journal of Southern History*, XII (1946), 3–23; Ralph A. Wooster, *The People in Power: Courthouse and Statehouse in the Lower South, 1850–1860* (Knoxville: University of Tennessee Press, 1969), *passim*, esp. Chap. 5, and *Politicians, Planters and Plain Folk: Courthouse and Statehouse in the Upper South, 1850–1860* (Knoxville: University of Tennessee Press, 1975), *passim*, esp. Chap. 5.
2. Chilton Williamson, *American Suffrage: From Property to Democracy* (Princeton: Princeton University Press, 1960).
3. The information in this section on political structure comes largely from state constitutions. The constitutions are most conveniently found in Francis Newton Thorpe (ed.), *The Federal and State Constitutions, Colonial Charters, and Other Organic Laws of the States, Territories, and Colonies New or Heretofore Forming in the United States of America* (7 vols.; Washington: Government Printing Office, 1909). I also made extensive use of Richard P. McCormick, *The Second American Party System: Party Formation in the Jacksonian Era* (Chapel Hill: University of North Carolina Press, 1966), 178–246, 287–303, 310–20 and the

North Carolina before 1800. By the 1830s each of these states made specific its commitment to white manhood suffrage, even though North Carolina retained one exception.[4] In 1810, by constitutional amendment, South Carolina dropped all property and tax-paying requirements. All the states that joined the Union in the nineteenth century—Alabama, Florida, Louisiana, Mississippi, Texas—gave the franchise to adult white males from the outset, except for Mississippi and Louisiana. Mississippi waited for only fifteen years after statehood before writing a democratic suffrage clause into her constitution in 1832. But Louisiana did not remove tax payment as a requirement for suffrage until 1845. In the South, only Virginia stood longer and more firmly by a restricted suffrage. Not until 1851 did Virginia, as a part of a broad constitutional reformation of the commonwealth's traditional political organization, confer the right to vote on all adult white males. Prior to the constitution of 1851 property qualifications had probably disfranchised between one-third and one-half of Virginia's white males.

After 1835 candidates for state offices generally had to meet no special qualifications. The practice in Virginia and South Carolina of maintaining property qualifications for legislators and governor to 1851 and to 1861 respectively was distinctly unusual. Louisiana dropped such requirements in 1845; and Tennessee, Georgia, and North Carolina dispensed with them in 1835. Mississippi had done the same three years earlier. Alabama, Arkansas, Florida, and Texas never had such provisions.

The states also turned over to the voters themselves the right of choosing their own leaders. Even before 1830 the voters chose presidential electors in all states except South Carolina, where the legis-

---

two books by Ralph A. Wooster cited in n. 1. The specific locations in Thorpe for state materials are: Alabama, I, 96–116; Arkansas, I, 268–87; Florida, II, 664–85; Georgia, II, 791–809; Louisiana, IV, 1380–1429; Mississippi, IV, 2032–2068; North Carolina, V, 2787–99; South Carolina, VI, 3258–69; Tennessee, VI, 3414–45; Texas, VI, 3547–68; Virginia, VII, 3812–52.

4. Until a constitutional amendment in 1856, North Carolina retained a freehold provision for voting for the state senate; this freehold requirement did not apply to the state house, to the governor, to presidential elections, to congressmen, to local officials.

lature retained that prerogative throughout the antebellum era. By the Jacksonian period governors also had to win the support of voters, not legislators. After 1830 only three of the older states kept that privilege in legislative hands. North Carolina's shift to a popularly elected governor in 1835 left only Virginia, where the same shift was not made until 1851, and South Carolina, where it was never made. The states that entered the Union after 1830, Arkansas, Florida, and Texas, all came in with constitutions stipulating the popular election of governors and presidential electors.

The second quarter of the nineteenth century also witnessed a powerful trend requiring state officers other than the governor as well as local officials to face the voters. As early as 1812 the justices of the peace in Georgia went before the voters of their county. In the mid-1830s Georgia and Tennessee thoroughly democratized local government; and the Mississippi constitution of 1832 specified popular elections for all state and county officials. In some states judges and militia officers received their commissions from the voters, though in others the legislature retained control especially over the bench. When Virginia in 1851 finally turned local government to local voters, only South Carolina kept control away from local citizens.

With few exceptions a democratic political structure pervaded the South from the 1830s to the war. These exceptions numbered but three. With Louisiana and Virginia joining the march by mid-century, only South Carolina refused to follow the democratic tune, but even that bastion had white manhood suffrage. Although a democratic structure by itself does not guarantee a democratic politics, it forms an essential part of such politics. To breathe life into inert form, the people or the voters must assert their power.

The power of voters comes from their voting. Voters in the antebellum South recognized that truth and acted on it by trooping to the polls in impressive numbers. Both in state elections and national or presidential elections, southern voters compiled an admirable record. The percentage of eligible voters in the South who cast ballots in presidential elections compared favorably—in fact almost exactly—to the percentage voting in the nation as a whole. Fewer than one-third of adult white males in the South voted in 1832 when Andrew Jackson smashed Henry Clay. But in 1836 one-half of those eligible exercised the franchise; then in 1840 and 1844 voter partici- pation reached beyond 75 percent. That kind of a turnout continued down to 1860, an election in which 69.5 percent of the southern voting population cast ballots. State elections generally brought out voters in equal, or even greater, numbers.[5] Such a performance provides indisputable evidence that southern politicians did not have passive constituents.

II

Politicians and both political parties in the South recited the cate- chism of the democratic faith and canonized the voters or the people as saints of the new religion. From podiums and editorial columns resounded the clear strains of the hymn: *"The Sovereignty of the People* is the great fundamental principle . . . to which we adhere." Southern politicians never tired of chanting "my reliance is on *the people.*" Paeans to "the virtues and intelligence of the people" re- verberated from the Potomac to the Rio Grande.[6]

The Jacksonian, or Democratic, party has traditionally been called the party of the people. Certainly in the South, Democrats made every effort to justify that definition. They reveled in their self-appointed mission as the voice of the people throughout the antebellum period. Singing out the Democratic creed, the Little Rock *Arkansas Banner* chorused, "The people are the only source of legitimate power." A Democratic convention in Texas echoed that

5. Richard P. McCormick, "New Perspectives on Jacksonian Politics," *American Histori- cal Review*, LXV (1960), 291–95; Green, "Democracy," 20 (according to Green, participation in the northern states totaled 69.7 percent); Brian G. Walton, "The Second Party System in Arkansas, 1836–1848," *Arkansas Historical Quarterly*, XXVIII (1969), 134, and "The Second Party System in Tennessee," *East Tennessee Historical Society's Publications*, No. 43 (1971), 25.

6. Jackson *Mississippian*, September 5, 1841; A. P. Upshur to Duff Green, February 23, 1844, in Green Papers, Southern Historical Collection, University of North Carolina; Robert H. White (ed.), *Messages of the Governors of Tennessee, 1796–1907* (8 vols.; Nashville: Tennessee Historical Commission, 1952–72), IV, 181.

cry when it proclaimed that "all power emanates from the people."
The venerable Richmond *Enquirer* constantly hammered away on
the theme that all Democrats acted for the people, the ultimate
judge of all public questions. As Governor Charles McDonald of
Georgia told Georgia legislators, "We, fellow citizens, are servants
of the people."[7]

Democrats always tried to brand their Whig opponents as
enemies of the people. Their cue came from the forceful language of
their great chieftain Andrew Jackson, who exclaimed, "a modern
Whigg [sic] . . . is synonimous [sic] to Federalism or aristocracy." In
1834 the New Orleans *Bee* condemned Whigs as aristocrats while
presenting the Democratic gubernatorial candidate as "OPPOSED TO
ODIOUS DISTINCTIONS—FRIENDLY TO POPULAR RIGHTS." North
Carolina Democrats called on the people to rise up and defeat the
evil intentions of the Federalists disguised as Whigs. Announcing
that Democracy signified "that the people govern," the chief Democratic newspaper in Georgia indicted the Whigs, or aristocrats, for
trying to relieve the people from the "troubles of government."
Thanking the citizens of Tennessee for electing him their governor
Andrew Johnson asserted that the Democratic party "correspond[ed] also to the Church Militant: both fight against error—one
in the moral, the other in the political field."[8]

Democrats expressed a fervent faith that "the will of the people in
the exercise of their constitutional and legal rights" would always
mean victory for their cause. Writing from the White House during
the first great Whig uprising, Andrew Jackson Donelson, President
Jackson's nephew and private secretary, discounted Whig pretensions. The Whigs "can do no harm," Donelson professed, because
"the great body of the people understand them and render all their
efforts harmless." Mississippi Democrats placed their trust in the

7. Little Rock *Arkansas Banner*, January 30, 1844; Houston *Telegraph*, March 2, 1848;
Richmond *Enquirer*, 1832–1854, *passim* (for a particular example see April 14, 1837); Milledgeville *Southern Recorder*, November 9, 1841.
8. Jackson to James K. Polk, February 7, 1845, in Polk Papers; New Orleans *Bee*, June 10,
1834; Raleigh *Standard*, December 9, 1837, April 3, 1839; Milledgeville *Federal Union*,
August 8, 1843; White (ed.), *Messages of Governors of Tennessee*, IV, 531.

"candid yeomanry of this State" who would surely defeat the Whigs, who were actually "tories in heart, soul and spirit."[9]

While the Democrats tried to gain exclusive rights to the mantle of the people, the Whigs made strenuous efforts to claim that mantle for themselves. When newly elected governor James C. Jones declared to the citizens of Tennessee in 1841 that "all political power must emanate from and concentrate itself in the hands of the people," he summarized the Whig creed. Never did the Whigs fall behind the Democrats as priests of democracy. "I shall at all times," Jones went on to tell his inaugural audience, "hold myself amenable to the bar of public sentiment." Searching for a gubernatorial candidate in 1834, a Georgia Whig editor wrote that "our candidate must emphatically be the people's candidate." Whigs in Mobile affirmed "that the Whigs of Mobile approve such measures only, as will promote the interest of the people." The Richmond *Whig* found the basic Whig truth in "the simple, the plain, the old-fashioned, the recognized in all ages, Republican maxim, that *the majority*, and *the majority only*, have a right to rule."[10]

Defiantly the Whigs denied any association with aristocracy or federalism; instead they shouted that the Democrats threatened "the subversion of civil liberty." According to the Richmond *Whig*, the Whig party never had any connection with federalism or Alexander Hamilton; rather the Whigs guarded the power of the people while Democrats tried to steal it. Georgia Whigs declared that their party truly befriended all of the people, even the poor, while the Democrats only masqueraded as a people's party. The Raleigh *Register* assured North Carolina voters that Whigs were devoted to "popular liberty" in contrast to tyranny-loving Democrats.[11]

9. Milledgeville *Federal Union*, October 17, 1837; Donelson to John Coffee, January 26, 1836, in Donelson Papers; Jackson *Mississippian*, April 12, 1839.

10. White (ed.), *Messages of Governors of Tennessee*, III, 464–65; Milledgeville *Southern Recorder*, July 30, 1834; Tuscaloosa *Independent Monitor*, March 9, 1840; Richmond *Whig*, November 21, 1845.

11. Woodville (Miss.) *Republican*, August 2, 1834; Richmond *Whig*, May 24, 1850; Milledgeville *Southern Recorder*, December 21, 1841; Raleigh *Register*, June 6, 1845.

In Whig rhetoric, party victories stemmed directly from "the people triumph[ing] over Rulers." Rejoicing over a gubernatorial victory in 1843, the Milledgeville *Southern Recorder* called the Whig win "the greatest triumph of the people (for it is their work, not that of demagogues) we have ever known in Georgia." Constantly Whig newspapers envisioned "the Thunder-tones of the people" striking down "the political wireworkers" and the "Office Party." Speaking for Whigs across the South the Raleigh *Register* placed its faith in the "Freemen of North Carolina" who would surely protect "THE LIBERTIES OF THE PEOPLE." [12]

Both parties paid equal homage to the same sovereign—the people or the voters. And neither party exhibited the slightest discomfort with the democratic politics they practiced so zealously. [13]

III

Southern politicians did not live and campaign in ivory towers; they acted out the praise-of-the-people songs by avidly currying the favor and the votes of those people. This practice of active campaigning had arrived in the South long before Jacksonian democracy. Even in the deferential society of colonial Virginia, men ambitious for office had to carry their case to the voters. In the prologue to *The Candidates,* Robert Munford's eighteenth-century comedy satirizing Virginia's electoral practices, "A Friend" informs the audience, "Here eager candidates shall call for votes." The play details the arduous efforts expended to cultivate voters by candidates both worthy and unworthy. In his sparkling account of political practices in George Washington's Virginia, Charles Sydnor underlined the reliability of Munford's depiction by entitling his chapter on cam-

---

12. Richmond *Whig,* June 11, 1839, January 1, 1841; Milledgeville *Southern Recorder,* October 10, 1843; Vicksburg *Tri-Weekly Whig,* August 13, 1840; Tuscaloosa *Independent Monitor,* June 22, 1847; Raleigh *Register,* June 2, July 21, 1835.

13. A common interpretation of Whigs has pictured them as aristocrats disdainful of the common herd; this antipathy helped comprise an antidemocratic bias. A good summary of this view can be found in Arthur Charles Cole, *The Whig Party in the South* (Gloucester, Mass.: Peter Smith, 1962), 67–70.

paigning, "Swilling the Planters with Bumbo." Sydnor reported that "Munford knew what he was writing about."[14]

Examples of the courtship that was paid to voters fill Sydnor's narrative. He tells of James Littlepage's quest for a seat in the House of Burgesses. Littlepage visited with worshippers at church services; he went on a house-to-house canvass to meet voters whom he could not find in assemblies; he "rode about . . . among the People." Finally he invited voters who lived more than a day's travel from the polling place to spend election-eve night beneath his roof. Littlepage won his seat in Hanover County in 1763. Thinking back, Colonel Landon Carter decided that his reelection bid had failed because he "did not familiarize [him]self among the people" but reported that his son had gone "amongst them and carr[ied] his Election." As James Madison remembered, it was commonly "the usage for candidates to recommend themselves to the voters . . . by personal solicitation." Sydnor concluded that without such exertions, aspiring politicians remained aspiring politicians. Successful candidates were those able to ingratiate themselves with the people or the voters.[15]

That necessity remained unchanged in the new century. Forging an identity with the voters occupied the thoughts and energies of politicians across the South. To attain a seat in the Mississippi legislature young John A. Quitman followed a course that became a part of the Abraham Lincoln legend. Attending a large gathering just prior to the election that would decide his future, Quitman astonished the crowd with his feats of leaping, boxing, wrestling, and foot racing. To cap an impressive performance, Quitman outshot the area's leading marksman. Then with a sure political touch he offered his prize, a fat ox, to the dejected loser and won the cheers and

14. [William Munford (comp.)], *A Collection of Plays and Poems, by the Late Col. Robert Munford of Mecklenburg County, in the State of Virginia* (Petersburg, Va.: William Prentis, 1798), xi; Charles S. Sydnor, *American Revolutionaries in the Making: Political Practices in Washington's Virginia* (New York: Free Press, 1965), Chap. 4 and p. 133 for the Munford comment.

15. Sydnor, *American Revolutionaries*, 47–48.

political support of the onlookers. As Quitman's biographer wrote, "from that moment the contest was decided."[16]

Quitman's athletic prowess may have been unique but his strategy was emulated everywhere. James Graham, a North Carolina Whig, wrote from his seat in the national House of Representatives to his brother William, also a successful office seeker: "I have always accomodated [sic] my *habits* and *Dress* to the People when electioneering.... I have always dressed chiefly in *Home spun* when among the people." Graham went on to say that since most voters were farmers, candidates should act accordingly. "If a Candidate be dressed Farmerlike he is well received and kindly remembered by the inmates of the Log Cabin, and there is no sensation among the children or the *chickens.*" Graham was not acting the patronizer but rather the adviser to his fellow Whigs on measures to combat Democratic charges that Whigs were snobs. Traveling through south-central Alabama in 1846, the eminent British scientist James Lyell saw southern democracy at work. One hopeful candidate informed Lyell that "he thought it a good policy to go every where on foot when soliciting votes, though he could have commanded a horse and the distances were great." Lyell also heard that one longtime legislator met defeat allegedly because his daughter had worn a fancy gown at a Mobile ball.[17]

In Andrew Jackson's own Tennessee cultivation of the voters reached a high art. Although Davy Crockett's memoirs consist of tall tales as well as actual events, his account of a legislative contest in 1821, even if apocryphal, makes a telling point. Crockett wrote that he based his campaign on entertaining the voters; the speeches he left to his opponent. His account of one campaign meeting reveals a

16. J. F. H. Claiborne, *Life and Correspondence of John A. Quitman, Major-General U.S.A., and Governor of the State of Mississippi* (2 vols.; New York: Harper & Brothers, 1860), I, 91–92.

17. Graham to William Alexander Graham, May 20, 1840, in J. G. de Roulhac Hamilton and Max R. Williams (eds.), *The Papers of William Alexander Graham* (5 vols.; Raleigh, N.C.: State Department of Archives and History, 1957–), II, 91–92; Charles Lyell, *A Second Visit to the United States of North America* (2 vols.; New York: Harper & Brothers, 1849), II, 62.

man completely in command of his political world. "I told them," Crockett recalled, "that there had been a little bit of speech in me a while ago, but I believed I couldn't get it out. They all roared out in a mighty laugh, and I told some other anecdotes, equally amusing to them, and believing I had them in a first-rate way, I quit and got down, thanking them for their attention." But Davy Crockett had only begun to destroy his opponent, for his story continues, "I took care to remark that I was as dry as a powder horn, and that I thought it was time for us all to wet our whistles a little: and so I put off to the liquor stand, and was followed by the greater part of the crowd." His opponent began his speech, but, alas, with few listeners. Running against the incumbent Governor James K. Polk, the Whig James Jones in 1841 captured audiences with what Charles G. Sellers, Jr., calls his "homely simplicity." Jones, in Sellers' words, "amble[d] to the stand stroking a coon skin and remarking in his comical manner, 'Did you ever see such a fine fur?'" That introduction guaranteed that Jones's audience accepted him as one of their own, a man of "rural pedigree."[18]

This pressing of the flesh, as Lyndon Johnson would later call it, brought forth great physical exertions from southern politicians. Henry Wise, who represented the Accomac District of Virginia in the United States Congress from 1833 to 1844, first as a Democrat then a Whig, claimed that no other congressman knew a district so well as he knew his. That Wise had a district cleaved by the Chesapeake Bay only spurred him to greater efforts. Every year he visited in every county on both shores even though he had "to travel by sail vessels and in canoes quite as much as by carriages." Wise turned his political career into a training session for a nautical one. "I became so familiar with every main, creek, island, and headland," he boasted, "so that I could pilot myself very well . . . by my knowledge generally of courses, distances, and bearings." The fervor of

---

18. [Davy Crockett], *Davy Crockett's Own Story: As Written by Himself* (New York: Citadel Press, 1955), 108–109; Charles G. Sellers, Jr., *James K. Polk* (2 vols.; Princeton, N.J.: Princeton University Press, 1957–), I, 438.

the 1848 presidential campaign in Louisiana caused Whig stalwart Seargent S. Prentiss to abandon caution and swim a rain-swollen river in order to make a scheduled rally. That swim, his brother believed, led directly to Prentiss's fatal illness.[19]

The practice of canvassing a district or a state appeared early and gained momentum. Usually, canvassing—or making a political speaking tour through a district or a state—began with one candidate. But quickly it became a joint endeavor of two or more contesting candidates. In 1835 Democrat Robert J. Walker of Mississippi spent months stumping the state urging voters to elect legislators who supported his candidacy for the United States Senate. In January of 1840 the major Whig newspaper of Louisiana, the New Orleans *Bee*, proudly announced that the Whig gubernatorial candidate was canvassing the state. A year later the Democratic and Whig contestants for the congressional seat from the Valley of Virginia covered their district, over 160 miles long, on horseback; during the six-week canvass the two candidates jointly appeared on the rostrum throughout the district. The gubernatorial canvass began in North Carolina in 1840, and in the 1844 campaign for governor both candidates toured the state speaking at numerous rallies and barbecues. A similar canvass appeared in Georgia in 1847 when the Democrat George Towns took to the stump. When the Arkansas Democratic Convention selected a gubernatorial nominee in 1852, it also resolved that the nominee canvass the state.[20]

Perhaps the most herculean campaign tours marked the tight gubernatorial battles in Tennessee fought between James K. Polk

19. Barton H. Wise, *The Life of Henry A. Wise of Virginia, 1806–1876* (New York and London: MacMillan, 1899), 103–104; *A Memoir of S. S. Prentiss*, ed. His Brother (2 vols.; New York: Charles Scribner, 1856), II, 455.

20. Edwin A. Miles, *Jacksonian Democracy in Mississippi* (Chapel Hill: University of North Carolina Press, 1960), 98–99; New Orleans *Bee*, January, 1840, *passim;* Alexander F. Robertson, *Alexander Hugh Holmes Stuart, 1807–1891: A Biography* (Richmond: William Byrd, 1925), 26–27; Raleigh *Standard*, summer, 1840, *passim;* Max Ray Williams, "William A. Graham, North Carolina Whig Party Leader, 1804–1849" (Ph.D. dissertation, University of North Carolina, 1965), 151–64; Milledgeville *Southern Recorder*, July 27, 1847; Little Rock *Arkansas Gazette*, May 7, 1852.

and his Whig opponents. During his first and only successful race for
the governorship in 1839, Polk, in a little over two months, rode
more than 1,300 miles while making forty-three scheduled speeches
and numerous impromptu addresses in thirty-seven of Tennessee's
sixty-four counties. Although Polk lost in 1843, he and his Whig
counterpart, James Jones, crisscrossed Tennessee for some 2,300
miles while speaking five or six hours almost every day. It took these
knights of the hustings four months to complete their arduous
crusade.[21]

Even though the canvass and the political speeches that accompanied it comprised the focal point of campaigning, antebellum
campaigns were not solemn occasions. Politicians injected a carnival
and holiday spirit into their serious endeavors. In the South as in the
rest of the country the Log Cabin campaign of 1840 transformed the
technique of political appeal. Even the oldest and most stable communities had no immunity. "This ancient commonwealth," observed the staid Richmond *Enquirer*, "is about to be stirred up from
her lowest foundations. Dinners, Clubs, Conventions, speeches,
Orators haranguing in all directions . . . are the order of the day."
And as the *Enquirer* emphasized, both Whigs and Democrats
plunged headlong into the melee. By the thousands the Whig faithful of Alabama met in a specially constructed log cabin in Tuscaloosa.
Flags, banners, street parades, and fervid oratory marked the Whig
uprising.[22]

Whigs worked mightily to excel with this technique. Providing
directions for the Whig effort in Virginia in 1844, the Richmond
Whig called for "County and District barbecues, lasting for several
days together, assembling the whole People, and bringing them into
converse, communion and interchange of thought" in addition to
"collecting distinguished public speakers." At such a rally in Baton
Rouge some twelve thousand Whigs gathered for food, balls,

21. Sellers, *Polk*, I, 370, 473.
22. Richmond *Enquirer*, July 3, 1840; John Rutherfoord to Andrew Stevenson, August 15,
1840, in Andrew Stevenson Papers, Division of Manuscripts, Library of Congress; Tuscaloosa
Independent Monitor, June 6, 1840.

parades, and speeches. Often the same strategy was pursued on a much smaller scale. Whigs in Shelbyville, Tennessee, "undertook to raise a 'Clay Pole' [in 1844] 145 ft. high—pole broke—took the pieces down to the blacksmith shop—bound them together and raised it 100 ft. high." Even in Shelbyville, Whigs had a rallying point. Across the South the party agreed that only "the strongest kind of stimulus" would arouse the multitudes of voters.[23]

The Democrats were not outdone. To arouse their faithful in the battle of 1844, Arkansas Democrats held a great barbecue in Little Rock. Attempting to cover all possibilities they "particularly solicited" the womenfolk and promised that "all necessary preparations will be made for their entertainment." In their difficult contest against Zachary Taylor in 1848, Georgia Democrats put on one of the greatest shows. In late August thousands upon thousands gathered at Stone Mountain for an overnight extravaganza. Attendance was undoubtedly increased by a special and substantial reduction in railroad fares; fares on all railroads were reduced to two cents a mile going to Stone Mountain with the return trip free. Bands, speeches, a huge barbecue, and more speeches entertained the assembled multitude. Great enthusiasm erupted for the *pièce de résistance*— the Democratic ladies of Chatham County sent up a cake one foot thick and three feet in diameter topped with raised gilt letters spelling out Cass and Butler. Of course most efforts were considerably less grandiose. A schoolteacher in central Tennessee recorded in his diary a Democratic tactic of 1844: "Yesterday the Democracy came into town [Shelbyville] with a long pole drawn by some 20 odd yoke of oxen, on one of which sat Joshua Scott playing a fiddle. After the pole was raised they sung—'damn old Clay and Frelinghuysen.'"[24] Always they tried.

23. Richmond *Whig*, July 12, 1844; New Orleans *Bee*, October 7, 9, 1844; Jason Niles Diary, August 17, 1844 (Southern Historical Collection, University of North Carolina); Alexander Porter to Jesse Burton Harrison, November 6, 1839, in Burton Harrison Papers, Division of Manuscripts, Library of Congress.

24. Little Rock *Arkansas Banner*, October 2, 1844; Milledgeville *Federal Union*, August 15, 22, 1848; Niles Diary, August 24, 1844.

Although this carnival atmosphere pervaded southern campaigns, the content of these political dramas equaled in importance their form. In Robert Munford's *The Candidates* after the voters had heard the claims of all the candidates, they chose the two, Worthy and Wou'dbe, who combined qualifications and integrity. Even the great self-proclaimed man of the people Davy Crockett found, much to his chagrin, that plying the voters with rum did not always insure victory. His 1835 race for the congressional seat from west Tennessee ended in defeat despite his ability to keep glasses filled.[25]

Time and again observers reported on the political awareness and attentiveness of voters who attended rallies and speeches. Making a campaign trek through southeastern Mississippi during the summer of 1841, J. F. H. Claiborne found "the sovereigns themselves" listening carefully to the orators; Claiborne specifically stated that the crowd did not stray from the speaker's platform. A political world away—southside Virginia in 1827—a northern-born Presbyterian minister was struck by the interaction between speakers and audience during stump-speaking occasions. Andrew Johnson, an alert and ambitious young Tennessee legislator, came to the conclusion in 1841 that "the day has passed by, when men aspiring to high places, can be sustained without making a fair expose of their of [sic] political creed when required by the people to do so."[26]

John S. Wise, the son of Henry Wise, characterized antebellum Virginia as a place "where everybody talked politics everywhere"; Wise need not have restricted his comments to one state, for the constant talk of politics reverberated throughout the South. In his 1860 description of southern society Daniel R. Hundley, a native southerner who had attended Harvard and lived in Chicago, as-

25. [Munford (comp.)], *Plays and Poems*, 50; [Crockett], *Crockett's Own Story*, 227–34.

26. J. F. H. Claiborne, "A Trip Through the Piney Woods," *Publications of the Mississippi Historical Society*, IX (1906), 519; John Hall (ed.), *Forty Years' Familiar Letters of James W. Alexander, D.D., Constituting, with the Notes, a Memoir of His Life* (2 vols.; New York and London: Charles Scribner and Sampson Low, Son, 1860), I, 99; Johnson to William Lowry, October 24, 1841, in Leroy P. Graf, *et al.* (eds.), *The Papers of Andrew Johnson* (3 vols.; Knoxville: University of Tennessee Press, 1967–), I, 34.

serted that the average southerner was "on the whole much better versed in the lore of politics and the provisions of our Federal and State Constitutions" than his northern counterpart. To Hundley the political discussions pervading "public barbecues, court-house-day gatherings, and other holiday occasions," produced exceptionally aware voters even among the "poor men in the South." The New Orleans *Bee* asserted that almost any southerner, "even if illiterate and shoeless," could talk intelligently about politics. The *Bee* attributed this ability to stump speaking. Stump speaking, the *Bee* argued, continually required politicians to show themselves to the public—a public rarely fooled by false claims and pretensions. At political rallies in Alabama "no orator dared to deceive." That opinion, the recollection of an avid young follower of Alabama politics, was based on personal experience. John W. DuBose, later the biographer of William Lowndes Yancey, went on to elucidate his observation. He emphasized the personal association between candidates and people stemming from the practice of traveling candidates visiting in private homes; from the personal identity of the citizens in a particular community with a candidate; from the circuit riding of lawyers, which familiarized many voters with individual attorneys who later came around asking for votes. The candidate's words from the stump also passed far beyond the range of his immediate audience. Those attending rallies talked politics as they headed homeward and "to those living on the highway who had been absent, they reviewed the events and sentiments of the day."[27] Then local newspapers gave full reports of speeches and rallies, reports which often found their way into the major newspapers of the state. Politicians had to live with what they said.

While the canvass became the visible sign of active parties, neither party neglected the less newsworthy and less glamorous

27. John S. Wise, *End of an Era* (Boston and New York: Houghton Mifflin, 1900), 30; D. R. Hundley, *Social Relations in Our Southern States* (New York: Henry B. Price, 1860), 201; New Orleans *Bee*, September 19, 1854; John Witherspoon DuBose, *The Life and Times of William Lowndes Yancey* (2 vols.; New York: Peter Smith, 1942), I, 79–80, 91–92.

work of political organization. In the South both parties exhibited a singular aptitude for organization; neither suffered from any congenital defects that enfeebled organizational efforts.[28] Although men uncomfortable with the fact and tactics of mass parties and politics undoubtedly belonged to both parties, they played a distinctly secondary role. Most who decried the alleged decay of political morality that supposedly accompanied the rise of parties remained outside of them. Those patricians and radicals, often individually the same, who lamented the decline of statesmanship watched the political contest from the sidelines. The one clear and critical exception was John C. Calhoun; he and his followers occupied a strategic position in southern politics, one that I will discuss in detail later. But the two major parties basically battled on equal terms, though in certain states, particularly Arkansas and Texas, Whigs remained considerably weaker than their Democratic opponents. Quite clearly, however, both parties recognized the centrality of organization and worked to build effective organizations. Whigs and Democrats worried about a strong partisan press; knew the value of conventions, local committees, and political propaganda; blamed defeats on the superior organization of the enemy.

The Baton Rouge *Gazette* cried, "Organize or you [Whigs] will suffer an inglorious defeat"; Whig leaders constantly reiterated that call. As early as 1835 the Richmond *Whig* urged Virginia Whigs to "Rouse yourselves for action . . . conquer not yourselves by division." Sixteen years later the *Whig* spoke with the same accent when it preached that without organization Virginia Whigs could never wield their legitimate influence. Far to the west Whigs in Arkansas worked for "complete organization" of their party. Without organization, as the Vicksburg *Whig* declared, no chance for victory

28. The story of Whig organization in the South that I have discovered provides little support for the contention that Whigs, for various reasons but especially devotion to personal leaders and an animus toward social trends of their time, were unable to organize as effectively as the Democrats. On this point see Lynn L. Marshall, "The Strange Stillbirth of the Whig Party," *American Historical Review*, LXXII (1967), 445–68.

existed. But with it, according to the Raleigh *Register*, the people would triumph over "the Political quacks."[29]

Whigs felt two foundations essential for a strong and efficient organization—partisan newspapers and active state and local bodies. The plethora of Whig sheets attested to the former as did the concern expressed over weak papers. When in 1850 a Whig newspaper disappeared from Little Rock, Arkansas Whigs worked to get a new one quickly, for it gave the central direction necessary for Whig activity. James Graham of North Carolina clearly stated this opinion: "The Press disseminates knowledge through the Country, and influences and *forms* public opinion." And in North Carolina in 1850, Graham believed that the Whigs "suffer[ed] greatly for the want of an efficient Press in the State, particularly at Raleigh; to which the Village Papers look for leading articles, stating clearly and concisely and in a popular manner the issues, reasons and arguments which divide the two parties."[30]

Even though the evidence from newspapers and private correspondence conclusively demonstrates that Whigs organized effectively and efficiently, some Whigs always decried their efforts while simultaneously praising and damning the organizational genius of the Democrats. A disconsolate Arkansas Whig castigated his Arkansas Whig brethren for "seem[ing] very indifferent to politics." Enemies of the Democrats often described them as "well drilled disciplined veterans." "They [the Democrats] are drilled regulars," wailed James Graham. "We are Raw and undisciplined militia."[31]

---

29. Baton Rouge *Gazette*, July 27, 1844; Richmond *Whig*, February 7, 1835, August 22, 1851; Little Rock *Arkansas Gazette*, November 8, 1843; Vicksburg *Daily Whig*, December 8, 1840; Raleigh *Register*, August 14, 1837.

30. Helena (Ark.) *Southern Shield*, September 21, 1850; Graham to William Alexander Graham, April 21, 1850, August 17, 1851, in Hamilton and Williams (eds.), *Graham Papers*, III, 320, IV, 187.

31. Charles F. M. Noland to Jesse Turner, February 23, 1848, in Jesse Turner Papers, William R. Perkins Library, Duke University; Mitchell R. King to Hugh S. Legaré, December 23, 1838, in Hugh S. Legaré Papers, South Caroliniana Library, University of South Carolina; Graham to William Alexander Graham, December 14, 1838, in Hamilton and Williams (eds.), *Graham Papers*, II, 27.

The reality of conventions, clubs, executive committees, correspondence committees, circulars, addresses, rallies, and, most important, victories belie such lamentations.

Democratic evaluations of the Whig organizational performance also undermine the singers of dirges. A Florida Democratic stalwart declared that "we do not support our men with the same zeal that Whigs do." In Arkansas the Little Rock *Arkansas Banner* said that Democratic organization was no match for the Whig, which always presented "a solid phalanx." Democrats in Mississippi considered their small margin of victory in 1836 a great triumph because the Whigs had made "extraordinary exertions." To James K. Polk one word summed up the reasons for the 1840 Whig victory in Tennessee—organization. In that same year the Raleigh *Standard* blamed the Democratic defeat in North Carolina's gubernatorial race to "the most perfect [Whig] organization."[32]

Not that the Democrats failed either to recognize the value of organization or work to build it. The New Orleans *Louisiana Courier* observed that Louisiana Democrats had sufficient numerical strength to control the state, but added bluntly that without organization numbers were of little avail. "No party can act efficiently without organization, and the more perfect, the better, the more certain is success," declared the Arkansas Democratic Convention of 1843. The Richmond *Enquirer* always an apostle of organization claimed that the greatest Democratic triumphs had been gained "by the agency of honest, fair party organization." To the *Enquirer* the practices of the patron saints Thomas Jefferson and James Madison had rendered the concept of organization "sacred." Sacred or not, all Democrats trumpeted the cry: "Organize for the next contest."[33]

32. John M. Smith (Monticello, Fla.) to Armistead Burt, June 23, 1846, in Armistead Burt Papers, William R. Perkins Library, Duke University; Little Rock *Arkansas Banner*, January 30, 1844; Jackson *Mississippian*, December 9, 1836; Polk to Robert B. Reynolds, November 18, 1840, in James K. Polk Papers, New York Historical Society; Raleigh *Standard*, August 26, 1840.
33. New Orleans *Louisiana Courier*, December 1, 1848; Little Rock *Arkansas Banner*, January 30, 1844; Richmond *Enquirer*, May 21, 1850; Milledgeville *Federal Union*, October 10, 1843.

Democrats like Whigs built a system based on committees, conventions, circulars, public addresses, and a partisan press. Competing for the partisanship championship, Democratic and Whig newspapers ended in a dead heat. Just as did their Whig counterparts, Democratic leadership worried when their press faltered. James K. Polk, who personally created the Democratic organization in Tennessee, found his sorest problem the absence of an effective party organ. When the chief newspaper in Arkansas, the Little Rock *Arkansas Gazette* changed owners and party affiliation in 1843, leading Democrats from around the state met in Little Rock "to take immediate steps for the establishment of a paper to advocate their principles." Thomas Ritchie, the dean of southern Democratic editors and chieftains, bemoaned the weakness of his party's press in Virginia. He wanted it strengthened. [34]

In organizational terms Whigs bested Democrats in some states while Democrats bested Whigs in others. [35] For example in Arkansas and Texas, the Whig organization had neither the effectiveness nor the staying power that the Democrats enjoyed. But in North Carolina and Tennessee the Whigs clearly outshone their enemies. In most states, however, organizations operated on a basis of equality. For a particular election one party might do a better job of organizing and getting out the vote than the other, but that success did not guarantee hegemony. With both parties working from the same basis and creating, for the most part, similar structures, election triumphs came from the enthusiasm generated by personalities and issues that fired the organization, not from the organization itself.

Quite clearly, then, political parties in the South developed into efficient machines run by expert political engineers. Whatever else

34. Polk to Frank Blair, October 3, 1835, in Blair-Lee Papers, Firestone Library, Princeton University; Little Rock *Arkansas Banner,* September 16, 1843; Ritchie to J. H. Pleasants, March 31, 1839, in "Unpublished Letters of Thomas Ritchie," *John P. Branch Historial Papers of Randolph-Macon College,* III (1911), 239.
35. The Democratic and Whig newspapers contain a mass of material on party organization. My purpose is not to describe details of party organization but to show that both Democrats and Whigs shared an abiding concern for it and acted effectively on that concern.

might be said about the development or lack of development in the society and economy of the antebellum South vis-à-vis the antebellum North, southern politicians definitely kept pace with their northern counterparts. Southerners created modern political vehicles that successfully negotiated the treacherous terrain of a political system based on white manhood suffrage and broad voter participation. At the same time neither the politicians nor the parties functioned in an hermetic laboratory. As legitimate offspring of southern society and culture, the values and mores of the South provided their blueprint. From the origins of the Jacksonian party, particular southern interests shaped the southern attitude toward parties and molded political behavior in the South.

3

The Flowering of Southern Sectional Politics

I

THE ELECTION OF 1832 reaffirmed Andrew Jackson's prodigious popularity and political power in the South. The general feebleness and ultimate collapse of the Barbour movement represented merely one illustration of Jackson's might. Besides vanquishing the Barbour effort, Jackson trounced Henry Clay and buried the National Republican party even deeper into oblivion. Clay did not even run so well as Adams had.[1] In three states—Georgia, Alabama, and Mississippi—no Clay ticket ever appeared. And in every other state, save one, Jackson bettered his 1828 showing. Only in Calhoun's fiefdom, South Carolina, which had no popular vote for president, did Jackson falter. Calhoun and his fellow nullifiers threw away South Carolina's electoral vote on their Virginia ally John Floyd. Nowhere did dissident Jacksonians and National Republicans fuse successfully. The chief effort was made in Virginia but to no avail; the ideological gulf was simply too wide.[2] No matter how opposed Virginians were to Jackson's tardiness on tariff reform or to his choice of Van Buren, they could not accept Clay's brand of nationalism.

That great victory in 1832 did not, however, preface continued unity among southern Democrats, but rather renewed and more traumatic disunity. After his reelection Jackson acted to give real momentum to an opposition that developed a substantial following as well as leaders. That combination, lacking in the Barbour move-

1. Edward Stanwood, *A History of the Presidency from 1788 to 1897* (New ed. rev. by Charles Knowles Bolton; 2 vols.; Boston and New York: Houghton Mifflin, 1926), I, 163–64.
2. Duff Green to James H. Pleasants, August 27, 1832, in Green Papers, Southern Historical Collection, University of North Carolina; Henry Clay to Francis T. Brooke, April 1, 1832, in Calvin Colton (ed.), *The Private Correspondence of Henry Clay* (New York: A. S. Barnes, 1856), 332–33.

ment, led to a new political organization that seriously challenged the Jackson party as the special party of the South. This powerful reaction, unthinkable in 1832, became a reality in 1835 and 1836. It derived from three separate but closely related episodes: the nullification crisis, the withdrawal of government deposits from the Bank of the United States, the accession of Martin Van Buren.

While many in the South viewed the lowered tariff of 1832 as a move in the right direction and applauded Jackson's call for even further reductions in his annual message of that year, doctrinaire antitariff men fulminated against what they called the president's lethargy on the tariff issue. The extremists were most numerous in Virginia and South Carolina. In the latter state, assisted by a unique political structure and an acute concern over slavery, they nullified the tariff with a theory of state sovereignty devised by Calhoun, and precipitated a national crisis. Jackson reacted by denouncing nullification as treason and nullifiers as traitors; then he asked Congress to stand with him if force proved necessary to crush this brand of treason.[3]

Jacksonian rhetoric in both the Nullification Proclamation and the so-called Force Bill made extensive claims for federal and presidential power. Herein lay the southern difficulties, for Jackson's language clearly violated the states' rights gospel. The Milledgeville *Southern Recorder* castigated the Nullification Proclamation as being "directly at war with the old State Rights defenders, the Jeffersonian Republicans." A self-styled "State-Rights" meeting in Milledgeville resolved that the proclamation and the Force Bill together "insidiously restor[ed] to the Federal party, the power which they lost under the elder Adams." The two measures, according to the resolutions, "have aimed a deadly blow at State Rights." These Georgians then reaffirmed the Old Republican doctrine as expli-

3. Richmond *Enquirer*, July 27, 1832, January 29, 1833; James D. Richardson (comp.), *A Compilation of the Messages and Papers of the Presidents, 1789-1897* (10 vols.; Washington: Government Printing Office, 1896–99), II, 598–99, 610–32, 640–56. For the South Carolina story see William H. Freehling's brilliant *Prelude to Civil War: The Nullification Controversy in South Carolina, 1816-1836* (New York and London: Harper & Row, 1966).

cated in the Virginia and Kentucky resolutions as "the great moral instruments" of federal-state relations and called for all true Republicans (or Democrats) to rally once again beneath that banner. "General Jackson's proclamation will not satisfy the South," a North Carolina friend told James K. Polk, because "It is thought to be an abandonment of the rights of the states." In ideologically sensitive Virginia, Jackson's new doctrine of federal power brought forth paroxysms of fear and anger. Governor John Floyd confided to his diary that the country was plunging into military despotism. To Thomas Ritchie, Jackson's actions endangered the existence of the party, for Virginians could not and would not accept the president's version of constitutionalism.[4]

And southerners spoke with one voice in demanding further tariff reduction. Urging tariff reform, the North Carolina legislature called the tariff of 1832 "impolitic, unjust, and oppressive." Similar language from Alabama branded the tariff as "unequal, unjust, and against the spirit, true intent and meaning of the Constitution." Thomas Ritchie's *Enquirer* asserted that "the South cannot acquiesce in *such an unjust and unequal system.*" Reducing the tariff became the formula both for redressing a general grievance and for heading off a confrontation between South Carolina and the federal government.[5]

Neither opposition to Jackson's hymn to federal power nor the claims for an even lower tariff signified that most southern Jacksonians supported either the theory of nullification or South Carolina's

4. Milledgeville *Southern Recorder,* December 27, 1832; the resolutions are printed in Charles Adam Gulick, Jr., *et al.* (eds.), *The Papers of Mirabeau Buonaparte Lamar* (6 vols.; Austin, Tex: A. C. Baldwin & Sons and Von-Boeckmann-Jones, 1921–27), I, 161–63; William J. Alexander to Polk, December 29, 1832, in Herbert Weaver *et al.* (eds.), *The Correspondence of James K. Polk* (3 vols.; Nashville: Vanderbilt University Press, 1969–), I, 593; Charles H. Ambler (ed.), "Diary of John Floyd," *John P. Branch Papers of Randolph-Macon College,* V (1918), 205–206; Ritchie to William C. Rives, January 6, 1833, in William C. Rives Papers, Division of Manuscripts, Library of Congress. The trauma among Virginia Democrats is underscored in a letter from Francis T. Brooke to Henry Clay, December 25, 1832, in Henry Clay Papers, Indiana University.

5. *State Papers on Nullification...* (Boston: Dutton and Wentworth, 1834), 201, 222; Richmond *Enquirer,* November 30, 1832.

specific actions. Most found Calhoun's theories too esoteric; as the venerable patriarch of Old Republicanism, Nathaniel Macon of North Carolina observed, a state could not simultaneously be both inside and outside the Union. Macon concluded that nullification had to be unconstitutional. Comparing South Carolina's course to that of a "rash young man," many southern Jacksonians felt that Calhoun and his associates had overreacted and recklessly endangered the Union. This question of union versus disunion captured the popular imagination and worked against the nullifiers. Jackson defined the crisis as such, and across the South the general view fit Thomas Hart Benton's description: "The mass of the people think the union is attacked . . . and that view is decisive with them." Calhoun himself received the same report from southern friends. Then, of course, to lend support to South Carolina meant, at least in part, to oppose Andrew Jackson. The force and popularity of Jackson's name presented a substantial stumbling block to nullifier partisans trying to encourage fellow traveling.[6]

Furthermore the nullifiers did not connect their crusade with a general threat to slavery. Nullifier rhetoric spoke of the evil tariff and of constitutional transgressions, not of slavery. William Freehling has convincingly shown that concern over slavery underlay the nullification impulse in South Carolina.[7] But that acute concern, based on the particular social structure and racial situation in the South Carolina low country, was not generally felt elsewhere. Outside of South Carolina, few saw nullification as a necessary protection for slavery. The inability and failure of the nullifiers to present openly their cause as an essential defense of slavery from outside

6. Macon to Bolling Hall, April 14, 1833, in Hall Papers; Henry St. George Tucker to N. B. Tucker, January 24, 1833, and Benton to N. B. Tucker, February 11, 1833, in "Tucker Correspondence," *William & Mary Quarterly*, 1st ser., XII (1903), 86, 92; Beverly Tucker to Hugh White, January 25, 1840, in Hugh White Papers, Division of Manuscripts, Library of Congress; Richardson (comp.), *Messages and Papers of the Presidents*, II, 640, 654–55; Jackson to James Buchanan, March 21, 1833, in James Buchanan Papers, Historical Society of Pennsylvania; Tomlinson Fort to Calhoun, July 15, 1832, in Tomlinson Fort Papers, Robert W. Woodruff Library, Emory University; Milledgeville *Federal Union*, February 14, 1833.
    7. Freehling, *Prelude, passim*.

assault eliminated any chance of their winning widespread popular support.

Even so southern Jacksonians recognized the potential danger to themselves and their party as well as to the South and the Union should the crisis explode. The prospect of armed conflict stemming from precipitate federal or presidential acts frightened southerners.[8] In such an event many of them expected fraticidal war, not only within the Union but in the southern states also. Sane men wanted to avert that kind of holocaust. Then southern Jacksonians would come under heavy political fire across the South if their leader and party invaded South Carolina. Individual Jacksonians would have to choose sides and the political unity in the South forged on the anvil of the Jackson party would disintegrate.

Virginia Democrats, and Thomas Ritchie particularly, led the campaign to keep the president *"cool."* Having already faced the Barbour defection and plagued with Old Republican ideologues who constantly harped on Jackson's ideological impurities, Ritchie feared that a typical Jackson response to the crisis would "prostrate" the party in Virginia. To Van Buren, to Frank Blair, editor of the administration newspaper, the *Globe*, in Washington, to William C. Rives, his Virginia comrade just arrived in Washington from the French mission, Ritchie "[spoke] with the utmost unreserve—for the times demand it." "Prudence," Ritchie emphasized to Blair, "must preside at the helm." Rives received an urgent message from Richmond "to impress upon our friends in the Administration the necessity of pursuing a *forbearing* as well as *decided* course towards South Carolina." To do otherwise Ritchie insisted would spread the already burning "flame of discontent." Writing to Rives in early 1833, Ritchie bared the danger—even Jackson's popularity in Virginia, he prophesied, "could not withstand the shock" of offensive action against South Carolina; Ritchie wanted the president to

---

8. Alexander Barrow to William S. Hamilton, February 19, 1833, Hamilton Papers; Barton H. Wise, *The Life of Henry A. Wise of Virginia, 1806–1876* (New York and London: MacMillan, 1899), 39–40; Milledgeville *Southern Recorder*, January 17, 1833.

wait on an "overt act from South Carolina," then get congressional approval before he used force.[9]

Although Jackson definitely did not back down from the threat of armed conflict, the evidence certainly indicates that he heard and heeded the anguished cries of Ritchie and others. His actions toward South Carolina have been thoroughly delineated by William Freehling. Freehling's account leaves no doubt that Jackson acted with moderation between December 1832 and March 1833—a moderation uncharacteristic of Andrew Jackson, who had a history of striking out promptly and savagely toward his enemies both real and imagined. Certain of his close advisers notably Van Buren, Roger B. Taney of Maryland, and William B. Lewis of Tennessee, men especially attuned to the plight of southern Jacksonians, advocated a temperate approach. Jackson's strategy—to wait and let the nullifiers make the first hostile move—suggests that these moderators definitely influenced him.[10]

In still three other ways, Jackson's moderation and his concern for a peaceable solution seem clearly evident. First, he made no effort to block the tariff compromise engineered by Clay and Calhoun. Earlier in an attempt to identify himself with the southern tariff stand he had declared for basic reductions in his annual message, and he even supported a tariff lower than the Clay-Calhoun pro-

9. Richmond *Enquirer,* November 30, 1832; Ritchie to Van Buren, June 25, 1832, in Van Buren Papers; Ritchie to Blair, undated [but obviously in the midst of the nullification crisis], in Blair-Lee Papers; Ritchie to Rives, an undated letter in late 1832 and on January 6, 1833, both in Rives Papers.

10. Freehling, *Prelude,* 265–95; Van Buren to Jackson, December 27, 1832, in John Spencer Bassett (ed.), *Correspondence of Andrew Jackson* (7 vols.; Washington: Carnegie Institution of Washington, 1926–35), IV, 506–508; Van Buren to Taney, undated [but obviously in the midst of the nullification crisis], in Roger B. Taney Papers, Maryland Historical Society; Ari Hoogenboom and Herbert Ershkowitz (eds.), "Levi Woodbury's 'Intimate Memoranda' of the Jackson Adminstration," *Pennsylvania Magazine of History and Biography,* XCII (1968), 512; Louis R. Harlan, "Public Career of William Berkeley Lewis," *Tennessee Historical Quarterly,* VII (1948), 136. For an argument that presents Jackson as taking a considerably less moderate course, as paying little attention to the South see both Richard Barnet Latner, "Andrew Jackson and His Advisers: White House Politics, 1829–1837" (Ph.D. dissertation, University of Wisconsin, 1972), Chap. 6, and James C. Curtis, *Andrew Jackson and the Search for Vindication* (Boston and Toronto: Little, Brown, 1976), Chap. 7.

posal.[11] Even so he could have easily opposed the efforts of Clay and Calhoun, two men he hated, for Andrew Jackson rarely allowed his visceral opponents a free hand in any endeavor, political or otherwise. Moreover, he never identified the heresy of nullification with the South or even with South Carolina. Instead he branded it as the unholy creation of the evil Calhoun and his cohorts who had misled a majority in their own state and a minority in several other states. Finally Jackson was a southerner; he did not relish the idea of bloodletting in his homeland. He realized that the conflict could not be restricted and that general civil war—a sectional one—might erupt. Thus he did all in his power and allowed others, even his arch enemies, to do all they could to find a peaceful solution.[12]

When South Carolina accepted the compromise tariff passed by Congress and signed by Jackson, the danger of military confrontation disappeared. Southern Jacksonians especially saw peaceful resolution as a joyous occasion. Still they and their party had not emerged from the crisis unscathed. In every state, formerly loyal Jacksonians, having condemned the president's claim for federal and executive power, now counted themselves in opposition. They cried against Jackson in language identical to that they had earlier used as Jackson men against Clay and Adams. Recognizing this irony Calhoun concluded that the nullification crisis had sparked "a new spirit" in the Jackson opposition.[13]

Alarm over Jackson's second move against the Bank of the United States—withdrawal of the federal deposits from the bank—spurred the southern opposition. Almost to a man the southern Jacksonians had cheered Jackson's first assault on the bank, his veto of the recharter bill in the summer of 1832. Initially Old Republicans viewed the bank battle as "fortunate for Republicans of the Old School," for

11. William B. Lewis to John Overton, December 2, 1832, in Overton-Claybrook Papers, Tennessee Historical Society; Andrew Jackson Donelson to John Coffee, December 18, 1832, in Donelson Papers; Freehling, *Prelude*, 288.
12. The argument that Jackson turned a deaf ear to the South misses, I think, the thrust of his policy. Yes, he was ready to fight but he left no stone unturned to avoid that outcome.
13. Calhoun to Bolling Hall, January 1, 1833, in Hall Papers.

they gave the bank a hatred equal to the protective tariff. John Tyler spoke for Old Republicans as well as for many southerners who simply thought of themselves as strict constructionists when he termed the bank "the original sin against the Constitution." Young Alexander Stephens branded it "the reptile" that deserved killing. Old Nathaniel Macon rejoiced over its destruction because like "nobles of the land" it had "exclusive privileges." To the Milledgeville *Southern Recorder,* Jackson's veto signaled a proper step in returning to the Constitution.[14]

Willie P. Mangum predicted that the effort to recharter the bank would find few friends among his fellow southerners in the United States Senate. The congressional votes on the bank recharter and on the attempt to override Jackson's veto bear out Mangum's prediction and clearly show the extent of southern antipathy to the bank. In the Senate but three southerners, only one of whom had been associated with the Jacksonians, voted for recharter, and just two of those three supported the futile attempt to defeat the veto. In the House, where no recorded vote occurred on the veto, southerners stood forty-three to seventeen (with six not voting) against recharter.[15] Disaffections in southern Jacksonian ranks because of the veto were few and insignificant.

But Jackson's acting to withdraw federal deposits from the bank in the autumn of 1833 sparked outrage below the Potomac. In this instance strict-construction southerners detected a gross abuse of power. The bank's charter stated that federal deposits could be removed only after investigation had revealed dereliction or mismanagement or similar violations in the bank's activities. A congressional committee had not found such errors; thus when Jackson

14. Richmond *Enquirer,* January 14, 1832; Tyler to Littleton W. Tazewell, June 23, 1834, in Tyler Papers; Journal Entry, May 8, 1834, in Alexander Stephens Papers, Division of Manuscripts, Library of Congress; Macon to Weldon Edwards, May 20, 1834, in Weldon Edwards Papers, Southern Historical Collection, University of North Carolina; Milledgeville *Southern Recorder,* July 26, 1832.

15. Mangum to Col. William Polk, February 11, 1832, in Polk Family of North Carolina Papers, Division of Manuscripts, Library of Congress; *Senate Journal,* 22nd Cong., 1st Sess., 345–46, 463; *House Journal,* 22nd Cong., 1st Sess., 1074–75.

announced he intended to withdraw the deposits, he stepped into the tyrant's role, even though he charged the bank with the abuse of power.

Formerly loyal southerners rushed to the attack. The Milledgeville *Southern Recorder* condemned withdrawal as a "mad course . . . and an unwarrantable usurpation of the powers of Congress." To United States Senator John Black of Mississippi withdrawal portended even greater disaster than either the Nullification Proclamation or the Force Bill. In Black's mind withdrawal destroyed constitutional government. A similar view came to Willie Mangum: "It is certainly," one of his North Carolina political friends wrote, "the most atrocious, high handed despotick [*sic*] measure, that ever was before assumed by the most absolute monarch."[16]

Virginians particularly cried out against withdrawal, which they feared as "a fearful proclivity of power toward the Executive Magistrate," an unconstitutional usurpation of power. Because it followed so quickly behind the nullification crisis, Thomas Ritchie worried that deposit withdrawal might fracture the Virginia Democratic party. Ritchie saw his nightmare realized, for withdrawal heralded a revolution in the Virginia General Assembly. By early 1834 the General Assembly, elected back in April, 1833, with a two-thirds administration majority, passed resolutions condemning Jackson's action by more than a two-to-one margin.[17] That legislative turnaround pointed toward the general political reverberations that would shake the Old Dominion in 1835 and 1836.

Henry Clay's move to have the United States Senate censure the

16. Milledgeville *Southern Recorder*, March 12, 1834; Edwin A. Miles, *Jacksonian Democracy in Mississippi* (Chapel Hill: University of North Carolina Press, 1960), 83; Tho. B. Littlejohn to Mangum, January 29, 1834, in Henry Thomas Shanks (ed.), *The Papers of Willie Person Mangum* (5 vols.; Raleigh: State Department of Archives and History, 1950–56), II, 72.

17. Armistead C. Gordon, *William Fitzhugh Gordon, A Virginian of the Old School: His Life, Times and Contemporaries, 1787–1858* (New York and Washington: Neale, 1909), 210–11, 216; Ritchie to William C. Rives, August 26, 1833, in Rives Papers; Lynwood M. Dent, Jr., "The Virginia Democratic Party, 1824–1847" (Ph.D. dissertation, Louisiana State University, 1974), 148, 151–52. Separate citations will not be given for state election results; I have used three basic sources for returns from gubernatorial, legislative, and congressional elections: newspapers, the *Tribune Almanac*, and secondary works.

president for removing the deposits clearly revealed the widespread southern antagonism to Jackson's plan. On March 28, 1834, nine southern senators from five different states voted for censure while only seven opposed it—a dramatic shift from the southern lineup on the bank recharter and veto.[18]

Jacksonian loyalists again found themselves defending the president from charges of usurping authority and backsliding from the South's venerated gospel of constitutionalism. Jacksonian stalwarts tried to make the popular veto and withdrawal two acts of the same play. The veto had been the bank's death warrant; withdrawal became the actual execution. Withdrawal, the president's defenders argued, was the only tactic that guaranteed the triumph of the country and the people over the bank. When apologies for Jackson's alleged high-handed course appeared, particularly in Virginia, they were always accompanied by claims of necessity. The bank presented such grave dangers to the republic that it had to be eliminated.[19] Although an energetic defense marked the Jackson spokesmen, they could not prevent the one critical result of the withdrawal episode—the opposition picked up momentum.

That momentum lost no force when Jackson secured Van Buren's succession by giving his vice-president the Democratic presidential nomination at the party's May, 1835, national convention. The opposition to Van Buren that had initially appeared in 1831 and 1832 reappeared. But neither Van Buren himself nor his nomination for the presidency generated any great new outbursts of defection or opposition. Men inclined to desert the Jackson party solely because of Van Buren's accession to power had in large part left by the campaign of 1832. Van Buren hurt the southern Democrats because he proved a particularly vulnerable candidate in a presidential campaign that focused on sectional and slavery issues. The desertion of

18. *Niles' Register,* XLVI (April 5, 1834), 88.
19. Richmond *Enquirer,* December 24, 27, 1833; Milledgeville *Federal Union,* October 15, 1833; Jackson *Mississippian* and New Orleans *Bee,* winter and spring, 1833 and 1834, *passim.*

thousands of Jacksonian voters in 1836 was caused by a combination of events beyond Van Buren's control, chiefly the rise of the abolition movement and the decision of southern Whigs to use it as their campaign issue. Still Jackson's insistence on Van Buren did little to help his beleaguered southern supporters. Van Buren as an individual or as a presidential candidate could not hold back the Whig tide. Instead Van Buren's candidacy completed the rupture of the Jackson party in the South. That rupture ended for a score of years the unchallenged supremacy of the Democrats in Dixie.

By 1834 the South no longer felt as one about the Jackson, or Democratic, party. Instead, numerous southerners had begun to perceive it as a spear aimed at the South rather than a shield defending the South. Although one can describe the Jackson party as primarily a southern vehicle in 1828 and even in 1832, that definition does not hold for Jackson's second administration.[20] However, neither Jackson nor his party completely spurned the South after 1832, for many southerners still counted themselves loyal Jacksonians. And after all, Jackson had listened to southern pleas—he worked to lower the tariff and he acted with uncharacteristic moderation during the nullification crisis. At the same time, his definition of federal and executive power did alienate former supporters, particularly the states' rights zealots. That disaffection, combined with the anger of Jackson politicos who lost favor with the president, weakened the Jackson coalition and afforded the dissidents a chance to chip away its bulk. Southern Democrats would reassert themselves and return the party to a straight and true

20. The historiographical boundaries are manned by Richard Brown and Richard Latner. In an influential article "The Missouri Crisis, Slavery and the Politics of Jacksonianism," *South Atlantic Quarterly*, LXV (1966), 55–72, Brown contended that the Jackson party was fundamentally a prosouthern party. Taking issue with Brown, Richard Latner in his dissertation (cited in n. 10 of this chapter) and article, "A New Look at Jacksonian Politics," *Journal of American History*, LXI (1975), 943–69, claims that the southerners had little influence in Jackson's White House. While I am inclined to agree with Brown, he overstates the case for Jackson's second administration; otherwise the early strength of the Whigs remains inexplicable. Latner, on the other hand, underestimates, in my judgment, both the southern origins of the Jackson party and Jackson's responses to the South during the nullification crisis and especially during the presidential election of 1836.

southern path by 1836. But the deviations between 1832 and 1835, clouding the party's southern identity, created a partial political vacuum in the South. Into this vacuum surged a new political force vigorously claiming for itself the southern mantle previously worn by the Jacksonians.

This new political formation, unearthed by the severe shocks that fractured the unity of Democrats, called itself the Whig party. Southern Whiggery bore little resemblance either to the old National Republican party or to the Barbour movement, though both groups embraced it. Of the two the Barbour movement had more direct and immediate influence because the southern Whigs quickly wrapped themselves in the flag of states' rights. The Whig party was not, however, simply a reincarnation of Barbourism. It differed from that earlier dissident movement in two critical ways: it dissociated itself completely from the Democratic party, and it captured a large popular following. In the new coalition the former National Republicans were silent and minority partners.

Coalition is certainly the right word for early Whiggism. All points of the opposition political compass turned to it as true north, the only available focus for anti-Jackson activity. Former National Republican newspapers like the Richmond *Whig* and the Raleigh *Register* quickly espoused the Whig line. Shifting to the Whig cause in 1834 were the four pronullification newspapers in Mississippi. The Whig journals also included formerly powerful Jacksonian sheets like the Milledgeville *Southern Recorder*. Then of course individual politicians and voters who had supported National Republicanism and who had defected for various reasons from the Jacksonians all put on the new Whig cap. As one of William A. Graham's Whig friends in North Carolina put it, "We have original Anti-Jackson men, the seceders from the Jackson party, and the Nullifiers[.]"[21] He spoke as well for Whiggery in every southern state.

---

21. Edwin A. Miles, "The Mississippi Press in the Jackson Era, 1824–1841," *Journal of Mississippi History*, XIX (1957), 10; James S. Smith to Graham, December 2, 1835, in J. G. de Roulhac Hamilton and Max R. Williams (eds.), *The Papers of William Alexander Graham* (5 vols.; Raleigh: State Department of Archives and History, 1957–), I, 401.

Although the new Whig party had diversity, southern Whigs clearly recognized and enunciated the states' rights orientation of their new party. Urging "let us all be Whigs" to both old-line National Republicans and dissident Jacksonians, the Woodville, Mississippi, *Republican*, at the same time, made clear the conditions of alliance: "if these parties do unite, it must be by the Nationals coming down to our standard of strict construction of the Constitution and by no other means." That "latter movement," the *Republican* had no doubt, "will take place." On the opposite boundary of the South, Edmund Tayloe, a Virginia Whig, concurred: "We can only counteract them [the Democrats]," he wrote to William Henry Harrison, "by rallying under the banner of State Rights. This must be our flag." Following suit the Richmond *Whig* jettisoned all National Republican trappings and blared forth states' rights Whiggery. Willie P. Mangum declared that the principles of states rights composed the foundations of the new party. The old Calhounite John Floyd, eagerly proselytizing for the Whigs in 1833, even tried to "detach [Henry Clay] from those Northern harpies" and return him to the fold of Jeffersonian politics and the South.[22]

Everywhere southern Whigs preached sermons on states' rights denouncing nationalism. Specifically they denounced Jackson's alleged executive usurpations, but they also blasted the nationalism that grew out of "the scholastic nonsense of John Quincy Adams." They made Jackson into a Federalist, who had maligned the Constitution in the spirit of the Adamses and Alexander Hamilton. National power became for southern Whigs the ultimate sin. Their rhetoric focused on national, not state, affairs.[23]

Not all of the disaffected Jacksonians were ideologically pure or for that matter even concerned about ideology. Certain important state leaders chose the opposition camp because they had lost favor and

22. Woodville (Miss.) *Republican*, September 6, 1834; Tayloe to Harrison, October 20, 1836, in William Henry Harrison Papers, Division of Manuscripts, Library of Congress; Richmond *Whig*, 1835 *passim*; Mangum to David L. Swain, December 22, 1833, in Shanks (ed.), *Mangum Papers*, II, 52–53; Floyd to William C. Preston, November 23, 1833, in John Floyd Papers, Division of Manuscripts, Library of Congress.
23. Richmond *Whig*, November 27, 1837.

influence with Jackson. Losing control of patronage in Mississippi and his position as the premier Jacksonian in his state, United States Senator George Poindexter moved into a new political home. In Jackson's own Tennessee, Congressman John Bell found his ambitions for higher office and increased power frustrated. His fellow congressman James K. Polk appeared to be the Tennessean favored by Jackson.[24] Poindexter and Bell, just as Berrien and Branch had done previously, struck out in opposition. All became Whigs, though Poindexter and Branch never attained the position in the party enjoyed by Bell and Berrien.

The course followed by these practical politicians provides indisputable evidence of the power and primacy of states' rights in southern Whiggery. Poindexter and Bell constantly harped on Jackson's power grabs that mutilated the original principles of Jacksonianism. In Georgia, John Berrien used states' rights arguments and nothing else to build a vigorous anti-Jackson party. Branch's work for Barbour in 1832 served as a foundation for states' rights Whiggery in North Carolina.[25] States' rights pleas became a panacea that had broad appeal, an appeal that went far beyond ideologues.

Now two parties rather than one claimed to speak for the South. The original Jackson party had been unique in the South because it contrasted so starkly with National Republicanism and John Quincy Adams. It had both a southern candidate and a southern platform whereas its opponents enjoyed neither of those advantages. But by 1834 the southern Whigs, the new opposition, proclaimed that they were more southern than the Democrats. Even in the midst of this confusing political topography one bench mark sharply delineates a critical boundary. The crisis of party upheaval occurred over na-

24. Miles, *Jacksonian Democracy*, 48–54; Alfred Balch to Andrew Jackson, October 31, 1834, in Andrew Jackson Papers, Division of Manuscripts, Library of Congress.
25. Poindexter to Felix Houston, March 9, 1834, in George Poindexter Papers, Mississippi Department of Archives and History; Joseph Howard Parks, *John Bell of Tennessee* (Baton Rouge: Louisiana State University Press, 1950), 100–101; Paul Murray, *The Whig Party in Georgia, 1825–1853* (Chapel Hill: University of North Carolina Press, 1948), 52–53; William S. Hoffman, "John Branch and the Origins of the Whig Party in North Carolina," *North Carolina Historical Review*, XXXV (1958), 299–315.

tional affairs. Between 1832 and 1836 southerners wrote about and talked about national questions almost exclusively. From podiums, editorial pages, and private correspondence the consuming interest was national politics. And a common denominator exists for all the rhetoric—strict construction and states' rights. Practically every politician who left a record of his decision for standing with the Democrats or moving with the Whigs pointed directly at that common denominator.[26] Even those who had no great commitment to the theory or ideology of states' rights spoke that particular southern language. Their chorusing the states' rights hymn testifies to its influence in the South.

This conclusion contrasts sharply with the view that the roots of southern Whiggery lay in opposition to Andrew Jackson's policies toward the second Bank of the United States, both the veto and withdrawal.[27] According to that interpretation the focus on financial matters had nothing to do with particular southern concerns including states' rights ideology; instead it indicated the urban, commercial, and nationalist outlook of the southerners who created the Whig party. In other words the Whig party was the old National Republican party with a new name. Although men with such an outlook undoubtedly joined the Whigs, those who insisted that the party must adopt their views played a distinctly minor and unimportant role in forging the identity of early southern Whiggery. The evidence presented in this chapter makes that point quite emphatically. Politicians who appealed to southern voters between 1833

26. John Y. Mason (Virginia congressman) to George Dromgoole, December 24, 1832, in Edward Dromgoole Papers, Southern Historical Collection, University of North Carolina; Francis Scott Key (writing from Tuscaloosa, Alabama) to Roger B. Taney, November 16, 1833, in Taney Papers; Thomas Ritchie to Andrew Stevenson, three letters in April 1834 [no day given], in Stevenson Papers; George Poindexter to Felix Houston, March 9, 1834, in Poindexter Papers; P. L. Rainwater (ed.), "The Autobiography of Benjamin Grubb Humphreys, August 26, 1808–December 20, 1882," *Mississippi Valley Historical Review*, XXI (1934), 238; J. S. Barbour to Willie P. Mangum, November 3, 1839, in Shanks (ed.), *Mangum Papers*, III, 21–22; J. F. H. Claiborne, *Life and Correspondence of John A. Quitman, Major-General U.S.A., and Governor of the State of Mississippi* (2 vols.; New York: Harper & Brothers, 1860), I, 111.
27. Charles Grier Sellers, Jr., "Who Were the Southern Whigs?" *American Historical Review*, LIX (1954), 335–46, is the basic statement on the economic origins.

and 1836 on a National Republican economic platform would have found neither listeners nor followers. And Southern Whigs of all persuasions recognized that fact. Thus even Whigs who were primarily interested in economic matters had to turn to states' rights and sectional issues to arouse southern voters against the Democratic party.[28]

Although Whigs espoused states' rights, a political cry that tended to rally southerners, that chorus alone did not make the Whigs such a powerful threat to the Democrats. While the old shibboleth of states' rights could arouse a certain, but unknown, number of southern voters, it could never generate the mass excitement and exuberance necessary to harness the energy of tens of thousands of southern voters behind the Whig cause. In 1833 and 1834 the Whig party stood on the threshold. It seemed to have three alternatives: the fledgling party could disintegrate amidst the ideological squabbles of National Republicans and nullifiers; it could prove incapable of growth and become an oversized Barbour movement; it could build on its early momentum and become a major party. That last possibility required a galvanizing issue, for no great popular figure in the Jackson image donned a Whig cloak. In fact none existed. The Whigs ended up taking the third course because they found their issue. The rise of an organized abolition movement in the North matched the growth of anti-Jackson sentiment in the South. The southern anti-Jackson men, the Whigs, went after the abolition issue with unabashed vigor and glee.

II

The rise of an organized, militant abolition movement in the United States is normally dated from 1831 when William Lloyd Garrison began the publication of his *Liberator* in Boston. By 1835 the South confronted this uncompromising opposition to slavery, which took

---

28. By the early 1840s, however, Sellers' characterization of southern Whiggery has more validity. Then southern Whigs identified themselves, albeit temporarily, with a nationalist economic program. See Chap. Five herein.

the form of petitions to Congress praying chiefly for emancipation in the District of Columbia and in abolitionist pamphlets sent by mail to southern communities. The South, always keenly sensitive to any outside intervention regarding slavery, was horrified. That this abolition crusade followed so rapidly the great slave revolt led by Nat Turner sent visions of cataclysm through the slave states.

Immediately and in unison the South struck back. Meetings to protest abolition in general and the incendiary publications (the name given by southerners to the abolitionist pamphlets) in particular were held in southern cities. In Charleston a group of irate citizens broke into the post office and burned the hated pamphlets. The South Carolina legislature declared that it was simply "impossible" for the South to permit the reception of abolitionist literature. Other state legislatures passed resolutions like those adopted in Virginia that affirmed that the South, or states in the South, retained sole control of slavery and that right must "be maintained at all hazards." "Upon this point," asserted the Georgia legislature, "there can be no discussion—no compromise—no doubt." In Louisiana governor and legislature agreed and moved for a southern convention to consider the crisis. United States Senator Hugh Lawson White of Tennessee told the Senate that slavery was "sacred" to the South. Never, proclaimed White, would southerners stand for any outside meddling with slavery.[29] This turmoil stemming from the collision between abolition and an aroused South exposed the raw nerve of slavery.

And the institution of slavery formed the bedrock of southern society. Perceptive as usual, Alexis de Tocqueville in the early 1830s recognized this centrality of slavery in southern society. From Tocqueville's time to break up of the Union nothing shoved slavery out of that central place. Practically every white southerner

29. *Niles' Register*, XLVIII (August 22, 1835), 444 ff, XLIX (January 2, 30, 1836), 245, 362–63; Freehling, *Prelude*, 340–41, 344; *Journal of the House of Representatives of the State of Louisiana, Twelfth Legislature: Second Session*, 2–3, 37–38, 54 and *Acts Passed at the First Session of the Thirteenth Legislature of the State of Louisiana*, 18–19; Nancy N. Scott (ed.), *A Memoir of Hugh Lawson White . . . (Philadelphia: J. B. Lippincott, 1856)*, 197–205.

agreed with Mississippi Governor John A. Quitman's assertion in his 1850 inaugural address: "This institution [slavery] is entwined with our political system and cannot be separated from it." Theresa Pulszky, accompanying Louis Kossuth on his southern tour in 1852, found slavery "so thoroughly interwoven with life and habits of Southerners that it 'form[ed] a part of their existence.'" To the Savannah physician and politician Richard Arnold slavery was no abstract question; for southerners it "involve[d] life and property, safety and security." Slavery meant "life and death to the South," wrote Colonel Arthur Hayne of South Carolina in 1835 to his friend Andrew Jackson. In January 1849 the General Assembly of Florida resolved unanimously that no division existed in the South on questions involving "the institution of slavery." To a Little Rock audience in the summer of 1850 United States Senator Solon Borland described slavery as "underlying as a sort of substratum, and inseparably connected with, the structure of all our institutions." "It affects," Borland emphasized, "the personal interest of every white man."[30]

For many southerners slavery also provided the foundation for their civilization; it became "the very foundation of Liberty." A broad-based intellectual defense became the cardinal goal of southern ministers, scientists, academicians, writers, and politicians. Together they agreed with William Gilmore Simms: "We believe also that negro slavery is one of the greatest and most admirable agents of Civilization."[31] By the hundreds and even the thousands, books, speeches, pamphlets, editorials, and sermons affirming the joy and value of slavery inundated southern readers and listeners. Many

30. Alexis de Tocqueville, *Democracy in America*, ed. Phillips Bradley (2 vols.; New York: Vintage, 1954), I, 370–419 *passim*; Quitman Inaugural Address, in John A. Quitman Papers, Department of Archives, Louisiana State University, Francis and Theresa Pulszky, *White, Red, Black: Sketches of American Society in the United States during the Visit of Their Guests* (2 vols.; New York: Redfield, 1853), II, 111–12; Arnold to the Reverend Chandler Robbins, August 15, 1837, in Richard H. Shryock (ed.), "Letters of Richard D. Arnold, M.D., 1808–1876," *Papers of the Trinity College Historical Society*, Double ser., XVIII–XIX (1929), 14; Hayne to Jackson, November 11, 1835, in Jackson Papers; Tallahassee *Floridian*, January 20, 1849; Little Rock *Arkansas Gazette*, July 26, 1850.

31. Alfred Huger to Joel Poinsett, September 1, 1838, in Joel Poinsett Papers, Historical Society of Pennsylvania; Simms to John Pendleton Kennedy, April 5, 1852, in John Pendleton Kennedy Papers, George Peabody Department, Enoch Pratt Free Library.

historians have cataloged and explicated the many facets of the pro-slavery argument. Even with their work, it is impossible to say how many southerners accepted or believed in the orthodox doctrine. But the number of true believers is of little import.

Although an indefinite number of white southerners refused to join the proslavery offensive, they remained steadfast behind slavery and reinforced the powerful hold it exerted on southern society. Concentrated in the upper South, especially in Virginia, these southerners followed the lead of men like Thomas Jefferson and John Randolph of Roanoke who, in an earlier day, had decried slavery as an evil but who had envisioned no remedy. More important, slavery was for them a southern problem not to be touched by outside hands. "In the name of wonder," Thomas Ritchie asked Martin Van Buren, "what business have our Brethren of the North with our Slaves?" While governor of Virginia in 1837, David Campbell spoke directly: "I am most decidedly opposed to any interference on the part of the non-slaveholding States or people about this question—*I do not even want their advice.*" For emphasis Campbell added, "I would not consent that any power upon earth should interfere with us about it." In 1835 the Richmond *Whig* admitted that it had supported a gradual emancipation program during the great Virginia debate of 1831, but the *Whig* declared that it lagged behind no man in opposing the abolitionists. They were outsiders and the South had no intention of ever allowing outsiders to make any decisions regarding slavery. A toast at a public dinner for Congressman Henry Wise summed up this view: "Slavery—Whatever differences of opinion may exist among us Virginians upon this vexed subject, we are unanimous on one point, a positive determination that no one shall think or act for us."[32]

This possessiveness spanned the South. Slavery was a misfortune

32. Robert McColley, *Slavery and Jeffersonian Virginia* (2nd ed.; Urbana, Chicago, London: University of Illinois Press, 1973), 124–32; Glover Moore, *The Missouri Crisis, 1819–1821* (Lexington: University of Kentucky Press, 1953), 252–57, 293–94; Ritchie to Van Buren, March 8, 1837, in Van Buren Papers; Campbell to Arthur P. Hayne, September 3, 1837, in Campbell Papers; Richmond *Whig*, October 23, 1835; Wise, *Wise*, 60–61.

said North Carolina's Kenneth Rayner to Congress in 1841, "But if it were ten times greater an evil than it is, we will never suffer those who are uninterested [northerners] in the matter to interfere with us." Calling emancipation "this delicate question," the Milledgeville *Federal Union* asserted, "the people of the South will be the keepers of their consciences, the protectors of their own interests, and the guardian of their own interests." During the abolitionist outburst of the mid-1830s the legislature of North Carolina resolved "with almost entire unanimity" that "North Carolina alone has the right to legislate over the slaves in her territory, and any attempt to change the condition, whether made by the congress, the legislatures, or the people of other states will be regarded as an invasion of our just rights." Declaring that the South could never liberate her slaves, Sam Houston of Texas, in his direct way, told the North to keep hands off.[33]

This unanimity of southern opinion certainly affected travelers in Dixie. E. A. Andrews of Boston visited northern Virginia in 1835 and quoted Virginians, even those who had supported emancipation Virginia style, as saying, "Our people have become exasperated, the friends of the slaves alarmed, and nothing remains, but that we should all unite in repelling the officious intermeddling of persons who do not understand the subject [read northerners] with which they are interfering." The Scotsman William Thomson reported conversing with planters who opposed slavery, but raised no hands against it because they saw no conceivable way of ending it. Joel Poinsett of South Carolina told Fredrika Bremer that though he felt slavery a "moral obliquity," he foresaw only one solution—the future. To Poinsett insurmountable difficulties barred any possible changes for the present. The peripatetic Frederick Law Olmsted found several southerners, particularly of the lower social classes, opposed to slavery in theory but he found all accepting it and none

33. For Rayner quote see Clement Eaton, *The Freedom-of-Thought Struggle in the Old South* (Rev. ed.; New York, Evanston, and London: Harper & Row, 1964), 287–88; Milledgeville *Federal Union*, April 11, 1833; *Niles' Register*, XLIX (January 2, 1836), 309; Amelia W. Williams and Eugene C. Barker (eds.), *The Writings of Sam Houson, 1813–1863* (8 vols.; Austin: University of Texas Press, 1938–43), VI, 172, 174.

working against it. A "poor white" in northeastern Mississippi told the traveler that he knew many who wanted slavery ended, but, the Mississippian continued, "it wouldn't never do to free 'em [the slaves] and leave 'em here [because] Nobody couldn't live here then." An Alabamian heading for Texas expressed identical sentiments: "I'd like it if we could get rid of 'em to yonst. I wouldn't like to hev' 'em freed, if they gwine to hang 'round."[34]

This kind of opposition really amounted to no opposition. Strong and positive assaults on slavery simply did not occur in the South. Impressed by this unity the world-traveled Englishman James Buckingham thought that it would be easier to attack popery in Rome, Mohammedanism in Constantinople, and despotism in St. Petersburg than to move against slavery in the South.[35]

Thus in practical terms it mattered little whether or not a southerner accepted or rejected the argument that slavery was a positive good. Standing "one and indivisible" on slavery, white southerners of all political persuasions and all social classes built a massive fortress around it. None could touch it but them, and they never did because even those who disliked slavery believed it untouchable and unchangeable. Any serious move against slavery was, as James H. Hammond, the South Carolina planter-politician, boldly put it, "a naked impossibility." This absence of even minimal dissent struck the historian of southern dissent Carl Degler, who described "an overall unity that embraces the diversity."[36] This conviction that slavery had to remain solely a southern concern made southerners

34. E. A. Andrews, *Slavery and the Domestic Slave-Trade in the United States* (Boston: Light & Stearns, 1836), 155–56; William Thomson, *A Tradesman's Travels in the United States and Canada, in the Years 1840, 41 & 42* (Edinburgh: Oliver & Boyd, 1842), 191; Fredrika Bremer, *The Homes of the New World; Impressions of America* (2 vols.; New York: Harper & Brothers, 1854), I, 287–88; Frederick Law Olmsted, *A Journey in the Back Country* (New York: Mason Brothers, 1860), 203, and *A Journey in the Seaboard Slave States, with Remarks on Their Economy* (New York: Dix & Edwards, 1856), 573.

35. J. S. Buckingham, Esq., *The Slave States of America* (2 vols.; London and Paris: Fisher, Son, *ca.* 1842), I, 183–84.

36. Jackson *Mississippian*, March 16, 1849, [James Henry Hammond], *Selections from the Letters and Speeches of the Hon. James H. Hammond of South Carolina* (New York: John F. Trow, 1866), 102; Carl N. Degler, *The Other South: Southern Dissenters in the Nineteenth Century* (New York, Evanston, San Francisco, London: Harper & Row, 1974), 3, and Chap. 1 *passim*.

acutely sensitive to any outside discussions or attacks on slavery and on any attempts to connect them with such views or movements.

From the Jackson period onward, southerners were quick to find even the worth of the Union wanting when it seemed to foster or harbor antislave sentiments. In the 1830s nullifiers and their extremist brethren continually spoke about the danger of the Union for southern interests. Repeatedly they, like James H. Hammond, declared that any government interference with slavery would "dissolve the Union." But the extremists did not cry out alone. Although Virginia Democrats worked hard to defuse the nullification crisis, their rhetoric often paralleled that of the nullifiers. William C. Rives, Virginia's loyal Jacksonian senator, asserted "that for the people of the non-slaveholding States to discuss the question of slavery, at all, is to attack the foundations of the union itself." From the pulpit of his Richmond *Enquirer*, Thomas Ritchie in 1833 preached that any tampering with slavery meant that the "Union [would] inevitably fall in pieces." Writing to Martin Van Buren four years later Ritchie declared that the South "would freely and voluntarily, coolly and deliberately withdraw from the Confederation" before allowing the federal government to strike against slavery. With outcries such as "The North must put down the fanatics, or the Union is gone like a wreath of sand before the flood tide," Whigs kept pace with Democrats. During the petition controversy in the House, Whig orators in clarion-call style emphasized that the Union did not come before southern determination to maintain slavery as a southern question.[37]

Later, when the issue of slavery in the territories erupted during the Mexican War, southerners equated their right to carry slavery into the territories with the existence of slavery itself.[38] To southern-

37. [Hammond], *Hammond Speeches*, 35; Rives to W. F. Ritchie, September 7, 1835, in Rives Papers; Richmond *Enquirer*, July 19, 1833, and Ritchie to Van Buren, February 11, 1837, in Van Buren Papers; Little Rock *Arkansas Advocate*, September 18, 1835; *Congressional Globe*, 24th Cong., 1st Sess., 77–78, 80–81 and in Appendix, 135, 298–300 and *Register of Debates*, 24th Cong., 1st Sess., 4010–28.

38. This point will be discussed in detail in Chap. Seven herein.

ers the exclusion of slavery from the territories by the federal government was just as unacceptable as emancipation. Freesoil and freesoilers became ogres in the exact image of abolition and abolitionists. The adamant southern stand against restricting slavery in the territories rested on constitutional theory, on considerations of political power, and on southern honor. Although southerners developed a constitutional defense of their position, political and psychological motives were paramount. Each reinforced the other. Southerners viewed the exclusion of slavery with hostility and horror, for they saw it as the preface to ultimate abolition. Moreover, they feared adoption of a restrictive policy as a first step toward permanent political inferiority, an inferiority that would eventually mean that the South could no longer protect its peculiar institution. Furthermore restriction branded southern society as un-American and dishonorable. Committed to slavery as the southerners were, they could not think otherwise. Restriction equaled insult and the southern code forbade accepting insults.

Because southerners never distinguished between free soil and abolition, the cry of restriction engendered all the charged emotion associated with the cry of emancipation. Talk and threats of restriction, just as talk and threats of abolition, stirred the innermost soul of southern society. Thus the emergence of the extension issue in the late 1840s only intensified the volatility of southern politics, a politics easily and often convulsed by any hint of outside moves against slavery.

Because slavery occupied such a crucial position in southern society, slavery dwarfed all other political issues. John Quincy Adams, who knew firsthand whereof he spoke, recognized in 1835 that the slave question was "paramount to all others" in the South. Southern politicians, Adams noted, "never failed to touch upon this key . . . and it has never yet failed of success." In that same year, Governor William Schley told his fellow Georgians that they could and did differ over the tariff and nullification, but not over slavery, the most important issue. To the South Carolina nullifier Thomas Cooper "the question of *Domestic Servitude* ultimately like Aaron's rod swallow[ed] up all the rest." Traveling in the South just before the 1840 presidential contest James Buckingham reported that when slavery took to the political field, all other issues fled. The slavery issue assumed "paramount importance" to southern parties and politicians, observed the Richmond *Whig* in 1846. Toward the close of the 1840s William P. Duval, a grand old man among Florida Democrats, described the tariff and banks as "mere subjects of policy" about which southerners "may honestly differ." But, Duval continued, "The slave question is the rock." [39]

Party partisans certainly tried to benefit from the political potency of slavery. Whigs constantly accused Democrats of trying "to make a party issue of the slavery question." Denouncing such tactics William B. Campbell, a Whig congressman from Tennessee, defined the congressional hassles over abolition in the late 1830s as an effort "by the Van Buren party & the Nullifiers to disturb the question of abolition." In 1850 the Raleigh *Register* proclaimed that southern Democrats had always engaged in "the aggravated *agitation* of the Slavery issue, as an end to be sought after." According to the Arkansas Whig, Charles F. M. Noland, southern Democrats "use[d] it for the purpose of injuring Whigs in advancing Democracy." Announcing that the Democrats "have ever used, and attempted to use, every question connected with the rights of the South, to a mere selfish political and party purpose," the leading Whig newspaper in Florida echoed Noland's charge. Democratic practices aroused the ire of the Vicksburg *Whig* while the Richmond *Whig* seemed resigned: "Agitation on the subject of Slavery has been a favorite game with the Locofoco party for many years." The general Whig assessment, in Alexander Stephens' pithy summary,

39. John Quincy Adams, *Memoirs of John Quincy Adams,* ed. Charles Francis Adams (12 vols.; Philadelphia: J. B. Lippincott, 1874–77), XI, 252; Milledgeville *Federal Union,* November 5, 1835; Cooper to Martin Van Buren, March 19, 1838, in Van Buren Papers; Buckingham, *Slave States,* I, 142; Richmond *Whig,* October 9, 1846; Duval to John J. Crittenden, November 26, 1848, in John J. Crittenden Papers, Division of Manuscripts, Library of Congress.

had Democrats using "the slave question for nothing but political capital."[40]

Although the Whigs continuously berated the Democrats for politicizing slavery, the Democrats, in turn, castigated the Whigs for attempting to make the slave issue their own. A rising North Carolina Democrat was disturbed because the Whigs adopted "rash measures in the hope of aiding the cause of *party.*" The Whig goal in 1835, according to William H. Haywood, Jr., was to "alarm the Southern feelings" by agitating the slavery question. The Raleigh *Standard* claimed that the slavery issue had become "an electioneering hobby" with Whigs. John H. Cocke, Sr., of Virginia decried Whig strivings "to lash up, & appeal to the morbid sensibility of the South." Florida Democrats protested vehemently against Whig attempts to use the slave issue for partisan advantage. In 1850 United States Senator James M. Mason, a Virginia Democrat, wrote that the slavery question had become "the touchstone of party" for Whigs in the South.[41]

Party politicians bedeviled each other in a personal way over the unending topic of slavery. Virginia Whigs tried to embarrass the prominent Democrat William C. Rives by publicizing certain comments on gradual emancipation that Rives had made in private correspondence. The North Carolina gubernatorial contest of 1840 found both sides plagued with efforts to connect each with abolition. Democrats tried to blemish the strongest Whig candidate "by representing that he had introduced Abolition memorials in the Legisla-

40. Edward J. Hale to William Alexander Graham, July 4, 1851, in Hamilton and Williams (eds.), *Graham Papers,* IV, 140; William Campbell to David Campbell, December 14, 1838, in Campbell Papers; Raleigh *Register,* January 9, 1850; Noland to Thomas Corwin, August 24, 1850, in Thomas Corwin Papers, Division of Manuscripts, Library of Congress; Tallahassee *Florida Sentinel,* May 30, 1848; Vicksburg *Tri-Weekly Whig,* June 2, 1849; Richmond *Whig,* October 1, 1852; Alexander Stephens to Linton Stephens, December 31, 1849, in Alexander Stephens Papers, Manhattanville College.

41. Haywood to William Gaston, December 5, 1835, in William Gaston Papers, Southern Historical Collection, University of North Carolina; Raleigh *Standard,* May 31, 1837; Cocke to William C. Rives, February 23, 1837, in Rives Papers, and also see C. W. Gooch to Levi Woodbury, October 10, 1835, in Levi Woodbury Papers, Division of Manuscripts, Library of Congress; Tallahassee *Floridian,* September 18, 1847; Mason to William C. Rives, February 4, 1850, in Rives Papers.

ture last winter." The Whigs responded in kind, for the Democratic nominee felt compelled to proclaim publicly that he opposed abolition "in any and every shape, form or fashion, except as the owners of slaves themselves desire"; Romulus Saunders' letter covered four newspaper columns. During the bitter gubernatorial race of 1851 in Mississippi, Henry Stuart Foote gave firsthand testimony on the use of slavery as an issue when he railed against his accusers: "I never voted with the Abolitionists—never—never—so help me God!"[42]

Candidates for national office also found themselves hounded by the omnipresent slavery issue. Opponents of Whig John M. Berrien's reelection to the United States Senate from Georgia worked zealously to cast doubt on Berrien's slavery stance. Evidently these efforts paid some dividends, if only briefly, for one of Berrien's supporters wrote the senator, "I was astonished to have it insinuated . . . that perhaps I was tainted with abolitionism" and just because he favored Berrien. In Arkansas both parties tried to elect congressmen by painting opponents with the abolition brush. In 1848 the Democrats charged the Whig candidate with supporting the Wilmot Proviso, but the Whigs, at least to their own satisfaction, proved the Democrats wrong. Then in 1851 while attacking the Democratic candidate for supporting restriction, the Whigs urged Arkansans to vote for their candidate with "his sturdy support of the true rights of the South."[43]

Aware that the slavery issue stirred up more excitement and enthusiasm than any other, southern politicians quite consciously invoked it as often and as forcefully in the 1830s as they did twenty years later. Many of them, in James H. Hammond's graphic language, "[thought] that you have to say but nigger to the South to set it on fire, as one whistles to a Turkey to make him gobble." Southern

42. Thomas Ritchie to Rives, August 23, 1834, in Rives Papers; William Alexander Graham to Willie P. Mangum, October 11, 1839, in Shanks (ed.), *Mangum Papers*, III, 19–20; Raleigh *Standard*, March 11, 1840; Jackson *Mississippian*, August 8, 15, 1851.

43. J. S. Peterson to Berrien, September 17, 1845, and C. B. Strong to Berrien, April 25, 1845, both in John M. Berrien Papers, Southern Historical Collection, University of North Carolina; Little Rock *Arkansas Gazette*, August 24, 1848; Helena (Ark.) *Southern Shield*, June 28, 1851.

politicians of all persuasions recognized that discussion of the slave question "excite[d] feelings allied to madness."[44]

III

The intimacy between the individual southerner and southern society had powerful implications for slavery as a political issue. While southern society defended slavery either as a positive good or a necessity, each mode of defense sprang from individuals who did not think of themselves apart from their society. Individual southerners defending slavery wove the fabric of societal unity. Accusations of unfaithfulness to southern civilization, the same as weakness or wavering on the slavery issue, brought forth immediate and vehement denials from all southerners, but especially from the politicians. They stood constantly under the glare of public scrutiny as they asked southern voters to let them speak for the South. As the most public of men their stance on slavery had to be crystal clear and beyond reproach.

The slavery question provided simultaneously the weapon of political victory and political destruction. Continuously accusing their opponents of abolitionist and freesoil connections southern politicians made rhetorical broadsides of such charges. And every politician who found himself or his party hit by one of these cannonades felt compelled to respond with an equally vigorous onslaught. This driving force engendered an increasing fury in charge and countercharge. Politicians caught up in the politics of slavery behaved as they did for two complementary reasons: first, they believed it politically astute and essential; second, they knew it necessary to maintain their identity as southerners.

That identity hinged on the idea of dignity and honor—dignity led to honor and honor required dignity. William Faulkner dramatized the pervasiveness and power of that idea in his brilliant story "An

44. Hammond to William Gilmore Simms, June 20, 1848, in James H. Hammond papers, Division of Manuscripts, Library of Congress; John H. Cocke, Sr., to William C. Rives, August 10, 1835, in Rives Papers.

Odor of Verbena."[45] Even though the story takes place during the Reconstruction years, the values and mores that influence the characters and action clearly come from the prewar South. Young Bayard Sartoris, faced with avenging the killing of his father, feels the pressure of a solid wall of community conviction. Honor demanded that he act. Whites of both the upper and lower social orders, men and women, the former slave, even the killer of Bayard's father all expect Bayard to observe the code that required a man to maintain and preserve his dignity (or independence) through action identifiable by the community. Bayard ultimately decides against killing; still he must face his father's killer in order to retain both his own dignity as well as his honor in the community. The values of the individual and those of the community reinforce each other to demand action.

Although Faulkner's genius enabled him to depict so powerfully the interaction among the code, the individual, and the community, contemporaries and historians recognized the power of those same forces. In a speech before the United States Senate in 1854 Albert G. Brown claimed that the "one standard of social merit" in the South was "integrity" or "an unsullied reputation." The honor and reputation of an individual, Brown informed the Senate, allowed him to stand "on a social level with all his fellows." The Scottish traveler William Thomson found southerners different from northerners. "They have a high sense of honor," Thomson wrote in 1842, "treating every white man as a gentleman, but rigidly exacting the same in return." Back in 1835 James H. Hammond used words like *virtue* and *courage* to define the primary forces in southern white society. According to John DuBose and Joseph Hodgson "a spirit of personal dignity and independence" dominated social relations in antebellum Alabama. Eugene Genovese has noted that white overseers often found themselves living in a social vacuum because "they were branded as lacking 'dignity'—no small charge in this quasi-traditional society." Although much of this language is

45. This story is a part of Faulkner's novel *The Unvanquished* (New York: New American Library, 1959).

vague and absolute precision is impossible, the existence and power of the forces it attempts to define cannot be denied.[46]

In his illuminating essay, "The Southerner and the Laws," Charles Sydnor admitted that imprecision, but concluded that the code—the honor and dignity—formed "the ideals of [the] society" and in so doing tells us "something of the nature of that society."[47] Sydnor observed that for many reasons southerners thought of themselves, not the state, as lawmakers and enforcers. An individual handled his own affairs without calling for help from any legal body, especially when his personal reputation was involved. And many southerners proclaimed slander a worse crime than murder. To them slander meant any implication that a person lacked honor either as an individual or in the community. Of course, as "An Odor of Verbena" demonstrates, the two were usually inseparable.

The code duello highlighted this emphasis on personal dignity and responsibility. For all of its elaborate etiquette and punctilio, the duel was based on individual responsibility and the determination to demand, and then accept it. Between 1830 and 1860 many southern public men either issued or accepted the challenge that led to personal combat, though many southerners, including some who fought, denounced this ritualized assassination. That it flourished in the face of denunciation and laws underscores the power of the code.[48]

46. M. W. Cluskey (ed.), *Speeches, Messages, and Other Writings of the Hon. Albert G. Brown, a Senator in Congress from the State of Mississippi* (Philadelphia: Jas. B. Smith, 1859), 336–37; Thomson, *Tradesman's Travels*, 20; [Hammond], *Hammond Speeches*, 45; John Witherspoon DuBose, *The Life and Times of William Lowndes Yancey* (2 vols.; New York: Peter Smith, 1942), I, 40, and Joseph Hodgson, *The Cradle of the Confederacy; or, the Times of Troup, Quitman and Yancey: A Sketch of Southwestern Political History from the Formation of the Federal Government to A.D. 1861* (Mobile: Register Publishing Office, 1876), 6–7; Eugene Genovese, *Roll, Jordan, Roll: The World the Slaves Made* (New York: Pantheon, 1974), 16.

47. Charles S. Sydnor, "The Southerner and the Laws," *Journal of Southern History*, VI (1940), 3–23.

48. Although historians have often commented on duels and dueling, none has yet made a thorough and penetrating study of the relationship between the duel and the values of southern society. For brief comments see Daniel J. Boorstin, *The Americans: The National Experience* (New York: Vintage, 1965), 206–12; John Hope Franklin, *The Militant South, 1800–1861* (Cambridge: Harvard University Press, 1956), 44–62; Guy A. Cardwell, "The Duel in the Old South: Crux of a Concept," *South Atlantic Quarterly*, LXVI (1967), 50–69.

Even though the duel touched chiefly the upper orders of white society, it symbolized a powerful force in the southern psychology—a force that permeated society. In the lower orders of white society, men guarded their dignity and honor with a jealousy and ferocity that matched the formal rules of the duel. The German commentator on American customs Francis Grund claimed that white southerners more than other Americans were conscious of dignity or independence. Determined to preserve their position above the slaves, white southerners "cherish[ed] doubly" their rights and independence. After cataloging the virtues, chiefly a fierce sense of independence, of the farm folk of northeastern Mississippi, Reuben Davis commented that any one of them would "knock down any [other] man who questioned his right to these privileges." Few observers have been more perceptive about the mores of the common whites of the antebellum South than Augustus Baldwin Longstreet. In his story "The Fight," Longstreet described the events following a verbal insult. When Billy Stallings offended Bob Durham's wife, Bob felt his honor blemished and in a ritual akin to the duel he challenged Billy. Billy freely admitted, "I've said enough for a fight." Thereupon the two Georgians commenced to settle their question of honor with fists and teeth. When he wrote about southern society in 1860, Daniel R. Hundley discussed the middle classes and the yeomen separately; even so he found a similar characteristic in each group. The middle-class man "[was] a man of the stoutest independence" and the yeoman, who "always possesse[d] a manly independence of character" had never "learned to fear mortal man" and would never allow himself to be humiliated. William Thomson had no doubt that southern "men of business and mechanics" more than their northern counterparts "consider[ed] themselves men of honour" and "more frequently resent[ed] any indignity shown them even at the expense of their life, or that of those who venture to insult them."[49]

49. Francis J. Grund, *The Americans in their Moral, Social, and Political Relations* (Boston: Marsh, Capen and Lyon, 1837), 375; Reuben Davis, *Recollections of Mississippi and*

This personal and community code had far-reaching political manifestations because the defense of the South and slavery was intimately connected with personal honor. With the white South united on slavery, failure to uphold the southern position became dishonorable, an intolerable badge for any southerner. The rhetoric of the slavery discussion points unmistakably to this conclusion. Southerners viewed with "horror" any connection between themselves and abolition sentiments as well as any attempt to make such a connection. They often described the conflict between abolition or free soil and slavery as one between submission and resistance. Certainly no honorable man wanted to be branded as a submissionist. The "manly spirit" of the South, in Hammond's words, made such a designation unthinkable. Southerners continually asserted that their duty required them to vanquish the insult of those who dared impugn slavery or the South. Anna Butler, preparing to live in Zachary Taylor's White House, told her family back in Louisiana that she did not "wonder that the southern gentlemen became so warm" because northerners constantly "insult and deride the South and its institutions." Thus when southern politicians found themselves accused of alliances with those who did denounce slavery and the South, they feared even *"seeming to submit* too much to Northern insolence and aggression."[50]

Such accusations usually charged the northern wing of either the Democratic or Whig party of working to injure or defame the South.

Mississippians (Boston and New York: Houghton Mifflin, 1899), 19; Augustus Baldwin Longstreet, *Georgia Scenes, Characters, Incidents, & C.* (Augusta: S. R. Sentinel Office, 1835), 53–66 and esp. 57–58; D. R. Hundley, *Social Relations in Our Southern States* (New York: Henry B. Price, 1860), 84, 198–99; Alex. Mackay, *The Western World; or Travels in the United States in 1846–47: Exhibiting Them in Their Latest Development, Social, Political and Industrial; including a chapter on California* (2 vols.; Philadelphia: Lea & Blanchard, 1849), II, 104; Thomson, *Tradesman's Travels*, 23–24.

50. Buckingham, *Slave States*, I, 184; Tallahassee *Floridian*, January 20, 1849; *De Bow's Review*, VIII (1850), 522; Milledgeville *Federal Union*, May 21, 1839; David L. Yulee to John C. Calhoun, July 10, 1849, in David L. Yulee Papers, P. K. Yonge Library, University of Florida; New Orleans *Louisiana Courier*, February 7, 1854; Anna Butler to Sara Butler, February 16, 1849, in Thomas Butler Papers, Department of Archives, Louisiana State University; William S. Archer to William A. Graham, February 4, 1851, in Hamilton and Williams (eds.), *Graham Papers*, IV, 25.

To a southern party man this indictment carried a condemnation equally as heinous as one against his person, for it accused him both of political association with an antisouthern group and of failure to defend the South. Accordingly, loyalty to party required defense of party, and that defense was as critically important as personal defense.

Politicians, the public men in the antebellum South, pushed the slavery issue to arouse southern voters and win elections in the South. Once brought out into the public light, the slavery issue could not be dismissed or shoved aside because it was not mere gasconade. Attacking and defending, southern politicians had to maintain their own sense of dignity—personal and in the community—just as did Bayard Sartoris. The rhetoric and reality of southern politics, then, fused seemingly disparate elements into an integrated, overpowering force—the politics of slavery. A modern, highly developed political mechanism, the parties, managed by professional politicians and based on a democratic political structure became one with an anachronistic social institution, slavery, and a particular code of personal and communal honor.

IV

Identifying itself as the South-Militant determined to protect the virtuous South from the iniquitous abolitionist foe, southern Whiggery launched its first political crusade. "Our domestic institutions," cried a group of Georgia Whigs, are threatened with "annihilation." According to southern Whigs that desperate situation demanded a southern president, one the South could trust. Pushing this theme the Richmond *Whig* asked, "Can the South be safe at a time like this, in voting for a President who has successively opposed all her principles?" Martin Van Buren was dangerous, the *Whig* charged, because he supported restricting slavery in Missouri back in 1820 and because he *"studiously conceal[ed]* his opinion upon the power of Congress to abolish slavery in the District of [Columbia]." The general Whig indictment of Van Buren described a man untrustworthy. As the Milledgeville *Southern Recorder* saw it, no southerner could hesitate in opposing a man who had consistently attacked the vital interests of the South regarding both the tariff and slavery. Denouncing those who tried to present Van Buren as a friend to the South, the Little Rock *Arkansas Advocate* made use of a homey analogy: "About such a friend as a pig in a garden. Heaven preserve Arkansas from *such* friends."[51]

Although southern Whigs carefully refrained from calling Van Buren an abolitionist, they constantly claimed that he had abolitionist friends and constituents. And they were able to place these claims before southern voters for an extended period because the Democrats had officially nominated Van Buren in May, 1835, some eighteen months before the presidential election. The Richmond *Whig* summed up the party's position: "We add, that in the present state of things—with the torch flaming—that the South would be mad to elevate to the Presidency any man who had such friends and allies—were he as valiant as Caesar and wise as Cato." And no southern Whig blessed Van Buren with those credentials. He was a devious politician who had no commitment to the South. The old charges of 1832 were replayed but with the added turbulence of the abolition controversy they appeared significantly more consequential. With Van Buren as a presidential nominee, the Democrats, according to the lexicon of southern Whigs, had turned their backs on the South in her hour of need. The Whigs, on the other hand, stood ready to defend the South and slavery with a native southern slaveowner as presidential candidate, Hugh Lawson White of Tennessee.[52]

From the earliest discussions of the presidential question southern Whigs urged that the next president be "generally acceptable to the South." The Jackson opposition in Georgia boomed one of their

51. Richmond *Whig*, January 5, 1836; Milledgeville *Southern Recorder*, January 6, December 15, 1835, May 10, 1836; Little Rock *Arkansas Advocate*, May 22, 1835.

52. Richmond *Whig*, June 30, August 7, 1835, September 16, 1836; Little Rock *Arkansas Advocate*, May 13, 1836.

own, the old states' rights zealot George Troup. John Tyler felt a southern candidate essential for the Whigs; without one he predicted any Whig hope for success "Absolutely one of gloom." In Washington talk abounded of a southern candidate to stop Van Buren in the slave states.[53]

From this general conviction that they needed a southerner, southern Whigs began to line up behind one man, Hugh White of Tennessee. In early 1834 Congressman James Graham informed his brother William, "I incline to White." In that same letter Graham indicated that congressmen from Virginia and Georgia were "very generally for White." A White drive in his native Tennessee gained momentum in that same year; a caucus of the Tennessee congressional delegation on December 23, 1834, produced a letter favoring White for the presidency supported by all but three of the delegation. The nomination of White by the Alabama legislature in January, 1835, seemed to end the talk of other candidates, for very quickly White became the Whig champion across the South.[54]

To determine exactly how the new coalition opposed to the Democrats decided on Hugh White is exceedingly difficult. No evidence suggests that union on White resulted from a decision by opposition leaders either northern or southern, in Washington or elsewhere, though from the first such men counted on White's strength in the South.[55] Undoubtedly the White movement began in Tennessee as early as 1833 as promotion for a favorite son without any anti-Jackson

53. Raleigh *Register*, September 23, 1834; Milledgeville *Southern Recorder*, April 30, 1834; Tyler to William Fitzhugh Gordon, November 9, 1834, quoted in Gordon, *Gordon*, 294; Nathaniel Niles to William C. Rives, January 20, February 11, 1835, in Rives Papers; John Sergeant to Nicholas Biddle, January 23, 1835, in Nicholas Biddle Papers, Division of Manuscripts, Library of Congress.

54. James Graham to William Alexander Graham, January 2, 1834, in Hamilton and Williams (eds.), *Graham Papers*, I, 278–79; Powell Moore, "The Revolt Against Jackson in Tennessee, 1835–1836," *Journal of Southern History*, II (1936), 335–59; *Niles' Register*, XLVII (February 7, 1835), 387.

55. See the Niles and Sergeant letters cited in n. 53 above; J. J. Crittenden to Orlando Brown, December 27, 1835, quoted in Mrs. Chapman Coleman (ed.), *The Life of John J. Crittenden, with Selections from His Correspondence and Speeches* (2 vols.; Philadelphia: J. B. Lippincott, 1871), I, 88–89; Henry Clay to Christopher Hughes, August 25, 1835, in Reeves Collection, William L. Clements Library, University of Michigan.

connotations. No evidence points to any central direction behind the movement and, because of the diffuse nature of the Whig party at the time, probably none existed.

Certainly White himself did not engage in high level negotiations with other southern or national leaders. He had little in common with Henry Clay or Daniel Webster, whose policies he had opposed all his public life.[56] White proudly identified himself as an Old Republican who had never wavered from the true faith. Moreover as a longtime personal and political friend of Andrew Jackson, White had been a Jacksonian stalwart both in Tennessee and in Washington where he sat in the United States Senate during Jackson's presidency. He stood with Jackson during the bank war on both veto and withdrawal as well as throughout the nullification crisis when he voted for the Force Bill. As late as December, 1833, Jackson, who had once invited White to live in the White House, still considered his old comrade a staunch political ally. In that year White even rejected presidential overtures from the Tennessee legislature because he feared that acceptance might endanger Jackson's strength in Congress. In 1834, perhaps in an effort to squelch the White presidential talk, Jackson offered his friend the vice-presidency on a ticket headed by Van Buren. White in 1836 declared, and there is no reason to dispute him, that his only difference with Jackson was the latter's determination to name his own successor.[57]

That difference, however, indicates that White did have presidential ambitions. As early as 1833 he had heard his name mentioned as next in line after Jackson. In January, 1835, a Virginia congressman wrote to William C. Rives that White was "obviously pleased at the prospect of his nomination" for the presidency. Evidently no disagreement existed in the White household, for a family

56. For a full account of White's life see Lunica Paul Gresham, "The Public Career of Hugh Lawson White" (Ph.D. dissertation, Vanderbilt University, 1943); Scott (ed.), *White*, contains numerous extracts from his correspondence and speeches.

57. Andrew Jackson to Martin Van Buren, November 16, 1833, in Van Buren Papers; Moore, "Revolt Against Jackson," 335–36; Scott (ed.), *White*, 334, 352; Charles G. Sellers, Jr., *James K. Polk* (2 vols.; Princeton: Princeton University Press, 1957–), I, 255.

friend reported that Mrs. White "is wonderfully elated at the idea of getting into the White House."[58] The willingness of White to accept the role of candidate in 1835 and his perseverance in the campaign through 1836 confirms those contemporary reports.

Certain of White's Jacksonian associates, including President Jackson, saw the White movement as little more than a vehicle used by Tennessee Congressman John Bell and the forces of the second Bank of the United States to camouflage their hopes for a new national bank. Bell did become a mainstay in the White campaign, though nothing indicates that he played the role either of initiator or of master wirepuller.[59] Also I have not detected any direct influence or intervention by the bank in any southern state. Thus White did not front for some kind of pro-bank cabal. Pro-bank men did favor him in Tennessee and elsewhere but they recognized the general unpopularity of their views and made no effort to push them in the South.[60] Additionally they composed a distinct minority in the coalition that formed behind White.

White's candidacy signaled that the old National Republican issues would not be dredged up; the major thrust would be an attempt to attract those Jacksonians already disaffected and to cultivate even more disaffection. The Richmond *Whig* defined the Whig effort as one "every Republican of the Old School can put in trust." Hugh White himself announced that his name had been placed before the *"Jefferson Jackson Republicans"*; if that meant "to be denominated 'new-born Whigs,'" White proclaimed, "we are content." National

58. John Y. Mason to Rives, January 10, 1835, in Rives Papers; John Campbell to David Campbell, March 5, 1835, in Campbell Papers.

59. Jackson to Felix Grundy, October 5, 1835, in Felix Grundy Papers, Southern Historical Collection, University of North Carolina; *The Autobiography of Martin Van Buren,* ed. John C. Fitzpatrick (Washington: Government Printing Office, 1920), 225 n.; Henry A. Wise, *Seven Decades of the Union* (Philadelphia: J. B. Lippincott, 1872), 161. Bell, though he stood with Jackson during the bank war, had definitely begun to judge the bank more favorably by 1834. Probably by 1835 he would have supported some kind of new charter, but he kept very quiet about his shift. Nicholas Biddle to Bell, May 2, 1834, in Biddle Papers; Parks, *Bell,* 68–69, 76–77.

60. Henry Clay to Francis T. Brooke, July 20, 1835, in Henry Clay Papers, William R. Perkins Library, Duke University and James Barbour to Clay, August 2, 1835, in Colton (ed.), *Clay Correspondence,* 398.

Republicans did hoist White's banner but for them as for the Old Republicans it flew over states' rights and slavery, not over economic and political nationalism. Almost to a man the disaffected Jacksonians rallied to the new cause. The South Carolina nullifiers represented the only noteworthy exception. Although the friends of Calhoun and nullification in Virginia, North Carolina, Georgia, Alabama, and Mississippi ardently supported White, Calhoun and his South Carolina confederates refused to commit themselves. Principle, they claimed, dictated their passiveness; White had voted for the Force Bill. Still the South Carolinians made it clear that they intended no public opposition; they knew their friends from the Potomac to the Mississippi were toiling for White. In fact they wished their associates "all good luck in the enterprise" of electing White.[61]

In two ways Whigs in the South made clear their goal of appealing to those southerners who had voted en masse for Jackson. Throughout the campaign the Whigs emphasized the true Jacksonian antecedents of their cause. Although they hammered away unceasingly at Van Buren, they never really made Jackson's character or personality a target. They proudly pointed to the *"original Jackson men"* in the new group. Of course White fit this scenario perfectly, for he had remained loyal to the Democratic party longer than many of his supporters. This direction insured a low profile for National Republicanism; in fact the Whig newspapers of 1835–1836 mention National Republicanism only to dissociate it from their endeavors.[62]

Southern Whigs also tried to capitalize on the claim by the Democratic party that it was the political personification of democracy.

61. Richmond *Whig*, February 13, 1836; Scott (ed.), *White*, 354; Calhoun to William F. Gordon, May 22, 1835, quoted in Gordon, *Gordon*, 298, and to Francis Pickens, May 19, 1835, in John C. Calhoun Papers, South Caroliniana Library, University of South Carolina; Duff Green to Calhoun, March 9, 1835, in John C. Calhoun Papers, Robert Muldrow Cooper Library, Clemson University; Wm. C. Preston to James H. Hammond, January 18, 1835, in Hammond Papers; John A. Quitman to his brother, October 17, 1835, quoted in Clairborne, *Quitman*, I, 139.

62. James Graham to William Alexander Graham, January 2, 1834, in Hamilton and Williams (eds.), *Graham Papers*, I, 278; Little Rock *Arkansas Advocate*, April 29, 1836; Richmond *Whig*, 1835–1836, *passim*.

Whigs chided the Democrats for attempting to hoodwink the voters by disallowing free choice and forcing Van Buren on them. The Virginia Whig Central Committee circulated a public address that condemned the Baltimore convention as a skillful plot designed to mask dictation; but, according to the address, the people were not duped, for the people, no more and no less, composed the opposition to Van Buren. Hugh White became "THE PEOPLE'S CANDIDATE FOR THE PRESIDENCY" in contrast to the dictated choice of the Baltimore convention. Southerners, Whigs proclaimed, always chose their own leaders. They bowed to orders from no one. The nomination of White by legislatures became the voice of the people speaking. The "PEOPLE'S ANTI-CAUCUS CANDIDATES" rang out from the Little Rock *Arkansas Advocate*. To the *Advocate* the people must either vote Whig or accept dictation. In Whig rhetoric the nomination of Van Buren became the abandonment of the democratic ideal. White proved a good choice on this point, for friend and foe attested to his popularity with southern voters. And White told those voters, "I will never yield to the dictation of one man living, but will willingly abide the expressed will of a majority" of the voters.[63]

While the appeal to old Jacksonians meant that the southern Whigs departed totally and forever from the narrow National Republican base and while the Whig self-identification with democracy and independence articulated a powerful force in southern life, neither the appeal nor the identification could arouse southern voters sufficiently to give the Whigs a chance of competing successfully against the Democrats. That conclusion does not stem from hindsight, for Whigs recognizing its truth worked vigorously the one issue that insured voter arousal and excitement—slavery and southern safety. Taking advantage of the volatile atmosphere created by

63. Richmond *Whig*, August 23, 1836; Little Rock *Arkansas Advocate*, April 29, 1836; Sam G. Smith to James K. Polk, February 3, 1835, in Polk Papers; Alfred Balch to Andrew Jackson, November 29, 1833, in Jackson Papers; John M. Berrien to Dr. Ambrose Baber, November 24, 1836, in Baber-Blackshear Papers, Ilah Dunlap Little Memorial Library, University of Georgia; Scott (ed.), *White*, 345.

the first crisis of abolition, southern Whigs determined to identify their future with slavery. Shunting aside any hint of economic issues, Whigs preached the potential danger to the South as the critical concern of southern politics and the southern voter. The White campaign relied on the "southern feeling, coexisting with slavery." The slogan of southern Whigs became: "The cause of Judge White is the cause of the South."[64]

Across the South, Whigs emphasized White's southern identity and what that identity meant to the South. Asserting that the slave question "will have a greater influence in the South, than any other circumstance in the contest," a Virginia leader, and one from the National Republican camp, told Henry Clay that in White's southernness lay Whig hopes in the Old Dominion. The Milledgeville *Southern Recorder* declared that "many who have hitherto been politically, opposed [to the Whigs], will be found united in the support of the Southern man, Southern rights and Southern interests." Proclaiming that the South must not "hold back" the Richmond *Whig* urged that all southern voters recognize that the Whig party and candidate represented the South. In an address in Northampton County, North Carolina, Willie P. Mangum asserted that White "possessed all the honesty of purpose, correctness of views, and clearness of comprehension that the South required." "I think our interests imperatively require a Slave holding President," exclaimed United States Senator Alexander Porter of Louisiana; every Southern Whig seemed to share that view. The *Southern Recorder* summed up the Whig message: "[White] will stand or fall with the people of the South for he is one of ourselves, and his own wife and children must be the participants of the weal or woe of the South."[65]

64. Nathaniel Niles to William C. Rives, January 20, 1836, in Rives Papers; Raleigh *Register,* December 22, 1835.
65. James Barbour to Henry Clay, August 2, 1835, in Colton (ed.), *Clay Correspondence,* 398; Milledgeville *Southern Recorder,* December 15, 1835, October 25, 1836; Richmond *Whig,* May 8, November 20, 1835, September 16, 1836; Porter to Jesse Burton Harrison, January 12, 1836, in Burton Harrison Papers.

In no southern state did any Whig-sponsored economic issue challenge the Whig effort to equate their cause with the fate of the South. Speaking bluntly John Tyler realized that "*no Bank man* can be elected." Agreeing, the Richmond *Whig* asserted that "the Bank is already decreed to go down" and defined the Whig campaign as an attempt "to band the whole South together, and once more present an unconquerable will to federal aggression." Omitting any reference to economics a Whig convention in North Carolina pointed up Whig strategy in the South when it resolved: "We wish not to excite feelings of sectional hostility, but things being equal, we deem it a safe rule in choosing a public servant, to take him who is identified with us in interest, and who in the administration of his office cannot injure us without injuring himself, rather than one who is not bound to us by such ties." This convention went on to report that because of the agitation of the slavery question "we deem it a matter of great importance to our safety and peace, to have a President who is with us on this great question." And as the Whig gubernatorial candidate Edward B. Dudley reminded his fellow North Carolinians: "Mr. Van Buren is not one of us. He is a Northern man... in soul, in principle, and in action."[66]

The sectional thrust of the White campaign caused difficulties between southern Whigs and their northern brethren. Northern Whigs in Congress had no dealings with White. Daniel Webster grumbled that "the movement of southern Whigs (as they call themselves) in Mr. White's favor had disgusted, deeply, the whole body of our friends in the North." Denouncing southern papers such as the Richmond *Whig* for presenting White and Van Buren as the only real choices, Webster asserted that in such a contest the North and East would vote for Van Buren. He urged that something be done to counter the mischief below the Potomac. While Webster com-

66. Tyler to William F. Gordon, November 9, 1834, quoted in Gordon, *Gordon*, 294; Richmond *Whig*, February 3, June 30, 1835; "Report and Resolutions of the Orange County Whig Meeting" printed in Hamilton and Williams (eds.), *Graham Papers*, I, 414–15; Raleigh *Register*, February 23, 1836.

plained, John Bell wondered whether or not his supposed northern compatriots would ever "learn common sense." The condemnation of White by northerners and their boosting of Webster as the proper and only alternative to Van Buren hurt the southern effort. According to Bell "the only argument urged with any effect against Judge White, in all the South and Southwest, by Van Buren's friends," was the cry that the race would end in the House where Webster, not White, would be the opposition choice. "Cannot something be beat in the heads of Webster's friends?" Bell asked. Unless the Webster people quieted down, Bell argued, the White movement might be prostrated.[67] Bell's ire and his eloquent pleading attest to the care that went into creating a prosouthern Whig party.

The conscious use by the southern Whigs of overtly sectional issues, not the candidacy of Martin Van Buren, generated the excitement of their campaign.[68] That particular campaign magnified tremendously Van Buren's liability to the southern Democrats. All Whig leaders in the South, no matter the specific road they had traveled into the party, went to southern voters with a direct and inflammatory sectional appeal.

Distress among southern Jacksonian politicians affirmed the success of the Whig strategy. In every southern state Democratic politicians parroted Thomas Ritchie's cry: "Judge White is cutting into our ranks." From far off Arkansas word came to President Jackson and to Congressman James K. Polk that "a great majority of the people still call themselves Jackson men; but still join the opposition in making war upon Mr. Van Buren." A Democratic loyalist in

67. Felix Grundy to John M. Bass. December 19, 1835, in Whitefoord Cole Collection; Webster to Nicholas Biddle, May 9, 1835, in Reginal C. McGrane (ed.), *The Correspondence of Nicholas Biddle Dealing with National Affairs, 1807–1844* (Boston and New York: Houghton Mifflin, 1919), 250–51; Bell to Gulian C. Verplanck, June 22, 1835, in Gulian C. Verplanck Papers, New York Historical Society.

68. To my mind Richard McCormick overemphasized the presence of Van Buren and underemphasized the character of the Whig campaign. See his *The Second American Party System: Party Formation in the Jacksonian Era* (Chapel Hill: University of North Carolina Press, 1966), 250–51, 338–40; cf. Burton W. Folsom II, "Party Formation and Development in Jacksonian America: The Old South," *Journal of American Studies*, VII (1973), 217–29.

Louisiana told his party's United States senator that the division in Democratic ranks caused by White's candidacy made him fearful that the Democrats would fail to carry the state. The extent of disaffection in Tennessee astonished Jackson's lieutenant Alfred Balch, who reported to his chief that those going over to White included many who were formerly among the president's "most zealous friends."[69]

While White partisans rejoiced that "this abolition question, takes well," Democratic leaders recognized the flag of sectional antagonism unfurled by the Whigs. Virginia's W. H. Roane noted that "their great effort is to excite Southern prejudice." Likewise a rising young Democratic leader in North Carolina identified the attempt to "alarm the Southern feelings" for "the cause of party" as the crux of the Whig campaign. Agreeing, Thomas Ritchie charged the Whigs with "attempting to convert the abolition question into a party movement." Democrats in Louisiana and Mississippi acknowledged that the Whig political offensive struck with fury because it used abolition and slavery as its main weapons. From Tennessee, James K. Polk informed Jackson that White's candidacy had been specifically designed to appeal to the South. The president did not need someone else to point out that fact to him; early in 1835 he defined the White movement as an opposition effort to capture the South.[70]

Southern Democrats gave abundant witness not only to their awareness of Whig strategy but also to their respect for its political

69. Ritchie to Frank Blair, March 27, 1835, in Blair-Lee Papers; Balch to Jackson, April 4, 1835, and Wm. L. Fulton to Jackson, February 19, 1836, in Jackson Papers; Archibald Yell to Polk, June 29, 1835, in Polk Papers: Joseph Walker to Charles Gayarré, November 15, 1835, in Charles Gayarré Papers, Department of Archives, Louisiana State University.

70. Duff Green to Richard K. Crallé, September 21, 1835, in Green Papers, Division of Manuscripts, Library of Congress; Roane to Frank Blair, May 7, 1835, in Blair-Lee Papers; William H. Haywood, Jr., to William Gaston, December 5, 1835, in Gaston Papers; Richmond *Enquirer,* September 4, 1835, and Wm. F. Ritchie to William C. Rives, August 23, 1835, in Rives Papers; New Orleans *Bee* and Jackson *Mississippian,* 1835–1836, *passim;* Powhatan Ellis to Levi Woodbury, January 22, 1836, in Woodbury Papers; Polk to Jackson, October 10, 1835, in Jackson Papers; Jackson to Joseph Conn Guild, April 24, 1835, in Bassett (ed.), *Jackson Correspondence,* V, 339–41.

astuteness. To a Mississippi Democrat, the Whig campaign embodied "the most subtle and efficient plans." Characterizing Whig strategy "as artfully diverting the minds of the People . . . [with] thorough political commotion" Virginia Congressman George C. Dromgoole asserted that nothing short of complete Democratic unity could hold back the Whigs. Peter V. Daniel, also of Virginia and a close associate of Ritchie, spoke for his Democratic comrades in every southern state when he called the White campaign "the cunningest, most capital, and efficient that wily politicians ever hatched."[71]

These men, feeling the pressure of the Whig onslaught, had made their decision to stand by the Jackson party without Jackson. Although various motives compelled that loyalty, all these politicians would act together and vigorously to insure that their party maintained their basic interests and survived. To pledge their continued allegiance to the Democratic party these southern Democrats had to accept Martin Van Buren as the party's presidential nominee. Such acceptance posed few problems for politicians friendly with Van Buren and confident both of his loyalty to their principles and of their power in the party. But for them Van Buren represented a political liability, not an asset, when they faced southern voters. Anti–Van Buren men in Virginia recognized that many of Jackson's "strong supporters" turned their backs on Van Buren. To an ambitious young Democratic politician in eastern Tennessee public disenchantment with Van Buren helped make doubtful his return to the legislature. When Governor William Carroll of Tennessee, a strong Van Buren partisan, ran for reelection in 1835, he decided to avoid combining his appeal with one for the unpopular Van Buren.[72]

71. R. W. Williamson to James K. Polk, October 11, 1835, in Polk Papers; George Dromgoole to Edward Dromgoole, Jr., February 17, 1835, in Dromgoole Papers; Daniel to Martin Van Buren, June 7, 1836, in Van Buren Papers.

72. Wm. F. Gordon to John Tyler, January 15, 1836, in Tyler Papers; Andrew Johnson to George W. Jones, December 25, 1836, in Leroy P. Graf, *et al.* (eds.), *The Papers of Andrew Johnson* (3 vols.; Knoxville: University of Tennessee Press, 1967–), I, 19; Wm. B. Lewis (recounting a conversation with Carroll) to Frank Blair, May 1, 1835, in Blair-Lee Papers.

The southern Jacksonian leadership that accepted Van Buren assumed a strong southern man would complete the Democratic ticket. Believing that their view prevailed in other parts of the Union as well as in the South, they thought a southerner would run with Van Buren for both national and party purposes. They did not take seriously enough the discussions in Washington that as early as 1834 pointed to Richard M. Johnson of Kentucky as Van Buren's vice-presidential partner. Many Democrats hoped that from such a geographic base Johnson could appeal to West and South. But Johnson's domestic arrangement—he lived openly with a mulatto mistress, who bore him two children—offended and enraged many southerners. Moreover, southern Jacksonian leaders feared that Johnson's candidacy would seriously jeopardize Van Buren's chances in the South. They told President Jackson so and urged him to turn to a southerner like Rives of Virginia or Carroll of Tennessee.[73]

In Virginia, the most important southern state and the linchpin of the Jackson party in the South, Johnson's probable candidacy angered the Democratic leadership. Virginia Democrats believed that the Jackson party had been built by them and New Yorkers to reconstruct the old Virginia—New York axis of Jeffersonian times. The Virginia builders expected this second system to follow the first, with Virginia leading the way as it had in the days of the Virginia dynasty. Jackson had been a means to an end, and they had to accept Van Buren because Jackson decreed it. But they were determined that Virginia would be next.

The Virginians, presumably, had good reason to be optimistic. Word came to the Old Dominion that William C. Rives, formerly Jackson's envoy to Paris and a United States senator from 1832 to 1834, enjoyed excellent prospects. Rives received reports as early as

73. William C. Rives to Martin Van Buren, June 2, 1835, in Van Buren Papers; New Orleans *Bee*, May 29, 1835; Raleigh *Standard*, June 5, 1835; Leland Winfield Meyer, *The Life and Times of Colonel Richard M. Johnson of Kentucky* (New York: Columbia University Press, 1932), 317–22, 407–13; Latner, "Andrew Jackson," 351–358; Alfred Balch to Jackson, December 19, 1834 and April 4, 1835, James K. Polk to Jackson, April 29, 1835, James Walker to Jackson, May 5, 1835, all in Jackson Papers.

1833 that Frank Blair and the Van Buren men found him eminently acceptable. Rives's backers, in turn, argued the case not only of their man, but also of the South.[74]

Then their plans went awry; Richard Johnson, not Rives, appeared to be the choice of the administration. A surprised Ritchie, who obviously had assumed that all was well, wrote Rives, "I had hoped the thing was fixed; and had given myself less concern than I ought about it." Still, on the very eve of the Democratic convention he pressed the claim of Rives and the South. To other Democratic leaders he urged that only with Rives on the ticket would the South be safe. The South, he stressed to Frank Blair, had "peculiar claims" on the rest of the party. He told Rives that "Peter V. Daniel has been induced by the urgency of the case to go to Baltimore and will take Washington in his way."[75]

Daniel's journey to Baltimore made no difference. In spite of a significant southern opposition, the administration pushed Johnson through. Most southern delegates voted for Rives; Virginia's delegation, reflecting Ritchie's disappointment, walked out. Later, Virginia Democrats, refusing to accept Johnson, made their own nomination of a southern man for vice-president, William Smith of Alabama; and a Van Buren–Smith ticket went on the Democratic ballot in Virginia.[76]

On the vice-presidential question the Jackson party rebuffed southern hopes. The rejection of Rives for Johnson seemed to replay the southern defeats on the Nullification Proclamation and on the withdrawal of federal deposits from the second Bank of the United States. The reports coming to Virginia from the convention emphasized that westerners and easterners had been much more

74. The vice-presidential hopes of Rives can best be followed in a series of letters from Rives's friend Nathaniel Niles. Pertinent letters, all in the Rives Papers are dated August 7, 31, 1833, January 3, 20, April 25, 1835.

75. Ritchie to Rives, May 19, 1835, *ibid.*; Ritchie to Blair, May 12, 1835, in Blair-Lee Papers.

76. *Niles' Register*, XLVIII (May 30, 1835), 228, XLIX (January 16, 1836), 329; Raleigh *Standard*, June 5, 1835; C. S. Morgan to Martin Van Buren, January 9, 1836, in Van Buren Papers.

adamant about Johnson than the southerners had been about Rives. Many nonsoutherners had made Johnson's nomination a *sine qua non* for continued party loyalty and the Van Buren men acquiesced. Probably Van Buren felt sure of his political connections with the southern leadership and Jackson believed that his own strength and name could hold his native section, though the president's thinking cannot be precisely delineated. Promptly after the convention Van Buren acted to reassure the Virginians of his loyalty and friendship. Jackson himself passed words of praise to the defeated Rives, including the soothing prediction that Rives would eventually be rewarded with the presidency.[77]

This vice-presidential affair, however, evidently taught the Virginians and the South a political lesson. Never again would southerners rely on assumptions; never again would pressure from the South be exceeded by that from elsewhere. Hereafter demands rather than assumptions characterized the relationship between the southern Democrats and their party. Certainly the course of both Van Buren and the administration between the convention and the election, a story told in the following pages, supports this conclusion. Then the Democratic party took on the distinctive southern color it had worn until 1832. And this time that hue would last until the cataclysm of 1860.

That the Virginia delegation walked out of the convention did not augur a party bolt. Their commitment to the party and their conviction that it was still the legitimate heir of Jeffersonianism precluded any such drastic action. When informing Rives of Johnson's nomination, Ritchie urged him to "keep perfectly cool," for "we must not divide our party." Previously Rives had written Van Buren that he would lead no crusade against Johnson.[78] Still the walkout and the

---

77. W. B. Slaughter (a member of the Virginia delegation) to William C. Rives, May 28 and June 12 (part of this letter recounts a conversation Slaughter had with Jackson), 1835, and Van Buren to Rives, May 26, 1835, all in Rives Papers.

78. Ritchie to Rives, June 5, 1835, *ibid.*; Rives to Van Buren, June 2, 1835, in Van Buren Papers.

subsequent nomination of Smith served notice on Van Buren that his Virginia allies did not take their defeat lightly. In the campaign that lay ahead Van Buren would be on trial in slave country.

In that campaign southern Democrats strove to counteract Whig efforts to brand their candidate and party as antisouthern, and their candidate and party strove to meet southern demands. Democrats did make a brief, but vain, attempt to make 1836 a referendum on the old Jacksonian–National Republican economic issues. Quickly, however, they realized that economics neither stymied the Whig charge nor diverted attention from Whig accusations. Attesting to this recognition was the hurried change of slogans by the Raleigh *Standard*. "THE PEOPLE *against* THE BANK" went on the *Standard*'s masthead on July 3, 1835; within two months it had been replaced by a statement from Van Buren declaring his undying opposition to any interference with slavery. That declaration remained on the masthead until the presidential election in November, 1836.[79] Realizing they had to meet the Whig challenge head on, southern Democrats presented Van Buren as a man attuned to southern needs and as a president who would stand by the South on slavery. He would lead a party committed to gratifying and protecting the South. Both Van Buren and the party performed as the southerners wanted.

Southern Democrats filled Van Buren's mails with reports of danger and demands for help. They described the prejudice held against him simply because he was a northerner; they warned that the Whigs attempted to identify him with the increased abolitionist activity. Joseph Watkins, a Ritchie subaltern, asked for hard facts to use in defending Van Buren from attack; Watkins wanted information on "those subjects about which, you know, the Southern people are very sensitive." Thomas Ritchie, deeply worried about the success of the Whig campaign, emphasized to Van Buren's confidant Silas Wright that such requests as Watkins' must be answered. "I cannot but believe," he wrote, "that [the questions] will be an-

79. Richmond *Enquirer*, March 7, 1835; Raleigh *Standard*, July 1835–November 1836.

swered as they wish it." Other loyal Democrats seconded Ritchie's view.[80]

A multitude of questions—though all had the same common denominator—concerned southern Democrats and filled the letters urgently posted to Van Buren. These concerns had nothing to do with economics. The White forces had attacked on a broad front. They interpreted Van Buren's actions in the presidential contest of 1812, during the Missouri crisis, and during the tariff debate of 1828 as distinctly antisouthern. Southern Democrats wanted facts to refute conclusively such charges. They also demanded concrete evidence that Van Buren opposed abolitionism, that he opposed sending the incendiary publications through the mails, that he opposed abolition of slavery in the District of Columbia.

Although Van Buren believed that he had made his friendship for the South clear, he heeded Ritchie's admonishment and poured answers southward. Not even his annoyance with the constant "cross-examination" from below the Potomac impeded his compliance with southern demands. In letters to private individuals and to newspapers he responded to southern cries. Van Buren agreed that the views attributed to him by the Whigs were "justly obnoxious to the slaveholding states." But he insisted on the falsity and perversity of such charges and emphasized that he had always held "an affectionate and just spirit toward the rights and interests of the South." To complement his individual efforts Van Buren published in 1836, and sent South, a thirty-two-page pamphlet including letters from the South, his replies, statements specifying his views on abolition, and his opposition to the abolition of slavery in the District of Columbia. [81]

80. The following letters to Van Buren are typical: Wm. Schley (Ga.), August 22, 1835, Byrd Brandon (Ala.), March 14, 1836, J. J. Lockhart (N.C.), September 6, 1835, Watkins to Silas Wright, January 29, 1835, Ritchie to Wright, March 2, 1835, Romulus M. Saunders to Martin Van Buren, August 25, 1835, all in Van Buren Papers; John Catron to Andrew Jackson Donelson, February 11, 1836, in Donelson Papers.

81. Van Buren to Samuel Gwin, July 11, 1834, William C. Rives to Van Buren, April 10, 1835, a copy of the pamphlet, all in Van Buren Papers; Van Buren to William C. Rives, April 1, 1835, B. F. Butler to Rives, May 26, 1835, both in Rives Papers; *Niles' Register*, XLIX (October 10, 1835), 93.

Southern Democrats made every effort to give the widest possible publicity to the prosouthern views of their candidates. A Van Buren article published in one newspaper quickly found its way to others. Editorials in Democratic papers abounded with such assertions as: Martin Van Buren "is as much the friend of Southern institutions and Southern interests as Hugh Lawson White"; Van Buren is "a FIRM FRIEND TO THE SOUTH." Several newspapers placed prosouthern and antiabolition statements from Van Buren at the top of their editorial columns. These quotations were normally in boldface print and were carried in every issue for several months prior to the election. [82]

In addition to public statements from Van Buren, southern Democrats also wanted action in Washington that would substantiate and reinforce their claim that their party remained a bulwark for the South. Democratic leaders made it clear to Jackson himself and to other administration officials that a distinctly prosouthern posture was essential wherever possible. [83] Failure to act, particularly on the abolition question, invited electoral disaster. To such cries the administration responded in a most positive fashion.

On three separate fronts the administration and the northern Democrats moved forthrightly southward. In 1835 and 1836 three new Andrew Jackson appointees took their seats on the United States Supreme Court. In 1835 Democratic Congressman James M. Wayne of Georgia assumed his position as associate justice; in early 1836 two additional Jackson appointees received Senate confirmation. Both Chief Justice Roger B. Taney of Maryland and Associate Justice Philip P. Barbour of Virginia, like their colleague Wayne, hailed from slave states. During the incendiary publications crisis Jackson acted in his normal vigorous way. In his annual message to

82. Milledgeville *Federal Union*, September 16, 1835; Richmond *Enquirer*, March 20, August 28, 1835; New Orleans *Bee*, June–November 1836; Jackson *Mississippian*, July–November 1836; Little Rock *Arkansas Gazette*, June–November 1836; Raleigh *Standard*, September 1835–November 1836.

83. Thomas Ritchie to Andrew Jackson, November 28, 1835, in Jackson Papers; Dabney S. Carr to Martin Van Buren, December 21, 1835, in Van Buren Papers; C. W. Gooch to Levi Woodbury, October 10, 1835, in Woodbury Papers.

Congress in December, 1835, he asked for legislation to restrict the use of the mails by abolitionists; he denounced those who would meddle with slavery; he said that southerners who received the abolitionist literature should either desist or get out of the South. He also instructed his postmaster general not to send the abolitionist pamphlets into the South unless specifically requested by citizens. As a southerner, Jackson knew that such requests would be practically nonexistent. The congressional actions of Van Buren and his associates clearly showed that he was moving in concert with Jackson. The administration and northern Democrats in the Congress also agreed with southerners on a strategy to shut off the abolitionist petitions to Congress. Although southern Whigs and Democrats differed on their approaches to this question, the Democratic party presented a united front based on what the southerners deemed essential. And southern Democrats knew that Van Buren acted with them on all counts.[84]

These triumphs, as the southern Democrats termed them, were trumpeted to southern voters. Pointing to the congressional debate over the incendiary publications, the New Orleans *Bee* declared that no doubt could exist about the position of Van Buren, the northern Democrats and the Democratic party on abolition. Thus, according to the *Bee*, Louisiana planters should know where to place their political trust. At the other end of the South the Richmond *Enquirer* made similar exhortations. The *Enquirer* lauded Amos Kendall, Jackson's postmaster general, whose "firm course" during the incendiary publication crisis "has endeared him to the South." Calling on Virginians to take pride in the Senate confirmations of Taney and Barbour as well as Virginia's own Andrew Stevenson as minister to Great Britain, the *Enquirer* kept the prosouthern stance of the ad-

---

84. Richardson (comp.), *Messages and Papers of the Presidents*, III, 175–76; Jackson to Amos Kendall, August 9, 1835, in Bassett (ed.), *Jackson Correspondence*, V, 360–61; Thomas Hart Benton, *Thirty Years' View or a History of the Working of the American Government for Thirty Years, from 1820 to 1850* (2 vols.; New York and London: D. Appleton, 1854), I, 587; George Rable, "Slavery, Politics, and the South: The Gag Rule as a Case Study," *Capitol Studies*, III (1975), 69–87, has the best account of the politics of the Gag Rule.

ministration before the public. Elated with the performance of the northern Democrats on the abolition petition issue, James K. Polk declared that all southerners must now realize that the Van Buren men "are sound upon that subject."[85]

While the southern Democrats proudly displayed the southern stance of both their administration and their northern comrades, they also began to move away from a purely defensive stance against the Whig onslaught. This Democratic counteroffensive, which gained momentum through the summer and fall of 1836, focused on the same themes the Whigs had been stressing since the beginning of 1835: democracy, slavery, and southern safety.

The national strategy of the new Whig party provided the southern Democrats their opportunity. Because of the diversity and the disagreement on issues that dominated early Whiggery, the fledgling Whig party supported three different men for the presidency: White in the South and William Henry Harrison of Ohio and Daniel Webster outside the South. The Whigs hoped that each of their three candidates would take enough votes from Van Buren to deny him a majority of the electoral votes and victory in the general election. If that meant throwing the election into the House of Representatives, so be it.

The southern Democrats characterized the Whig strategy as an undemocratic ploy designed to take from the people their right to choose the president. Picturing 1836 as a possible replay of 1824, the Democrats denounced the Whig policy as the scheme of unscrupulous politicians to frustrate the will of the people. Southerners, Democrats exhorted, expected and demanded the right to make their own choice without the threat of a deadlocked election. On this tack Democrats never attacked White personally; they simply declared that he had no chance of winning. Even if the South stood by him, the Democrats argued, no other section would. Thus, in Democratic rhetoric, a vote for White became a vote for deciding the

85. New Orleans *Bee*, August 12, 1836; Richmond *Enquirer*, March 19, 1836; Polk to William R. Rucker, February 22, 1836, in Polk Papers.

election in the House. Democrats knew that southerners remembered 1824, the last House-decided presidential contest, when it seemed that political manipulation had robbed Andrew Jackson and placed the New Englander John Quincy Adams in the White House. The Democratic refrain had southern votes for White turning into congressional votes for Harrison or Webster—equal evils.[86]

Harrison and Webster became equal evils because the southern Democrats identified both men as distinct threats to the South. Democratic orators and editors spent little time on Webster because no southerners, not even Whigs, defended him from charges of federalism and abolition. But southern Whigs found Harrison to be eminently acceptable should White stumble. Thus the Democrats zeroed in on Harrison. According to them, Harrison embodied the worst of Alexander Hamilton and William Lloyd Garrison. The Democrats described him as a Federalist and abolitionist just as dangerous as Webster. He became an "ultra emancipationist" who left his native Virginia for the West because of antipathy to slavery. In fact the Democrats painted Harrison with the same strokes the Whigs had colored Van Buren—a northern man tainted with abolition, a man southerners could not trust. Beware, the Democrats urged southern voters; the South must protect itself. As the New Orleans *Louisiana Courier* observed, knowledge of the connection between Harrison and abolition makes "an irresistable appeal to the people of this state—and it will be answered in the right way, for we are not yet chained and yoked to the car of negrophiles."[87]

The campaign rhetoric had come full circle. Whigs found them-

86. Little Rock *Arkansas Gazette*, October 25, 1835; New Orleans *Bee*, July 11, 1836; Jackson *Mississippian*, March 25, August 19, 1836; Richmond *Enquirer*, September 16, 23, 1836; "Address of the Giles County [Tennessee] Van Buren Committee to the Voters of Tennessee" printed in Editors of the Union and American (eds.), *Speeches, Congressional and Political, and Other Writings of ex-Governor Aaron V. Brown of Tennessee* (Nashville: J. S. Marling, 1854–[55]), 444–53.

87. Milledgeville *Federal Union*, October 25, November 1, 1836; Raleigh *Standard*, September–October, 1836; New Orleans *Bee*, August 1, September 26, 1836; Richmond *Enquirer*, September 16, October 21, 1836; New Orleans *Louisiana Courier*, September 26, 1836.

selves assaulted with the same weapon they had used against the Democrats. And it both disturbed and hurt them. With few exceptions southern Whigs were stalwart White men; they did not run him as a ringer for Harrison or anyone else. Only in Virginia did a separate movement for Harrison complete with a Harrison convention appear, but it sprang from the transmontane region more identified with the trans–Ohio West than with the South. Even so, it agreed to work in Virginia with the dominant White men.[88]

Still southern Whigs preferred Harrison to Van Buren. They said they wanted White to win and believed he could win. But if White faltered, Harrison was completely safe for the party and for the South. According to the southern Whigs a vote for Harrison in either the electoral college or the House would not betray the campaign they had run. Southern Whigs began to defend Harrison's record and stance on slavery just as the Democrats had defended Van Buren's. Harrison was a Virginian with deep roots in the South; he had supported the South against restricting slavery in Missouri; he had even tried to take slavery across the Ohio River into the old Northwest Territory. Southern Whigs asked what more could southerners want from a prospective president. By the autumn of 1836 Whig newspapers championing Harrison's safety read like Democratic ones extolling Van Buren's loyalty to the South and the southern view of slavery.[89] Now the Whigs had to defend as well as attack while the Democrats added attack to their overall posture of defense.

This late Democratic move against Whig strategy and Harrison probably hurt the White campaign, though a precise assessment is impossible. Even so the Whigs and White made a tremendously impressive showing at the ballot box. Van Buren's popular vote total exceeded White's by only 4,182; Van Buren won 50.7 percent of the

88. Dent, "Virginia Democratic Party," 202–203, 210–12. *Cf.* Duff Green to Richard K. Crallé, May 10, 1835, in Green Papers, Division of Manuscripts, Library of Congress.
89. Richmond *Whig,* summer and fall, 1836, *passim;* Milledgeville *Southern Recorder,* summer and fall, 1836, *passim.*

popular vote, White 49.3 percent. Whig votes came from old National Republicans, from disaffected Democrats, and from the substantial number of voters who had not gone to the polls in 1832 but did cast ballots in 1836, though precisely how much of the Whig vote came from each source is unclear.[90] The result of the election, however, is clear indeed. Although the southern Whigs failed to elect White or to stop Van Buren, they placed themselves securely on the southern political map. They won almost half the popular vote and carried two states, Tennessee and Georgia, in their first southwide race; the National Republicans had never managed more than 20 percent of the popular vote and had never carried a state. Not surprisingly southern Whigs came out of the 1835–1836 campaign eagerly looking to the future.

The first great battle fought between Democrats and Whigs in the South spotlighted the politics of slavery. Waving the flag of political democracy, slavery, and sectional danger, southern Whigs charged out of the political wilderness to contention. As the Democrats recognized, "a real 'White' speech-roared against... Dictation, abolition, and in short against Van."[91] The impact of the Whig charge sent the once omnipotent Democrats reeling. The Democrats hurried to defend themselves and galvanize their administration into action. Afterwards they tried to countercharge under the same banner the Whigs had raised; only then did they manage to stymie the Whig drive and force the challengers to defend as well as attack.

Out of the charge and countercharge that reverberated through the South the political rhetoric employed by both parties became a dynamic force itself. When the Whigs used it to gain initial momentum, they forced the Democrats to respond in an identical

90. William C. Rives to James Buchanan, September 13, 1836, in Buchanan Papers; Lewis Dishough to Willie P. Mangum, March 23, 1836, in Shanks (ed.), *Mangum Papers*, II, 410; John Bell to Gulian C. Verplanck, June 22, 1835, in Verplanck Papers; Willie P. Mangum to Henry Clay, March 26, 1838, in Clay Papers, Indiana University; W. Dean Burnham, *Presidential Ballots, 1836–1892* (Baltimore: Johns Hopkins University Press, 1955), 252, 254. Hereinafter all presidential election figures are from this source.

91. Jos. C. Herndon to James K. Polk, May 25, 1836, in Polk Papers.

idiom, defensively first, then offensively. Neither party could stand outside or beyond that rhetoric, for it embodied and articulated the basic forces in southern society. Thus the initial contest between Democrat and Whig generated the political rhetoric and the strategy that would drive politics in the South for the life of the parties.

4 Tippecanoe and Tyler and Slavery, Too

I

MARTIN VAN BUREN's victory did not mark any relaxation of the firm southern stance taken by the administration or by Van Buren himself. On the day before he left office Andrew Jackson placed another southerner on the United States Supreme Court when he awarded a newly created seat to John Catron, one of his Tennessee lieutenants. Van Buren took the oath of office from Chief Justice Roger B. Taney on the eastern portico of the Capitol; more appropriate would have been some spot on the southern wing.

When he spoke to the nation for the first time as president, Van Buren dealt in platitudes and generalities except when he discussed slavery.[1] After twelve paragraphs of homilies Van Buren turned directly to slavery. In this portion of his address he reaffirmed the commitments of the campaign. He urged his listeners—and the nation—to follow "the justice and patriotism" of the Founding Fathers by "calming excited passions" that had disrupted the generous and fraternal feeling that characterized the era of the founding. According to Van Buren the Fathers recognized that slavery was and ought to remain a local institution controlled by local, not federal, interests. While not using these precise words, his pledge to oppose congressional action both on slavery in the District of Columbia and on any attempts to interfere with slavery in the states makes his meaning crystal clear. His statement of general principle could have served for Thomas Ritchie or, for that matter, John C. Calhoun: "I desire," Van Buren affirmed, "to declare that the principle that will govern me in the high duty to which my country calls me is a strict

---

1. James D. Richardson (comp.), *A Compilation of the Messages and Papers of the Presidents, 1789–1897* (10 vols.; Washington: Government Printing Office, 1896–1899), III, 313–20.

adherence to the letter and spirit of the Constitution as it was designed by those who framed it." That principle he amplified by explicitly embracing limitations on national power and reaffirming the rights of the states. Then, Van Buren closed by pledging that the United States desired the friendship of all nations and by praising the glory of his predecessor. Neither of these brief statements, however, undermined or confused the major thrust of the substantive part of the inaugural.

Van Buren's declarations brought forth praise from the South. The Raleigh *Standard,* the leading Democratic paper in North Carolina, announced its particular pleasure that the views expressed on slavery in the inaugural "correspond[ed] with [Van Buren's] former avowals." Emphasizing its delight the *Standard* proclaimed that no one could legitimately brand Van Buren as an enemy of the South; quite to the contrary he was a true and loyal friend. Even the old nullifiers praised Van Buren's declarations. From Thomas Cooper, former president of South Carolina College and one of the most radical ideologues among the nullifiers, came the opinion that "your pledges on the abolition question are felt and approved: they will tell greatly in your favor in the South." Cooper went on to assert that most of South Carolina shared his feelings.[2]

When Van Buren turned to his cabinet, he maintained his southern orientation. His decision to retain Jackson's cabinet left him with little to work with, for only one vacancy existed, in the War Department. Southern Democrats did not fail to let the administration know that they expected a southern appointment. "The mass of the Southern people would feel more confidence in the good disposition of the administration," Richard E. Parker of the Richmond Junto told Van Buren, "by seeing in the cabinet men born amongst them entertaining, if you will, the same prejudices." To Speaker of the House James K. Polk a North Carolinian wrote that putting a southerner in the cabinet post would "have a greater tendency to remove

2. Raleigh *Standard,* March 8, 1837; Cooper to Van Buren, March 27, 1837, in Van Buren Papers.

false impressions, as regards Mr. V. Buren's sincerity towards the South" than anything else the new president could do. Van Buren either listened or agreed or both, for he never hesitated; he wanted a southerner. First he tried to convince William C. Rives to join his official family. That effort failed, for Rives demanded the State Department occupied by John Forsyth of Georgia. Van Buren had determined to fill the War Department post but make no other changes. Thus he said no to Rives and added to the anger of a man disappointed since the failure of his vice-presidential candidacy back in 1835. When the overture to Rives collapsed, Van Buren turned to Joel R. Poinsett of South Carolina. Poinsett accepted the offer and served throughout Van Buren's term.[3]

Although the specifics of the inaugural and the cabinet focused on the South, economic concerns quickly engulfed the new Van Buren administration. Only two months after Van Buren's inauguration, financial debacle gripped the country. The Panic of 1837, the gravest economic catastrophe since 1819, surprised few. Many political leaders, both Democrat and Whig, had feared and predicted the onset of a panic or depression. The crash stemmed from the frenzied expansion that had marked the nation's economy in the 1830s. This economic expansion was tied directly to territorial expansion in the West, which meant rising cotton prices, rising demands and prices for land, a tremendous demand for credit. The unending cry for credit led to numerous new banks chartered with slight concern for financial stability.

No central institution governed or controlled this headlong advance. Andrew Jackson destroyed the second Bank of the United States, an institution that had exercised some control, but he put nothing in its place. Instead by increasing the assets of local or pet banks with federal revenues, he probably multiplied the speculation

3. Parker to Van Buren, February 7, 1837, in Van Buren Papers; W. D. Mosely to Polk, January 17, 1837, in Polk Papers; undated memorandum written by Rives recounting cabinet discussion with Van Buren, in Rives Papers; James C. Curtis, *The Fox at Bay: Martin Van Buren and the Presidency, 1837–1841* (Lexington: University Press of Kentucky, 1970), 53–54.

that spearheaded the onrushing economy. Finally recognizing the general economic dangers and hoping to brake speculation, Jackson in 1836 promulgated the specie circular which required that all public land be paid for in gold and silver. While this order probably curtailed speculation, it exacerbated the pressures faced by the nation's financial institutions. It placed a particularly heavy burden on eastern banks that had to face tightening credit from European creditors, especially the Bank of England, at the same time their own specie reserves were being transferred to the West because of the specie circular. Finally on May 10, 1837, banks in New York City, unable to meet the increasing demands for specie, closed their doors. Banks across the country rapidly did likewise; trade ground to a halt; prices plummeted; debtors faced huge obligations with less money.

Van Buren's response to the panic set off a bitter party and congressional struggle that dominated the politics of his administration. As a solution to the crisis Van Buren proposed a total divorce between the federal government and banks. To accomplish this goal he advocated the creation of the Independent or Sub-Treasury. Under this plan the government would be its own depository; neither a national bank nor state banks would hold federal deposits. Immediately Whigs stormed that Van Buren's Independent Treasury meant tyranny by the executive in the tradition of Andrew Jackson—executive tyranny because the executive branch would control the national revenues. This battle over financial and economic issues affected southern politics chiefly in three ways: one effect was relatively minor and distinctly temporary; the other two had more immediate impact and more significant long-term implications.

The attacking Whigs received allies from the president's own camp. A few Democrats, both northern and southern, refused to support the Independent Treasury scheme. Like the Whigs they insisted that the nation's banks must be directly involved with holding the revenues. Calling themselves Conservatives these dissident

Democrats did not become Whigs in the beginning. This Conservative revolt assumed serious proportions in only one southern state, Virginia.[4] In Virginia the Democrats who opposed the Independent Treasury came together under the leadership of one of Virginia's leading Jacksonian stalwarts, William C. Rives. The motives behind Rives's actions, which led him into the Whig party in 1840, remain problematical. Most probably his disappointment over the vice-presidential nomination of 1835 and his inability to come to terms with Van Buren on a cabinet position contributed to his Conservative course, but clear-cut evidence does not exist. In Virginia the Conservative movement caused great anxiety and serious political problems for the Richmond Junto in particular and for the Democratic party in general. Although Rives never returned to the Democratic fold, the revolt had largely spent itself by 1840. The Democratic party came out of the Conservative difficulties still powerful; it was able to blunt Whig efforts to make Virginia a Whig state. Thomas Ritchie and his associates even managed to hold Virginia for Van Buren in 1840—no mean feat when faced both with Rives's defection and the force of the Whig campaign.

Just as the panic made economic questions central for Van Buren's administration, it also brought them to the forefront in state politics. Everywhere in the South, Whigs and Democrats divided over banking and related financial issues.[5] Thus the panic gave a new salience to economic concerns in southern state politics because partisan division over state economic policy had been largely absent since the birth of the Whig party. Although financial matters dominated state politics for roughly a half dozen years between the late 1830s and the early 1840s, they played practically no part in the presidential election of 1840. In that great contest neither Whigs nor Democrats used

---

4. Lynwood M. Dent, Jr., "The Virginia Democratic Party, 1824–1847" (Ph.D. dissertation, Louisiana State University, 1974), Chap. 6; James Roger Sharp, *The Jacksonians versus the Banks: Politics in the States after the Panic of 1837* (New York and London: Columbia University Press, 1970), Chap. 9.

5. For a full discussion of economic issues in the states see Chap. 5 herein.

economics in their appeals to southern voters. Instead they refought the battle of 1836.

The panic and Van Buren's reaction to it also prompted the return of John C. Calhoun to the Democratic party. Announcing his support of the Independent Treasury in September, 1837, and obviously pleased with Van Buren's ringing reaffirmation of states' rights in the presidential message proposing the Independent Treasury, Calhoun moved back under the old Jacksonian colors. He did not come alone. His followers, for the most part, also ended their liaison with the Whigs and put on the Democratic uniform. That move had a tremendous impact on southern politics generally and on the Democratic party especially. With Calhoun in the Democratic fold the southern identity of the party was secure. Now Van Buren had a powerful ally, for John C. Calhoun, no matter what else he was, was clearly identified with the South. Historians have differed on whether Van Buren or Calhoun stood as the dominant figure in the new alliance, on which man compromised principle and program.[6] For the purposes of this story that debate is largely irrelevant. The crucial point is the southern identity of the Democratic party, and on that point no doubt can exist.

II

John C. Calhoun commanded a powerful influence in southern politics. He was venerated—the New Orleans *Bee* eulogized him as "the statesman, orator and patriot, the purest and most upright of all the public men in the present age." He was hated—a Whig congressman from Tennessee castigated him as "the most unprincipled and reckless Roman of them all." He was followed—calling him "the Pilot," Franklin Harper Elmore, a South Carolina disciple, declared, "all confide in Mr. Calhoun, or will be controlled by his views." He was distrusted—the Richmond Junto viewed with sus-

6. For the two interpretations see Curtis, *Fox at Bay*, 98–99, 119, n. 38, and Charles M. Wiltse, *John C. Calhoun* (3 vols.; Indianapolis and New York: Bobbs-Merrill, 1944–51), II, Chap. 24.

picion his conversion from the broad nationalism of his early career
to the extreme states' rights stance that marked his later activities;
speaking for his colleagues Thomas Ritchie said that he had "no
confidence" in Calhoun "as a *politician.*"[7]

But all, even his opponents, respected both his intellectual prowess and his political strength. Although disgusted with Calhoun's
"metaphysical delusions," the eminent Charlestonian Hugh S. Legaré still considered him "By far the fittest man in the country for the
presidential chair." James H. Hammond, who followed Calhoun
though secretly resenting his control of South Carolina politics, condemned what he saw as Calhoun's selfishness, but admired Calhoun's ability to see "great principles & truths clearly." While the
Richmond Junto looked askance on Calhoun's embrace of the doctrines of 1798, they held their public tongues because of Calhoun's
political might in Virginia. During the tense days of 1849 Howell
Cobb, the Georgia Democrat, wrote to his wife: "I shall look upon it
as a national blessing" if "our Heavenly Father" decided to call
Calhoun "*home.*" Five months later, because of his opposition to
Calhoun's Southern Address, Cobb found himself in an extremely
precarious political position. His desperate struggle for political survival eloquently attested to the political force of the great South
Carolinian.[8]

During the life of the second party system, that force had an

7. New Orleans *Bee*, April 2, 1850; William B. Campbell to David Campbell, January 3,
1838, in Campbell Papers; Elmore to Armistead Burt, October 2, 1845, in Calhoun Papers,
Robert Muldrow Cooper Library, Clemson University; Andrew Stevenson to Ritchie,
January 1, 1840, Letterbook, in Stevenson Papers, and Ritchie to William C. Rives, June 5,
1838, in "Unpublished Letters of Thomas Ritchie," *John P. Branch Historical Papers of
Randolph-Macon College*, III (1911), 228.
8. Legaré to Alfred Huger, December 15, 1834, in *Writings of Hugh Swinton Legaré . . .*,
ed. His Sister (2 vols.; Charleston: Burges & James, 1846), I, 217; Hammond to William
Gilmore Simms, November 1, 1847, and Hammond Diary, 1841–46, entry June 10, 1842,
both in Hammond Papers; John Bragg to [Martin Van Buren], October 10, 1842, in Donelson
Papers; Cobb to his wife, February 8, 1849, in Cobb-Erwin-Lamar Papers, Ilah Dunlap Little
Memorial Library, University of Georgia; Cobb to James Buchanan, June 2, 1849, in Ulrich B.
Phillips (ed.), *The Correspondence of Robert Toombs, Alexander H. Stephens and Howell
Cobb* (Washington: Government Printing Office, 1913), 159; Cobb to Robert J. Walker, June
2, 1849, in Robert J. Walker Papers, New York Historical Society.

unsettling effect on southern politics because Calhoun rejected the rules that guided the conduct of the regular party men. Those politicians were southern men just like Calhoun, and they were also committed to defending southern doctrines and institutions, especially slavery. But the politics of slavery that captivated Democrat and Whig alike came out of southern culture and produced a rhetoric and an electoral strategy designed for the South and southern voters. Most southern politicians were chiefly concerned about the success of their party, both in their home states and in Washington. They saw the rhetoric of slavery as a political weapon to best the opposing party in the South. Accordingly, they aimed it at southern, not national audiences. Calhoun, on the other hand, cared most about maintaining the parity of the South as a section in the Union. Although Calhoun wanted support from southern voters, his major goal was to confront the North with demands, to force public concessions from northern politicians in Congress.

For two critical reasons southern party men wanted to maintain close relations with their northern associates. Recognizing that they lived in a nation but came from a section that had particular concerns, the party men grounded their strategy for protecting the South and slavery on gaining national power through cooperation with northerners. A national party, in this view, precluded a sectional assault on slavery, particularly since the southerners required the northerners to let them control the slavery issue. The prize southerners could offer northerners, and covet for themselves as well, was political power and the rewards that ensued from it. Political power stemmed from political victory and national political power from national political victory. That desire for power, for both noble and ignoble reasons, motivated all political leaders, Whig and Democrat, northern and southern. To northerners the price demanded by southerners for political alliance seemed reasonable: southern control of a sectional or southern question in turn for assistance in the quest for national power. This blueprint for alliance worked reasonably well until the late 1840s when more and more northerners began to identify slavery as a national, not a sectional, question. As a result northern politicians became increasingly unwilling either to let the South set the tone of the slavery discussion or even to allow the South to go its own way. Instead they began demanding that the South follow where they led.

The southern party men did not want to alienate their northern fellows by constantly and publicly testing them on slavery. The sectionalism of political campaigns involved each party's trying to damage the other's image and credibility in the South by connecting the respective northern halves with antislavery and antisouthern views. The party men did not think of the politics of slavery as disrupting their own party but rather as insuring the defeat of the opposition party. Continually pushing the slave question in Congress could possibly fracture the political alliances that permitted southern politicians to hold national power. Northern politicians forever facing public challenge from the South might react by annulling their political alliance or by taking positions on sectional questions that would make it impossible for southern party men to defend their northern connection before southern voters. Either result was unacceptable to the party men, for each meant the loss of political power or danger for the South or both.

Calhoun found the basic concept of the party men fraught with peril. In his mind they wrote a fatal prescription for the South because they failed to appreciate both the numerical superiority of the North and the potential political power of antislavery ideology. Calhoun always emphasized the minority position of the South, and he was convinced that "a large portion of the northern states believed slavery to be a sin." He feared the time when the more powerful North would feel "an obligation of conscience to abolish it."[9] With that conviction he saw as death warrants the political guarantees for southern safety so proudly displayed by the party men.

9. Calhoun to Committee for Barbecue for W. C. Preston, July 24, 1838, printed in Richmond *Whig*, August 21, 1838, and Richard K. Crallé (ed.), *The Works of John C. Calhoun* (6 vols.; New York: D. Appleton, 1854–57), II, 483–84, 628.

The inevitable result of the dominion of party he read in his interpretation of Virginia history. To Calhoun, Virginia had been the great mother—of the South, of states' rights principles, of the correct reading of the Constitution. "Her true political position," he wrote to a Virginia friend, "is to stand at the head of the South." But Virginia politics was the domain of one of Calhoun's greatest antagonists, Thomas Ritchie. The two men were not opposed in ultimate conviction, for they both professed faith in the doctrines of 1798; nor did they disagree on the primacy of protecting the South and slavery. But on the strategy to gain these common goals they clashed fundamentally. Ritchie was as committed to the party solution as Calhoun was committed against it. On Ritchie, Calhoun placed a fearful responsibility. According to Calhoun, Ritchie's loyalty to party "must detach her [Virginia] from her old associates; alienate her from old & glorious doctrines; and finally corrupt her morals & debase her character." Party, he wrote to Benjamin Watkins Leigh, had caused "the proudest and most firmly established heretofore in her political principles of all the Slave holding states, [to] sink down virtually into a colony of N. York." With that last allusion to Ritchie's fast adherence to Martin Van Buren, Calhoun pointed to "the fall of Virginia." If only Virginia faltered, the prognosis might not be so gloomy, but Calhoun saw Virginia as a microcosm of the South. If Virginia's fall from so lofty a pinnacle be permanent, Calhoun was convinced "the doom of the South is sealed."[10]

To rescue Virginia and to keep the rest of the South from repeating her experience Calhoun wanted to substitute for the fatal political guarantee an open, public declaration from the North. As Calhoun envisioned that declaration, it would come from the Congress and would abide by his and the South's theory of the sanction and

10. Calhoun to Thomas W. Gilmer, July 28, 1843, in [Lyon G. Tyler (ed.)] "Original Letters," *William and Mary Quarterly*, 1st ser., XX (1911), 9–10; Calhoun to Leigh, May 22, 1835, in Benjamin Watkins Leigh Papers, Alderman Library, University of Virginia; Calhoun to Littleton W. Tazewell, January 16, 1834, in John C. Calhoun Papers, Division of Manuscripts, Library of Congress.

protection given to slavery by the Constitution. To that end he proclaimed the gospel of 1798; only the restoration of "the old State rights Republican doctrine of '98," he announced, could save the South and the Union.[11] To Calhoun the constitutional Union entailed a small federal establishment which incorporated a narrow view of federal power. Thus slavery would always remain in southern hands.

Calhoun acted as well as talked. He spared no effort in his quest for constitutional guarantees clearly and publicly enunciated by the North—guarantees that in his mind would insure "permanent security" for the South.[12] Although Calhoun believed that the Constitution protected the South, he asserted that the rise of abolition necessitated a reaffirmation of that protection. With the Congress as his chief forum he strove during the 1830s for new constitutional pledges during the petition controversy and during the abolition debates of 1837 and 1838. Later he placed the annexation of Texas and the debate over the Wilmot Proviso in this same context.

Adamantly opposed to the politics of accommodation practiced by the party men he urged a politics of confrontation. As he wrote to his son in 1837: "I think the sooner the issue is made the better for us [the South] and the country." That was no isolated expression; time and again he told his associates the South must act and act immediately.[13] To insure southern success when the confrontation occurred Calhoun worked to unify the South. In his scheme unity was essential for confrontation, for without unity no confrontation

11. Calhoun to Thomas W. Gilmer, July 28, 1843, in "Original Letters," 9; Calhoun to Robert Y. Hayne, November 17, 1838, in J. Franklin Jameson (ed.), *Correspondence of John C. Calhoun* (Washington: Government Printing Office, 1900), 416; Calhoun to Henry W. Conner, April 20, 1848, in Henry W. Conner Papers, Charleston Library Society (all other Conner citations will be to this collection unless otherwise noted); Wiltse, *Calhoun*, II, 368, 370–71.
12. Calhoun to Robert Y. Hayne, November 17, 1838, in Jameson (ed.), *Calhoun Correspondence*, 416.
13. Calhoun to James Edward Calhoun, December 20, 1837, and to Robert Y. Hayne, November 17, 1838, *ibid.*, 386, 416; Calhoun to Franklin H. Elmore, November 24, 1840, in Franklin H. Elmore Papers, Division of Manuscripts, Library of Congress; Calhoun to Henry W. Conner, December 16, 1847, and April 20, 1848, in Conner Papers; William C. Preston to Henry M. Boyer, January 11, 1839, in William C. Preston Papers, Division of Manuscripts, Library of Congress.

would occur. "It is time," he told his Alabama friend Bolling Hall as early as 1833, "the South should overlook all minor differences and unite as one man in the defense of liberty." In a public letter written in 1838 he defined southern unity "not only as necessary to our prosperity and safety, but indispensable." He felt southern oneness "a point of vital importance" so that the South "cannot fail to control the other and more divided sections." As late as 1847 he was urging the organization of an "apparatus in the South" to lead the "defense of our rights & institutions."[14]

How to attain the unity he so desperately wanted was a problem he never solved. He tried to get a southern convention that would draft a statement of principle or demands and present it to Congress; he hoped for a southern party; finally toward the end of his life he moved reluctantly toward secession. Secession had not been his goal, for he truly loved the Union—but only a Union that nurtured the South. Only twelve years before he died he described to his daughter the grave difficulties in secession. His words were eloquent and prophetic: "how many bleeding pours [*sic*] must be taken up in passing the knife of separation through a body politick [*sic*], (in order to make two of one) which has been so long bound together by so many ties, political, social and commercial." To avoid taking what he termed "the final step" he used all of his mental and political powers.[15]

But everywhere Calhoun turned he met the implacable force of party. Party divided the South and turned its attention away from the critical issue of abolition and the oncoming deluge. Parties in the South, as Calhoun saw them, had no commitment to principle: "*The exclusive object of both parties in electing the President is to obtain the spoils.* They are both equally ready to *sacrifice any other consid-*

14. Calhoun to Hall, March 25, 1833, in Hall Papers; Richmond *Whig*, August 21, 1838; Calhoun to James Iredell, July 21, 1837, in John C. Calhoun Papers, William A. Perkins Library, Duke University; Calhoun to Wilson Lumpkin, December 26, 1841, in Jameson (ed.), *Calhoun Correspondence*, 500; Calhoun to Henry W. Conner, August 25, 1847, in Conner Papers.

15. Calhoun to James Edward Calhoun, December 20, 1837, and to Anna Maria Clemson, January 25, 1838, both in Jameson (ed.), *Calhoun Correspondence*, 386, 391.

eration." Because of "the trammels of party," he lamented, "our [southern] people have been lulled into a false security by party papers and party leaders on both sides, who take a far deeper interest in the result of a presidential election, than in what relates to the interest and safety of the South."[16]

This enmity toward parties led Calhoun to a general theory delineating their evil. Near the end of his life he tried to put his antiparty views in systematic form; much of his famous *A Disquisition on Government* is devoted to an indictment of parties and the debilitating effect they have on government. Throughout the pages of *A Disquisition* he presents democracy gone to ruin because of the selfishness and small-mindedness of scheming party politicians. But, as William Freehling has shown, his system was wracked with inconsistency—Calhoun never decided whether the politicians themselves or the interest groups they represented really controlled government.[17] That inconsistency in logic, however, takes nothing away from the sincerity of his convictions.

Convinced of the absolute correctness of his views Calhoun felt it his duty to force the South out of her apathy, to awaken the South to the siren song of the party men. In his own mind principle dominated his every action. As early as 1832 he described himself as leading the fight for liberty. Those who opposed him he branded as men who "intend unqualified submission." Defining party politics and party struggle as ephemeral he announced in 1838, "I have higher objects, and a more sacred duty to perform." In 1847, only three years before his death, he still hoped that he and his followers could force principle on the corrupt parties.[18]

16. Calhoun to Ellwood Fisher, February 14, 1848, in Calhoun Papers, South Caroliniana Library, University of South Carolina; Calhoun to Robert M. T. Hunter, June, n.d., 1837, in Jameson (ed.), *Calhoun Correspondence,* 371; Calhoun to E. S. Dargan, May 14, 1847, in Calhoun Papers, William R. Perkins Library, Duke University.
17. Crallé (ed.), *Calhoun Works,* I, 1–107; William W. Freehling, "Spoilsmen and Interests in the Thought and Career of John C. Calhoun," *Journal of American History,* LII (1965), 25–42.
18. Calhoun to Waddy Thompson, Jr., July 8, 1832, to Micah Sterling, February 26, 1838, and to Eustis Prescott, September 5, 1847, all in Calhoun Papers, South Caroliniana Library, University of South Carolina.

While Calhoun wrapped himself in the purity of principle, his Democratic and Whig opponents in the South characterized his activities quite differently. He was condemned as a man consumed by ambition, a voracious ambition for the presidency. That ambition, not principle, led to the efforts for a southern party he wanted to lead. One modern biographer has even used that theme as the basic motive in Calhoun's life.[19] If, to his enemies, ambition replaced principle, then his politics of confrontation also came under attack. "Mr. Calhoun is incessantly agitating," declared James Louis Petigru, the distinguished Charleston attorney who opposed Calhoun in their native state. Thomas Ritchie echoed Petigru's declaration in his own analysis: "Mr. Calhoun is for agitation, agitation." Henry Clay, in 1837, used the word *mischievous* to define Calhoun's agitating. In the mid-1830s both John J. Crittenden and the Milledgeville *Federal Union* condemned Calhoun's taking extreme ground and then claiming it as the only true southern position. President James K. Polk berated Calhoun for "blindly mount[ing] that topic [slavery] as a hobby." Calhoun and his men were "anxious to get up an excitement upon the *Slave* question," Alexander Stephens wrote to his brother Linton in 1847. The Richmond *Whig* summed up this view of Calhoun when it dubbed him "John Crisis Calhoun."[20]

19. William Gilmore Simms to James H. Hammond, May 1, 1847, in Mary C. Simms Oliphant, *et al.* (eds.), *The Letters of William Gilmore Simms* (5 vols.; Columbia: University of South Carolina Press, 1952–56), II, 310; James L. Petigru to Hugh S. Legaré, May 25, 1838, in James L. Petigru Papers, South Caroliniana Library, University of South Carolina; John S. Eaton to Abraham Venable, December 18, 1847, in Abraham Venable Papers, Southern Historical Collection, University of North Carolina; J. J. Barbour to Thomas Ritchie, June 13, 1846, in Thomas Ritchie Papers, Division of Manuscripts, Library of Congress; Gerald M. Capers, *John C. Calhoun—Opportunist: A Reappraisal* (Gainesville: University of Florida Press, 1960).

20. Petigru to Hugh S. Legaré, November 20, 1833, quoted in James Petigru Carson, *Life, Letters and Speeches of James Louis Petigru: The Union Man of South Carolina* (Washington: H. L. & J. B. McQueen, 1920), 53; Ritchie to Martin Van Buren, July 2, 1838, in "Unpublished Letters of Ritchie," 230; Clay to Peter B. Porter, December 24, 1837, in Peter B. Porter Papers, Buffalo Historical Society; Mrs. Chapman Coleman (ed.), *The Life of John J. Crittenden, with Selections from His Correspondence and Speeches* (2 vols.; Philadelphia: J. B. Lippincott, 1871), I, 108; Milledgeville *Federal Union*, March 11, 1836; Milo Milton Quaife (ed.), *The Diary of James K. Polk during His Presidency, 1845–1849* (4 vols.; Chicago: A. C. McClurg, 1910), II, 348; Stephens to Linton Stephens, January 13, 1847, in Stephens Papers, Manhattanville College; Richmond *Whig*, December 29, 1848.

Although the party men bitterly resented Calhoun's politics of confrontation, they responded by participating as well as condemning, for they knew as well as Calhoun that the politics of slavery destroyed those judged faithless. Although they often opposed his particular measures, they entered his debate. The reaction to the resolutions Calhoun proposed in the Senate on December 27, 1837, illustrates the predicament of the party men. The resolutions, six in number, reiterated the states' rights constitutional arguments; declared that slavery was a local institution and, as such, must be protected from outside interference by the general government; condemned as "a direct and dangerous attack on the institutions of the Slave-holding States" any moral assault on slavery. Whig Congressman William B. Campbell of Tennessee wrote to his uncle, "It was the desire of the South to avoid any debate upon the question of Slavery," but when Calhoun introduced it, southerners felt compelled to speak. Senator Robert Strange, Democrat of North Carolina, reported that he advised against the introduction of the resolutions. Strange went on to say, however, that if the resolutions came to a vote, he would vote for them. Even Henry Clay found himself forced to take the slavery offensive because of Calhoun's action. Assiduously cultivating southern support for a presidential try in 1840, Clay came forward with his own resolutions affirming his steadfastness and soundness on slavery. [21]

Calhoun's power in South Carolina permitted him to follow any political course he chose. No other contemporary southern politician enjoyed a comparable domination of his constituency. In South Carolina the second party system never took hold. Although a few South Carolinians identified themselves as Whigs, no organized Whig party existed. And the Democrats were generally loyal to Calhoun rather than to any conception of a national party, a fact exemplified by the absence during Calhoun's lifetime of an official

---

21. Wiltse, *Calhoun*, II, 371; William Campbell to David Campbell, January 3, 1838, in Campbell Papers; Richmond *Whig*, January 2, 1838, and Raleigh *Register*, January 8, 1838. For Clay see pp. 122–24 herein.

South Carolina delegation at any Democratic national convention. Unity in South Carolina, as Calhoun believed and informed his disciple Franklin Elmore, made it "impossible for the opposition to take any course with the least prospect of success, unless we should concur." Believing that political solidarity in his own state was essential for his larger purpose, he expended great efforts to forge unity in South Carolina behind his leadership. In this task he unquestionably succeeded. The divisiveness of the nullification period was forgotten; South Carolina became one. From the mid-1830s to his death in 1850 he controlled his state absolutely. All who opposed him he deposed. That fact of political life was clearly recognized by his South Carolina opponents, who wrung their hands in frustrated impotence.[22]

That Calhoun had able and loyal lieutenants, not just in South Carolina but spread throughout the South, magnified his influence. His following was particularly strong in Virginia where his ideological forthrightness attracted older luminaries like Littleton Waller Tazewell and capable young politicians like Robert M. T. Hunter, who was elected speaker of the national House of Representatives in 1839. From the late 1830s to 1845 the Calhoun faction of the Virginia Democratic party, or the Chivalry as it was known, was a powerful minority that Thomas Ritchie and the Richmond Junto had to placate. After 1845 the Chivalry replaced the junto as the dominant force in the Virginia Democracy—a transition symbolized by the election of Hunter and his Calhounite colleague James M. Mason to the United States Senate in 1847. In Alabama the Calhoun forces,

22. Calhoun to Elmore, November 24, 1840, in Elmore Papers, Division of Manuscripts, Library of Congress; Calhoun to Committee for Barbecue for W. C. Preston, July 24, 1838, printed in Richmond *Whig*, August 21, 1838; Joel Poinsett to James B. Campbell, October 20, 1836, in Samuel Gaillard Stoney (ed.), "The Poinsett-Campbell Correspondence," *South Carolina Historical and Genealogical Magazine*, XLII (1941), 150–51; William C. Preston to John J. Crittenden, January 23, 1844, in Crittenden Papers; James L. Petigru to Daniel Webster, December 6, 1850, in Daniel Webster Papers, Division of Manuscripts, Library of Congress. For an interesting, though not wholly convincing, attempt to explain South Carolina's unique political world, see James M. Banner, Jr., "The Problem of South Carolina," in Stanley Elkins and Eric McKitrick (eds.), *The Hofstadter Aegis: A Memorial* (New York: Alfred A. Knopf, 1974), 60–93.

composed of talented and prominent men, "exerted no little influence." J. Mills Thornton, in his recent study of Alabama politics, concluded that the Calhounites gave the Democrats their margin of victory in the state. After Calhoun's move to the Democrats in 1837, regular Democrats in Mississippi made concerted efforts to wed the Calhoun men to their banner through "union" conventions and by declaring Calhounites acceptable as Democratic candidates. Success came in 1839. The old nullifier John A. Quitman, the leading Calhounite in the state, aligned with them; a state convention of regulars and Calhoun men passed resolutions that praised the Virginia and Kentucky resolutions and Calhoun. The marriage insured Calhoun influence and Democratic hegemony in Mississippi. Even in Louisiana the voice of John C. Calhoun was not silent. Democrat John Slidell reported the Calhoun group "not very numerous, but sufficiently active and devoted to make itself felt."[23]

In those states and elsewhere most Calhoun men went with the Democrats. After Calhoun's return to the Democratic fold in 1837 most of his followers followed their leader. During Calhoun's loose connection with the Whigs between 1834 and 1836 many Calhoun men had acted with that party. Certainly in Virginia, in Georgia, in Mississippi, and in Alabama most Calhounites backed Hugh White, and generally they had supported anti-Jackson men and measures in those states. But Calhoun's announcement in 1837 ended that affiliation, though the Whigs did not give up their Calhounite partners without a struggle. Mississippi Whigs paid court to them just as did the Democrats, but the Democrats gave more concrete political rewards and also, of course, had the example of Calhoun himself. Proclaiming "We have followed and admired and loved John C. Calhoun," the Richmond *Whig* urged both Calhoun and his Virginia

23. Dent, "Virginia Democratic Party," Chaps. 7–8; William Garrett, *Reminiscences of Public Men in Alabama for Thirty Years with an Appendix* (Atlanta: Plantation, 1872), 49, and Jonathan Mills Thornton III, "Politics and Power in a Slave Society: Alabama, 1806–1860" (Ph.D. dissertation, Yale University, 1974), 49, 190–93; Edwin Arthur Miles, *Jacksonian Democracy in Mississippi* (Chapel Hill: University of North Carolina Press, 1960), 147, 152; Slidell to James Buchanan, March 21, 1847, in Buchanan Papers.

followers to stay away from the party of the Force Bill and the Nullification Proclamation. The true home of honest states' rights men, the *Whig* insisted, was the Whig party. When it realized that Calhoun was lost, the *Whig* stated that the Whigs never deserted Calhoun or his principles; instead he had deserted both his friends and his principles.[24] The pleas of the *Whig* evidently had some effect, for the Whig party retained in Virginia a stronger element of the Calhounite following, led by John Tyler, than in any other state.

Politicians in the South wooed Calhoun because they recognized his power and because they knew his followers could be a disruptive force. Although the Calhounites gave Alabama Democrats their margin of victory in the state, the "faction was difficult to control." The distress of a stalwart among Alabama Democrats, Congressman George S. Houston, testified to the potency of the Calhounites. He wrote Howell Cobb in 1846 that his district was going to a Calhoun man and he feared that the opposition of the Calhounites had finished him politically "for years if not forever." Although the junto men in Virginia basically disliked Calhoun, they kept their personal feelings to themselves. They knew they stared directly down the barrel of the Calhoun gun. Thomas Ritchie, particularly, made every effort to cultivate the Calhoun men. He never belittled them during or after state party fights, and he never spoke publicly against Calhoun. During the heated contest between the Calhoun men and the junto backers of Van Buren in 1842 and 1843, Ritchie's *Enquirer* always spoke of the Calhounites in a most complimentary fashion. In fact Ritchie went out of his way in early 1845 to urge president-elect James K. Polk not to "wound Mr. Calhoun in the slightest degree."[25]

24. Richmond *Whig*, August 28, 1838, December 20, 1839.
25. Thornton, "Politics and Power," 49; Houston to Cobb, June 26, 1846, in Phillips (ed.), *Correspondence of Toombs, Stephens and Cobb*, 166–67; John Bragg to [Martin Van Buren], October 10, 1842 (recounting numerous conversations with Virginia leaders), in Donelson Papers; J. S. Barbour to John C. Calhoun, December 18, 1844, in Chauncey S. Boucher and Robert P. Brooks (eds.), *Correspondence Addressed to John C. Calhoun, 1837–1849* (Washington: U.S. Government Printing Office, 1930), 271; Richmond *Enquirer*, March 7, 1842, February 3, 1844; Ritchie to Polk, February 17, 1845, in Polk Papers.

Even in North Carolina, a state where they had little strength, the Calhoun men forced everybody else to reckon with them. In 1842 the Democrat Bedford Brown was the heavy favorite to win a United States Senate seat from the legislature. The Democrats controlled the legislature, and overwhelmingly they favored Brown. When the balloting began, Brown and the Whig contender William A. Graham polled roughly the same number of votes with a third candidate, another Democrat, receiving only half as many votes as Brown. Brown, however, was an ardent backer of Martin Van Buren, then locked in a struggle with Calhoun for the 1844 Democratic nomination. Thus the Calhoun men, nominal Democrats all, determined to stop Brown, no matter the cost. Refusing to give Brown the votes that would have given him a majority, they succeeded. Eventually recognizing the obduracy of the Calhounites, Brown withdrew; that move paved the way for a compromise candidate all the Democrats supported and elected. A bitter man, Brown blamed his defeat directly—and correctly—on Calhoun. Democrats outside North Carolina also noted that the Calhoun forces only played by their rules.[26] Party victory and party safety meant little to them if they believed either the victory or the safety endangered their position.

Across the South politicians talked about Calhoun's power. To Joel Poinsett, Calhoun's new alliance with the Van Buren administration meant that "the strength of the South [was] united." In 1844 the Tennessean John Catron, viewing southern politics from the United States Supreme Court, defined Calhoun's strength as "a vast & controlling power in the South."[27] Although Calhoun and his followers worked mostly with Democrats, their activities had a significant impact on Whigs as well. The Calhounite pressure on the Democrats to satisfy their demands on sectional issues inevitably

26. Brown to David S. Reid, September 20, 1842, in David S. Reid Papers, North Carolina Department of Archives and History; Raleigh *Standard*, December 14, 21, 28, 1842; Cave Johnson to James K. Polk, December 18, 1842, January 29, 1843, in Polk Papers.

27. Poinsett to James B. Campbell, October 17, 1837, in Stoney (ed.), "Poinsett-Campbell Letters," 165; Catron to James K. Polk, June 8, 1844, in Polk Papers.

resulted in Democratic pressure on the Whigs to equal the Democratic performance. Such comprised the dynamics of the politics of slavery.

Calhoun increased his power still further through his personal involvement with parties, especially the Democratic party. Although he disdained them intellectually, he acted with them—at times and always on his own terms. "Our true role," he lectured James H. Hammond, "is to enter into an alliance with no party, but to act with any for the time moving in the same direction, without deflecting in the least from our principles, or doctrines." Never did he give any party sincere loyalty. After 1836 he broke even the loose ties he had maintained with the Whigs. When he renewed his association with the Democratic party in 1837, he claimed the Independent Treasury won him. He saw it as a boon to the South because it would eliminate the danger of consolidated financial power in the North that he considered so inimical to southern interests. And there can be no doubt that he worked avidly for its passage; friend and foe alike testified to the energy and time he expended for it.[28] Even so he remained his own man. In the midst of the battle over it he evinced little confidence in the Democratic party. Confiding to Hammond in January, 1840, he wrote, "My reliance is on the power, which circumstances has [sic] placed in our control." As Calhoun saw it, the Democratic party was dependent upon him for political success.[29] That such a view was grandiose or overly sanguine or probably both does not erase the conviction of the holder.

28. Calhoun to Hammond, April 20, 1840, in Jameson (ed.), *Calhoun Correspondence*, 452; Francis P. Blair to Andrew Jackson, February 8, 1839, in John Spencer Bassett (ed.), *Correspondence of Andrew Jackson* (7 vols.; Washington: Carnegie Institution of Washington, 1926–35), VI, 3; William C. Preston to Willie P. Mangum, March 28, 1838, in Henry Thomas Shanks (ed.), *The Papers of Willie Person Mangum* (5 vols.; Raleigh: State Department of Archives and History, 1950–56), II, 517; Daniel Webster to Nicholas Biddle, February or May, 1838, in Reginald C. McGrane (ed.), *The Correspondence of Nicholas Biddle Dealing with National Affairs, 1807–1844* (Boston and New York: Houghton Mifflin, 1919), 301.

29. Calhoun to Hammond, January 25, 1840, in Hammond Papers; Calhoun to Virgil Maxey, December 26, 1841, in Galloway-Maxey-Markoe Papers, Division of Manuscripts, Library of Congress.

When Calhoun made his greatest try for the presidency in the early 1840s, he did not change his rules at all. He made it crystal clear that his party loyalty and his party regularity depended on events going his way.[30] The regular Democrats watched him warily; cognizant of his strength in the various southern states, they feared that he would use some pretext to pull out of the party, take his followers with him, and smash their hopes for 1844. He did pull out, after a fashion, but he neither sabotaged nor attempted to sabotage the Democratic party. He did, however, assist in wrecking Van Buren's plans for 1844. That success was almost victory enough, for he was more ecstatic after Polk's winning the Democratic nomination than at any other time between Jackson's election in 1828 and his own death in 1850. Yet only two years after rejoicing over that victory he broke with President Polk over the Mexican War and spent his last remaining years, appropriately, outside the party fold.

Thomas Ritchie in 1834 described perfectly Calhoun's relations with the parties: "The Southern Achilles will have every thing his own way—or he is determined to withdraw from the action, and leave to others the glory of sacking Troy."[31] To the party men like Ritchie, Calhoun embodied ruin, for he strove to unravel their finely woven fabric. On that count they were right, but in the long run they followed his pattern. They played the party game with their northern associates only so long as they, both Democrats and Whigs, wrote the rules concerning the South and slavery. Although his strategy differed from theirs, they too were caught up in the politics of slavery. Within five years after his death most southern Whigs acted on his premises and the southern Democrats followed in another five.

John C. Calhoun was consumed by ambition; he was an ideologue; but he also saw with laserlike perception the plight of slavery and the South.

---

30. See Chap. Five herein; Martin Van Buren, *The Autobiography of Martin Van Buren*, ed. John C. Fitzpatrick (Washington: Government Printing Office, 1920), 389–95.
31. Richmond *Enquirer*, August 8, 1834.

III

While Van Buren's inaugural pledges and Calhoun's return affirmed the southern stance of the Democratic party, southern Whigs had no comparable symbols signifying the southern orientation of their party. At the same time they had no intention of losing the momentum of the White campaign. Having built their impressive edifice on the solid foundation of the politics of slavery, they knew that its maintenance depended on their loyalty to that politics.

Even so the southern Whigs realized that to challenge successfully the Democrats on both a national and a sectional basis required closer coordination among all Whigs. The three-headed ticket of 1836, or even a two-headed one, could not be repeated if they wanted to succeed in the nation and the South. They knew that White had been hurt by Democratic charges that he could not win, that he was a stalking horse for others unfavorable to the South. The obvious way to insure concert was a national convention of the Whig party. The Democrats had already used it twice and nothing else seemed so plausible. But in the aftermath of the White campaign southern Whigs did not embrace the convention idea without trepidation. As Willie P. Mangum told Henry Clay, "We the Whigs in No. Ca. have rendered that mode of nomination a good deal unpopular." Mangum's statement points to the issue that Whigs across the South as well as in North Carolina had made of what they called the "dictation": the nomination of Van Buren by the Democratic national convention back in 1835. Southern Whigs had used that issue to picture themselves democratic in contrast to their opponents, and they did not want to risk losing that image. Additionally some of them feared that in a convention northerners might forget about special southern needs and force candidates or platforms that would throw the southerners to the Democratic wolves.[32]

---

32. Mangum to Henry Clay, March 26, 1838, in Clay Papers, Indiana University; Mangum to Duff Green, October 10, 1837, in Green Papers, Division of Manuscripts, Library of Congress; Henry Clay to Peter B. Porter, January 5, 1838, in Porter Papers.

Finally, by 1838 most southern Whigs had come to accept the necessity for a convention. They seemed to agree with Henry Clay, who stressed to his Virginia friend Francis T. Brooke "the immense importance of a convention." Clay urged southern Whigs to give up their "repugnance to Conventions" and join with the rest of the party to give the Whig presidential candidate legitimacy and unity of support. The Richmond *Whig* echoed Clay's call by pleading with Whigs to support a Whig national convention. While the *Whig* admitted that a convention was not perfect, it insisted that every other nominating technique had even greater faults. Such pleas were heeded, for when congressional Whigs decided to hold a national party convention in Harrisburg, Pennsylvania in December, 1839, southern Whigs said aye. A North Carolina associate of William A. Graham spoke the mind of many of his fellows when he wrote:

> I hope the Whigs will by no means repudiate the ideas of sending Delegates to Harrisburg; if we are to cut ourselves loose from the Whig party of the North let us hear it from some one who can speak with authority, for as to prevalent opinion that the dictu [*sic*] of isolated persons, as it were, are to constitute our rule of action, I myself cannot come into it. Our strength and success consist in Union & as this Harrisburg Convention was proposed as a sort of middle ground upon which to reconcile the distracted opinions and preferences of the Whigs, let the South meet them there and I guarantee that the meeting will be productive of most beneficial results.[33]

Actually a national convention was the only way for southerners to insure that a single Whig presidential candidate was satisfactory to them. This concern became more than academic when news from the East brought word that Daniel Webster was eager for the nomination and that Webster supporters had already begun to make efforts in his behalf. This news was correct. And the southerners

---

33. Clay to Brooke, April 2, 1839, in Henry Clay Papers, Division of Manuscripts, Library of Congress; Clay to Willie P. Mangum, May 31, 1838, in Shanks (ed.), *Mangum Papers*, II, 525; Richmond *Whig*, June 18, 1839; James W. Bryan to Graham, January 3, 1839, in J. G. de Roulhac Hamilton and Max R. Williams (eds.), *The Papers of William Alexander Graham* (5 vols.; Raleigh: State Department of Archives and History, 1957–), II, 29–30.

realized that a Webster candidacy meant doom for them. They knew the politics of slavery would annihilate a Webster Whig party. As one of them predicted, "if he [Webster] is to be the candidate, the South will be thrown by irresistable [*sic*] necessity into the arms of the President [Van Buren and the Democrats]."[34]

Southern Whigs looked to Harrisburg to give them not a Webster but a candidate made for the politics of slavery. Their first success had come with a southern slaveholder, Hugh White; naturally their first choice for 1840 was another slaveholder. For 1840 southern Whigs worked not for a local hero like White but for a national figure, Henry Clay. With practical unanimity southern Whigs trumpeted Clay's name. The Raleigh *Register* asserted that Clay was distinctly the favorite of the southern Whigs and the only Whig contender who could command the electoral vote of North Carolina. George Bryan, that rare species, a practicing South Carolina Whig, urged John Pendleton Kennedy of Maryland to do all he could for Clay because no other Whig had a chance in the South. On the western boundary of southern Whiggery both the New Orleans *Bee* and the Vicksburg *Whig* blared forth the name of Clay just as often and just as loudly as their eastern brethren.[35]

This rush to Clay did not signify that southern Whiggery had become National Republicanism reincarnated. It meant exactly the opposite; Henry Clay was coming to the southern Whigs and coming without qualification. The Henry Clay that captured southern Whiggery between 1837 and 1839 had jettisoned political and economic nationalism, embraced states' rights, and joined John C. Calhoun on the front lines defending slavery. He told southerners that he no longer urged a new national bank; instead he would follow the

34. Sydney Nathans, *Daniel Webster and Jacksonian Democracy* (Baltimore and London: Johns Hopkins University Press, 1973), 107, 109, 114–15; George Bryan to Henry Clay, July 14, 1837, in Clay Papers, Division of Manuscripts, Library of Congress. See also Hamilton C. Jones to Willie P. Mangum, December 22, 1837, in Shanks (ed.), *Mangum Papers*, II, 513–14 and Richmond *Whig*, July 14, 1837.

35. Raleigh *Register*, February 12, 1838; Bryan to Kennedy, July 14, 1837, in Kennedy Papers; Vicksburg *Whig*, April 18, 1839 (daily), and July 13, 1839 (tri-weekly); New Orleans *Bee*, January 7, 1839.

lead of the people. No longer did he stand as the apostle of protection; he was committed to the compromise tariff of 1833 with its decreasing duties. With unmistakable clarity he identified himself as a true son of the South in his attitude toward slavery and abolition. [36]

In 1838 and 1839 Clay moved forcefully toward the South on slavery. He identified Calhoun's resolutions of December, 1837, as, at least in part, an attempt to trap him between the northern and southern wings of his party. Reacting swiftly, Clay placed himself squarely in the southern camp. He moved to amend Calhoun's resolutions with his own. In them he denounced the abolitionists for "endangering the rights and security of the people of the District [of Columbia]"; he asserted that any move toward abolition in the district would be "a just cause of alarm to the people of the slaveholding States, and have a direct and inevitable tendency to disturb and endanger the Union." He also condemned any moves toward abolition in Florida Territory and in "any district of the country, set apart for the Indian Tribes, where it now exists, because of the serious alarm and just apprehensions which would be thereby excited in the States sustaining that domestic institution." Although Clay's language did not take the moral tone of Calhoun's and though he hedged on constitutional questions, he certainly affirmed the rights of slavery and castigated the abolitionists. And although the Calhounites accused him of "straddling the Slave Question," southern Whigs proudly paraded his fidelity to the South and her peculiar institution. [37]

Clay, however, did not rest on the laurels of these resolutions. Almost a year after he introduced them he assumed his full southern

36. Richmond *Whig*, August 21, 1838; Lyon G. Tyler, *The Letters and Times of the Tylers* (3 vols.; Richmond and Williamsburg: Whittet & Shepperson, 1884–85, 1896), I, Chaps. 19–20.

37. Clay to Peter B. Porter, January 10, 1838, in Porter Papers; *Senate Journal*, 25th Cong., 2nd Sess., 125–27; Francis W. Pickens to James H. Hammond, January 13, 1838, in Hammond Papers.

stature in a major Senate speech he delivered on February 7, 1839. This speech even impressed the Calhounites.[38] Lambasting those he called "ultra-abolitionists," he termed their activities dangerous to the continued existence of the Union. Turning to the Constitution, he almost became a Calhounite. He asserted that Congress had no power over slavery in either the states or the District of Columbia, though he qualified the district question by saying that others could interpret the constitutional provisions differently. But to do so, he hurried to say, was "a violation of implied faith," "a breach of trust." Moving far away from his nationalist views he even denied that the commerce clause gave the federal government any power over the interstate slave trade. Declaring that constitutional power was intended "to secure peace and harmony among the States," Clay insisted that Congress could not use it to touch the slave trade, for such action would cause turmoil, not harmony. Furthermore, he asserted that when a slave was recognized as property, the law of movable property applied and that law permitted no interference from Congress on the interstate movement of bondsmen. In sum Clay told his fellow senators and the nation that the Constitution did not apply to slavery except for representation and direct taxation. Certainly the Fathers understood it that way; otherwise it would never have been ratified by the South.

Although Clay presented a traditional southern brief on the constitutional protection and sanctity of slavery, he did not defend the institution as a positive good. In this part of his speech he sounded like those southerners of an earlier time who deprecated slavery but who deplored interference with it even more. He held to his belief that slavery was inherently evil, but he did not condemn southern slaveholders because, in his mind, they had no feasible alternative to maintaining slavery. For the great South and Southwest any talk of

---

38. Calvin Colton (ed.), *The Works of Henry Clay: Comprising His Life, Correspondence and Speeches* (10 vols.; New York and London: G. P. Putnam's Sons, 1904), VIII, 135–59. Francis W. Pickens to James H. Hammond, February 8, 1839, in Hammond Papers.

abolition was impossible. Emancipation there, even gradual emancipation, according to Clay, meant either black domination or race
war, equal catastrophes.

In a great irony Clay proclaimed slavery essential for American
liberty. Clay reached this point when he said the United States
could not exist without slavery, for the South, he believed, would
choose slavery over the nation, if forced to make that kind of choice.
Thus abolitionists, not slaveowners, became the great enemies both
of liberty and the Union. They, not the slaveowners, threatened
Clay's beloved Union. If abolitionists persisted with their nefarious
program, Clay declared, a war against them and for the Union would
be clearly justified.

Private assurance to southern Whig leaders accompanied these
public declarations. In a letter to Willie P. Mangum, Clay termed
"ridiculous" charges connecting him with abolition. He pointed out
that abolition newspapers in the North condemned him because
they knew "the Slave interest will have in me a firm supporter."
Reporting a conversation with Clay, Henry Wise paraphrased Clay's
views on slavery and constitutional guarantees: "He [Clay] was a
slaveholder himself, identified with the South in that interest; and so
inexpedient and bad in faith did he deem the *exercise* of the power
of abolition by Congress, that he would justify its resistance by
force of arms. Thus, then, practically he would be with the most
ultra of strict constructionists, though he might fundamentally differ
with them as to the principles at the bottom of all these questions."[39] Simply, from the public podium and through personal
contacts Clay told the South he was theirs.

Without question the southern Whigs responded. Clay as the
great friend of the South rang out from Whig newspapers across the
South. They covered their columns with full reprints of the 1839
speech. The Raleigh *Register* praised Clay for moving "boldly" in

39. Clay to Mangum, May 31, 1838, in Shanks (ed.), *Mangum Papers*, II, 526; Barton H.
Wise, *The Life of Henry A. Wise of Virginia, 1806–1876* (New York and London: MacMillan,
1899), 88–90.

favor of slavery with his resolutions "fearless of the consequences."
To the *Register* the proper course for the South was clear: "If our
slaveholding people wish to avoid a political connexion [*sic*] with the
Abolitionists, they must cast their votes against Martin Van Buren."
The *Register* thought the 1839 speech "must endear him [Clay] to
every Southern man." Glorying in the condemnation of Clay by
abolitionist newspapers, the Richmond *Whig* challenged the Democrats to produce a candidate as true to the South as Henry Clay.
Clay's 1839 speech brought forth resplendent rhetoric from the New
Orleans *Bee*. "It is the dirge of abolition," cried the *Bee*, "that hide-
ous monster may shake its gorgon head but its twisted snakes hiss in
vain." The arch disciple of states' rights, John Tyler, told Clay that
their views meshed; Tyler said that he and other Virginia Whigs saw
Clay as the champion of the South and states' rights. Southern
Whigs seemed to agree with the Darien, Georgia, physician who
remarked in 1839 to the actress-turned-plantation-wife Fanny
Kemble Butler that "he inclined vehemently to Mr. Clay as one on
whom the slaveholders could depend."[40]

Clay, in turn, was confident he could depend on them to push him
toward his goal, the presidential nomination to be awarded by the
Harrisburg convention. As early as January, 1838, he informed his
close friend Peter Porter that "beyond all question, I should obtain
every vote in that quarter [the South], looking to the present state of
public opinion." His proslavery offensive in 1838 and 1839 did nothing to lessen his confidence.[41]

The Harrisburg convention proved Henry Clay accurate. Every
southern delegation cast its vote for him on the first ballot. That solid
backing gave Clay the lead in a three-way contest. He had 103 votes

40. Raleigh *Register*, January 15, September 17, 1838, February 25, 1839; Richmond
Whig, August 14, 1838; New Orleans *Bee*, February 26, 1839; Tyler to Clay, January 25, 1838,
in Clay Papers, Division of Manuscripts, Library of Congress and Tyler to Clay, September
18, 1839, Frederick M. Dearborn Collection, Houghton Library, Harvard University; Frances Anne Kemble, *Journal of a Residence on a Georgia Plantation in 1838–1839* (New York:
Harper & Brothers, 1863), 62.
41. Clay to Porter, January 5, March 4, and December 27, 1838, all in Porter Papers,
Buffalo.

while his rivals William Henry Harrison and Winfield Scott had 94 and 57, respectively. But the victory Clay so hungered for escaped him. After that first ballot, his opponents combined behind Harrison, and the transplanted Virginian from north of the Ohio River defeated his counterpart from the southern shore. The convention had not acted as either Clay or the southern Whigs wanted. Clay was bitter in defeat. In contrast his southern supporters showed little distress over his failure. Even before Harrisburg, some of them had spoken of Harrison's acceptability should Clay stumble.[42] Initially northern Whigs pushed Harrison's candidacy. Back in 1836 he had made a strong showing in the middle states and the old Northwest. Whig managers from the North believed that he could win many more votes than Clay because no important group of northern voters opposed him. Southerners gleefully leapt upon the Harrison bandwagon.

Southern Whigs knew Harrison from 1836, and they were confident that he could succeed in the politics of slavery. Besides the Harrisburg convention in deciding against the promulgation of a national platform left southern Whigs unencumbered with any distasteful or dangerous party issues. Reporting Harrison's triumph the Raleigh *Register* admitted that Clay had been its first choice, but quickly the *Register* went on to say that Harrison satisfied in every respect. In Virginia, in Alabama, in Louisiana, and across the South, Whigs echoed the *Register*'s declaration. In accepting Harrison as their candidate southern Whigs made clear that they took him on southern grounds. Harrison was eminently safe for the South, announced the New Orleans *Bee*. For proof the *Bee* told its readers that both Benjamin Watkins Leigh and James Barbour of Virginia had placed their name in Harrison's column. Neither would have done so, according to the *Bee*, if there had been the slightest doubt regarding Harrison's safety. William A. Graham also invoked

42. *Niles' Register*, LVII (December 14, 1839), 248–52; Henry A. Wise, *Seven Decades of the Union* (Philadelphia: J. B. Lippincott, 1872), 170–71; William A. Graham to Willie P. Mangum, October 11, 1839, in Shanks (ed.), *Mangum Papers*, III, 19.

Leigh's name when he informed a fellow North Carolina Whig that "Mr. Leigh declares that he, H[arrison], has no principle adverse to the South." Writing from Washington, James Graham assured his brother William that Harrison had no connections with abolition. Proclaiming support for Harrison the editor of the Tuscaloosa *Independent Monitor* identified himself as "belong[ing] to the States Rights school as taught by Mr. Jefferson, and more recently by Gov. Troup." Stephen Miller then placed Harrison squarely beside himself on those hallowed southern principles.[43]

Confidence that Harrison stood as a true soldier guarding the South helped make the State Rights party of Georgia a full member of the Whig community. The State Righters had acted with the Whigs since the break up of the Jackson party between 1833 and 1835; moreover they carried Georgia for Hugh White in 1836. Even so they refused to give up completely their State Rights identity and merge totally with Whiggery. Staying away from Harrisburg, these Georgians called for the nomination of their own George Troup. After Harrison's nomination the Milledgeville *Southern Recorder* insisted that the State Rights party ought to remain steadfast for Troup.[44] But certain leaders of the party disagreed. The old anti-Jacksonian John M. Berrien, Congressman William C. Dawson, the young Robert Toombs, and others believed that the State Righters should become full-fledged Harrison men and Whigs. As political leaders and aspiring leaders, these men wanted recognition as leaders of the Whig party, not just Georgia politicians. To gain that status required their supporting the candidate of the party rather than the local Troup ticket. At the same time they wanted and needed their state to move with them.

These men made their move to bring Georgia under Harrison's

43. Raleigh *Register*, December 14, 1839; Richmond *Whig*, December 13, 1839; Tuscaloosa *Independent Monitor*, March 9, 1840; New Orleans *Bee*, December 23, 1839, January 7, 1840; Graham to James W. Bryan, December 14, 1839 and James Graham to William A. Graham, December 22, 1839, both in Hamilton and Williams (eds.), *Graham Papers*, II, 71–72.

44. Milledgeville *Southern Recorder*, June 25, December 17, 1839.

banner by identifying Harrison with the cause of the South. Political ambition and calculation underlay their strategy, to be sure. But only in part, for these men were sincerely concerned about the position of the South as well as their own goals. Dawson in Washington wrote Berrien: "I am now satisfied that Genl. Harrison is not the least tinctured with abolition." Dawson continued that he had "the fullest assurance" that a Harrison cabinet "will be perfectly satisfactory to the Slave holding & Planting interest." Emphasizing that he had not rushed his decision, Dawson went on, "You know on this subject I feel deep solicitude & I am not mistaken—my time has been spent in ascertaining this fact." In conclusion he reported that the opinion of Georgia would be "properly & honorably respected" by a Harrison administration.[45] Security for the South and personal power and influence—Dawson was confident of the twin goals of the southern party men.

In Georgia, Berrien agreed with Dawson and led the campaign to carry the State Rights party all the way into the Whig camp. To a fellow State Righter, Berrien confessed that he had come to favor Harrison because Harrison had "warm Southern feelings, and on many subjects [was] politically friendly to the South." Troup, as-sured of Harrison's safety, was asked to step aside; a Harrison-Tyler electoral ticket was suggested. This campaign won converts, for in May, 1840, the *Southern Recorder* pulled back from Troup and urged all Georgians to join in sounding the tocsin—Harrison, the true and safe candidate for the South. Then in June the Georgia State Rights party met in convention and endorsed the Harrison-Tyler ticket.[46]

While Harrison received the plaudits of the South, his vice-presidential running mate shared them. To southern Whigs, John Tyler was a comrade of long standing. He had been denouncing

45. Dawson to Berrien, February 20, 1840, in Berrien Papers.
46. Berrien to Joseph H. Lumpkin, April 27, 1840, in Joseph H. Lumpkin Papers, Ilah Dunlap Little Memorial Library, University of Georgia; Milledgeville *Southern Recorder*, May 5, 19, June 1, 2, 1840.

Democrats since 1832, and in 1836 he had appeared as a vice-presidential candidate on the Hugh White ballot in several southern states. Tyler won his nomination more because of his identity as a Clay man than for his identity as a southerner. Of course in Harrisburg in December, 1839, one would have been hard put to separate the Clay supporters from the southerners. And though the convention participants disagreed on many particulars concerning the vice-presidential nomination, they tended to agree on three points: the convention desperately wanted a Clay loyalist for the second spot in order to reconcile and win the support of the Kentuckian and his followers; only southerners were seriously considered because they were the leading Clay men; Tyler stood close to the top, if not at the top, of the list of possible choices.[47] With Tyler beside Harrison, Whigs in slave country were jubilant.

Unlike their Whig counterparts southern Democrats had no qualms about a national convention and no concern about a presidential candidate. After two national conventions, both blessed by Andrew Jackson, all Democrats, including southerners, accepted the national party convention as the right and proper method for selecting the national standard-bearers. The southerners joined their northern brethren in agreeing that Martin Van Buren deserved a second term. Following the example of the sainted Jefferson, Jackson had served two terms; two terms seemed normal and natural. Besides, as far as the southern politicians were concerned, Van Buren had stood foursquare with them: his inaugural and the course of his administration confirmed the campaign pledges of 1836; in 1838 his influence came down on the southern side during the congressional debate on abolition sparked by Calhoun's resolutions; he strengthened the southern presence in the cabinet; he

47. Wise, *Seven Decades*, 159–61; Harriet A. Weed (ed.), *Life of Thurlow Weed, Including His Autobiography and A Memoir* (2 vols.; Boston: Houghton Mifflin, 1883), I, 482; Benjamin W. Leigh to Editors of Richmond *Whig*, [December 3, 1841], printed in [Lyon G. Tyler (ed.)], "John Tyler and the Vice-Presidency," *Tyler's Quarterly Historical and Genealogical Magazine*, IX (1927), 89–95.

gave his only two Supreme Court appointments to southerners, John McKinley of Alabama in 1837 and Peter Daniel of Virginia in 1840. They had no reason to challenge his desire for another four years in the White House.

The southern Democrats, however, did not want everything to remain the same. They demanded someone other than the incumbent Richard M. Johnson as Van Buren's running mate. Back in 1835 the southerners, especially the Virginians, opposed the selection of Johnson chiefly because of his living openly with his mulatto mistress and their children. But then their opposition had come too late and been too meek. As 1840, and its May national convention approached, the southerners had not changed their minds about Johnson. In fact many were disgusted with what one of them termed Johnson's "nightly revel and riot upon the charms of a bright eyed mulato [sic]"—and " in sight of the capitol."[48] This time southerners were determined to eliminate Johnson.

Early in Van Buren's presidency the southern campaign to dump Johnson got underway. William Haywood, Jr., of North Carolina told James K. Polk in March, 1838, that Johnson must go, and to insure success "early action" was essential. Writing to James Buchanan two months later, Richard E. Parker, an intimate friend of Ritchie's, called Johnson "a dead weight" and insisted that he be dropped. In early 1839 the old Jacksonian John Catron argued that Johnson definitely should be replaced. By early 1840 southern Democrats stood almost in unison with Andrew Jackson, now the Tennessee planter, who lent his prestige and influence to the effort to throttle Johnson. To a group of Tennessee Democrats, Jackson declared that Johnson "would weaken and distract our party in the south, south west." Jackson also informed Frank Blair, still editing the *Globe*, the administration organ in Washington, that no southern state would support Johnson. Clearly these views reached and registered with the administration, for two months prior to the con-

48. Samuel H. Laughlin to James K. Polk, April 29, 1840, in Polk Papers.

vention Joel Poinsett reported to a South Carolina friend that the South would not concur in the renomination of Johnson.[49]

Although southern Democrats stood practically as one against Johnson, no unity existed on the name of his replacement. In February, 1840, the Virginia Democratic convention endorsed Polk, who definitely mounted the most vigorous effort to capture southern support for the vice-presidency. Even though Polk had the widest range of supporters as well as the backing of Andrew Jackson, he was by no means the only man considered. Thomas Ritchie made private soundings for his fellow Virginian, Andrew Stevenson. Both the Milledgeville *Federal Union* and the New Orleans *Louisiana Courier* pushed John Forsyth, Van Buren's secretary of state and a Georgian. Still others spoke of Alabama's William R. King.[50]

When the Democrats met in Baltimore, they did as the southerners desired. Richard M. Johnson was deprived of a second nomination as vice-president, even though some close to the administration feared the reaction from the West and the North. But in his place the Democratic convention put no new face; instead, with southerners blocking all attempts at even pro forma votes for Johnson, it decided to let each state party choose the man it preferred.[51] While the

49. Haywood to Polk, March 10, 1838, Polk to A. O. P. Nicholson, January 13, 1838, both in Polk Papers; Parker to James Buchanan, May 21, 1838, in Buchanan Papers; Catron to Andrew Jackson Donelson, January 4, 1839, in Donelson Papers; St. George L. Sioussat (ed.), "Diaries of S. H. Laughlin, of Tennessee, 1840, 1843," *Tennessee Historical Magazine*, II (1916), 46; Jackson to Blair, February 15, 1840, in Bassett (ed.), *Jackson Correspondence*, VI, 50–51; Poinsett to Dr. Jos. Johnson, March 12, 1840, in Joel R. Poinsett Letters, Henry D. Gilpin Collection, Historical Society of Pennsylvania. Cf. Little Rock *Arkansas Gazette*, October 30, 1839, and May 27, 1840.

50. Charles G. Sellers, Jr., *James K. Polk* (2 vols.; Princeton, N.J.: Princeton University Press, 1957–), I, 399–414; Theophilus Fisk to James K. Polk, February 21, 1840, Cave Johnson to James K. Polk, February 27, 1840, Alfred Balch to James K. Polk, September 2, 1839, all in Polk Papers; Raleigh *Standard*, January 15, 1840; Francis W. Pickens to James H. Hammond, February 28, 1840, in Hammond Papers; Sioussat (ed.), "Laughlin Diaries," 46; James K. Polk to David Hubbard, April 5, 1840, in George W. Campbell Papers, Division of Manuscripts, Library of Congress; Ritchie to Stevenson, May 15, 18[39], in Stevenson Papers; Milledgeville *Federal Union*, May 19, 1840; New Orleans *Louisiana Courier*, May 9, 1840.

51. Poinsett to Dr. Jos. Johnson, March 12, 1840, in Poinsett Letters, Gilpin Collection; Cave Johnson to James K. Polk, February 27, 1840, in Polk Papers; *Niles' Register*, LVIII (May 9, 1840), 150–51.

southerners did not get a southern vice-president, they did accomplish their main goal—the removal of Richard Johnson.

With Johnson out of the way and with an incumbent president pledged by word and deed to their particular concerns, southern Democrats prepared for battle with Harrison and Tyler.

IV

The presidential contest of 1840, the Log Cabin campaign, is one of the most famous elections in American history, and it gave birth to what is probably the most familiar campaign slogan, "Tippecanoe and Tyler, Too." In the antebellum South, that election has a special importance because it confirmed the politics of slavery as the primal force in southern politics. The political battle in 1840 amplified and magnified the images and metaphors that had captured southern politics during the first great Whig-Democratic clash. To be sure, the South participated fully in the revolution in electioneering techniques heralded by the Log Cabin campaign. That campaign carnival was in itself an essential ingredient in the politics of slavery, for it cemented the close bond between the politician and the voter in addition to underscoring the need for a politics of excitement. It also provided an even larger arena for the rhetoric that articulated the most fundamental concerns of southern society. The election of 1840 in the South can best be understood through a slight, though crucial, addition to the famous slogan—"Tippecanoe and Tyler and Slavery, Too."

In 1840 the politics of slavery dwarfed all economic issues even though Van Buren's administration had been consumed by the panic and the concomitant debate over banks and the Independent Treasury. The partisan division over banking and financial policy that had begun to dominate state politics did not intrude into the presidential contest. Southern Democrats hardly mentioned the Independent Treasury; neither did they make more than feeble and sporadic efforts to fill the horizon of a Whig victory with a new national bank. When they did mention a bank, they normally did so as a part of a more general attempt to tie the Whigs to federalism and centralism. And these infrequent notices were buried under the rhetoric of slavery.[52]

Southern Whigs did not rush to fill the economic vacuum left by the Democrats. Of course the depression and the failure of recovery under Van Buren created a favorable political atmosphere for the Whigs, but the point remains that they did not base their campaign or their case for Harrison on any economic grounds. When they did talk about economics, they insisted, just as they had done back in 1836, that Whiggery did not represent a rebirth of National Republicanism. Presenting Harrison, in the states' rights, strict-construction gown worn by Hugh White, southern Whigs said Harrison's economics were like White's. Harrison favored neither a new national bank nor a protective tariff. On the tariff he stood with Clay and Calhoun behind the compromise tariff of 1833 with its decreasing duties. Rumors that Harrison favored a bank were promptly denounced as false. After affirming that Harrison opposed another national bank, the Richmond *Whig* declared he would never change "unless it be shown to be absolutely necessary for the management of the nation's finances." Although that qualification might be considered a bit of a hedge, it certainly kept Harrison outside the ranks of the probank men.[53] By making no issue of economics the southern Whigs made it plain that financial matters were distinctly secondary to the question of southern safety and security.

Although southern Whigs evinced little interest in economics, they did exclaim about the rights of the people. According to the Whig creed, gaining independence and freedom required throwing

52. The generalizations in this and the following paragraph are based on all the Democratic and Whig newspapers I read. For specific examples of the Democratic use of economics see Little Rock *Arkansas Gazette*, September 23, 1840; "An Address to the Democrats of Virginia, 1840," [written by Thomas Ritchie], printed in *John P. Branch Historical Papers of Randolph-Macon College*, III (1911), 263–70; Jackson *Mississippian*, October 3, 1840; New Orleans *Louisiana Courier*, October, 1840, *passim*.

53. Raleigh *Register*, April 17, 1840; Richmond *Whig*, June 12, 1840. Of the seven Whig newspapers I read for the 1840 campaign only the New Orleans *Bee* ever intimated that it favored a new national bank; and even in the *Bee* the few editorials supporting a national bank were buried under an avalanche of slavery-related ones.

off the Democratic yoke. "Strike off these manacles of a cold-blooded party despot and restore your sons to freedom," shouted the Richmond *Whig.* "Expel from the Capitol the man who would subjugate them and you." The New Orleans *Bee* called Harrison's campaign the great march of the people. To the Vicksburg *Whig* another race by Van Buren meant that the old evil of dictation still lived, for once again the dictated choice of Andrew Jackson, not the free choice of the people, threatened the republic. And when Harrison won, the Richmond *Whig* saw the victory as "the triumph of the People over an Administration which felt power and forgot right."[54]

As ironclad evidence that the Democrats intended to usurp every right of the people, southern Whigs pointed to the militia reorganization proposed by Joel Poinsett, Van Buren's secretary of war. In an effort to improve the efficiency of the militia and to strengthen the armed forces, Poinsett advocated more centralized direction of training. But his innocent reform became, in Whig rhetoric, "this most audacious grasp after the most dangerous power." "ONE STEP TOWARDS FURTHER MONARCHY," cried the New Orleans *Bee.* With what Whigs called an oversized standing army, an all powerful central government would have an immense military force to stamp out popular liberty and threaten the safety of the South.[55]

The safety of the South, the potential danger to slavery—this shibboleth became the great Whig cry of 1840 just as it had been four years earlier. Long before the presidential contest of 1840, long before the Harrisburg convention, southern Whigs began reconnoitering for their second explosive foray in the politics of slavery. In 1838 a Whig congressional hopeful in Tennessee brought to the stump the old Whig charges against Van Buren. Even before Van Buren was inaugurated the Richmond *Whig* declaimed against the "faithless

54. Richmond *Whig,* March 6, November 13, 1840; New Orleans *Bee,* 1840, *passim;* Vicksburg *Tri-Weekly Whig,* July 7, 1840.
55. Milledgeville *Southern Recorder,* April 28, September 8, 1840; New Orleans *Bee,* June 30, 1840. Also see Richmond *Whig,* March 31, April 10, and June 5, 1840; Vicksburg *Tri-Weekly Whig,* June 23, 1840. Details of Poinsett's plan can be found in Curtis, *Fox at Bay,* 199.

promises" of Van Buren and his supporters. No matter if Van Buren
be inclined toward the South, he must, according to the *Whig*,
ultimately side with the North. Southerners, then, took a perilous
risk if they put their trust in him. Midway between 1836 and 1840
the Milledgeville *Southern Recorder* both looked back and peered
ahead. Declaring that in Georgia the election of 1836 turned on the
slavery question, the *Recorder* predicted the same paramount issue
in 1840. As Georgians had repudiated Van Buren once, they would
do it again. Once again the *Recorder* paraded the facts of Van Buren's
misdeeds toward the South. "The first solid reason" for southerners
to support Van Buren did not exist. Instead, as the *Recorder* emphasized, every reason to distrust him did.[56]

When the Harrisburg convention gave them their own candidate,
the southern Whigs reaffirmed their electoral strategy. Upon receiving news of the Harrisburg nominations, the editor of the New
Orleans *Bee*, newly a Whig paper, articulated his conception of
Whig campaign strategy. Writing to John J. Crittenden, Alexander
C. Bullitt admitted that he expected Clay's nomination. Clay, he
thought, fitted perfectly the needs of southern Whigs whereas Harrison's candidacy meant more work "to produce a Harrison sensation
in the South." But that prospect neither frightened nor demoralized
Bullitt. To Crittenden he spelled out his course: "I will go to work to
show Van Buren[']s connection with the abolitionists and try to put
the locofocos on their defense."[57] Whether other Whig editors and
speakers agreed with Bullitt's assessment of Harrison's candidacy
cannot be determined, but, no matter, for they all moved down an
identical road.

The Whig assault on Van Buren in 1840 basically repeated the
charges of 1835 and 1836. Whig newspapers bombarded southern

56. A. O. P. Nicholson to Felix Grundy, October 8, 1838, in Felix Grundy Papers,
Southern Historical Collection, University of North Carolina; Richmond *Whig*, January 6,
1837; Milledgeville *Southern Recorder*, March 20, April 24, May 1, 1838, July 9, 1839.

57. Bullitt to Crittenden, December 21, 1839, in Crittenden Papers. In 1839 the *Bee*
changed owners and politics; from 1839 to the demise of Whiggery in Louisiana, the *Bee* was
the leading Whig newspaper in the state.

voters with cries challenging Van Buren's loyalty to the South. From Virginia to Arkansas the refrain never varied, though different verses portrayed different outrages. Van Buren supported restriction during the Missouri crisis; Van Buren advocated Negro suffrage in New York; Van Buren admitted that Congress had the right to abolish slavery in the District of Columbia; Van Buren and his northern supporters were in collusion with abolitionists. Concluding all the specific accusations were declarations that southerners could not trust Van Buren. For evidence to support these indictments southern Whig editors used excerpts from northern papers, from congressional debates, from the journal of the New York constitutional convention of 1821. Then, seemingly in opposition to all the specific accusations, southern Whigs pictured Van Buren as a devious man. For evidence of his duplicity, they contrasted his efforts to portray himself as a friend of the South with his supposed enmity toward the South and slavery. Southern Whigs never claimed that Van Buren embraced abolition directly; they did claim that his deeds put him in that camp. As Whigs saw it, that embrace would have been the manly course for Van Buren to follow. In sum, as Bullitt's *Bee* proclaimed, "doubt, mystery and suspicion enshroud Van Buren." Thus southerners who demanded a man of conviction and honor must look elsewhere.[58]

At every turn southern Whigs presented William Henry Harrison as the complete opposite of Van Buren. Harrison was a native southerner who understood and respected the particular needs of the South. According to Whig rhetoric, that identity forged in his Virginia birth and upbringing was crucially important. In the words of the Milledgeville *Southern Recorder* it meant that Harrison would surely act as "the conservator of [southern] domestic institutions." In a letter to a Harrison rally in North Carolina, Hugh S. Legaré declared it unthinkable for "a man born and educated in the South"

<hr>

58. Such charges pervaded every Whig newspaper. For specific examples see Richmond *Whig*, June 19, July 3, September 11, 1840; Raleigh *Register*, January 3, May 1, 1840; Milledgeville *Southern Recorder*, May 19, July 14, 1840; Tuscaloosa *Independent Monitor*, April 17, 1840; Vicksburg *Tri-Weekly Whig*, June 16, 1840; New Orleans *Bee*, March 17, May 29, 1840; Helena (Ark.) *Southern Shield*, September 18, 1840.

not to be "trusted by the South" to defend southern institutions and rights.[59]

Although promoting Harrison as a native undoubtedly assisted the Whig cause, it by no means comprised the whole, or even the bulk, of the Whig case for him. Southern Whigs made much of Harrison's past actions regarding slavery, and generally they reported accurately. They pointed out, back in 1804, he favored relaxing the restrictions against slavery in the old Northwest Territory. With great relish they described Harrison's course in the Missouri crisis when he publicly supported the South and voted against restriction even though it hurt him politically in Ohio. Gleefully they contrasted Harrison's action in this instance with that of Van Buren, who maintained a public silence even though he probably favored the southern position. Advancing to the 1830s southern Whigs proudly displayed extracts from two Harrison speeches, one given in Ohio in 1833, the other in Indiana in 1835, in which Harrison declared that Congress had no power over slavery either in the states or the District of Columbia unless the concerned states requested congressional action. He also asserted that abolition societies, regardless of their motives, were both dangerous and unconstitutional. Describing the Ohio address, the Richmond *Whig* exulted, "The entire portion of the speech relating to abolition, breathes the most ardent and devoted attachment to the rights and institutions of the South." The Indiana speech demonstrated conclusively, according to the Raleigh *Register*, "[Harrison's] soundness on the subject of slavery." The *Register* called on every southerner, particularly the Van Buren men, to read it and "contrast the views, therein boldly set forth, with the temporizing, vacillating opinions of [Van Buren] on the same question."[60]

Summing up the Whig thrust the Tuscaloosa *Independent*

59. Milledgeville *Southern Recorder*, September 29, 1840; Legaré to Sponsors of Harrison Rally in Salisbury, N.C., June 12, 1840, in Hugh S. Legaré Papers (Personal Papers Miscellaneous), Division of Manuscripts, Library of Congress.

60. These claims, just as the anti-Van Buren charges, pervaded the Whig newspapers. The quotations come from the Richmond *Whig*, March 24, 1840, and the Raleigh *Register*, January 3, 1840.

Monitor asserted, "Mr. Van Buren has not the remotest hold upon
Southern confidence, while Gen. Harrison is a 'tower of strength' to
Southern institutions." This campaign crusade was no sometime
thing; from the Harrisburg convention in December 1839 to the
election almost a full year later these accusations and claims filled
southern Whig newspapers. Hardly a single issue failed to take up
the cudgels on some aspect of the sectional campaign. Often a paper
picked out a particular statement of Harrison's and kept it on the
masthead for an extended period. The Raleigh *Register*, for example, printed on its masthead in bold-face capital letters from January
17, 1840 to the election the following quotation from Harrison's
Indiana speech: "NEITHER THE STATES WHERE SLAVERY DOES NOT
EXIST, NOR THE GOVERNMENT OF THE UNITED STATES, CAN WITH-
OUT ASSUMPTION OF POWER, AND THE VIOLATION OF A SOLEMN
COMPACT, DO ANYTHING TO REMOVE IT, WITHOUT THE CONSENT
OF THOSE IMMEDIATELY INVOLVED."[61]

Southern Democrats never hesitated in accompanying once again
their Whig counterparts into the thickets of the politics of slavery.
They also began before the Log Cabin campaign officially got
underway. Aware that southern Whigs hoped Henry Clay would
carry the Whig banner in 1840, the Democrats set out to infect Clay
with the germ of abolition. After considering Clay's stand on various
issues the Jackson *Mississippian* concluded that on all counts Clay's
beliefs were antisouthern; even worse they found him "a dupe of the
abolitionists" on questions referring directly to slavery. The Mil-
ledgveille *Federal Union* condemned Clay as "the Whig, Abolition
and Latitudinarian candidate." Clay was alleged to be intimately
associated with northern Whigs who were, in the opinion of the
Raleigh *Standard*, traitors to the South; thus southerners must take
heed and turn their backs on Clay and his nefarious associates.
Predicting a Whig ticket composed of Clay and a northerner, proba-

61. Tuscaloosa *Independent Monitor*, May 8, 1840; Raleigh *Register*, January 7–October
9, 1840 (the last issue before the election in the microfilm edition of the *Register* prepared by
the North Carolina Department of Archives and History).

bly an abolitionist, James K. Polk relished the prospect of having such opposition in Tennessee. He was sure it guaranteed an easy Democratic win.[62]

When the Harrisburg convention produced Harrison, not Clay, southern Democrats immediately leaped upon him. Unlike Hugh White, whom they could not attack directly on the slavery issue, Harrison hailed from a free state. By definition, that made him a superb target. With Harrison as the focus of their assault the Democrats mounted an offensive aimed at identifying the Whigs with antislave sentiments. Simultaneously they reasserted their party as the only true southern party. Andrew Jackson's contemptuous phrase, "Harrison with his abolition principles," became the Democratic watchword. Thomas Ritchie called Harrison "the Abolition Candidate"; the New Orleans *Louisiana Courier* simply declared him an abolitionist. According to the *Federal Union* the great danger posed by Harrison was not his incompetence but his identity with the abolitionists. Tennessee Democrats based their campaign on tying Harrison to the abolitionists. Southern Democratic editors headlined editorials with such declarations as: "HARRISON AN ABO- LITIONIST, MORE PROOF."[63]

For that proof southern Democrats managed to build a shaky case at best. They brought out that Harrison as a young man in Virginia had belonged to an emancipation society; then they implied that he had worked for emancipation ever since. They quoted from an 1822 address in which Harrison declared himself a friend of liberty. They claimed that Harrison had said emancipation was a subject dear to his heart. These accusations pervade Democratic papers of 1840, yet

---

62. Jackson *Mississippian*, March 2, June 22, 1838; Milledgeville *Federal Union*, April 16, 1839; Raleigh *Standard*, January 3, April 11, 1838, and February 6, April 3, June 5, 1839; Polk to A. O. P. Nicholson, January 13, 1838, in Polk Papers.

63. Jackson to William B. Lewis, May 22, 1840, in Jackson-Lewis Correspondence; Ritchie to Senior Editor of the Richmond *Whig*, February 18, 1840, printed in "Unpublished Letters of Ritchie," 242; New Orleans *Louisiana Courier*, January 25, 1840; Milledgeville *Federal Union*, March 3, 1840; Paul Herbert Bergeron, "The Jacksonian Party on Trial: Presidential Politics in Tennessee, 1836–1856" (Ph.D. dissertation, Vanderbilt University, 1965), 134; Little Rock *Arkansas Gazette*, July 8, 1840.

all in all their indictment touched many items but pursued few. The weakness of their claims did nothing to impede the forcefulness of their charges.[64]

Southern Democrats did not base their case against Harrison's candidacy solely on his supposed abolitionist sentiments. Some Democrats even admitted that Harrison himself probably did not subscribe to the tenets of abolitionism. In fact that mattered little, for his party was filled with northerners friendly to abolition as well as outright abolitionists. Thus a vote for Harrison became a vote for the destruction of southern institutions. The Milledgeville *Federal Union* put the issue squarely: the Democrats were acting "to *save* the South from vassalage to the North." "We are fighting," declared the *Federal Union,* "a great battle for the maintenance of our liberties and institutions." Alabama Democrats equated voting for the Whig ticket with "meanly sacrific[ing] the dignity and honor, as well as the rights, and interests and safety of [our] State and its people[.]" Thomas Ritchie's *Enquirer* spared no effort to arouse the South to the impending danger: "Wake up, freemen of Virginia! Your altars, your firesides, your liberties are in danger!" "Can the South sleep on the very verge of the volcano?" As the election approached, Ritchie exploded his most powerful charge: "PEOPLE OF THE SOUTH You will find out, (will it be too late?) that Whiggery and Abolition are BOTH ONE throughout the Northern, middle, and Northwestern States." Ritchie and his fellow Democrats denounced any southerner who supported such a party as a man who had sold out the South, who had no honor, who was a traitor to his own people.[65]

As the Democrats smashed at Harrison and his party as dangers to the South, they emphasized the safety and security of their candi-

64. For examples of the attack on Harrison, see Little Rock *Arkansas Gazette,* July 8, 1840; New Orleans *Louisiana Courier,* May 29, 1840; Richmond *Enquirer,* July 10, 1840; Jackson *Mississippian,* July 24, 1840.

65. Milledgeville *Federal Union,* August 18, 1840; "Address to the People of Alabama," quoted in John Witherspoon DuBose, *The Life and Times of William Lowndes Yancey* (2 vols.; New York: Peter Smith, 1942), I, 88–89; Richmond *Enquirer,* July 24, September 18, October 17, 1840.

date Van Buren and their party. As Thomas Ritchie put it in an address to Virginia Democrats, "[Van Buren] has always been characterized as 'the Northern man with Southern feelings.'" A toast read at a public dinner in Williamsburg, Virginia, concurred: "Martin Van Buren on abolition—He is as true to the South as the Needle to the Pole—there is no 'North Bend' in him." Southerners, announced the New Orleans *Louisiana Courier*, "have always found [Van Buren] ready to declare in favor of their domestic policy,— their vital interests." In sum Van Buren was a man "so acceptable to the South." And the Democratic party—it embodied the principles and goals of the South; its great mission was to protect the South and its institutions. [66]

Even with such an impassioned attack on Harrison and the Whigs and such an ardent defense of Van Buren, southern Democrats still found it impossible to wrest the political initiative away from the Whigs. Expecting a South united against Harrison they were surprised at the effectiveness of the Whig charges against Van Buren. [67] Although precise and clear-cut proof on the question of initiative is elusive, a close reading of the record of 1840 leaves no doubt of its accuracy. The Democrats found themselves bridled not so much by Harrison or by the Whigs as by their own candidate Van Buren. In many ways 1840 replayed 1836. Van Buren came under heavy attack from the Whigs, and the Democrats were forced to expend much energy defending him. Four years had done little to endear Van Buren to southern voters or to convince them of his safety.

From southern Democrats, Van Buren received letters identical to those posted to him in his first presidential race. In March, 1840, W. F. Leak, chairman of the Democratic convention of Richmond County, North Carolina, wrote to Van Buren at the direction of the

66. "Address to Virginia Democrats," 265; Robert Anderson to Frank Blair, July 13, 1840, in Blair-Lee Papers; New Orleans *Louisiana Courier*, March 3, 1840; Milledgeville *Federal Union*, March 3, 1840.

67. Cave Johnson to James K. Polk, December 16, 1839, in Polk Papers; Wm. H. Haywood, Jr., to Martin Van Buren, August 15, 1840, in Van Buren Papers; Little Rock *Arkansas Gazette*, July 8, 1840.

convention. Leak admitted to Van Buren that Richmond County Democrats had no evidence connecting him with abolition; "yet we are firmly persuaded that the highly excited and Sensitive condition of the publick mind at the South, requires at [your] hands, a renewal of the Same Sentiments and pledges as were contained in [your] letter of the 6th of March 1836, addressed to Junius Amis & others [of North Carolina]." An elector from Murfreesboro, Tennessee, wanted to know exactly where Van Buren stood on abolition in the District of Columbia and on the interstate slave trade. From Irwinton, Alabama, came a request for new statements on congressional power over slavery and on the morality of slavery. Carefully and patiently Van Buren responded to these calls; often he replied by directing his correspondents to his 1836 declarations. Even with these repeated assurances Van Buren found it impossible to convince the mass of southern voters of his trustworthiness. As the Raleigh *Register* observed, Van Buren's words might satisfy committed Democrats, but "the *people* of the Southern States will require stronger proof of devotion to their interests."[68] The *Register* did not indicate what kind of proof it meant. Surely Van Buren had done all that any southerner could ask. But regardless of what he said or did, even embracing Calhoun, it never seemed enough.

Van Buren was not without sincere friends in the South, friends who were convinced that he kept the well-being of the South foremost in his mind. From the days when he helped create the Jackson party, Van Buren had a group of devoted associates, especially in Virginia and Tennessee. In 1833 Romulus Saunders of North Carolina believed that Van Buren united qualifications for the presidency "vastly superior" to those of any competitor with a genuine devotion to "the old democratic principles." On the eve of Van Buren's presidency a freshman South Carolina congressman

68. Leak to Van Buren, March 21, 1840, H. Yoakum to Van Buren, June 8, 1840, Alexander R. Crawford to Van Buren, June 17, 1840, Van Buren to Leak, March 27, 1840, Van Buren to Louisville, Ky. Democratic Committe, April 21, 1840, all in Van Buren Papers; Raleigh *Register*, April 17, 1840.

found him "frank-urbane, very kind in his manner, and very favorable to Southern interests and institutions." To Felix Grundy, Van Buren "[could and would] do more than any other man to put down this dangerous and disorganizing spirit [abolition]." Before Van Buren approached him about a cabinet position, Joel Poinsett "regard[ed] Van Buren as the safest man we can have to secure our southern interests." Richard E. Parker summed up the feelings of these men when he said, "I am so much Mr. VB's friend that I would make great sacrifices to serve him."[69]

And supporting Van Buren in slave country often placed his friends in precarious political positions. Although immensely popular in the South, Andrew Jackson could not transfer that appeal to his chosen heir. Occasionally men such as Ritchie and James K. Polk had to tell Van Buren that political reality forbade their public embrace of him. Prior to his first race for governor of Tennessee, Polk begged Van Buren to postpone a scheduled Tennessee visit, lest the popular antipathy toward Van Buren hurt his election chances. With little exaggeration the old Democratic hand John Catron put his finger directly on Van Buren's problem: he was unpopular "with all classes—essentially so with the people at large; rest assured little less so, with leading politicians; and what is more, clearly so, with the rank & file of our political friends." As Roger B. Taney wrote to Andrew Jackson, "For all of [Van Buren's] talents & integrity of purpose, he wants some essential qualities of a leader, & was manifestly lacking in popularity from the time he entered upon the office of President." His lack of popularity and the inability of his support-

69. Joseph Hobson Harrison, Jr., "Martin Van Buren and His Southern Supporters," *Journal of Southern History*, XXII (1956), 438–58; Wm. Carroll to Andrew Jackson, February 7, 1832, J. A. Eaton to Andrew Jackson, March 13, 1832, both in Jackson Papers; Saunders to Thomas Ruffin, November 4, 1833, in J. G. de Roulhac Hamilton (ed.), *The Papers of Thomas Ruffin* (4 vols.; Raleigh: Edwards & Broughton, 1918–20), II, 107; John P. Richardson to Col. James Chesnut, January 15, 1837, in Williams-Chesnut-Manning Papers, South Caroliniana Library, University of South Carolina; Grundy to Col. Holeman, January 18, 1838, in Felix Grundy Papers, Manuscript Division, Tennessee State Library and Archives; Poinsett to James B. Campbell, January 6, 1837, in Stoney (ed.), "Poinsett-Campbell Letters," 155; Parker to James Buchanan, May 21, 1838, in Buchanan Papers.

ers to project an appealing image of him to southern voters severely handicapped Van Buren when he entered the swirl of southern democratic politics.[70]

Added to that near mortal liability Van Buren had the worst public image of any major political figure of his time. After all his nicknames, the Little Magician and the Red Fox of Kinderhook, were neither ennobling nor endearing. In the nation and definitely in the South he was named as the original devious, unprincipled politician. In 1832 John Randolph of Roanoke declared Van Buren unsuitable for the presidency because "he is too great an intriguer & besides wants personal dignity & character." Similar sentiments had helped spawn the Barbour movement. Again and again from the vice-presidential contest of 1832 to the mid-1840s southern commentators, both political figures and private citizens, found him unprincipled; they denigrated him for being politically dishonest. To discover Van Buren's principles, according to one, "would be a riddle worthy of the sphinx." Many agreed with James H. Hammond who exclaimed that he would trust Van Buren no "further than I can see him." In describing a political opponent an Alabama Whig editor captured this uneasy feeling: "He is oily and plausible, with precisely that character to make a politician of the Albany [or Van Buren] school."[71]

Thus already unpopular Van Buren was perceived by many southern voters as a charlatan. In democratic politics anywhere this combination would be a distinct liability. In the politics of slavery it was lethal. With Van Buren, southern Democrats faced a two-fold

70. Ritchie to Van Buren, April 30, 1831, Van Buren to Andrew Jackson, February 17, 1839, both in Van Buren Papers; Polk to Andrew Jackson, February 7, 1839, in Jackson Papers; Catron to Mrs. James K. Polk, January 7, 1840, in Polk Papers; Taney to Jackson, June 19, 1844, in Stanley Horn Collection, Manuscript Division, Tennessee State Library and Archives. Van Buren himself, after his loss to Harrison, seemed to understand that he was unable to cope with popular politics. Curtis, *Fox at Bay*, 208–209.

71. Randolph to Andrew Jackson, March 18, 1832, in Jackson Papers; Hugh S. Legaré to G. Kemble, December 21, 1839, in Legaré Papers; Thomas Douglas, *Autobiography of Thomas Douglas, Late Judge of the Supreme Court of Florida* (New York: Calkins & Stiles, 1856), 117; Tuscaloosa *Independent Monitor*, December 1, 1838, September 18, 1844; Hammond to Francis W. Pickens, May 15, 1839, in Hammond Papers.

problem. First they had to deal with his unpopularity; then they had to contend with his reputed dishonesty and deviousness, characteristics that would hardly endear a northerner to a people particularly concerned with guarding their special interests. That the letters coming to Van Buren from southerners in 1836, in 1840, and again in 1844 covered the same ground emphasized their predicament. Facing these obstacles southern Democrats engaged in a mighty crusade to convince southern voters that they could safely place their trust in Martin Van Buren.

Southern Democrats in the Congress as well as administration officials joined the drive to make Van Buren a winner. Upon Van Buren's official renomination in May, 1840, congressional Democrats from Alabama drafted and sent to their state an "Address to the People of Alabama." The address urged Alabamians not to degrade themselves and their state by voting for Harrison, for the ascendency of the Whigs "would be fatal to the rights and institutions of the South." Van Buren and the entire Democratic party, proclaimed these Democrats, had proved themselves loyal to southern principles and deserving of the trust the South gives to her own. In midsummer a group of slave-state congressmen and senators met in the Capitol under the chairmanship of Senator William R. King of Alabama. At this meeting a committee of one from each slave state was appointed to draft an "Address to the People of the Slaveholding States." Widely publicized in the South, this address made largely the same points discussed by the Alabama Democrats. According to the address a Whig victory portended ruin for the South because it meant the triumph of abolitionist principles. Southern salvation rested only with Van Buren and the Democrats, who had conclusively demonstrated their steadfastness to southern rights. Secretary of the Treasury Levi Woodbury claimed in a letter to the North Carolina Democrat Bedford Brown that the South would "commit suicide, by voting for an abolitionist [Harrison]." Only the Democrats, Woodbury lectured, protected the South. Joel Poinsett prayed that the South would not deliver itself into the hands of her mortal enemies by supporting Harrison and the Whigs. "I hope & trust," he confided to a close friend in South Carolina, "something may yet be done to save our people of the slave holding States to a sense of the danger."[72]

The danger many southerners sensed, however, came not from Harrison or the Whigs, but from Poinsett's militia recommendations. In their accustomed fashion the Democrats had attempted to wrap themselves with the blanket of the people while simultaneously clothing the Whigs with the Federalist-aristocratic label. Although they continued to preach on that text, the Democrats found themselves cast in the role of devil for attempting to supplant holy liberty with an unholy standing army that endangered the republic and the South. No matter that Whigs wildly exaggerated the result of Poinsett's proposed militia reorganization; their accusations fell on listening ears. Distressed, southern Democrats advised Poinsett that Whigs had made headway with their claims. Thomas Ritchie wanted Poinsett to send him a public letter denying Whig charges and explaining fully what his proposal entailed.[73]

Poinsett replied to Ritchie's satisfaction; then he went a step further. He prepared a pamphlet defense of his proposed reorganization. In this pamphlet, which he sent South, he talked about military needs, but came down hardest on slavery. He explained to a Charleston friend his belief that wide circulation of the pamphlet would "produce a beneficial effect in the South & throughout the Slave holding States." Although it is impossible to measure the impact of Poinsett's pamphlet, he has to get high marks for the way he fitted a militia bill into the politics of slavery. He pictured his proposals as but another step in the efforts of the Democratic party and the Van

72. DuBose, *Yancey,* I, 88–89; *Richmond Enquirer,* September 8, 1840; Jackson *Mississippian,* October 3, 1840; Woodbury to Brown, September 11, 1840, in Bedford Brown Papers, William R. Perkins Library, Duke University; Poinsett to Dr. Jos. Johnson, September 28, 1840, in Poinsett Letters, Gilpin Collection.

73. Richmond *Enquirer,* December 14, 1839; Milledgeville *Federal Union,* May 26, 1840; Little Rock *Arkansas Gazette,* September 23, 1840; Ritchie to Poinsett, May 29, 1840, in Poinsett Papers; Bedford Brown to Poinsett, September 23, 1840, in Poinsett Letters, Gilpin Collection; Richard E. Parker to James Buchanan, May 4, 1840, in Buchanan Papers.

Buren administration to protect southern institutions. His plan would insure trained, armed southern men to protect the South—and the South must protect itself—if the need should ever arise. In other words an army of southern citizens would be in place and ready to deal swiftly with any slave uprising. Thus the Democrats were insuring, not subverting, the rights of the southern people.[74]

This stupendous effort by Poinsett and his southern brethren to overcome the Whigs and return a united South to the Democratic fold failed. The Democratic party was quite clearly a southern-oriented party in which southerners had place and influence. But southern Whigs could legitimately make the same claim for their party, and they did not have to carry the weight of a Van Buren candidacy. The results of 1840 demonstrated conclusively that 1836 was no accident; the Whigs had come to southern politics to stay. The South shared in the huge outpouring of new voters that marked the 1840 contest with the popular vote in the South going up some 69 percent over the 1836 total. And the Whigs claimed a significantly larger share of the political newcomers than did the Democrats. While the Democratic vote increased between 1836 and 1840 by a substantial 56 percent, the Whig vote shot up by an astounding 82 percent. The Whigs held Georgia and Tennessee, the two states they had carried in 1836, and added three new states, Louisiana, Mississippi, and North Carolina. Of the four states that went for Van Buren, the Whigs came very close in Virginia, which they lost by only 1,120 votes out of 85,484 cast, and made a respectable showing in Alabama (46 percent) and Arkansas (43 percent). Calhoun delivered South Carolina for Van Buren. In all the Whigs won 53 percent of the popular vote. Two-party politics had definitely come to the South.

74. Poinsett to Ritchie, June 5, 1840, Ritchie to Poinsett, June 10, 1840, in Poinsett Papers; Richmond *Enquirer*, June 5, 12, August 29, September 5, 1840; Raleigh *Standard*, June 24, 1840; Poinsett to James B. Campbell, September 26, 1840, in Stoney (ed.), "Poinsett-Campbell Letters," XLIII (1942), 30; [Joel R. Poinsett], *Letter of the Hon. J. R. Poinsett To His Fellow-Citizens of Charleston* [Washington: n.p., 1840].

Although southern voters divided their political allegiance between the two parties, each party maintained an identical and wholehearted commitment to the politics of slavery. In the midst of the campaign John Tyler reported, "The Southern mind is evermore kept in a state of excitement" by the abolition rhetoric. "Never," said Tyler, "have I known the Southern mind so deeply agitated." In a graphic account of the political battle George Troup described both parties as "now in the very act of cutting one another's throats in the controversy as to which of the two belongs the higher degree of abolitionism[,] a point yet undecided."[75] The Democrats, the Whigs, the South all bowed to the politics of slavery.

75. Tyler to Charles B. Kirkland, July 15, 1840, in Simon Gratz Collection of Administration Papers, Historical Society of Pennsylvania; Troup to Edward Harden, August 4, 1840, in Edward Harden Papers, William R. Perkins Library, Duke University.

5 The Great Aberration

JUBILANT SOUTHERN WHIGS joined with their fellows across the country in celebrating the great victory of 1840. Not only did the Whigs elect their president, they also elected a Whig Congress. All Whigs had talked of the general improvement in the government that would occur in a Harrison administration. But the precise ingredients in the expected reformation are difficult to identify, because the Whigs themselves had never been specific about their goals for the Harrison presidency. Certainly the southern Whigs had been either vague or silent about the national measures that had dominated Van Buren's administration. Only on questions relating to slavery and southern safety had southern Whigs made clear, straightforward claims for their candidate and party. Most probably the chief reason for Whig joy was Whig anticipation of holding power and garnering its rewards. No longer the political outs, they had become the political ins.

The mist of uncertainty clouded the new president just as it did the goals of his party. During the campaign Harrison had made little effort to specify or clarify his position on any question. The southern Whigs, of course, presented him as a strict constructionist committed to defending the southern position on slavery. Because Harrison died only one month after taking office, where he would have stood on major issues remains a mystery. Generally Harrison has been written off as little more than a cipher who would have followed wherever the Whig titans Clay and Webster led. Perhaps, but Harrison had never been a cipher before 1841; and he impressed certain southern Whigs with his intention to be his own man. Moreover, shortly after his inauguration, he told Clay that he intended to be

149

president in fact as well as in name.[1] Thus what Harrison as president would have been like no one will ever know.

The death of Harrison brought John Tyler into the spotlight, and he became the first vice-president to accede to the presidency without benefit of election. After some discussion of whether he should conduct himself as an acting president or whether he should behave as if he had been elected, the latter view prevailed. Tyler himself never doubted that he had the constitutional duty and right to serve for the remainder of Harrison's term, to March 4, 1845, with all the powers of the presidency, and the precedent has not been seriously challenged in the subsequent 137 years.

Although many Whigs had vague notions about Harrison's views, none should have had any doubts about John Tyler's stance on public questions. A public man for many years, Tyler had always clung steadfastly to the tenets of Old Republicanism, Virginia brand. He never tired of insisting that only the principles embedded in the Virginia and Kentucky resolutions provided a proper blueprint for constitutional and republican government. Claims for the economic and political powers of the central government, whether made by National Republicans or by Andrew Jackson, he considered both unconstitutional and dangerous. That Tyler cast the only vote in the United States Senate against the Force Bill demonstrates his commitment to his convictions. And during the 1840 campaign he repeatedly expressed this devotion to the Virginia principles.

Tyler's rock-ribbed commitment to those principles, to strict construction and states' rights, underlay the breach between him and his party.[2] That conflict erupted when a special session of Congress,

1. The most thorough study of Harrison is Freeman Cleaves, *Old Tippecanoe: William Henry Harrison and His Time* (New York and London: Charles Scribner's Sons, 1939). William C. Preston to Willie P. Mangum, March 28, 1841, in Henry Thomas Shanks (ed.), *The Papers of Willie Person Mangum* (5 vols.; Raleigh: State Department of Archives and History, 1950–56), III, 130; Harrison to Clay, March 13, 1841, in the Clay Papers, Division of Manuscripts, Library of Congress.
2. George Rawlings Poage, *Henry Clay and the Whig Party* (Chapel Hill: University of North Carolina Press, 1936), Chaps. 3–7 has a superb account of the Tyler-Whig break. In my summary I have depended heavily upon Poage and upon Sydney Nathans, *Daniel Webster*

called by Harrison, met on May 31, 1841. When the 27th Congress convened in special session, it had a Whig majority in both houses and one senator who intended to use that majority to his own ends. Henry Clay was determined to place the direction of the Whig party solely in his own hands. He would be president in fact, even though another and lesser man, in his view, occupied the White House. Clay intended that either Tyler and Secretary of State Daniel Webster, his premier cabinet officer, follow the lead of Henry Clay or both be damned. During the special session which lasted through the summer till mid-September, Clay spurned all attempts to arrive at a compromise between Tyler and himself, between president and the Whig majority in Congress. Instead he insisted that all Whigs, including the president, toe his mark or be banished.

Although the evidence does not give a totally clear picture of Clay's motives, he evidently was convinced that the special session provided the opportunity to gain control of the party. Aware of his power in the Congress, Clay used it to put Tyler and his administration on the defensive. He feared that Webster, not Clay, would become the leading figure in the party if the administration gained the political initiative. From the beginning Clay envisioned relations between Tyler's White House and the Congress as an adversary proceeding. Clay's actions, admirably detailed by George R. Poage, lead to the inescapable conclusion that he wanted a break between the Whig majority in Congress (or himself) and the administration. Using every weapon at his command—including influencing congressional action through his mastery of procedure, aiming alternately a soothing and stinging tongue at his fellow Whigs, utilizing a friendly press to condemn those Whigs he deemed wavering— Clay lashed the congressional Whigs into a cohesive unit responsive to his will. Then, with the congressional majority doing his bidding, he could write the membership rules for Whiggery. These rules

---

and Jacksonian Democracy (Baltimore and London: Johns Hopkins University Press, 1973), Chap. 7. Nathans devotes considerable attention to attempts, encouraged by Webster, to reach a compromise.

would automatically make him the Whig leader, for any in the administration who left the president would have to come to Henry
Clay.

   In this enterprise Clay reverted to his traditional platform of economic nationalism, the platform of National Republicanism. He obviously felt more comfortable with this program, which he had called
his own for most of his public life, than with the states' rights pose he
had adopted in the late 1830s. Besides, states' rights had not won
him the prize he sought, the Whig presidential nomination. Now in
the summer of 1841 he proclaimed the platform of economic
nationalism the platform of the Whig party. As the first legislative
action of the new Whig administration Clay demanded the scrap-
ping of the Independent Treasury and the creation of a new national
bank. The Whigs in Congress, under the sting of his verbal and
political whip, repealed the Independent Treasury and passed a
bank bill that would have recreated the second Bank of the United
States. Problems promptly arose with the president; Tyler had opposed a national bank all his public life, and he had no intention of
changing direction just because he had become president. The evidence does indicate that he might have agreed to a scaled-down
bank that could set up branches in the states only if individual states
authorized such branches. But all attempts at compromise, led by
Webster, came to naught. Clay remained an implacable foe of any
compromise, and Tyler, pressed by Virginia comrades, began to feel
that his principles and his honor required that he not deviate from
his lifelong aversion to any kind of national bank. In the end both
Clay and Tyler got their way. Congress passed Clay's bill; Tyler
vetoed it. Clay, then, kept Congress from quickly passing a bill Tyler
might have accepted and forced on it a bill he knew Tyler would
reject. Tyler, nervous that his principles were somehow being
mocked, vetoed the second bank bill. With that second veto, on
September 9, the entire cabinet, except for Webster, resigned.
Then the Whigs in Congress caucused and read John Tyler out of the
Whig party. The party, so recently united and triumphant, seemed
in a shambles.

Whigs reacted as Henry Clay hoped. Frustrated and angry because they saw party division and rupture occurring almost at the moment of the long-awaited victory, Whigs felt that fate had replaced triumph with debacle. Fearing that the entire party might disintegrate yet unwilling to line up behind an accidental president who opposed the will of the Whig congressional majority, Whigs turned to the man who seemed to stand firm amidst the winds of political destruction, who provided a focus and a platform in the midst of uncertainty. Facing impending chaos, caused in no small part by Clay, the Whigs searched for stability and Clay provided it.

II

Southern Whigs joined the general Whig move to Henry Clay. During the summer battle between Clay and Tyler some, particularly Virginians, urged compromise[3]; but when the break came the southern Whigs sided with Clay. The great majority of them in House and Senate voted as Clay voted. The southerners in Tyler's cabinet resigned just as did their northern counterparts. Senator Willie P. Mangum of North Carolina presided over the caucus of congressional Whigs that read John Tyler out of the Whig party.

Following the purge of Tyler, southern Whigs cast the president in the role of villain. They condemned him with language normally reserved for enemies of the South. Willie Mangum thought *traitor* best fit Tyler. The Tuscaloosa *Independent Monitor* excoriated Tyler for stealing the fruits of the great victory of 1840. Tyler's greatest sin, according to the New Orleans *Bee*, was his duplicity. The Richmond *Whig* asserted that Tyler ought to be impeached for "the safety of the Republic." Southern Whigs rained their verbal blows on Tyler, but words alone were not enough for one angry North Carolinian who exclaimed, "Jno. Tyler deserves to atone for his unmanly vile treachery, in the merciless hands of the hangman."[4]

3. Richmond *Whig*, July 2, 9, 1841.
4. Willie Mangum to Priestly H. Mangum, August 10, 1842, in Shanks (ed.), *Mangum Papers*, III, 376–77; Tuscaloosa *Independent Monitor*, September 22, 1841; New Orleans *Bee*,

Fear that Tyler's course would destroy the Whig party prompted these vicious outbursts. From the tense summer months of 1841 on into 1842, southern Whigs anguished over the fate of their party. Congressman William B. Campbell expected the party to suffer; he wrote that differences with Tyler could mean "we have lost all that we gained by our victory last November." Full war with Tyler, Willie Mangum predicted in August 1841, would entail an "explosion." That explosion, in the view of Mississippi's Sergeant S. Prentiss, might result in "the destruction of the Whig party, which will immediately be broken up into factions, and probably fall an easy prey to the united and unprincipled energies of the Democratic or Loco-foco party." This possibility of Whigs as Whigs fighting Whigs as *"Tylerites"* disturbed an Arkansas Whig chieftain. As late as the summer of 1842, southern Whigs still spoke of their party as in an "anomalous state" because of the battle with Tyler.[5]

The shattering impact of the bitter break with John Tyler affected southern Whigs in two critical ways. First, after the break Clay became, in the words of the New Orleans *Bee*, the "shining mark" for southern Whigs. Before 1841 had run its course Whigs across the South praised Clay for his steadfastness to party and principle. As early as the winter of 1842 both Willie Mangum and William A. Graham urged North Carolina Whigs to make a public declaration of their intention to back Clay as the next Whig presidential nominee. By the summer of 1842 Whigs in Georgia and Mississippi boomed Henry Clay as the party's savior and salvation.[6]

October 15, 1841; Richmond *Whig*, May 31, 1844; William C. Preston to Waddy Thompson, undated, in Waddy Thompson Papers, Division of Manuscripts, Library of Congress; Little Rock *Arkansas Gazette*, May 24, 1843; Priestly H. Mangum to William A. Graham, May 12, 1842, in J. G. de Roulhac Hamilton and Max R. Williams (eds.), *The Papers of William Alexander Graham* (5 vols.; Raleigh: State Department of Archives and History, 1957–), II, 308.

5. Campbell to My Dear Wife, August 11, 1841, in Campbell Papers; Mangum to C. L. Hinton, August 13, 1841, in Shanks (ed.), *Mangum Papers*, III, 215; *A Memoir of S. S. Prentiss*, ed. His Brother (2 vols.; New York: Charles Scribner, 1856), II, 203; A. Fowler to Jesse Turner, December 27, 1841, in Turner Papers; John M. Berrien to Dr. Ambrose Baber, July 2, 1842, in Baber-Blackshear Papers.

6. New Orleans *Bee*, September 17, 1841; Richmond *Whig*, September 24, 1841; Raleigh *Register*, December 10, 1841; Mangum to Charles P. Green, March 2, 1842, in Shanks (ed.),

From this early date no one else challenged Clay's position as the knight and shield of southern Whig forces. Attachment to Clay brought both political solidarity within the party as well as psychological relief from the fears of party dissolution. This state of affairs did not escape the notice of both the Democrats and the Tyler adherents. Discounting the possibility of genuine devotion, the Raleigh *Standard* slammed the Whigs for their "Gross and servile adulation of Henry Clay." Viewing the political scene as a member of Tyler's reconstituted cabinet, the Virginian Abel P. Upshur saw Whigs glorifying "party drill [or regularity]" in their march behind Clay.[7]

This second avowal of Clay contrasted sharply with the first. In the late 1830s Clay had come South as a supplicant bearing states' rights and strict construction as gifts to the southern Whigs he courted. But in the early 1840s Clay, brandishing National Republicanism, his American System, including a national bank and a protective tariff, demanded that southerners accept his platform along with him. Southern Whigs did not hesitate; with the eagerness of converts they recited their new creed. Spokesmen for the new faith existed even before the irrevocable parting with Tyler,[8] though the mass of southern Whiggery embraced Clay's economic nationalism only in the aftermath of the Tyler crisis.

There can be no doubt that a fundamental ideological transformation occurred among southern Whigs. During the early 1840s southern Whigs in Congress affirmed their commitment to a new party line by voting overwhelmingly for Clay's financial issues whenever they appeared on the congressional docket. Clay himself pointed directly to that shift in a letter to Whigs in Charlotte County, Virginia. Commenting on the principles enunciated by

---

Mangum Papers, III, 291–92; Graham to Daniel M. Barringer, January 18, 1842, in Barringer Papers; Robert Toombs to John M. Berrien, July 6, 1842, in Berrien Papers; Vicksburg *Tri-Weekly Whig*, July 14, 1842.

    7. Raleigh *Standard*, December 13, 1843; Upshur to Duff Green, April 6, 1842, in Green Papers, Southern Historical Collection, University of North Carolina.

    8. New Orleans *Bee*, April 22, 1841.

those Virginians, Clay congratulated them for "renouncing pre-conceived prejudices and antipathies, [and] candidly reviewing their former opinions adverse to a protective tariff." Although Clay in that letter talked about the tariff, not a national bank, southern Whigs cried for a new national bank just as they found new virtues in a protective tariff. Trumpeting its support for Clay's "great measures" the Vicksburg *Whig* in 1842 announced its approval of both a national bank and a tariff. In that same year the Richmond *Whig* pronounced a national bank and a protective tariff the most important items in the Whig lexicon. Proclaiming their implementation critical for national well-being, the *Whig* called for the election of Clay, the guardian of Whig principle. A national bank was essential, according to the Little Rock *Arkansas Gazette*, for the restoration of economic prosperity. The New Orleans *Bee* injected national economic issues into the 1842 state elections in Louisiana. Urging a strong Whig turnout, the *Bee* declared that Democratic control of the Louisiana legislature meant a new Democratic United States senator and, thus, one less vote for a protective tariff. The Whig state convention of North Carolina in 1843 adopted resolutions supporting both a national bank and a tariff. In addition the convention nominated William A. Graham as the Whig candidate for governor. In his letter accepting the nomination Graham emphasized his agreement with the resolutions passed by the convention. [9]

Even in Georgia, where they had reluctantly given up their separate State Rights party identity only in 1840 and only then because Harrison was presented to them as the hero of states' rights, the Whigs exulted over their new doctrine. The 1843 Whig state

9. Joel H. Silbey, *The Shrine of Party: Congressional Voting Behavior, 1841–1852* (Pittsburgh: University of Pittsburgh Press, 1967), 52–56, 62–66, and Thomas B. Alexander, *Sectional Stress and Party Strength: A Study of Roll-Call Voting Patterns in the United States House of Representatives, 1836–1860* (Nashville: Vanderbilt University Press, 1967), Chaps. 4–5; Clay to Clement Carrington *et al.*, January 23, 1844, in Henry Clay Papers, Indiana University; Vicksburg *Tri-Weekly Whig*, October 4, 1842; Richmond *Whig*, June 7, 1842; Little Rock *Arkansas Gazette*, November 8, 1843; New Orleans *Bee*, June 27, 1842. The resolutions and Graham's letter are in Hamilton and Williams (eds.), *Graham Papers*, II, 455–64.

convention meeting in Milledgeville found previously unseen advantages in a tariff. Not only did the convention go on record favoring a tariff, it also announced that Georgia favored a national bank.
Calling such a bank an honorable institution, these Whigs to support
their changed position even called on the authority of the United
States Supreme Court, an institution they had never before ten-
dered much respect. Georgia Whigs, and all their southern
brothers, agreed with the definition of southern Whiggery provided
by a Tennessee Whig newspaper in 1843 when it called Tennessee
"A WHIG STATE—A NATIONAL BANK STATE—A TARIFF STATE—A
CLAY STATE."[10]

Just as southern Whigs and southern Democrats differed over the
need and value of another national bank, party differences over the
role and behavior of banks dominated state politics in the South
during the early 1840s.[11] Banking had not always been a primary
issue between Whigs and Democrats; in fact, prior to the Panic of
1837 banking had played practically no part in Democratic-Whig
political divisions in any southern state. In the older and more settled states a quiet banking system remained almost invisible politically. In the newer and more rapidly growing states of the Southwest
everyone, Democrat and Whig alike, clamored for more credit and
for the banks to supply it. Looking back at the formation of banks in
Arkansas, the Democratic Little Rock *Arkansas Gazette* commented, "no party question was raised; it was deemed indispensable
that we should have institutions of the kind."[12]

---

10. Milledgeville *Southern Recorder*, August 29, 1843; Paul H. Bergeron, "The Election
of 1843; A Whig Triumph in Tennessee," *Tennessee Historical Quarterly*, XXII (1963), 135.
    11. Gene Wells Boyett, "The Whigs of Arkansas, 1836–1856" (Ph.D. dissertation,
Louisiana State University, 1972), 77–80, 124–28, 154–60, 173–75, 265–70; George D. Green,
Finance and Economic Development in the Old South: Louisiana Banking, 1804–1861 (Stan-
ford: Stanford University Press, 1972), 129–30; Milton Sydney Heath, *Constructive
Liberalism: The Role of the State in Economic Development in Georgia to 1860* (Cambridge:
Harvard University Press, 1954), 205–23; Charles G. Sellers, Jr., *James K. Polk* (2 vols.;
Princeton, N.J.: Princeton University Press, 1957–), I, 324–25, 345, 363–65, 385–92, 439,
475–78; James Roger Sharp, *The Jacksonians versus the Banks: Politics in the States after the
Panic of 1837* (New York and London: Columbia University Press, 1970), Chaps. 3, 9.
    12. Little Rock *Arkansas Gazette*, February 12, 1840.

When the Panic of 1837 struck, it delivered a thunderous blow, not only to economic prosperity in the South, but also to southern banks. While farmers and planters suffered grievously because of the collapse of prices and mounting debts, bankers and banks also faced severe trials. The panic ended the political unity that had governed the relations between banks and politics since the mid-1820s. It also undermined the general public acceptance of banks or, at the least, public indifference to them. As a result of the panic many banks failed; the banks that did not fail had to suspend specie payments, that is refuse to redeem bank notes or paper money for coin, in order to remain open. Suspension hit various states and various banks at different times between 1837 and 1841. Often banks suspended, then resumed specie payment, then suspended all over again. Suspension spawned angry popular and political outcry; banks moved to the forefront of partisan politics across the South. The banking issue arose in 1838 and 1839 and grew more powerful in the early 1840s, though it played absolutely no part in the Log Cabin campaign. Between 1841 and 1845, torrents of words about banks filled southern newspapers, podiums, and legislatures from Virginia to Arkansas. Politicians, editors, bankers, private citizens spoke with several tongues: demagogic, arcane, responsible, irresponsible, intelligent, idiotic, but all had political overtones.

The debate over banking focused on four basic areas. Pro and antibank men argued over whether banks should exist at all. Suspension aroused a great deal of attention. Pointing to the evils of suspension antibank men cried against paper money, against bank notes. They insisted that only hard money, metallic coins, should be authorized by the states. Furthermore, they demanded that the states require banks to resume specie payment or lose their charters. In opposition, probank men termed bank notes an essential part of economic activity; a turn to hard money they pictured as a great folly. On the question of ending suspension they asserted that the banks knew best. They argued that the state might suggest, even prod, but that banks should retain great influence on the decision to resume or to suspend in order to maintain fiscal health of the banks and the society. According to their argument a general collapse of the banking system must result in a collapse of the entire economy.

Those two aspects of the banking question spanned the South; two others had a more limited application. Many states had both state banks and private banks. The private banks were just that, private; most often they operated with a state charter but with little or no state regulation and no state duties. The state banks, on the other hand, often had directors selected by the legislatures and performed certain duties such as fiscal agent or depository for the state government. When banking became a political issue, the question of whether state banks or private banks should dominate the banking scene became a disputed one particularly in Georgia and Alabama. Dominating the banking dispute in Arkansas and Mississippi was the problem of bonds. Back in the halcyon days before the panic, legislatures in both states had authorized the good name of the state to back bonds that were sold to help get banks underway. After the catastrophe set off by the panic, the affected banks could pay neither the principal nor the interest due on these bonds. Thereupon the pro-bank spokesmen called on the states to make good their pledge and redeem the bonds. Denouncing such proposals as efforts by plutocrats to rob hard-working citizens, antibank forces campaigned for legislatures to repudiate those bonds.

Although events and issues in the states were not identical, a general political pattern did exist. Whigs supported the banking position; Democrats opposed the banking position. Those who urged elimination of all banks were, without exception, Democrats as were those who preached that only hard money led to economic salvation. Likewise Democrats took the lead in denouncing suspension and demanding that legislatures require resumption. Wherever a contest between state banks and private banks occurred, Democrats generally supported the state banks and worked to dissolve the private ones. And in Arkansas and Mississippi the Democrats led the campaign for repudiation.

Whigs, in contrast, defended the right of banks to exist. In Whig rhetoric banks became the partners of the citizenry in the common quest for economic prosperity. Thus, as the Whigs saw it, banks must control, ultimately, the timing of suspension or resumption, for a mistake could destroy the banks and permanently harm society. As for hard money, Whigs viewed it at best as wrong-headed or at worst as criminally stupid. Opposing repudiation of state-sponsored bank bonds Whigs asserted with the Mississippi Whig convention of 1843 that "to repudiate these bonds *now* by the State, would be repugnant to law, and would cover the State with the infamy and disgrace."[13]

Not every Democrat, however, agreed with every other Democrat on every feature of the banking question. The most extreme antibank Democrats condemned banks as leeches on the body politic. An editorial in the New Orleans *Louisiana Courier* summed up this view: "BANKING—This is one of the greatest of modern humbugs; it gives to a few privileges not enjoyed by kings, by which they can make cities, gain thousands, and command labors of millions, for pieces of paper, printed and signed." On the other hand many Democrats believed with the Raleigh *Standard* that properly managed banks with a concern for the public welfare had a legitimate place in society.[14] As a party the Democrats in both Arkansas and Mississippi opposed state redemption of bank bonds, though a few Democrats in each state joined with the Whig call for redemption of those bonds. Democrats in Alabama divided over the fate of the Bank of Alabama; a majority of Democrats in the legislature wanted to retain it, but in 1842 a minority joined with the Whigs to kill it.

Neither did southern Whigs stand as one man with one mind regarding banks. Whigs normally followed the New Orleans *Bee* in defining the interests of the state, the people, and the banks as identical. Arkansas Whigs, however, make the exception that proves

13. Vicksburg *Daily Whig*, June 16, 1843.
14. New Orleans *Louisiana Courier*, February 18, 1837, January 2, 1841, December 5, 1843; Raleigh *Standard*, January 11, February 8, 1843.

the rule. Along with their Democratic opponents, they heaped abuse upon the banks of Arkansas, though they did oppose repudiation. But from that general agreement the Whigs diverged. When Louisiana passed her important banking law in 1842, the act was rightly associated with the Whigs; even so Whig legislators did not vote in unison on all its provisions. Some Whigs agreed with Dudley S. Jennings of Mississippi that banks and bonds represented good incarnate. This brand of Whig pictured opponents of banks and bonds as satanic anarchists out to undermine morality and wreck society. More moderate and politically astute Whigs adopted the view put forth by the Richmond *Whig*: "Above all, we hope not to see the Whig party, under any romantic and mistaken conception of public duty, wreck their influence by an undiscriminating defense of corporate bodies [banks], which are both odious to the mass of the people, and deserve to be so."[15]

Although all Democrats and Whigs did not have precisely the same attitudes toward the place of banks in southern society, each party assumed recognizable and different stances toward banks and related fiscal questions. Certainly Democratic and Whig politicians and newspapers perceived the Democrats as less friendly to banks, and Whigs as more friendly to banks. Votes in state legislatures clearly show that Whig legislators assumed a distinctly probank posture in contrast to Democratic legislators, who voted time and again for restrictive bank charters, for abolition of banks, for forced resumption of specie payment, for repudiation of bonds. Moreover no leading probank spokesman identified himself with the Democrats. Likewise no major antibank figure colored himself Whig.

Thus in the early 1840s party divisions on state banking issues reinforced the national division over economic policy. On the national level southern Whigs backed Clay economics including a na-

15. New Orleans *Bee*, January 27, 1842; Dudley S. Jennings, *Nine Years of Democratic Rule in Mississippi Being Notes Upon the Political History of the State, from the Beginning of the Year 1838, to the Present Time* (Jackson: Thomas Palmer, 1847); Richmond *Whig*, January 3, 1843.

tional bank while in the states they counted themselves as friends of banking. The Democrats, in contrast, found both a national bank and state banks politically objectionable. It did seem that economic issues had taken control of southern politics.[16]

Southern Whigs opened the election year, 1844, emphasizing their commitment to their new economics. A public letter to the people of Arkansas drafted by the Whig state convention in January focused on the three pillars of transformed southern Whiggery: a national bank, the protective tariff, and Henry Clay, the great statesman of the age. Extolling the glories of the first two, the letter presented Clay as the only man who could secure positive congressional action on them. In neighboring Louisiana the Whig state convention took almost identical action; meeting in February it adopted an address underscoring the importance of Clay's platform. The nation must endorse Clay and economic nationalism or face degradation and ruin. A Whig campaigner in Virginia hoped "to make an impresssion" by stressing the tariff and the other "great questions" to Virginia voters. In the midst of a southern tour Henry Clay, in March, wrote John J. Crittenden that he had not encountered a single southern Whig who balked at the principle of a protective tariff. Southern Whiggery in truth had turned itself upside down.[17]

From the Potomac to the Mississippi the Whig cry resounded— Henry Clay and economic nationalism. Through the spring of 1844 southern Whigs gave infrequent and rather perfunctory notice to any specifically sectional issues. Occasionally a Whig editor reminded his readers that Clay was a slaveowning southerner, but he never dwelled on the fact nor did he attempt to make it much of an issue.[18] The reader who has been immersed in southern Whig

16. The primacy of banking as a state issue was distinctly temporary; see pp. 228–30 herein.

17. Little Rock *Arkansas Gazette*, January 31, February 2, 1844; New Orleans *Bee*, February 26, 1844; Alexander H. H. Stuart to John P. Kennedy, February 22, 1844, in Kennedy Papers; Clay to Crittenden, March 24, 1844, in Crittenden Papers.

18. For example, see New Orleans *Bee*, November 7, 1843 and Baton Rouge *Gazette*, January 6, 1844.

newspapers since the early 1830s cannot help but feel that he has come upon a different political universe. The rabid sectional rhetoric that denoted the Whig press during the campaigns of 1836 and 1840 has disappeared, has vanished. Southern Whigs seemingly had abandoned the politics of slavery for the politics of economics— a national bank, a protective tariff.

This about-face by the southern Whigs did not escape ridicule by the Democrats. In 1844 the Democratic Central Committee of Virginia asked the obvious question. Were the Whigs sincere in their new confession of faith? After all, as the committee's address indicated, through 1840 the Whigs in Virginia had presented themselves as anti–national bank and antitariff. After 1840, however, the Whigs had abandoned that traditional Republican ground; instead they proclaimed the benefits of a classic Federalist program. Pointing to Whig shifts on the tariff the Milledgeville *Federal Union* declared itself perplexed about the exact position held by Georgia Whigs on the tariff. As the *Federal Union* correctly noted, Georgia Whigs had previously denounced the tariff. In fact not until after the break with Tyler did they change sides on the tariff.[19]

The questions posed by the Democratic Central Committee of Virginia and by the *Federal Union* as well as by other southern Democrats do not lend themselves to easy answers. Quite obviously a marked transformation had occurred in the ranks of southern Whiggery. Willie P. Mangum of North Carolina is a superb illustration. In 1838 Mangum swore to a fellow North Carolinian that he supported neither a national bank nor a protective tariff.[20] Mangum's career in the 1830s bears out his oath. He joined in Jackson's destruction of the second Bank of the United States; he worked vigorously in the states' rights, antibank campaign run for Hugh White in 1836; in the late 1830s he favored the states' rights version of Henry Clay for the Whig presidential nomination. As a United States senator in 1841, however, he acted as one with Clay in the

19. Richmond *Enquirer*, March 8, 1844; Milledgeville *Federal Union*, May 5, 1846.
20. Raleigh *Standard*, August 10, 1842.

battle against Tyler; he even chaired the caucus that separated John Tyler from the Whig party. In the aftermath of that political blood-letting he became a leading spokesman for the revised Clay brand of southern Whiggery. Mangum's course was followed by many other Whigs below the Potomac. He and most of his fellow southern Whigs faced a cruel dilemma in 1841. Of course for a few no dilemma existed at all. The Whigs who had come from National Repub-licanism and had never given up economic nationalism welcomed the opportunity to speak their old familiar language. But this group represented a distinct minority in southern Whiggery. The great majority of southern Whigs faced a wrenching experience. To con-demn such men as hypocrites or charlatans who shifted with the political winds is easy but not helpful. Although some undoubtedly played fast and loose with political ideology, only a hardened cynic could attribute the revolution in southern Whiggery to such crass-ness. Just as certainly, some southern Whigs, prodded by the extent and longevity of the panic or depression, changed their minds about the value of a tariff and a national bank. Even though it is impossible to be specific about the number of such converts, their number could not have turned Whiggery around. Neither political obtuse-ness nor ideological conversion provides an adequate explanation for the course followed by southern Whigs.

Southern Whig politicians were political men faced with a politi-cal crisis. Investigating their possible alternatives provides the most practical way to understand their behavior. After Clay forced the bank issue and precipitated the break with Tyler, southern Whigs had three alternatives. They could hang on with Tyler; they could turn to the Democrats; they could follow Clay—which included standing on his platform. The first alternative was really no alterna-tive at all for active and ambitious public men. Moving to Tyler led initially into some kind of political limbo and ultimately straight to a political dead end. By 1841 party had become ingrained in the American and southern political scheme; without a party politicians wandered in the political wilderness. And southerners knew they would wander alone, for Clay commanded the allegiance of most northern Whigs. Besides, Tyler had been branded a traitor to their party. Joining the Democrats offered even less, for turning to the former enemy involved giving up the fight of almost a decade. That battle, carried on in numerous state contests and through two presidential elections, had instilled pride and belief in the Whig party. Such convictions did not vanish overnight.

Standing by Clay, on the other hand, meant the survival of the party and the opportunities and rewards that went along with an established party. And critically important, the issue or set of issues involved in the decision to go with Clay concerned economics. Nowhere did the sanctity of slavery or the safety of the South appear; as southern Whigs saw it the reoriented Whig party posed no threat to slavery or to the South or, ultimately, to them as southern politicians. Although the southern Democrats might deride them for reversing their positions on a national bank and a protective tariff, Democrats could not brand them as traitors to the South. Thus southern Whigs saluted their new flag and with a whoop fell in to march behind Henry Clay.

Exulting over their leader Clay and zealous for their platform, southern Whigs approached 1844 with a heady confidence. No longer anguishing over the possibility of party disruption, they looked forward euphorically to the presidential election set for the fall of 1844. Perhaps the escape from political destruction so many of them had feared prompted them to discount the possibility of defeat. Perhaps the fervent conviction of new believers inculcated in them an unswerving faith in victory. From wherever it came, no Whig had the slightest doubt that his candidate and his party would win. Clay himself told his southern correspondents that all was well, that all was even better than well. In Clay's letters the Democrats were always losing strength and heart; the Whigs in contrast were always surging forward. He and his comrades would surely smash the Democrats just as they had done in 1840. Clay's tour through the South in the winter and early spring of 1844—from New Orleans to

Mobile, to Montgomery, through Georgia to Savannah, to Columbia and Charleston and through North Carolina into Virginia—was a triumphant march. All along his route admiring throngs feted him and paid him homage. A participant, albeit a partisan one, reported that even in Charleston, the citadel of Calhoun, that "there ha[d] been no such procession—no such ball—no such turning out of the citizens to shake hands with any man—since Lafayette." Southern Whigs began to tell one another that the Democrats "despaired" of carrying the South. In a letter written on April 3, 1844, a Kentucky Whig senator caught the extravagance of this mood perfectly: "Clay the high comb cock. The election begins & ends. Clay is President and the nation redeemed."[21]

III

In contrast to their Whig counterparts, southern Democrats found themselves in a quandary regarding the presidential question. Although Tyler tried to make himself attractive to southern Democrats, few took him seriously as a possible Democratic presidential nominee. They gave Tyler applause for standing firm against the Whigs, but that applause did not lead to a political embrace of the president. Tyler seemed little more than a sideshow exhibit to the main attraction playing before southern Democrats: Van Buren and Calhoun vying for attention and support.

Once again southern Democrats wrestled with the political enigma of Van Buren. He commanded the loyalty and respect of many southern Democratic leaders, but, as in 1840, many evinced doubts about his ability to win in the southern political arena. They feared that the "old charges [would] be revived again." In Arkansas the top Democratic vote-getter, Archibald Yell, declared that Van

21. Clay to Pierce Butler, August 9, 1842, in Pierce Butler Papers, South Caroliniana Library, University of South Carolina; Clay to Willie P. Mangum, June 7, 1844, in Shanks (ed.), *Mangum Papers,* IV, 134; George Bryan to John P. Kennedy [April, 1844], in Kennedy Papers; Robert Toombs to John M. Berrien, January 28, 1844, in Berrien Papers; J. T. Morehead to James W. Webb, April 3, 1844, in Willie P. Mangum Papers, Department of Archives, Louisiana State University.

Buren "has the Confidence of our leading men here but they have no greater love for the man—they think him rather *cold blooded!*" North Carolina Congressman Romulus Saunders felt another Van Buren candidacy "all wrong" because it would hurt southern Democrats. The Mississippian William Gwin, an old crony of Jackson's, shared Saunders's concern. Several Georgia Democrats informed Howell Cobb that with Van Buren heading the ticket they would have an extremely difficult time preventing Georgia from giving her vote to Henry Clay. After losing to the Whigs in both 1836 and 1840, Tennessee Democrats were especially eager to place Andrew Jackson's own state back in the Democratic column. But as Andrew Johnson wrote: "There is one thing Certain to my minde [sic] and that is, that the State cannot be carried for Mr. Vanburen [sic]." A multitude of Johnson's Tennessee cohorts echoed his conviction.[22]

While distress over Van Buren's ability to win votes dominated the thoughts of many southern Democrats, others saw his candidacy in a different light. Longtime and loyal political friends like Thomas Ritchie, Bedford Brown, Andrew Jackson Donelson, and Andrew Jackson himself worked in Van Buren's behalf.[23] These men remained convinced that because of Van Buren's devotion to Democratic principles and to the South he deserved another chance at the White House. More traditional political motives also operated. Some politicians, among them Van Buren's enemies as well as his

22. Cave Johnson to James K. Polk, May 20, 1842, Yell to James K. Polk, March 6, 1842, Gwin to James K. Polk, November 5, 1842, A. Anderson to James K. Polk, September 14, 1842, and J. P. Hardwicke to James K. Polk, November 13, 1842, all in Polk Papers; Saunders to David S. Reid, February 17, 1842, in Reid Papers; James M. Kelly to Cobb, February 8, 1844, W. C. Daniell to Cobb, February 8, 1844, James Jackson to Cobb, April 11, 1844, all in Howell Cobb Papers, Ilah Dunlap Little Memorial Library, University of Georgia (all future Cobb citations are to this collection unless otherwise noted); Johnson to Robert B. Reynolds, September 9, 1843, in Leroy P. Graf *et al.* (eds.), *The Papers of Andrew Johnson* (3 vols.; Knoxville: University of Tennessee Press, 1967–), I, 121.

23. Charles Henry Ambler, *Thomas Ritchie: A Study in Virginia Politics* (Richmond: Bell Book & Stationery, 1913), 228–29; Brown to Weldon Edwards, July 25, 1843, in Edwards Papers; Donelson to Martin Van Buren, December 21, 1842, in Andrew Jackson Donelson Papers, Tennessee Historical Society; Jackson to Frank Blair, November 25, 1842, in John Spencer Bassett (ed.), *Correspondence of Andrew Jackson* (7 vols.; Washington: Carnegie Institution of Washington, 1926–35), VI, 178.

friends, were convinced that Van Buren would win the nomination regardless of what his opponents might do; such a conviction undoubtedly worked in Van Buren's favor.[24] Additionally a few leading southerners aspiring for a vice-presidential spot, either for themselves or their friends, pushed for Van Buren, for they believed he had to choose a southerner to run with him. The list of southern vice-presidential aspirants in 1844 almost duplicated that of 1840.

Again James K. Polk mounted the greatest effort to gain Van Buren's attention and secure the vice-presidential nomination.[25] Polk knew that his chances depended on a Van Buren triumph. If any southerner got the number one spot, then number two would have to go to a nonsoutherner. Even Polk's second consecutive defeat for governor of Tennessee in 1843 failed to relax his dogged persistence to attain national office. As the most influential Tennessee Democrat, excluding only Jackson who sponsored him, he managed to keep Tennessee away from Van Buren's enemies, even though Van Buren inspired little enthusiasm among Polk's Tennessee comrades.

In two other states a similar phenomenon occurred. Thomas Ritchie wanted his Richmond Junto associate Andrew Stevenson to get the vice-presidential plum. That wish reinforced his decision to remain loyal to Van Buren by insuring that Virginia Democrats held to the Virginia-New York axis. Friends of William R. King did likewise in Alabama. Hoping that King would become the first Alabamian to win the nation's second highest office, they kept the Alabama Democracy safe for Van Buren until the state convention of December 1843 resolved to support a Van Buren–King ticket.[26]

24. For example see Dixon H. Lewis to Richard K. Crallé, March 14, 1842, in Crallé Papers, Division of Manuscripts, Library of Congress; Robert M. T. Hunter to John C. Calhoun, December 19, 1843, in J. Franklin Jameson (ed.), *Correspondence of John C. Calhoun* (Washington: Government Printing Office, 1900), 908; James K. Polk to Heiss and Hagan, January 21, 1844, in John P. Heiss Papers, Tennessee Historical Society; Andrew Johnson to A. O. P. Nicholson, February 12, 1844, in Graf *et al.* (eds.), *Johnson Papers,* I, 149.

25. Sellers, *Polk,* II, Chap. 1.

26. Ambler, *Ritchie,* 228; John M. Martin, "William R. King and the Vice Presidency," *Alabama Review,* XVI (1963), 41–43.

The threat that Van Buren's friends tried to stave off came chiefly from John C. Calhoun. Although some Democrats attempted to maintain a neutral stance and others, particularly in Virginia and Tennessee, tried unsuccessfully to stir up enthusiasm for Lewis Cass of Michigan, the major competition for southern support was between Van Buren and Calhoun. In 1842 and 1843 Calhoun mounted his greatest campaign to win the presidency. His road to the presidential mansion ran through the Democratic party. Striving to get northern support for his candidacy he and his friends created a national campaign committee in Washington; they also dangled the vice-presidential prize before prominent northern Democrats like Silas Wright of New York and Levi Woodbury of New Hampshire.[27]

Even with these efforts Calhoun based his hopes chiefly on unifying southern Democrats behind a fellow southerner. Evidence abounded that many of those southern Democrats, leery of another race with Van Buren, wanted to strike against the New Yorker with one of their own. Tennessee Congressman Cave Johnson, Polk's close friend who acted as his eyes and ears in Washington, reported to Polk as early as May 1842 that a group of southern Democrats in Congress intended "to thrust [Van Buren] aside" with one of their own. Southerners working to depose Van Buren insisted that the South needed a southern president. To Van Buren came reports describing these activities designed to undermine his southern strength.[28] These political movements chiefly benefited John C. Calhoun.

27. John Slidell to Robert Walker, December 2, 1842, in John Slidell Letter, Howard-Tilton Memorial Library, Tulane University; New Orleans *Louisiana Courier*, February 7, 1843; J. Rutherfoord to William C. Rives, November 25, 1843 and William B. Lewis to William C. Rives, July 12, 18, 1843, all in Rives Papers; Sellers, *Polk*, II, 8–14, 22; Dixon H. Lewis to Richard K. Crallé, May 10, 1842, in Crallé Papers, Robert Muldrow Cooper Library, Clemson University; Francis W. Pickens to Samuel Ingham, June 18, 1842, in Francis W. Pickens Papers, South Caroliniana Library, University of South Carolina.

28. Johnson to Polk, May 20, July 20, 1842, in Polk Papers; John P. Richardson to Robert Barnwell Rhett, January 21, 1842, in Robert Barnwell Rhett Papers, Southern Historical Collection, University of North Carolina; Andrew Jackson Donelson to Van Buren, December 21, 1842, in Donelson Papers, Tennessee Historical Society; Tho. J. Pew to Van Buren, May 14, 1843, in Van Buren Papers.

These movements generated optimism in the Calhoun camp throughout 1842 and much of 1843. In March, 1842, Francis W. Pickens, a key associate in South Carolina, described Calhoun's chances as excellent. A year later Calhoun himself announced that "zeal, energy and discretion [would] ensure success." The Calhounites had a solid basis for this positive outlook. Operating in most southern states, Calhounite agents reported their cause advancing smartly toward the goal of southern unity behind Calhoun. Although his people carried his message to all of the South, Calhoun put his greatest hopes on Virginia; in his mind Virginia should lead the South. And in Virginia his devoted coterie of able lieutenants headed by Robert M. T. Hunter, James M. Mason, James A. Seddon, and William Fitzhugh Gordon toiled tirelessly in his behalf.[29] If Virginia came in on his side, Calhoun believed that southern unity and his election to the presidency would become reality, not just a dream.

Calhoun recognized that Van Buren represented a formidable obstacle to his success. Van Buren's control of state organizations in both North and South posed the greatest danger to Calhoun's aspirations. In the South, Van Buren did not exercise personal control over the various state parties, but he had fast friends, like Thomas Ritchie, in critical positions. Moreover, those like James K. Polk who hoped to gain from his victory had enormous influence. Add to that total those who stood against Calhoun, or at least not for him, because of their conviction that Van Buren would be the ultimate winner, and the hurdles Calhoun faced become more understandable.

To counter Van Buren's organizational strength the Calhoun forces came up with a three-pronged proposal. Two of the three

29. Pickens to George McDuffie, March 14, 1842, in Pickens Papers; Calhoun to Franklin H. Elmore [March], 19, 1843, and Pickens to Calhoun, July 19, 1843, both in Calhoun Papers, South Caroliniana Library, University of South Carolina; Ker Boyce to Calhoun, October 21, 1842, and B. Boykin to Calhoun, October 12, 1842, both in Calhoun Papers, Robert Muldrow Cooper Library, Clemson University. For the Virginia story see Lynwood M. Dent, Jr., "The Virginia Democratic Party, 1824–1847" (Ph.D. dissertation, Louisiana State University, 1974), Chaps. 7–8, and James A. Seddon to William C. Rives, April 8, 1943, in Rives Papers.

advocated reforming important parts of the national convention procedure. First the Calhounites wanted delegates to the national convention elected by congressional districts, not on a statewide basis. Then they urged abolition of unit-rule voting by state delegations in the convention; instead they proposed that each delegate vote as an individual. These two reforms were intended to give the Calhounite minority a clear voice and a full vote. Finally the Calhounites wanted a late convention date to give them time to round up as much support as possible. They suggested May of 1844 rather than the autumn, 1843, date desired by the Van Buren forces.

Despite Calhoun's hopes his plans failed. Triumphs did occur; in June, 1843, the Georgia Democratic convention named Calhoun as its choice for the Democratic nomination. But his proposals for reforming delegate selection and voting procedures fell on deaf ears. And in Virginia the state Democratic convention meeting in March 1843 delivered him a stunning blow. Responding to Thomas Ritchie's baton the convention turned down the Calhounites on every count. It rejected a late national convention, elimination of the unit-rule, and election of delegates by congressional district. The Georgia endorsement became more and more conspicuous by its loneliness; of the other southern states only South Carolina gave her official blessing to Calhoun's candidacy. The coup de grace came in December when Congress convened. In overwhelming numbers the Van Buren forces blitzed the Calhounite minority and gained complete control of congressional Democrats by electing Van Buren stalwarts to all key congressional posts. In the South and in the nation Calhoun was beaten and he knew it. Unwilling to lose in a national convention he decided early in December 1843 to withdraw from the contest.[30]

When Calhoun gave up the fight, he railed against the nominating process and called on his followers to abandon Van Buren. That such a course probably meant defeat for the Democrats and Van Buren

30. Milledgeville *Federal Union*, June 13, 1843; Richmond *Enquirer*, March 7, 11, 1843; Charles M. Wiltse, *John C. Calhoun* (3 vols.; Indianapolis and New York: Bobbs-Merrill, 1944–51), III, 146–47.

bothered Calhoun not at all. Party loyalty counted for nothing, he declared, when sacred principles were at stake. "The object now is, not victory," he wrote to Robert M. T. Hunter, "but to preserve our position and principles; the only way, under [the] circumstances, by which we can preserve our influence and the safety of the South." [31] To Calhoun personal defeat meant that principle had been subverted and the South endangered, for adherence to principle by the Democrats and the party's concern for the safety of the South would have guaranteed his triumph. Here, as before, Calhoun identified principle with himself and castigated those opposed to him as unprincipled lovers of office and lucre.

That Calhoun, faced with rejection by the party, might try to torpedo it had troubled Democratic party men all along. Anticipating such an outcome the Virginia Democratic convention of 1843 read out of the party in advance "any individual, however eminent" who refused to support in advance the choice of the national convention. The reference to Calhoun, though he was not named, was unmistakable. The possibility that Calhoun might scuttle the party also distressed James K. Polk. If Calhoun pulled out, Georgia Democrats feared losing any chance for carrying their state for Van Buren. Even Henry Clay reported that his intelligence indicated the Calhoun men would turn against the party if it rejected their leader; such information added to Clay's confidence. The Democrats and Clay had good reason for their respective anxiety and hope. Not only did Calhoun consider such action, at least some of his loyal disciples were prepared to follow him. [32]

Although Calhoun's initial reaction was to secede from the party and try to take his followers with him, he eventually decided on a

31. Calhoun to George McDuffie, December 4, 1843, and to Robert M. T. Hunter, December 22, 1843, both in Jameson (ed.), *Calhoun Correspondence*, 552–57.

32. Richmond *Enquirer*, March 11, 1843; Polk to Andrew Jackson Donelson, October 19, 1843, in Donelson Papers; W. C. Daniell to Howell Cobb, March 19, 1844, in Cobb Papers; Clay to John M. Clayton, May 27, 1843, in Clayton Papers; see n. 31 in this chapter and Percy Walker to Joseph Lesesne (both Alabama Calhounites), December 10, 1843, in Joseph Lesesne Papers, Southern Historical Collection, University of North Carolina.

different tack. He realized that asking his supporters outside of South Carolina to forsake the Democratic party was a request that they commit political suicide. Although loyal to him they did not have the secure political bastion that South Carolina afforded him. Furthermore he knew that any such crusade would mean a general purge of his supporters and, consequently, his influence from the party. Thus, still hoping that he could somehow keep the nomination from Van Buren, he allowed his closest associates to moderate the public letter announcing his withdrawal from the contest. The final shaping of the public announcement took a bit of time so the "Address of Mr. Calhoun to His Political Friends and Supporters" did not appear publicly until early February, 1844. It had a much more conciliatory tone than Calhoun's letters of two months earlier. His lieutenants had softened the address, for they had no interest in wandering in the political wilderness.[33]

The southern Democratic party men made it easier for the Calhounites to maintain close ties with the Democratic party by reassuring them that the party still offered political and ideological sanctuary. As the southern Democrats saw it, retaining the Calhoun connection was essential for their political success. Besides, Calhoun's basic principles of states' rights and defense of the South posed no embarrassments to the southern Democrats. Leading the conciliators Thomas Ritchie left no avenue unexplored in his quest to hold the Calhounites with the Democracy. Ritchie constantly reassured Calhoun's friends in Virginia of his respect for them. To them he always spoke of Calhoun in the highest terms; to them he

33. Calhoun to James Edward Calhoun, February 14, 1844, in Jameson (ed.), *Calhoun Correspondence*, 569–70; Wiltse, *Calhoun*, III, 147–48; for the "Address" see Richard K. Crallé (ed.), *The Works of John C. Calhoun* (6 vols.; New York: D. Appleton, 1854–57), VI, 239–54.

By this time Calhoun knew of John Tyler's intention to push the Texas question (see pp. 184–89 herein). That knowledge did not, however, cause him to reconsider his decision to withdraw. In the winter of 1844 no one knew whether or not Texas could derail Van Buren or what the Democratic convention would do if it did. Calhoun had no intention of risking what he considered the humiliation of a convention defeat. If the convention had ended up drafting him, he would undoubtedly have accepted the nomination, but his days as an active candidate were over.

iterated and reiterated that he and they shared allegiance to the same political creed. He even told Hunter that he had new commitments from Van Buren that guaranteed the New Yorker's loyalty to the southern cause. After Calhoun's withdrawal Ritchie engineered the great love feast that characterized the Virginia Democratic convention of February 1844. At that convention Ritchie made one of the few public speeches of his career; in the speech he warmly embraced the Calhoun men as fellow believers in the holy Jeffersonian gospel. Ritchie's wooing of the Calhounites spread beyond Virginia's borders. He urged Georgia Democrats to follow Virginia's example and welcome the Calhounites to their proper home, the Democratic party.[34]

Thomas Ritchie did not act alone. Responding to pressure from the South, the northern Van Burenites agreed to postpone the national convention until May, 1844, the date desired by the Calhounites. The Milledgeville *Federal Union,* as if following Ritchie's advice, praised the result of the Virginia convention. According to the *Federal Union* the Calhoun men had acted nobly in overcoming their disappointment. Declaring that such action deserved applause, the *Federal Union* called on Calhounites in every state to emulate their Virginia comrades. Far to the west the Little Rock *Arkansas Banner* spoke the same language. Praising Calhoun, it called on all Calhoun men to remain with their principles in the Democratic party. And the party, the *Banner* assured the Calhounites, would honor them.[35]

34. Robert M. T. Hunter to Calhoun, November 7, 1842, in Calhoun Papers, Robert Muldrow Cooper Library, Clemson University; Albert Rhett to Calhoun, August 17, 1843, in Calhoun Papers, South Caroliniana Library, University of South Carolina; Thomas Ritchie to Gentlemen, May 16, 1843, in Robert M. T. Hunter Papers, Alderman Library, University of Virginia; Robert M. T. Hunter to Calhoun, February 6, 1844, in Jameson (ed.), *Calhoun Correspondence,* 929; Richmond *Enquirer,* February 6, 1844; Thomas Ritchie to Howell Cobb, February 8, 1844, in "Three Letters from Thomas Ritchie to Howell Cobb," *John P. Branch Historical Papers of Randolph-Macon College,* III (1912), 354.

35. James C. N. Paul, *Rift in the Democracy* (Philadelphia: University of Pennsylvania Press, 1951), 63–65; Milledgeville *Federal Union,* February 13, 1844; Little Rock *Arkansas Banner,* February 20, 1844; New Orleans *Louisiana Courier,* January 12, 1844.

Such overtures helped hold Calhoun and let the southern Democrats present a united front. In early 1844 all appearances indicated that the front would undoubtedly benefit Martin Van Buren; he had successfully withstood the Calhoun challenge. Across the South, Democrats agreed with their great chieftain Andrew Jackson that Van Buren for the third time would carry the party's colors into battle against the Whigs. Even confidants of Calhoun informed Van Buren that he could depend upon them. Although all seemed well with southern Democrats, rumors persisted that an anti-Van Buren conspiracy still existed.[36] According to this murky scenario unhappy Calhounites and others chronically dissatisfied with Van Buren still conspired to block the New Yorker no matter the cost to the party. It seemed impossible to shut off permanently the anti-Van Buren undercurrent.

Still, as spring blossomed across the South, all signs pointed to a Van Buren-Clay presidential battle. And once again the Whigs held the political initiative, though this time, unlike 1836 and 1840, they trumpeted national economic issues, not particular sectional topics. Southern Democrats, absorbed with the Van Buren-Calhoun contest, had given little thought to issues except to reaffirm their undying opposition to a national bank and a protective tariff. The endorsement of the Calhoun faction by the regular party men guaranteed that Democrats would loudly decry the evils of protection. Thus almost without thinking the southern Democrats prepared to answer Clay's nationalism with their time-honored Jeffersonian-Jacksonian program of states' rights and no national economic institutions. Clay and Van Buren believed the campaign would follow such a pattern; both men were supremely confident that they controlled events. Neither of them gave much thought to the man who would in fact be author of the drama of 1844—John Tyler.

36. Jackson to E. G. W. Butler, February 9, 1844, in Gayarré Papers, Howard-Tilton Memorial Library, Tulane University; James H. Hammond to Van Buren, December 24, 1843, and Robert Barnwell Rhett to Van Buren, February 26, 1844, both in Van Buren Papers; Cave Johnson to James K. Polk, February 25, 1844, in Polk Papers.

IV

John Tyler had more influence on southern politics than any other southern politician between Andrew Jackson and the demise of the second party system. Only John C. Calhoun was at all comparable. Although historians have generally relegated Tyler to the second rank among presidents, they have failed to appreciate the enormous consequences of his determination to maintain his political life or, at the least, his political ideology.[37] More than any other man, John Tyler caused both the political death of Martin Van Buren and the destruction of the new Clay Whig party in the South. By fundamentally altering the pattern of the 1844 campaign as devised by Van Buren and Clay, Tyler guaranteed the continued supremacy of the politics of slavery in the South. As a result of Tyler's course the shift of southern Whigs away from sectional particularism to economic nationalism had but a short life. Because of his actions the effort made by southern Whigs between 1842 and 1844 to substitute a politics of economics for the politics of slavery became the great aberration of antebellum southern politics.

Two basic motivations governed Tyler's political life as president. First he wanted, if possible, to remain president after his term expired; second, in all his political actions and calculations he never strayed from his native southern orientation. Nothing suggests that Tyler thought of himself as a caretaker president who would simply fill out Harrison's term and go happily back to his Virginia plantation. He might have to return to Williamsburg and Charles City County after March 4, 1845, but not without fighting to retain his residence in the White House. Immediately after Harrison's death Tyler insisted that he was the president in fact, not some kind of figurehead. His inaugural address intentionally left open the question of a second term. Then in his duel with Clay and the Whig-dominated Congress he acted as a strong chief executive in the mode

37. A recent exception is Frederick Merk; see especially his *Slavery and the Annexation of Texas* (New York: Alfred A. Knopf, 1972).

of Andrew Jackson. In the aftermath of his break with the Whig party he assembled a cabinet of his own persuasion loyal to him. Finally from late 1841 on into 1844 he tried to develop a strategy that would enable him to succeed himself as president.

In planning for his political future, Tyler found himself in an exceedingly difficult position. He was a man without a party in a political world dominated by two powerful national parties, the Democratic and the Whig. Tyler had no future with the party that made him vice-president. To him the Whig party of Henry Clay offered nothing but undying enmity. Tyler and his advisers realized that he had to turn elsewhere for political sustenance. That left only two alternatives: the Democrats or a third party. Tyler clearly thought about a third party. He spoke of reforging the old Jeffersonian Republican party; in his mind that entailed, as one of his most trusted friends put it, "bring[ing] parties to some ground of principle."[38] Thomas W. Gilmer might also have added that such a reorganization would be intended to allow John Tyler to retain the presidency.

In Tyler's effort to build a new political organization based on his principles and behind his leadership he looked to both the old parties for recruits. For Tyler, political patronage served as the prize he offered Whigs and Democrats alike for joining him in the interparty world.[39] Party loyalty, after all, had not been the most important feature of Tyler's political career. An original Jackson man, he broke with the Democrats during the nullification crisis. Then less than a decade later he parted company with his second party, the Whig. Even before the creation of the Jackson party, he differed with

38. Tyler to Littleton W. Tazewell, October 24, 1842, in Tyler Papers; Tyler to Alexander Gardiner, July 11, 1846, Abel P. Upshur to Nathaniel B. Tucker, December 23, 1841, and Thomas W. Gilmer to Franklin Minor, August 7, 1841, all quoted in Lyon G. Tyler, *The Letters and Times of the Tylers* (3 vols.; Richmond and Williamsburg: Whittet & Shepperson, 1884–85, 1896), II, 154, 341–42, 707; Cave Johnson to James K. Polk, February 27, 1842, in Polk Papers; William B. Campbell to David Campbell, June 17, 1841, in Campbell Papers.

39. Abel P. Upshur to Nathaniel B. Tucker, December 23, 1841 and undated, both quoted in Tyler, *Tylers*, II, 154, 248–49n; Daniel Webster to Nicholas Biddle, March 11, 1843, in Reginald C. McGrane (ed.), *The Correspondence of Nicholas Biddle Dealing with National Affairs, 1807–1844* (Boston and New York: Houghton Mifflin, 1919), 345.

Thomas Ritchie and the Richmond Junto over the value of loyalty to any political organization. And in fact none claimed his allegiance except his own conception of the original Jeffersonian party.

Even as he strove to build his third party, Tyler recognized that it would be exceedingly difficult to construct a political instrument that could seriously challenge, much less replace, either the Democratic or Whig party. That recognition did not cause Tyler to give up all hope for his new party, but it did lead him to explore the opportunities, if any, offered by the Democrats. When Tyler stood firm and vetoed Clay's bank bill, southern Democrats cheered him. Thomas Ritchie's *Enquirer* set the tone of the southern Democrats when it proclaimed: "We hail it with gratitude." "President Tyler," cried the Milledgeville *Federal Union*, "is a man of history." Andrew Jackson added his name to those applauding the second president to face down a Henry Clay-sponsored national bank.[40] All these Democrats praised Tyler for his tenacious hold to common principles. Although accolades aplenty came Tyler's way, no Democratic spokesman suggested, or even hinted, that John Tyler might make a magnificent Democratic president. The southern Democrats were delighted to see Tyler smash the Whigs, but they proffered neither promises nor rewards to the president who had once deserted them. If Tyler wanted to become a major Democratic leader, if he entertained thoughts of winning the Democratic presidential nomination, he would have to do more than block Henry Clay's legislative program.

Through all of his political activities Tyler revealed himself as thoroughly southern. He was a southern politician totally committed to the traditional southern shibboleths of strict construction, states' rights, and defense of the South. Over a long political career he had never wavered from that standard. And Tyler made clear that his accession to the presidency had not decreased his devotion to his old creed. Shortly after assembling his own cabinet he wrote: "The

40. Tyler to Littleton W. Tazewell, October 24, 1842, in Tyler Papers; Richmond *Enquirer*, August 20, September 17, 1841; Thomas Ritchie to Robert M. T. Hunter, March 29, 1842, in Hunter Papers; Milledgeville *Federal Union*, August 24, 1841; Tyler, *Tylers*, II, 292.

new Cabinet is made up of the best materials. Like myself they are all original Jackson men and mean to act upon Republican princi- ples."[41] From that description Tyler obviously omitted the one holdover from Harrison's cabinet, Daniel Webster. Moreover, to a man of Tyler's background and thinking the phrase "Republican principles" was a convenient way to capsule the southern shib- boleths that guided his political life.

From the earliest days of his presidency Tyler looked to the South to sustain him. Although Tyler tried to build a national following to support his course, his chief political advisers were all southerners. In fact his most intimate confidants—Abel P. Upshur of his cabinet and Thomas Gilmer and Henry Wise of the Congress—all came from Virginia and the states' rights tradition of that commonwealth, from the same political milieu that bred John Tyler. The two most important intellectual counselors of the president and his intimate circle, Judge Nathaniel Beverly Tucker and Professor Thomas R. Dew, were both deeply committed to Virginia Republicanism and to southern institutions. That both Tucker and Dew lived in Williamsburg and taught at the College of William and Mary, Tyler's alma mater, underscored the single vision that controlled Tyler's thoughts and actions. The most important non-Virginians who had ready access to the president and his Virginians included the mercu- rial Duff Green, a vehemently prosouthern apostle of Calhoun, and Calhoun himself, who was especially close to Upshur. The Tyler circle maintained close relations with Calhoun, who was not only privy to the important political decisions of the Tyler administration, but also counseled it on the key issue of Texas annexation.[42] Admir-

41. Tyler to Thomas Cooper, October 18, 1841, in Tyler Papers; Tyler to Andrew Jackson, September 20, 1842, in Jackson Papers; Tyler to Andrew Jackson Donelson, November 15, 1841, in Donelson Papers; Tyler to John Rutherfoord, June 23, 1841, in John Rutherfoord Papers, William R. Perkins Library, Duke University; Duff Green to Tyler, September 10, 1841, in Green Papers, Southern Historical Collection, University of North Carolina.
42. Tyler to William C. Rives, May 8, 1841, in Rives Papers; Francis W. Pickens to James H. Hammond, April 13, 1841, in Hammond Papers; Virgil Maxcy to John C. Calhoun, December 31, 1843, in Calhoun Papers, Robert Muldrow Cooper Library, Clemson Univer- sity; Thomas W. Gilmer to John C. Calhoun, December 13, 1843, quoted in Tyler, *Tylers*, III, 130–32; Merk, *Slavery*, Chap. 1 *passim*; pp. 184–89 herein.

ing Calhoun, Tyler and his advisers thought much like the South Carolinian. Like Calhoun the Tyler men believed the capture of the South an essential preface to any national political victory.

Thus Tyler's preoccupation with the South in his search for political salvation is not at all surprising. Galvanizing a potent following in the South could lead, theoretically, in either of the two directions Tyler had open. A pro-Tyler southern constituency could form the basis of a third party or, more likely, it could propel Tyler toward leadership of the Democratic party. But when Tyler and his men looked South in 1842 and 1843, they found grave difficulties. Martin Van Buren, the odds-on Democratic favorite, had great strength in most southern states. Not the least of these was Tyler's own Virginia where Thomas Ritchie and the Richmond Junto provided Van Buren with his most powerful southern base. To short circuit Van Buren's southern machine would require an issue to arouse southerners and make it possible for Tyler to emerge as the champion of the South. As Tyler and his advisers knew from their early Whig experience, such an issue had to touch on the South's most responsive political chord—only something related directly and dramatically to slavery could do that. To be most effective the scenario ought to show Tyler defending the South and slavery against some kind of dangerous outside threat.

Even if the Tyler men discovered their issue, however, they faced another, and seemingly insurmountable, obstacle—John C. Calhoun. To replace Calhoun as the champion of the South was by definition all but impossible, especially when he was actively cultivating southern support in his campaign for the Democratic nomination. Moreover Calhoun had a powerful following in the state Tyler knew best, his own Virginia. Besides, Tyler and especially his most confidential advisers had little reason to try to thwart the hopes of the political leader they most admired. As Abel Upshur put it, "No *southern* man can hesitate between Mr. Calhoun & any other man." Rather than fight Calhoun, the Tyler managers decided to join forces with him. Although not absolutely conclusive, the contemporary evidence strongly suggests that the Tyler men and the Calhoun men worked in conjunction for the common benefit of both.[43] Since both camps agreed on issues and both shared the same goal, the defeat of Van Buren, such an arrangement provided no real difficulties. As both Calhoun and Tyler saw it, to defeat Van Buren would return the Democratic party to first principles and, not incidentally, to their control. Calhoun's decision to pull out of the race did not end this alliance, for into the spring of 1844 both Tyler and Calhoun, a member of Tyler's cabinet from March, 1844, still retained hopes of stopping Van Buren.

Tyler with Calhoun's aid acted to change the direction of the southern Democracy. If their plans succeeded, Van Buren would either lose out to a candidate they considered more principled and more southern oriented or Van Buren would have to come to them. For, whoever the Democratic candidate, he would run on the Tyler-Calhoun platform. Thus John Tyler acted squarely as a practitioner of the politics of slavery when he drove for the annexation of Texas.

43. Upshur to Green, July 11, 1842, February 23, 1844, and Green to Upshur, January 19, 1844, all in Green Papers, Southern Historical Collection, University of North Carolina; William B. Lewis to William C. Rives, March 15, 1843, in Rives Papers; Willie P. Mangum to James W. Webb, December 6, 1842, in Mangum Papers; Wiltse, *Calhoun*, III, 114–15, 177–78.

6 The Explosion of Texas

I

JOHN TYLER early cast his eyes upon Texas. In the autumn of 1841, just after the final break with the Whig party, Tyler questioned Secretary of State Daniel Webster about the practicability of annexing Texas by treaty. In 1842 he instructed Waddy Thompson, his representative in Mexico, to sound out the Mexican position on an American move toward annexation. These two initiatives did not result from off-hand thoughts. From the beginning of his presidency he considered the acquisition of Texas a primary goal of his administration.[1]

The question of annexing Texas did not appear for the first time when Tyler broached it to Webster. The issue had initially emerged back in 1836 when Texas successfully revolted from Mexico and declared herself independent.[2] The victorious Texas revolutionaries, American emigrants to a man, actively solicited annexation by the United States. President Andrew Jackson, a friend of Texas and particularly of Texas chieftain Sam Houston, wanted to attach Texas to his country. But Jackson, recognizing the possible adverse political ramifications, held back. He realized that annexation might endanger the unity of the Democratic party by antagonizing northern Democrats opposed to increasing the territory of slavery. And slavery, southern style, did exist in Texas. Democratic solidarity, as Jackson knew, was necessary to elect Martin Van

1. Tyler to Webster, October 16, 1841, in Webster Papers, Division of Manuscripts, Library of Congress; Sydney Nathans, *Daniel Webster and Jacksonian Democracy* (Baltimore and London: Johns Hopkins University Press, 1973), 206; Lyon G. Tyler, *The Letters and the Times of the Tylers* (3 vols.; Richmond and Williamsburg: Whittet & Shepperson, 1884–85, 1896), II, 254; Henry A. Wise, *Seven Decades of the Union* (Philadelphia: J. B. Lippincott, 1872), 182.

2. James C. Curtis, *The Fox at Bay: Martin Van Buren and the Presidency, 1837–1841* (Lexington: University Press of Kentucky, 1970), Chap. 8.

Buren president. A fractured party pitted against northern Whigs using annexation against Van Buren might defeat Jackson's hand-picked successor.

Political considerations also governed President Van Buren's attitude toward Texas. Although not personally enthusiastic about Texas, Van Buren worried most about the political shoals underlying any move to acquire Texas. He knew northern opposition would do neither his party, his administration, nor himself any political good. Accordingly he refused to heed the urgings of southern Democrats, including prominent ones like Thomas Ritchie, pushing for the annexation of Texas. Talk of Texas receded when the Panic of 1837 enveloped the administration. Although certain southern Democrats had proposed annexing Texas, annexation never became a public question in the South during either Jackson's or Van Buren's administration. Southern Democrats, acceding to the wishes of their presidents, made no issue of it.

In contrast to his predecessors in the White House, John Tyler felt no political impediments when he grasped Texas. Instead, political reality, as Tyler perceived it, propelled him toward Texas. For Tyler and his intimate circle of advisers, no other issue had so much political potential. The annexation of Texas presented properly to the nation, but especially to the South, offered the possibility of a popular rising behind John Tyler. The Tyler men saw no other issue creating that situation. With Texas, Tyler could become the national champion of expansion and increased economic opportunity. In the South, always the focus of Tylerite vision, Tyler could become the guardian of slavery and southern safety.

In the spring of 1843, Tyler prepared his administration for action. Then he began to reach out for the political prize he had coveted since 1841. Annexing Texas would necessarily require diplomatic as well as political action because Texas claimed to be an independent nation. And Tyler's chief diplomat, Daniel Webster, was wary, at the least, of any moves toward annexation. Webster's resignation as secretary of state in May, 1843, came in no small part because, as

Tyler's son later wrote, "it was necessary to have in the office of Secretary of State one who would go the full length of the Texas question." Tyler replaced Webster with Hugh S. Legaré of South Carolina. When Legaré died after only a month as secretary *ad interim*, Tyler transferred Abel Upshur from the navy department. With either Legaré or Upshur the Texas question was, as Henry Wise put it, "in safe Southern Hands."[3] Thus Tyler had made all preparations to launch his campaign for Texas.

Tyler's pursuit of Texas did not, however, depend solely upon political calculations. As Frederick Merk showed, Tyler's Texas offensive really gained momentum in the summer of 1843.[4] The catalyst that sparked the administration's diplomatic and political activity was a report from Tyler confidant Duff Green, then in London. In July and August, Green informed Tyler, Upshur, by then secretary of state, and Calhoun that Great Britain intended to back Texas financially and politically in return for the abolition of slavery in Texas. Professor Merk took pains to show that Green grossly misrepresented British intentions. But the Tyler men accepted Green's assessment without hesitation even though corroboration of his fears did not come from the American minister in England, Edward Everett.

Green's warnings fit into Tyler's annexation plans so perfectly that the meshing tempts one to argue that Tyler sent Green to London in the spring of 1843 expressly to produce the report he actually made. Certainly Tyler's previous actions and his hopes for Texas suggest that possibility. Such an hypothesis readily explains why Tyler and his associates required no substantiating evidence from Everett or anyone else. They knew what Green was going to tell them before they received his message. This conspiratorial interpretation, however, has severe problems. First the manuscript record—on the Tyler-Green relationship and Texas it is relatively full—provides no

3. Tyler, *Tylers*, II, 263–64; Wise, *Seven Decades*, 221.
4. Frederick Merk, *Slavery and the Annexation of Texas* (New York: Alfred A. Knopf, 1972), Chap. 1.

evidence to support a conspiracy thesis. Professor Merk, who thoroughly investigated Tyler's secret diplomacy and his using Green as a presidential agent, produced no such evidence; neither has my own research.[5] Of course one could maintain that Tyler gave Green verbal instructions and swore him to eternal secrecy. Green himself provides the difficulty for this theory. A voluble man, he kept few political secrets from his intimate friends. It seems most unlikely that Green never uttered a word about this aspect of his mission to either Calhoun or Upshur. But from none of the three does any hint come that Green went to London with his Texas letter already written.

Calhoun and Upshur pose the second problem for a conspiracy interpretation. A genuine and sincere alarm pervades the responses each of them made to Green's revelations. Any indication of expectation or foreknowledge simply does not exist, even in their private correspondence. Both could be dismissed as complete charlatans and hypocrites, but such condemnation has no basis either in their personalities or in the historical record. Tyler, to be sure, could have kept his directions to Green secret from them. But Upshur, his confidential friend as well as Green's, was in the cabinet when Green left for England. And Upshur had taken over the State Department before Green's letter arrived in Washington. It seems inconceivable that Upshur would not have received from either Tyler or Green some glimpse into any secret plotting between the president and his secret agent.

Although it is highly improbable that Green headed to England with his Texas letter in his baggage, it is quite possible, even probable, that he hoped somehow to connect the British commitment to abolition with Texas. To link English abolitionism to Texas would give Tyler's script for annexation an effective and dramatic ending. Aware of Tyler's Texas hopes and sharing Tyler's views on slavery and abolition, Green would certainly have been alert for signs of a

5. Frederick Merk, *Fruits of Propaganda in the Tyler Administration* (Cambridge: Harvard University Press, 1971), 3–35 *passim*, esp. 17–23.

connection. Thus when Green discovered what appeared to him convincing evidence of the England-abolition-Texas triangle, he hurried his news back to his friends. Tyler and his associates welcomed Green's letter because it met their political needs so perfectly. But its specific contents caused genuine alarm because Green asserted that he had uncovered a real danger—British abolitionism did intend to absorb Texas.

With Green's warning before them the president and his advisers viewed the acquisition of Texas as critical for the preservation of slavery and southern safety. That Everett did not corroborate Green's findings bothered the Tyler men not at all. After all the British had ended slavery in their West Indian possessions, and Green, as dedicated to slavery as his comrades on this side of the Atlantic, would know an abolition move when he saw it. As for Everett, he was from Massachusetts; to the Tyler men no more need be said. Letters passing between Upshur and Calhoun pictured "the very existence of the South" as dependent upon obtaining Texas with slavery intact. Upshur viewed Texas as "*the* question of the day" and "the great object of [his] ambition." To these men southern civilization was at stake because they believed that abolition in Texas, in their minds a certainty if they failed to act, would lead inevitably to abolition and cataclysm in the South. In the aftermath of annexation Calhoun declared, "I am proud to have my name associated with [annexation.]"[6]

Convinced that the South was in mortal danger, the Tyler men set out to alert the South to its peril. Calhoun had advised Upshur that "the attention of the people of the South ought to be turned to the subject." They believed that a publicity campaign would produce the desired reaction. As Upshur told Calhoun, "nothing more is necessary to insure success than that the South be true to itself. I

6. Upshur to Calhoun, November 8, 1843, in Calhoun Papers, Robert Muldrow Cooper Library, Clemson University; Calhoun to Upshur, August 27, 1843; Upshur to Nathaniel Beverly Tucker, October 10, 26, 1843, all quoted in Merk, *Slavery*, 21, 234; Calhoun to Thomas J. Rusk, August 12, 1845, in Thomas J. Rusk Papers, Eugene C. Barker Texas History Center, University of Texas.

trust that no southern representatives will be found so blind or so tame of spirit as not to be worthy of the present great occasion." This aroused South would look to Tyler as its political hero. Calhoun caught this political aspect when he wrote that Tyler's course "ought to be unanimously and decidedly supported by the South."[7] Here is the politics of slavery at work—politicians, for political and ideological reasons, stridently warning the South of threats to southern safety and expecting the reaction to those warnings to form the basis of political support.

Not that Tyler forgot the rest of the country. Although his attention seemed riveted southward, he hoped to bring northerners as well as southerners to his side. To win northern support for Texas the Tyler men presented Texas as a land of economic opportunity for northern commerce and manufacturing. Texas cotton would enrich the North. Additionally Tyler's spokesmen denied that expansion into Texas meant expanding slavery. In fact, according to the Tyler message, it meant exactly the opposite. Economic forces would soon cause a transfer of slaves from the East to Texas; then economic forces would cause the ultimate abandonment of slavery in Texas. This script then placed the former slaves on the road to Mexico and Latin America. Thus Texas would act as a conduit to rid the United States of slaves and blacks. The single most important weapon in this Tyler arsenal was a pamphlet written by Democratic Senator Robert J. Walker of Mississippi, an ardent expansionist and a personal friend of Tyler's. Walker's *Letter of Mr. Walker, of Mississippi, Relative to the Annexation of Texas* written in January, 1844, had a circulation of millions.[8]

Tyler himself declared Texas a national issue. In his message to Congress accompanying the annexation treaty he insisted that the

7. Calhoun to Upshur, August 27, 1843, quoted in Merk, *Slavery,* 22; Upshur to Calhoun, November 30, 1843, in Calhoun Papers, Robert Muldrow Cooper Library, Clemson University; Calhoun to George McDuffie, December 4, 1843, in J. Franklin Jameson (ed.), *Correspondence of John C. Calhoun* (Washington: Government Printing Office, 1900), 555.

8. Merk, *Fruits,* Pt. 2, has a good discussion of this effort; Walker's pamphlet is conveniently reprinted on pages 221–52.

entire nation would benefit from bringing Texas under the flag. "My
view of [Texas]," Tyler informed one of his sons in 1850, "was not
narrow, local, or bigoted. It embraced the whole country and all
its interests." Tyler saw Texas as a national issue because he saw
no conflict between the nation and slavery. Slavery, to Tyler, was
an integral part of the nation. Although he attempted to show northerners that Texas held rewards for them, he did not shirk from
annexing more slave territory. Back in that 1841 letter to Webster,
Tyler acknowledged that slavery was the chief objection to bringing
in Texas. But he rejected it as a legitimate basis for opposition because slavery already existed in the United States.[9] And believing,
as he and his advisers did, that slavery was either a good or a necessity, they had no reason to hold back. This view of the legal and
moral relationship between slavery and the nation was distinctly a
Calhounian and southern view.

After he left the White House, Tyler complained that Calhoun, as
secretary of state, forced slavery to the front of annexation and made
it and the administration "a mere Southern agency." But slavery was
not more important to Calhoun than to Upshur, or for that matter
even to Tyler. Calhoun was just a more forceful man than either of
his two Virginia comrades. Also he had no interest in downplaying
slavery for any northern audience. Calhoun always wanted to assert
what he considered the rights of the South and demand that the
North adhere to them; Texas gave him another opportunity. Besides
Tyler certainly knew what both Upshur and Calhoun thought about
slavery and how each conducted the Texas negotiations. Tyler definitely did not think himself an enemy of Calhoun, whom he finally got
into his cabinet following Upshur's death in February 1844. He had
tried as early as 1842 to bring Calhoun into his official family. And in
September 1843, Duff Green, privy to Tyler's thoughts, had urged

9. James D. Richardson (comp.), *A Compilation of the Messages and Papers of the Presi-
dents, 1789–1897* (10 vols.; Washington: Government Printing Office, 1896–99), IV, 308–309;
John Tyler to Robert Tyler, April 17, 1850, quoted in Tyler, *Tylers,* II, 483; Tyler to Daniel
Webster, April 17, 1850, in Tyler Papers.

Calhoun to come into the cabinet so that he could have active control of Texas strategy.[10]

Counting on the South, hoping for the North, Tyler moved on two fronts—one public, the other private—in his quest for Texas.[11] Events occurring on both fronts would have an enormous impact on southern parties and politics. On the private front Tyler initiated secret negotiations for an annexation treaty with Texan representatives in Washington. He hoped for a treaty which he could present to the Senate as a *fait accompli*. Simultaneously he began a massive public campaign emphasizing the great benefits Texas would bring to the United States. The administration and its supporters used friendly newspapers, public letters, and pamphlets to stress the advantages of an American Texas. Thus, by early 1844 the future relationship of the United States and Texas became an open, publicly discussed issue.

II

Texas as a political issue came from the Tyler-Calhoun combine which had much closer ties to southern Democrats than to southern Whigs. And that alliance had, in part, designed Texas to stir up southern Democrats in an attempt to undermine Martin Van Buren's hold on the party. Also the southern Democrats, unlike their Whig counterparts, had no particular platform or campaign strategy that generated enthusiasm either among the party's leaders or voters. What the Democrats did have was a candidate who excited few of them. Tyler and Calhoun hoped to provide an issue or an "explosion," as Robert M. T. Hunter frankly termed it, that would simul-

10. Tyler to Alexander Gardiner, June 17, 1847, quoted in Tyler, *Tylers*, II, 426; Charles M. Wiltse, *John C. Calhoun* (3 vols.; Indianapolis and New York: Bobbs-Merrill, 1944–51), III, 87, 138, 161–63; Green to Calhoun, September 29, 1843, quoted in Duff Green, *Facts and Suggestions, Biographical, Historical, Financial and Political, Addressed to the People of the United States* (New York: Richardson & Co., 1866), 85.

11. For an account of both the negotiations and the public relations campaign see Merk, *Slavery*, Chaps. 1–3.

taneously inflate the enthusiasm of southern Democrats and deflate the prospects of Van Buren.[12]

In Democratic circles there was talk of Texas before the presidential year, but a general discussion did not occur until 1844. In Washington in 1843 the Tyler administration found helping hands among a few non-Calhounite southern Democrats. Tennessee Congressman Aaron V. Brown angled to bring Andrew Jackson into the Texas camp and Mississippi Senator Robert J. Walker eagerly adopted the product for which he would become a major salesman. At a Democratic dinner in King William County, Virginia in the fall of 1843, Tyler-Calhoun partisans "broached the question of Texas." To Andrew Stevenson, who reported the episode to Martin Van Buren, the introduction of Texas portended "a deep excitement" that would shake the party.[13]

After the turn of the year, when the administration's publicity campaign picked up momentum, Texas became the chief topic of conversation among southern Democrats. In Stevenson's colorful colloquialism, "the *Cat* [was] out of the bag." Democratic editors across the South began the chant for Texas. Thomas Ritchie's imperative, "The annexation of Texas must be met," set the tone of the southern performance. Similar declarations of action sprang from Democratic stalwarts from Raleigh to Little Rock, from Nashville to New Orleans. The Raleigh *Standard* asserted that the South would stand unanimously for annexation. According to the Milledgeville *Federal Union* no self-respecting Democrat or southerner could possibly oppose the acquisition of Texas. Speaking for Democrats in a state bordering the Republic of Texas, the Little Rock *Arkansas Banner* declared: "We are a decided and uncompromising advocate of the annexation of Texas." The Nashville *Union* proclaimed that the prospect of annexation gripped the South with powerful tenta-

12. Hunter to John C. Calhoun, December 19, 1843, in Jameson (ed.), *Calhoun Correspondence*, 908.
13. Charles G. Sellers, Jr., *James K. Polk* (2 vols.; Princeton, N.J.: Princeton University Press, 1957–), II, 50–51, 53–55; Stevenson to Van Buren, October 8, 1843, in Van Buren Papers.

cles. As early as February the Jackson *Mississippian* aligned itself
with the most ardent pro-Texas advocates. In Louisiana, where
interest in Texas had always been high and the newspapers had
carried Texas stories for a decade, the New Orleans *Louisiana
Courier* carried the Democratic message for Texas.[14]

In late April the Tyler administration advanced still another step
with Texas by completing the negotiations for annexation. The goal
of Calhoun, Upshur, and Tyler had been reached—an agreement
that would make Texas part of the United States, protect the South,
and foil Great Britain. Tyler urged that the Senate maintain the
same secrecy in its deliberations that had marked the administration's diplomacy; but an opponent of annexation, the abolitionist
Senator Benjamin Tappan, Democrat of Ohio, leaked the treaty and
accompanying documents to the press. Now all was in the open—
not just the publicity campaign but a signed treaty also. As a result
the annexation debate was no longer an academic or theoretical
proposition; instead annexation had become something tangible. Its
existence on paper had only to be ratified by the United States
Senate in order to exist in fact. The submission of an actual treaty
added urgency to the southern debate.

Shortly after the treaty went to the Senate, Secretary of State
Calhoun sent along two official letters he had written to Richard
Pakenham, the British minister in Washington. Protecting slavery
had always been a part of the Texas picture, but with the Calhoun-
Pakenham letters the prominence of slavery was dramatized. In
them Calhoun expressed deep concern over the British interest in
general abolition. To Calhoun such an attitude could only entail the
gravest problems for the United States. He repeated the Tyler refrain that abolition in Texas would lead inevitably to abolition in the
South. That, in turn, would endanger the security of the United

14. Stevenson to Martin Van Buren, October 8, 1843, in Van Buren Papers; Richmond
Enquirer, March 29, 1844; Raleigh *Standard*, April 3, 1844; Milledgeville *Federal Union*,
February 27, April 9, 1844; Little Rock *Arkansas Banner*, April 10, 1844; Nashville *Union*,
April 6, 1844, quoted in Sellers, *Polk*, II, 67; Jackson *Mississippian*, February 21, 1844; New
Orleans *Louisiana Courier*, April, 1844 *passim*.

States. Thus for self-preservation the United States had concluded a treaty of annexation. Not content to talk only about his government's policy Calhoun went on to provide a lengthy defense of slavery. Slavery as morally and constitutionally a legitimate part of the United States now stood at the forefront of the entire Texas question. After Calhoun's performance no one could possibly evade the equation: annexation equaled defense of slavery.[15]

Although submission of the treaty placed another weapon in the arsenal of the pro-Texas men, they had even more powerful armament to aid them in their campaign to woo southern Democrats. The patron saint and great hero of southern Democrats added his potent name to those clamoring for Texas. In a characteristically forceful manner Andrew Jackson shouted, "We must regain Texas, *peacefully if we can, forcibly if we must.*" Jackson began his labors for Texas in 1843, though his role became public only in the spring of 1844. In February, 1843, he bemoaned his failure to annex Texas while he was president; "I shall ever regret it," he wrote Van Buren. In that same month he wrote to Aaron Brown that he considered annexation essential for national security. In both these letters the fear that Great Britain would descend upon Texas dominated his thoughts. Jackson was convinced that his old enemy of 1815 once again threatened the lower Mississippi Valley and the Union. And once more Andrew Jackson announced his willingness to use the sword against Redcoats. He vigorously supported President Tyler's annexation plans and told him so.[16]

---

15. Calhoun to Pakenham, April 18, 27, 1844, both printed in *Senate Documents*, 28th Cong., 1st Sess., No. 341, pp. 50–53, 65–67. For a discussion of Calhoun's motivation, see Appendix A herein.

16. Jackson to William B. Lewis, September 18, 1843, in John Spencer Bassett (ed.), *Correspondence of Andrew Jackson* (7 vols.; Washington: Carnegie Institution of Washington, 1926–35), VI, 230; Jackson to Van Buren, February 12, 1843, in Van Buren Papers; Jackson to Brown, February 12, 1843, printed in Richmond *Enquirer*, March 22, 1844; Tyler, *Tylers*, II, 285.

Although Jackson authorized its publication, the letter to Brown was not published until a year after its composition; the Texas men held it until the most opportune moment. But the delay in no way distorted Jackson's views on Texas. The evidence cited in this and the following note makes that point conclusively. *Cf.* Sellers, *Polk*, II, 51–52 and James C. N. Paul, *Rift in the Democracy* (Philadelphia: University of Pennsylvania Press, 1951), 82–83.

While alleged British malevolence roused the martial spirit of the old warrior, the threat thus identified led Jackson directly to a genuine concern for the safety of southern institutions. In a letter to Sam Houston he expressed approval of the veil of secrecy Tyler used to cover the treaty negotiations. Secrecy was essential, according to Jackson, to prevent John Quincy Adams, "that arch fiend," and other abolitionists from mounting a public campaign against ratification. He called ratification and annexation crucial for the South. Failure to annex, which to him guaranteed British penetration into Texas, would endanger slavery. He informed Frank Blair that the time had come for the South "to take the alarm" and rise up to protect her institutions and safety. These views stated in private letters did not remain private. Some were printed; Jackson wrote others expressly for publication. Southern Democratic spokesmen constantly invoked Jackson's name in their cries for Texas. They called on southern Democrats to rally once more around their old chief.[17]

Jackson never felt that he spoke exclusively as a southern partisan. Quite to the contrary, he insisted that annexation was not a narrow sectional question—"we must and will have Texas, with, and in our *glorious Union.*"[18] For Jackson, as for Tyler, slavery was a national institution; for him a threat to slavery was a threat to the nation. In this regard Jackson shared the feelings even of Upshur and Calhoun.

To all these pleas the southern Democrats responded. In early May when Dixon Lewis, the Calhounite senator from Alabama, urged meetings to agitate for Texas, he described what was already taking place. The Little Rock *Arkansas Banner* reported Texas meetings replete with resolutions in every Arkansas county. Every issue of the Milledgeville *Federal Union* in May noted similar meetings

17. Jackson to Houston, March 15, 1844, in Amelia W. Williams and Eugene C. Barker (eds.), *The Writings of Sam Houston, 1813–1863* (8 vols.; Austin: University of Texas Press, 1938–43), IV, 265–67; Jackson to Blair, May 7, 1844, in Jackson Papers; Richmond *Enquirer*, March 22, April 16, 1844; Raleigh *Standard*, March 27, 1844; Little Rock *Arkansas Banner*, April, 1844; *Niles' Register*, LXVI (June 15, 1844), 241.

18. Jackson to James K. Polk, June 29, 1844, in Bassett (ed.), *Jackson Correspondence*, VI, 299.

throughout Georgia. A tour of northwestern Georgia by a Democratic congressman turned up overwhelming sentiment for annexation. John H. Lumpkin claimed that he met only two men not enthusiastic for Texas. A Democratic politician in North Carolina predicted that 90 percent of "our population" eagerly advocated Texas. A Democratic elector in Tennessee attributed his selection to his promise to fight for Texas. From all over Tennessee letters telling of the popular surge for Texas came to James K. Polk. Among Virginia Democrats, Texas became the issue of the moment.[19]

The Tyler-Calhoun strategy had definitely succeeded. They had counted on Texas "unsettl[ing] all calculations as to the future course of men & parties." In Dixon Lewis' picturesque image, they hoped to see southern public opinion "boil & effervesce & [illegible] more like a volcano than a cider Barrel." They got their wish. A month after graphically depicting his hopes for the future Lewis confidently claimed, "The question of Texas annexation is swallowing up all others even the Presidential election." In early April the Raleigh *Standard* announced that the Texas issue "seems to be absorbing every other question." At the end of that same month an old Virginia friend informed Van Buren that "The Texian [sic] question has grown up rapidly in the South to a size and extent of which you can form no just idea—and it is still increasing." Acknowledging that it had tried to discuss the tariff, the Milledgeville *Federal Union* admitted, "it is rendered less interesting by the absorbing topic of Texas." Another observer of the Georgia scene foresaw that "The Texas question will soon become the absorbing & all engrossing subject." The old Tennessee Jacksonian Alfred Balch employed an appropriate image; Texas had become "a political conflagration rag-

19. Lewis to Franklin H. Elmore, May 9, 1844, in Franklin H. Elmore Papers, Southern Historical Collection, University of North Carolina; Little Rock *Arkansas Banner*, April, May, 1844; Milledgeville *Federal Union*, May, 1844; Lumpkin to Howell Cobb, April 18, 1844, in Cobb Papers; Jno S. Strange to David S. Reid, May 12, 1844, in Reid Papers; Joseph C. Guild, *Old Times in Tennessee with Historical, Personal, and Political Scraps and Sketches* (Nashville: Tavel, Eastman & Howell, 1878), 165; for examples of Polk's correspondence see John H. Bills to Polk, May 12, 1844, and H. Yoakum to Polk, May 13, 1844, both in Polk Papers; for Virginia see pp. 200–201 herein.

ing through the whole South-West." Thomas Ritchie, who had watched political issues come and go for forty years, recognized the power of Texas. Nothing, he told Howell Cobb, could "stop the current of public sentiment in the South." [20]

Without any doubt Texas struck a popular chord in the South unmatched by any political issue since the initial outburst of abolition activity back in 1835 and 1836. Anyone reading southern newspapers for the 1840s cannot help but notice the rapid shift in the spring of 1844. For the two previous years the papers were full of state and national financial matters. Then with a rush Texas crowded out discussions of economics. And the pervasive local meetings discussing Texas plus the letters from local political figures pouring into state leaders leave no doubt that the newspapers were talking about a topic that had captivated southern opinion.

Although the Tyler administration's publicity campaign undoubtedly pushed Texas to the forefront of southern discussion, a public relations offensive alone could never have brought forth such a powerful reaction. That kind of reaction came because the Texas issue reached to the wellspring of southern society. When Calhounites defined annexation as "vital to the Safety of the South and the prosperity of our institutions," they heard regular southern Democrats echoing them. When they denounced opposition as the desire of the North "to impair and injure the institution of slavery by all the means in its power," they found themselves proclaiming in unison with the regular southern Democrats. Congressman Andrew Johnson of Tennessee spoke directly: "Texas must com [sic] in to the Union." A public meeting in New Orleans resolved that "the peace of the country, and the safety of the Southwest forbid Texas staying

20. Lewis to Richard K. Crallé, March 19, 1844 in Crallé Papers, Division of Manuscripts, Library of Congress; Lewis to Bolling Hall, April 15, 1844, in Hall Papers; Raleigh *Standard*, April 3, 1844; William H. Roane to Van Buren, April 30, 1844, in Van Buren Papers; Milledgeville *Federal Union*, May 14, 1844; Wilson Lumpkin to Howell Cobb, April 4, 1844, in Cobb Papers; Balch to Van Buren, May 22, 1844, in Van Buren Papers; Ritchie to Cobb, May 6, 1844, in Ulrich B. Phillips (ed.), *The Correspondence of Robert Toombs, Alexander H. Stephens and Howell Cobb* (Washington: Government Printing Office, 1913), 56.

in a precarious situation, liable to fall a prey to the ambitions of states with interests hostile to ours." The South had a "deep stake" in "this matter [annexation]," according to Mississippi Democrat Powhatan Ellis. A South Carolina friend of Calhoun phrased the same sentiment even more dramatically: "On it hinges the very existence of our Southern institutions." To Mississippians assembled in January, 1844, to hear his inaugural address as governor, Albert G. Brown identified the source of this strident language: "Annex Texas to the United States, and you give to the South a degree of influence in the councils of a nation which will enable her to assert her rights with confidence, and maintain them with independence, and secure Mississippi [read any southern state] peace in the exercise of her domestic policy, and a proud independence as a separate member of the confederacy." Anyone disagreeing with that interpretation of annexation submitted to "open insults" and "grinding oppressions" from the enemies of the South and was by definition "more wedded to *Abolition* than to the honor and interests of their country."[21]

The Tyler-Calhoun message on Texas had done its work. That message had posited for the South simple alternatives: annex Texas or face impending ruin.[22] Many southerners foresaw a real threat to slavery because they accepted the Tyler-Calhoun contention that

21. James A. Seddon to Richard K. Crallé, April 28, 1844, in Crallé Papers, Robert Muldrow Cooper Library, Clemson University; Armistead Burt to Benjamin F. Perry, January 30, 1844, in Benjamin F. Perry Papers, Alabama Department of Archives and History; Johnson to David T. Patterson, April 13, 1844, in Leroy P. Graf *et al.* (eds.), *The Papers of Andrew Johnson* (3 vols.; Knoxville: University of Tennessee Press, 1967–), I, 161; James E. Winston, "Louisiana and the Annexation of Texas," *Louisiana Historical Quarterly*, XIX (1936), 93–94; Ellis to Robert J. Walker, March 23, 1844, in Munford-Ellis Family Papers, William R. Perkins Library, Duke University; James Gadsden to Calhoun, May 3, 1844, in Jameson (ed.), *Calhoun Correspondence*, 952; M. W. Cluskey (ed.), *Speeches, Messages, and Other Writings of the Hon. Albert G. Brown, a Senator in Congress from Mississippi* (Philadelphia: Jas. B. Smith, 1859), 66; L. A. Hoe to John C. Calhoun, May 11, 1844, in Chauncey S. Boucher and Robert P. Brooks (eds.), *Correspondence Addressed to John C. Calhoun, 1837–1849* (Washington: Government Printing Office, 1930), 227; Little Rock *Arkansas Banner*, December 23, 1843.

22. Although the argument discussed in this and the following paragraphs did not emerge full grown in the spring of 1844, its component parts germinated across the South. Few speeches, editorials, or private letters failed to mention at least some part of it. Occasionally the general outline appeared all at once as in Albert G. Brown's inaugural. See especially the sources cited in notes 18, 21, 22, and 47 of this chapter.

Texas, if not annexed, would become a dependency of England. Southerners saw England not only as an old enemy and a powerful rival of the United States but also as the international leader of the abolition crusade. Texas under British domination would quickly become abolitionized just like England's West Indian colonies. Then the dread disease would spread rapidly eastward. After all both Arkansas and Louisiana physically touched Texas. Such a terrible outcome might take time, but that did not diminish the terror of the prospect. Moreover long before abolition conquered the South, the mere existence of a free Texas would serve as a magnet and a haven for runaway slaves. Thus, an abolitionized Texas threatened the very existence of southern slave society.

Although the spectre of abolition loomed ominously over the Texas horizon, it was not the only danger perceived by southerners. The pro-Texas rhetoric linked annexation with southern honor and independence. Identifying opposition to annexation with abolition enabled pro-Texas southerners to claim that failure to annex would blemish southern honor. The southern escutcheon would carry a mark of indignity because opponents of annexation by disallowing southern expansion branded the South inferior to the rest of the country. Thus, failure to annex Texas threatened southerners not only with the destruction of their social system but also branded them as un-American pariahs. Because slavery was so deeply embedded in southern culture, any move against it became a challenge to southern honor.

Texas also served as a symbol for the future. If annexation were blocked—and in the rhetoric only abolition would do it—then southerners would have to face the resulting political and economic realities. That the nation would continue to expand seemed a foregone conclusion. Not only did the Louisiana Purchase extend to the Rocky Mountains but already there was talk of an American Oregon. Thousands of square miles existed for the creation of more free states. The South and slavery were circumscribed by the Missouri Compromise, which effectively blocked slavery in the remainder of the Louisiana Purchase. Thus, Texas provided a possible way of maintaining political parity. If the drive for Texas were stymied, southerners could only conclude that the North, spurred on by the abolitionists, had no intention of letting slavery grow. The ultimate political outcome could only be unmitigated disaster—disaster because abolition and the North would inevitably turn against the slave states themselves, it would only be a matter of time and power. A South bound within its borders could only count the hours to the cataclysm.

The issue of land was also wrapped up in Texas. Southerners, as did northerners, moved from east to west, to the open spaces beyond. The nation was embarked on a great western march that definitely included the South. Since 1815 settlers had poured into Alabama, Mississippi, Louisiana, Arkansas, and Florida. Texas was next; to shut off Texas meant telling southerners no more marching for you. Such a command entailed breaking the habits of a generation. It also placed in jeopardy the independence of southerners. A confined man became a dependent man; he no longer controlled his destiny.

This threat to social system, to political and geographical independence became inextricably tied to personal honor and independence. Barricades to continued political self-control and to movement went up because of slavery. In effect southerners felt themselves being told you must accept restrictions and inferiority because you are different and inferior—inferior because slavery is a stain upon the nation. This accusation challenged southern honor because southerners believed themselves and their society honorable. Such a challenge demanded a powerful response: *"In the name of the South, then, we demand Reannexation."*[23]

In the midst of the excitement and turmoil generated by the force of Texas, Martin Van Buren's public letter opposing immediate annexation became the epicenter for the massive shocks that reverber-

23. Richmond *Enquirer*, April 16, 1844.

ated throughout the southern Democracy. Aware that Henry Clay viewed annexation with disfavor, southern Democrats in the early spring of 1844 eagerly awaited a public statement from the Whig leader. When it came on the morning of April 27, they rejoiced. As Cave Johnson characterized the reaction of southern Democrats, "we were in high spirits confident of riding over him in the South rough shod." Glee quickly became dismay, for on the afternoon of the twenty-seventh—and in the midst of Johnson's letter writing— the Washington *Globe* printed a Van Buren letter, dated April 20, defining his stance on Texas. Van Buren's letter, though it differed from Clay's in particulars, ended up in the same camp. He, too, opposed the annexation of Texas unless Mexico agreed. And everyone knew that Mexico was adamantly opposed.[24]

The reaction of the South was instantaneous; from every direction came cries that southern Democrats must find another candidate, a pro-Texas one. Georgia Democrats moaned to Howell Cobb that Van Buren's letter "prostrated all our hopes." The Milledgeville *Federal Union* agreed that Van Buren could never carry Georgia. In Mississippi such regular Democrats as Henry S. Foote and such Calhounites as John A. Quitman as well as the entire congressional delegation turned away from Van Buren. The burden of an anti-Texas candidate convinced Archibald Yell that he faced imminent defeat in his try for a congressional seat, even in heavily Democratic Arkansas.[25]

Although the anti–Van Buren storm had few boundaries, it caused particular disruption in Tennessee and Virginia, where Democratic leaders and the Democratic party had been especially close to Van Buren. In Nashville the "jollification" reigning after the arrival of

24. *Niles' Register*, LXVI (May 4, 1844), 152–57; Johnson to James K. Polk, April 28, 1844, in Polk Papers.

25. James Jackson to Cobb, May 7, 1844, and Albow Chase to Cobb, May 4, 1844, both in Cobb Papers; Milledgeville *Federal Union*, May 14, 1844; John Edward Gonzales, "The Public Career of Henry Stuart Foote (1804–1880)" (Ph.D. dissertation, University of North Carolina, 1957), 32; J. F. H. Claiborne, *Life and Correspondence of John A. Quitman, Major-General, U.S.A., and Governor of Mississippi* (2 vols.; New York: Harper & Brothers, 1860), I, 214; Sellers, *Polk*, II, 62; Yell to James K. Polk, June 21, 1844, in Polk Papers.

Clay's letter turned into "astonishment and confusion" when Van Buren's appeared. Quickly a delegation headed out to the Hermitage to inform Jackson and get his advice. James K. Polk, the active leader of the Tennessee party, was called from his home in Columbia up to Nashville for consultations with Jackson and other party notables. Most agreed that Van Buren must change his mind or be replaced. To nominate him on an anti-Texas platform would be a disaster, for he could never receive the support of the South. A pro-Texas and anti–Van Buren fire raged through the Tennessee Democracy.[26]

"It put me aback," was Thomas Ritchie's reaction. Ritchie said "the deepest anxiety" overcame him; he wondered, "God knows what we are to do." Ritchie knew that the Texas fire was running rampant among the Virginia Democrats. He received letters from all over Virginia attesting to the power of Texas. An anti-Texas candidate would demoralize Virginia Democrats and give the state to Clay. Hurriedly Ritchie gathered his closest associates. The Richmond Junto had helped Van Buren build the Jackson party; it had helped put him atop the Democratic party. It had kept Virginia loyal to him through the Barbour affair, through the Rives vice-presidential disappointment, through the Conservative defection, through the Calhoun campaign. Now over Texas it decided that loyalty must end. In the blunt words of James A. Seddon: "Mr. Van Buren has utterly killed himself with all parties in Va." Ritchie's *Enquirer* published an address from the state Democratic Executive Committee telling Virginia Democrats to reconsider their commitment to Van Buren. To Van Buren himself an anguished Ritchie

26. Guild, *Old Times*, 164–65; A. O. P. Nicholson to John P. Heiss, May 8, 1844, in A. O. P. Nicholson Papers, Manuscript Division, Tennessee State Library and Archives; Polk to Cave Johnson, May 13, 1844, in St. George L. Sioussat (ed.), "Letters of James K. Polk to Cave Johnson, 1833–1848," *Tennessee Historical Magazine*, I (1915), 239–41. One leading Tennessee Democrat held back from the anti-Van Buren tirades. Ironically it was the man who would gain most from the Texas issue, James K. Polk. Polk's circumspection was based on his vice-presidential ambitions; even so, he recognized the power of Texas and never spoke publicly against it. And his private efforts to hold Tennessee Democrats to Van Buren were singularly ineffective. Sellers, *Polk*, II, 72–76.

wrote on May 5, "The last ten days have produced a condition of political affairs, which I did not believe to be possible." No longer, Ritchie concluded, could Virginia support Van Buren. [27] The New York–Virginia alliance was broken at last; never again would it be rebuilt. In wrecking the axis, Texas sealed the political fate of Van Buren.

The furious anti–Van Buren reaction among southern Democrats spilled over into the Democratic national convention which began in Baltimore on May 27. In Baltimore the overwhelming majority of southern delegates had two goals: to stop Van Buren and to get a pro-Texas platform. In order to prevent Van Buren's nomination, the southerners were determined to hold the convention to the traditional rule that nomination required a two-thirds majority. Van Buren commanded a simple majority and could win if the two-thirds rule were overturned. But when his managers tried to remove it, the South stood firm in opposition, and with Virginia casting the deciding votes the convention maintained the rule. [28] Martin Van Buren would not be the Democratic nominee. Although united against Van Buren, southerners had no particular favorite to replace him. Southern votes were divided among several men, though Lewis Cass of Michigan, who had come out for annexation, polled the largest number in the early ballots. When Polk's name first came up on the eighth ballot, he garnered a few southern votes. On the ninth when Polk won the nomination, southerners joined the stampede to him.

27. Ritchie to George C. Dromgoole, April 28, May 5, 1844, both in Dromgoole Papers; for conferences see James Glenmore to George C. Dromgoole, May 17, 1844, *ibid.* and A Faithful Follower & Friend [in Richmond] to Van Buren, May 1, 1844, in Van Buren Papers. The letters to Ritchie from Austen Brockenbrough, April 21, 1844, from William Byars, April 27, 1844, from Thomas J. Randolph, May 4, 1844, from James McDowell, May 6, 1844, from W. M. Watkins, May 7, 1844, from John R. Edmonds, May 12, 1844, are all in "Virginia and Texas, 1844," *John P. Branch Historical Papers of Randolph-Macon College*, IV (1913), 117, 118, 124–34; Seddon to Richard K. Crallé, April 28, 1844, in Crallé Papers, Robert Muldrow Cooper Library, Clemson University; Richmond *Enquirer*, May 10, 1844; Ritchie to Van Buren, May 5, 1844, in Van Buren Papers.

28. For full accounts of the convention see Sellers, *Polk*, II, 79–100 and *Niles' Register*, LXVI (June 1, 1844), 211–18. The southern delegates voted sixty-nine to five for the two-thirds rule; all five negative votes came from North Carolina.

Southern Democrats had a candidate to their liking and also a platform. The convention went on record clearly supporting the Texas position of John Tyler and John C. Calhoun. It made expansion more than a southern hobby by including with the call for Texas a demand for sole American occupation of Oregon. With candidate and platform both immersed in the rhetoric of Texas, southern Democrats were ready for Henry Clay and his new Whig party.

Southern Democrats had responded so ferociously to Van Buren's letter because they believed they had so much at stake. Between 1842 and 1844 they had watched their Whig opposition grow in confidence and unity. They knew the Whigs were convinced that the presidential contest would crown their efforts of the previous two years. Already the Democrats had ironclad evidence of Whig strength. In state elections in 1843 and early 1844 Whigs had sent Democrats scurrying for political cover. Only in Louisiana where the Democrats, despite Whig control of the legislature, elected their first governor in 1842 and three of four congressmen in 1843 did the reverse seem to hold true. In 1843 voters in Georgia and Tennessee had elected Whig governors and Whig-controlled state legislatures. While the Democrats enjoyed relatively comfortable margins in Alabama, Mississippi, and Arkansas, state financial issues had severely strained the party in each state. Those same issues only cemented Whig unity. Better news did not come in 1844. In April, 1844, the Virginia Whigs surprised and shocked Ritchie and the Democrats by winning the legislative elections. Confident that they would retain the governorship and win back the legislature they had lost in 1842, North Carolina Whigs looked forward to their state elections scheduled for the summer of 1844. Facing this Whig surge southern Democrats found themselves stuck with an unpopular candidate, who had clearly demonstrated on two previous occasions that he could not arouse southern voters. To these hard-pressed Democrats, Texas seemed a godsend—politics and ideology meshed in a way unmatched since 1828. But just as they began to savor what Texas could mean, Van Buren, in one stroke, took it away. He forced southern Democrats to choose between him and Texas; they never hesitated.

Van Buren and his intimate northern friends reacted angrily to the southern defection. "Texas is all now—tariff nothing," boomed Thomas Hart Benton, "Van Buren & his friends are kicked off— Tyler & Texas is the word—and all the rest may go to the devil." Van Buren himself believed, or at least claimed to believe, in 1844 and later, that he had been defeated by a conspiracy. He felt that by the end of 1843 he had vanquished all opposition in the South fairly, and, as a result, all southern Democrats should have been good party men and remained loyal.[29] A conspiracy did exist, but only if that term be applied to the Tyler-Calhoun efforts. They did refuse to accept Van Buren's seeming triumph, but they, not the regular Democrats, forcibly injected Texas into the bloodstream of the southern Democracy. The southern Democrats responded to the political and ideological potency of the injection.

Rather than conspire against Van Buren the regular Democrats kept him informed about the growing importance of Texas. As early as the fall of 1843 when Andrew Stevenson reported on the excitement Texas could cause in Virginia, he warned that the South would not allow Van Buren to remain silent on Texas. Stevenson closed, "Forewarned, forearmed!" By the spring of 1844 Van Buren could not have doubted the pertinence of Stevenson's counsel. The letters that arrived from the South repeating the same old questions about Van Buren's views on slavery and southern rights also asked about Texas. Van Buren also knew that his old patron Andrew Jackson had added his powerful voice to the Texas chorus. Letters to Van Buren in April from Silas Wright, his close friend and watchman in Washington, charted the growing power of Texas and its effect on southerners in Congress. Ritchie told Wright, in a March letter

29. Benton to James McDowell, May 6, 1844, in James McDowell Papers, William R. Perkins Library, Duke University; Van Buren to Frank Blair, October 5, 1844, in Blair Family Papers, Division of Manuscripts, Library of Congress; *Autobiography of Martin Van Buren*, ed. John C. Fitzpatrick (Washington: Government Printing Office, 1920), 8.

Wright forwarded to Van Buren, that Van Buren must announce for Texas or "*all is gone.*" Thus when Van Buren decided to come out against immediate annexation, he knew where the southerners stood and what they wanted from him.[30]

Southern Democrats expected Van Buren to do what he had always done. In the campaign of 1835–1836, during the congressional debates in 1838 on Calhoun's slavery resolutions, and in 1840 Van Buren had always struck the pose the southerners had prescribed for him. In 1844 they acted as they always had and expected Van Buren to do the same. As they saw it, a declaration for Texas was simply the obverse of a declaration against abolition—and Van Buren had never let them down on the latter point. As Andrew Jackson explained to one of Van Buren's New York friends, "The Texas question was an absorbing one in the south, and was necessary to be respected in the selection of candidates by those who are governed by the will of the people."[31] Jackson as a good southerner obviously placed considerably more importance on the will of the southern people than on those in the North.

In the end northern opinion governed Van Buren's final decision. Although he had no great personal desire for annexation, he felt the necessity of holding his native political base required that he refuse the South. He and his associates felt that they had long stood by the South. In fact their loyalty to the South had begun to raise difficulties for them among northerners. Their enemies harped on the readiness of Van Buren and his lieutenants to follow the southern lead, a posture that hurt the North. That the prosouthern history of Van Buren never gained him the support of much of the South further irritated his northern associates. Even so in his Texas letter Van

30. Stevenson to Van Buren, October 8, 1843, in Van Buren Papers; Jefferson Davis to Van Buren, March 25, 1844, in Haskell M. Monroe, Jr., and James T. McIntosh (eds.), *The Papers of Jefferson Davis* (2 vols.; Baton Rouge: Louisiana State University Press, 1971–), II, 140; Jackson, Mississippi Democratic Association to Van Buren, April 13, 1844, A. Walker (New Orleans) to Van Buren, April 25, 1844, Wright to Van Buren, April 1, 29, 1844, Ritchie to Wright, March 20, 1844, all in Van Buren Papers.

31. Jackson to Benj. F. Butler, June 24, 1844, in David Rankin Barbee (ed.), "A Sheaf of Old Letters," *Tyler's Quarterly Historical and Genealogical Magazine*, XXXII (1950), 87.

Buren tried to keep open an avenue toward the South by opposing only immediate annexation, not annexation itself. He counted on "what I have said and done in respect to the rights of the South" to hold his southern friends. He did not expect the southerners "to distrust [his] fidelity to the principles I have announced" because of that one letter. [32]

He miscalculated. He had done much for them, but the southerners could not and did not let him rest on past laurels. As the southerners understood the party compact, they exercised total control of slavery-related questions and certainly Texas fit that category. They saw Texas as essential both for their own political needs and for the South. They could not accept a presidential candidate who broke their rules, even Van Buren. In the words of a Virginia Democrat, Van Buren had violated "the *sanctum sanctorum.*" [33] Van Buren had accepted southern directions so long as the slavery question remained essentially sectional, but in 1844 his constituency in New York and the North perceived its current manifestation, Texas, as a national issue and a threat. In truth Van Buren was a casualty of the politics of slavery.

While those politics destroyed Van Buren, they helped a seemingly washed-up Tennessee politician win the Democratic presidential nomination. Behind James K. Polk the southern Democrats forged a unity they had not known since 1828. After his nomination Polk courted John Tyler; the courtship succeeded during the summer when Tyler gave up all thoughts of a third-party race. The southern Tylerites joined Polk's army. John C. Calhoun was euphoric. He and his closest associates were convinced that finally the Democratic party had returned to its pristine purity. They identified Polk as a guardian of sacred principle, a staunch defender of the South, a friend, a political and ideological soul mate. Back in

32. Gouverneur Kemble to Joel Poinsett, October 18, 1840, in Poinsett Papers; Van Buren to Frank Blair, September 12, 1842, in Blair Family Papers; Van Buren to Benj. F. Butler, May 20, 1844, in Van Buren Papers.
33. J. S. Barbour to John C. Calhoun, May 16, 1844, in Boucher and Brooks (eds.), *Calhoun Correspondence*, 229–30.

South Carolina after attending the Baltimore convention Francis W. Pickens crowed, "We have triumphed. Polk is nearer to *us* than any public man who was named. He is a large Slave holder & plants cotton—*free trade*—Texas—States rights *out & out.*" Calhoun threw his personal efforts into the Polk campaign as he had done for no presidential candidate since Andrew Jackson in 1828. When Robert Barnwell Rhett threatened to break the united Calhounite front by dredging up nullification talk in South Carolina, Calhoun promptly disowned and crushed his efforts. Throughout the campaign the Calhounite enthusiasm remained high. In September, Francis Pickens, reporting on an interview with Polk, concluded, *"all is safe for us."*[34]

Unified and enthusiastic about their candidate, southern Democrats turned with jubilation to the presidential campaign itself. The triumph of Texas within the party "ha[d] awakened new energies in the Democracy here, and enkindled an enthusiasm in the great body of the people, that must, in Nov., overwhelm our adversaries." The Raleigh *Standard* proclaimed that with Texas the Democrats of North Carolina had their Whig opponents on the run. A Democratic organizer in Tennessee summed up this new confidence when he wrote: "We will sweep everything before us. We *feel* it—we *know* it. The excitement on the Texas question is carrying and sweeping down every resistance."[35]

III

Texas ensnared southern Whigs, though Henry Clay tried to lead them away from its clutches. Upon hearing in the fall of 1843 that Tyler's campaign to annex Texas had begun in earnest, Clay made known his opposition to annexation, though he made no immediate

34. Tyler, *Tylers*, II, 337–50; Sellers, *Polk*, II, 134–37; Pickens to Henry Conner, May 29, 1844, in Henry Conner Papers (photostats), Division of Manuscripts, Library of Congress; Calhoun to Francis Wharton, July 14, 1844, in Jameson (ed.), *Calhoun Correspondence*, 601; Wiltse, *Calhoun*, III, 187–92; Pickens to James Edward Calhoun, September 14, 1844, in Pickens Papers.

35. Correspondence Committee to Andrew Jackson, July 23, 1844, in Graf *et al.* (eds.), *Johnson Papers*, I, 171–72; Raleigh *Standard*, October 23, 1844; Gideon Pillow to Henry Horn & J. K. Kane, July 2, 1844, quoted in Tyler, *Tylers*, III, 139.

public declaration. During his southern tour in the late winter and early spring of 1844 he professed to find "indifference or opposition to the measure of annexation" in the South. "Of one thing you may be certain," he wrote to John J. Crittenden from Savannah, "that there is no such anxiety for annexation here at the South as you might have been disposed to imagine." Near the end of that journey Clay prepared his famous Raleigh letter opposing annexation. From Raleigh he forwarded it to Washington for publication. "I feel perfectly confident in the ground which I have taken," Clay announced. At that time he anticipated running against Van Buren, who, he felt reasonably certain, shared his feelings on Texas.[36] In sum Clay in late April did not consider Texas an important campaign issue, and he reached that conclusion after traveling across much of the South.

All southern Whigs did not share Clay's assessment of the political impact of Texas. A large pro-Texas meeting held in New Orleans on April 24 had a distinctly bipartisan cast with Whigs very much in evidence. The Whig speaker of the state House of Representatives served as chairman of the meeting while Alexander C. Bullitt, editor of the New Orleans *Bee*, delivered the major address. One of the Texas negotiators in Washington found that "some Southern Whigs" responded most positively to talk of annexation. From Richmond, Virginia, Benjamin Watkins Leigh reported in mid-April, "The public mind here is very full of Texas." According to the Vicksburg *Whig* the Texas issue "has tended greatly to excite the public mind." At the end of April the Milledgeville *Southern Recorder* gave its reading of the southern political pulse: "The public mind is at this moment almost wholly engrossed with the Texas question. It seems to swallow up all the others."[37]

36. Clay to John J. Crittenden, December 5, 1843, quoted in Mrs. Chapman Coleman (ed.), *The Life of John J. Crittenden, with Selections from His Correspondence and Speeches* (2 vols.; Philadelphia: J. B. Lippincott, 1871), I, 207–10; Clay to Willie P. Mangum, April 14, 1844, in Henry Thomas Shanks (ed.), *The Papers of Willie Person Mangum* (5 vols.; Raleigh: State Department of Archives and History, 1950–56), IV, 102; Clay to Crittenden, March 24, April 17, 19, and 21, 1844, all in Crittenden Papers.

37. Winston, "Louisiana and Texas," 93–94; J. Pinckney Henderson to Thomas J. Rusk, April 16, 1844, in Rusk Papers; Leigh to Willie P. Mangum, April 17, 1844, in Shanks (ed.), *Mangum* Papers, IV, 104; Vicksburg *Weekly Whig*, April 8, 1844; Milledgeville *Southern Recorder*, April 30, 1844.

Even though Clay's assessment of southern opinion on Texas differed radically from that of both Democrats and many Whigs, the
two seemingly dissimilar views can be reconciled. The first explanation is chronological. The Texas rampage did not gain full force until
April; by then Clay had already reached the Atlantic seaboard. He
was just a bit too early for the heat of Texas to sear him. The second
and far more important explanation lies in the nature of Clay's tour.
Even if Clay did pass through the Southwest before Texas had grown
beyond the brushfire stage, one would expect a politician of his
ability and experience to sense the potential fury of Texas. But Clay
did not. He moved through the South like a conquering hero.
Everywhere lionized and immersed in adulation, Clay had little
reason to seek out or even to think about unpleasantness. And for
him Texas could not be pleasant. It also seems probable that Clay
assumed himself invincible, though such a hypothesis cannot be
conclusively proved. He shared—in part, created—the overwhelming confidence that pervaded southern Whiggery. He was
their hero, who was leading them to certain victory. He and they
acted as though he had already been elected. Nothing unwanted or
uninvited, like Texas, could crash into either the personal psychology of triumph or the political caravan of victory. In his overconfi-
dence Clay forgot the riot that dramatic sectional issues could spark
in southern politics.

The events following publication of the Raleigh letter reinforced
Clay's predilection to downplay or disregard Texas. As he expected,
Van Buren joined him in publicly declaring against annexation.
Texas did seem like nothing more than a desperate ploy of the
ignominious Tyler. Clay's southern supporters certainly lavished
praise upon the Raleigh letter. "Bold and statesman like," the cry of
the Baton Rouge *Gazette* echoed across the South. In Washington,
Clay had even more firsthand evidence that he had not misread the
southern temper regarding Texas. Southern Whigs in the United
States Senate stood in almost perfect unity with their northern comrades against John Tyler's treaty. Throughout May and early June

southern and northern Whigs fought vigorously and ultimately successfully to defeat the handiwork of the hated Tyler. In the end only one, John Henderson of Mississippi, of nine southern Whigs broke ranks and voted for ratification. As Clay saw it, Texas was inconsequential. Accordingly he informed a key northern Whig: "I am sure you will be pleased to hear from me that I am firmly convinced that my opinion on the Texas question will do me no prejudice at the South."[38]

The southern front, however, was not so quiet as Clay reported—and wanted to believe. Although the southern Whigs stood by their candidate and his platform, they were not immune to the political and psychological impact of Texas. The same newspapers that cheered the Raleigh letter also acknowledged the depth of pro-Texas feeling among southerners. Admitting that the people of Arkansas favored annexation, the Little Rock *Arkansas Gazette* declared that it shared that sentiment. But, the *Gazette* insisted that the circumstances of Tyler's treaty were all wrong. Annexation should await more favorable conditions, which included chiefly getting some kind of advance assurance of Mexico's agreement or acquiescence in order to preclude any chance of war. Similar statements came from Whig newspapers across the South.[39]

Consequently southern Whigs found themselves in an extremely difficult political position. Politically they opposed the Democrats and wanted to win with Clay and their economic platform. At the same time they could not totally oppose the issue raised by the political enemy, the Democrats. Texas struck too deeply and too surely; as southerners, southern Whigs responded to it. The Little

38. Baton Rouge *Gazette*, May 11, 1844; Raleigh *Register*, May 3, 1844; Milledgeville *Southern Recorder*, May 7, 1844; Vicksburg *Weekly Whig*, May 13, 1844; Merk, *Slavery*, 68–82; Clay to Thurlow Weed, May 6, 1844, quoted in Harriet A. Weed (ed.), *Life of Thurlow Weed, Including His Autobiography and a Memoir* (2 vols.; Boston: Houston Mifflin, 1883), II, 120.

39. Little Rock *Arkansas Gazette*, May 24, 1844. See also New Orleans *Bee*, June 6, 1844; Milledgeville *Southern Recorder*, May 7, June 25, 1844; Richmond *Whig*, June 28, 1844; Tuscaloosa *Independent Monitor*, May 15, 1844, quoted in Stephen F. Miller, *The Bench and Bar of Georgia: Memoirs and Sketches, with an Appendix, Containing a Court Roll from 1790 to 1857, etc.* (2 vols.; Philadelphia: J. B. Lippincott, 1858), II, 384.

Rock *Arkansas Gazette* asked the question that troubled the southern Whig leadership, "Will they [southern Whig voters], in their
sudden passion for Texas, forget their fondly cherished principles,
and abandon their leader at the very moment when victory is about
to perch upon his banner?" Far to the east the Raleigh *Register*
revealed an identical concern. A resolution passed by a convention
of Whigs from Georgia's fourth congressional district underscored
the predicament of southern Whigs: "*Resolved,* that though we are
unanimously in favor of a pacific annexation of the Republic of Texas
to the United States, yet we will not suffer the question of im-
mediated [*sic*] annexation to be forced upon us, to our distraction, or
dismemberment, by the diversified Democracy in our Union,
whose object is to establish available issues to themselves at the
expense of discord in our ranks." That resolution was passed on June
3; three weeks later the state Whig convention unanimously iterated: "That we are in favor of the annexation of Texas to the United
States, at the earliest practicable period consistent with the honor
and good faith of the nation." Throughout Mississippi local Whig
clubs and conventions proclaimed the same message.[40]

When the southern Democrats leaped into the presidential campaign with a pro-Texas candidate and a pro-Texas platform, the
Whigs realized that the Democrats intended to make Texas the issue
in the South if at all possible. Initially the Whigs berated Polk as a
political nobody and ridiculed the Democrats for daring to use such
a political pigmy to challenge Henry Clay.[41] At the same time,
however, they recognized that Texas might transform Polk into a
political giant and scuttle the Whig economic platform. Democrats,
the Richmond *Whig* told its readers, "have but one hope for [Polk] in
the South; and that is he may be able to ride the Texas humbug with
success." The *Whig* tried to appear confident that such an outcome
was impossible, but its columns carried more and more Texas-

40. Little Rock *Arkansas Gazette,* June 12, 1844; Raleigh *Register,* July 19, 1844; Milledgeville *Southern Recorder,* June 25, July 2, 1844; James E. Winston, "The Mississippi
Whigs and the Annexation of Texas," *Southwestern Historical Quarterly,* XXIX (1926), 170–
71.
41. Sellers, *Polk,* II, 100–101.

related items. And privately Virginia Whigs admitted, "we begin to fear old Virginia is in danger, with the Texas question hanging over us." In Tennessee, Ephraim Foster remained confident, though he found "the Texas question is the only hobby of our adversaries." To William B. Campbell that fact made the Tennessee outcome doubtful because "this rascally Texas question will mislead some." A Georgia Whig described Texas "as the only difficulty we have." From northern Alabama a Whig stalwart reported that one-fourth of his district had gone to the Democrats on the Texas issue alone. A Whig editor in Tuscaloosa had earlier informed Clay, "the Texas question, forming a new issue, is pushed here with great assiduity by the Democrats." The Vicksburg *Whig* declared that Mississippi Democrats "have concentrated all their might upon 'immediate Annexation'— this is the sole hobby of the party, *fons et origo,* of the principal creed."[42]

This Texas blitz ravaged Whig unity. The strongest reaction was defection. Although turning to the Democrats never became endemic, it did happen, particularly in the Southwest. In Alabama, Mississippi, and Louisiana some Whigs, including former Alabama Congressman George W. Crabb, agreed with Mississippi's Felix Huston. In a public speech Huston, the law partner of Mississippi's best-known Whig Seargent S. Prentiss, identified himself as a true Whig and a firm believer in Whig principles. Even so, convinced that annexation was essential, Huston "was willing to surrender any thing else for that—to drop Mr. Clay—for his opposition to the measure and support any body at all—no matter whom, who favored it." Others tried to diminish the importance of Texas. "The Texas question alarms only at a distance," asserted John J. Crittenden. Agreeing, the Tuscaloosa *Independent Monitor* editorialized in August that Texas had run its political course. Still other Whigs ham-

42. Richmond *Whig,* June 4, 1844; J. J. Fry to William C. Rives, July 3, 1844, in Rives Papers; Foster to John J. Crittenden, July 13, 1844, in Crittenden Papers; William Campbell to David Campbell, July 9, 1844, in Campbell Papers; S. H. Wales to William C. Rives, June 29, 1844, in Rives Papers; H. M. Cunningham to Alexander Stephens, October 21, 1844, in Stephens Papers, Division of Manuscripts, Library of Congress; Stephen F. Miller to Clay, June 20, 1844, quoted in Miller, *Bench and Bar,* II, 386; Vicksburg *Weekly Whig,* August 5, 1844.

mered away with the message that Texas was a humbug, a false issue invented by Tyler and the Democrats to subvert the legitimate economic issues propounded by the Whigs.[43]

There were more variations on a theme. Some denounced annexation as a threat to slavery and the South. Whigs who took this position followed the lead of United States Senator Alexander Barrow of Louisiana and Waddy Thompson of South Carolina, a former minister to Mexico. In public letters both Barrow and Thompson argued that annexation endangered the South because the rich lands of Texas would spark a massive exodus of slaves from the older slave states. This slave drain, according to Barrow and Thompson, would make free states of the border slave states relatively quickly; and inevitably that trend would follow the southwestward march of the slaves. In addition the enormous production of cotton and sugar in Texas would depress the price of those critical staples. Thus, economic prosperity and social security for the South required the defeat of annexation. Other Whigs tried to make of Texas a union-disunion issue. They claimed a Calhounite cabal had made Texas in the image of nullification to threaten the sanctity of the Union; all who loved the Union must put down Texas until the Calhounite taint on annexation was removed.[44] Yet another response, and the one occurring most often in the Whig press, agreed with the Democrats that Texas ought to be annexed. But to the Whigs the Democratic timing was askew. This argument, which had often accompanied the defense of Clay's Raleigh letter, demanded additional diplomatic preparations as well as guarantees against war.[45]

---

43. William Garrett, *Reminiscences of Public Men in Alabama, for Thirty Years with an Appendix* (Atlanta: Plantation, 1872), 53; James Kimmins Greer, "Louisiana Politics, 1845–1861," *Louisiana Historical Quarterly,* XII (1929), 404; Huston speech quoted in McIntosh (ed.), *Davis Papers,* II, 175–76; Crittenden to Waddy Thompson, July 1, 1844, in Waddy Thompson Papers, South Caroliniana Library, University of South Carolina; Tuscaloosa *Independent Monitor,* August 28, 1844; Alexander Stephens to James Thomas, May 17, 1844, in Phillips (ed.), *Toombs, Stephens, Cobb Correspondence,* 58; Richmond *Whig,* June 4, 1844.

44. *Niles' Register,* LXVI (July 13, 1844), 316–19; New Orleans *Bee,* June 3, 1844; Arthur Charles Cole, *The Whig Party in the South* (Gloucester, Mass.: Peter Smith, 1962), 114–15.

45. This argument appeared periodically in every Whig newspaper.

No matter the particular Whig response, each one added to the rhetorical dominance of Texas; even those who claimed Texas a false issue talked about it. While it is impossible to enumerate precisely the number of Whigs making a specific response, the result of the general Whig reaction is clear enough. References in the Whig press to national economic issues, especially a national bank and a protective tariff, decreased through the summer. Texas crowded them out. More and more editorials and letters referred to Texas. In newspapers like the Richmond *Whig* and the Milledgeville *Southern Recorder* the domination of Texas was almost complete. The Raleigh *Register*, on the other hand, evinced a determination not to let Texas completely blot out the economic issues; in the *Register*, Texas had to share billing, but even that sharing was a victory for Texas and the Democrats. The Democrats had forced the Whigs to adopt their vocabulary. Weaning the Whigs away from their economic rhetoric and economic issues, the Democrats gained the rhetorical and political initiative in southern politics, a position they had not enjoyed since before 1835.

Exceptions to the triumph of Texas rhetoric did exist, but the uniqueness of the exceptions emphasizes the victory of Texas. On the extreme western boundary of southern Whiggery, in Arkansas and Louisiana, the major Whig newspapers maintained the economic issues as primary. In both states—Louisiana, where the Whigs had been and were still strong, and Arkansas, where they had always been a distinct minority—a practical unanimity existed on Texas. Almost everybody was for it. Newspapers in both states, particularly in Louisiana, had reported fully on Texas affairs for a decade. Aware of the universality of Texas sentiment and the hopelessness of any antiannexation talk, the New Orleans *Bee* and the Little Rock *Arkansas Gazette* never stopped telling their readers that economic questions ought to govern their politics.

Although the southern Democratic speeches and editorials of the campaign inundated southern voters with the pro-Texas arguments that had dominated their rhetoric since the early spring, they did add one new ingredient to their pro-Texas agenda. The same political force that influenced Van Buren to break his prosouthern pattern assumed considerable importance in the northern Whig campaign against Polk and Texas. Polk and Texas, in the hands of northern Whigs, became the incarnation of an evil South out to destroy liberty and constitutionalism. This approach by his northern supporters created problems for Clay in the South because it fueled the southern Democratic campaign against him. Such tactics enabled the southern Democrats to claim that anybody opposing Texas had to be either in league with abolitionists or dupes of abolitionists. Having already satisfied themselves that they had conclusively demonstrated how critical Texas was for the South, southern Democrats filled their newspapers with claims that northern Whigs were determined to deprive the South of justice. News stories and editorials carrying headlines such as "THE COALITION BETWEEN THE CLAY PARTY, AND THE ABOLITIONISTS OF THE NORTH AND NORTHWEST" abounded. In this manner southern Democrats "poured forth a torrent of abuse upon Mr. Clay and his friends, branding them as abolitionists, who, to strengthen their cause in the North, were willing to destroy the prosperity of the South." Thus no self-respecting southerner could vote for Clay. To do so would mean voting directly against southern interests and also for southern degradation since the abolitionists condemned the South as evil and individual southerners as personally reprehensible.[46]

This Democratic message assumed its most cogent form in a pamphlet brought out by the indefatigable Robert J. Walker. In September, Walker published his second major pamphlet on Texas, *The South in Danger.* [47] This pamphlet in particular and the southern Democratic case for Texas in general provide a glimpse into the future, for they outlined the political and psychological responses

46. Richmond *Enquirer*, August 2, October 19, 1844; Raleigh *Standard*, August 21, October 9, 1844; Jackson *Mississippian*, July 26, September 13, 1844; speech of Henry S. Foote at Port Gibson, Mississippi, on July 1, 1844, quoted in McIntosh (ed.), *Davis Papers*, II, 176.
47. Walker, *The South in Danger* (Washington: n.p., 1844).

that would dominate the southern reaction to the problem of slavery in the territories. In *The South in Danger*, Walker aimed directly at southern voters. "There never was," Walker screamed, "a period when the South was in so much danger as at this moment." The imminent danger resulted from conscious efforts by northern Whigs who, in their eagerness to elect Clay, courted abolitionists. As a result the Whig party had been largely abolitionized. To prove his contention Walker included copious extracts from northern Whigs and abolitionists indicating that they shared common principles, including adamant opposition to the annexation of Texas. In the face of this diabolical alliance Walker insisted that Clay must be defeated, for his victory would mortally endanger the South. As for southern Whigs, Walker declared he counted on their assistance in the battle against Clay because they were southerners before they were Whigs. He concluded by placing a fearful responsibility on the southern Whigs: "Reflect, then, Whigs of the South, our brethren and fellow-citizens, before you sink us all together into one common abyss of ruin and degradation."

In this pamphlet Walker played to the deep-rooted southern preoccupation with honor and to the southern determination to maintain control of their destiny. He emphasized that the northern Whigs had joined with the abolitionists "in holding up the South to obloquy and reproach." According to Walker, northern Whigs now preached the abolitionist gospel that slavery "disgraced and degraded" southerners. These unholy priests condemned the annexation of Texas because it would expand and perpetuate slavery, "*an evil and a curse.*" Then Walker stepped from a disgraced South to a politically inferior South. Walker proclaimed that individual southerners, Democrat and Whig, proud of their southern identity and of their southern institutions must defend their honor by opposing those who would besmirch it. This same act of defense would also insure that the South retained control over its destiny and institutions. Walker reached this point by arguing that the acquisition of Texas was necessary for the South to maintain political parity in

Washington. If Texas were not annexed, then the South would become a minority in the Senate just as it had already become in the House. And, in Walker's picture, no one could doubt the ultimate outcome of an unchecked northern congressional majority. Thus when the South defended southern honor, it protected southern political power and ultimately southern control over the future of the South. Walker's powerful brief summarized the southern Democratic case. It also added to the tremendous pressure on the southern Whigs.

When the southern Democrats hurled words like *traitor* and *treason* at Clay and his party, southern Whigs reacted angrily. And on this question southern Whig ranks knew no division. Bristling at such barbs they shouted that Clay, a son of the South, would never betray his people or his section on Texas or any other issue. They exclaimed that Clay, like any other good southerner, abhorred abolitionists. Denouncing all southern Democratic efforts to brand Clay and the Whig party as "unfavorable to Southern institutions, and opposed to Southern interests," Seargent S. Prentiss spoke for all southern Whigs. Any such charge, Prentiss averred, was "as insulting as it is false."[48]

The pressure squeezing southern Whigs reached to Henry Clay himself. In an effort to bolster his southern supporters and his own image before southern voters Clay again took up his pen. Twice, on July 1 and July 27, he wrote public letters designed to refurbish his southernness. He supplemented them in early September with a public statement, first published in a Lexington, Kentucky newspaper, reemphasizing his adamant opposition to abolition.[49] Al-

48. Prentiss' speech is quoted in James Elliott Walmsley, "The Presidential Campaign of 1844 in Mississippi," *Publications of the Mississippi Historical Society,* IX (1906), 191–92. See also New Orleans *Bee,* November 7, 1843; Vicksburg *Weekly Whig,* November 11, 1844; Little Rock *Arkansas Gazette,* July 10, 1844; Tuscaloosa *Independent Monitor,* June 19, 1844, quoted in Miller, *Bench and Bar,* II, 385.

49. The Alabama letters dated July 1 and July 27, 1844, are printed in *Niles' Register,* LXVI (August 3, 1844), 372 and (August 31, 1844), 439. On the Lexington statement see *ibid.,* LXVII (October 12, 1844), 83, and Sellers, *Polk,* II, 147.

though both the July letters were responses to inquiries from Alabama Whigs, each reached a considerably wider audience through publication. In the first Alabama letter and the Lexington statement he emphatically denied the charge that he had wooed the abolitionists: "As to the idea of my courting the abolitionists, it is perfectly absurd." He claimed, on the contrary, to have been "abused by them more than any other public man in the United States." That first letter tried to downplay Texas by calling it "a bubble blown up by Mr. Tyler." In contrast the Texas issue filled the second Alabama letter. Therein Clay maintained his old position that the time was not propitious for annexation, but he hastened to add: "I have, however, no hesitation in saying that, far from having any personal objection to the annexation of Texas, I should be glad to see it." Although Clay qualified his endorsement of Texas by saying annexation should only come without war and with the support of the entire country, he emphasized that the existence of slavery in Texas did not provide legitimate grounds for excluding Texas from the Union. While Clay had by no means come all the way to the Democratic position, he had bent to the necessity of southern politics.

As the campaign closed, the Democratic issue of Texas had driven Whig economic issues from the center ring of the southern political arena. The politics of slavery reigned once again as the monarch of southern politics. Not only did Texas smash the politics of economics, it also gave the South to Polk. Although it is impossible to prove that Polk would have lost in the South without Texas, the southern Whigs blamed their woes on Texas. "Upon it all our losses in the South & West occurred," wrote Leslie Combs of Kentucky, friend of Clay and Crittenden. Combs even believed that the Whigs held Kentucky only because of Clay. The Richmond *Whig* had no doubt that Texas threw over the Whig economic platform and controlled the campaign. The Raleigh *Register* agreed that Texas had routed the Whig economic issues. Even the New Orleans *Bee,* where economic issues had remained primary, admitted that Texas had been just as important as the tariff in determining the outcome.[50] And after being immersed in Whig and Democratic letters and newspapers I can only concur with the Whigs. To my mind the most striking element in the manuscript record is the shift in attitude. Because of Texas the divided, dispirited Democrats became united and jubilant. Because of Texas the united, jubilant Whigs became, albeit more slowly, fragmented and dispirited.

The returns themselves also indicate that Texas helped the Democrats immensely. In spite of experiencing severe problems in most state elections in 1843 and 1844, the Democrats carried all but two southern states. And Tennessee they lost by only 267 votes while North Carolina went to Clay by just over 4,000 votes. The total number of voters in the South increased by 59,103 between 1840 and 1844, but that increase benefited only the Democrats. Polk's vote exceeded Van Buren's by almost 26 percent; in contrast Clay polled 1,599 fewer votes than Harrison. Thus new voters cast Democratic ballots. In fact Clay received a smaller percentage of the southern popular vote than any of five Whigs who ran for president in the South, except for the last one, Winfield Scott. No state issues had arisen to give that kind of boost to the Democrats; on the basis of the two previous years state issues should have helped the Whigs. Even so, Clay's Alabama letters and his Lexington statement with their forthright declaration against abolition and their hesitant, qualified support of annexation probably enabled Clay to hang on to Tennessee and perhaps even North Carolina. Although such an assertion cannot be proven, it does not seem unlikely that those letters could have swayed the few critical votes, especially the 134 that would have made Tennessee a Democratic state. And in Tennessee at least one Democratic manager was convinced they had that effect.[51]

50. Combs to John M. Clayton, November 30, 1844, in Clayton Papers; Richmond *Whig*, May 2, 1845; Raleigh *Register*, February 7, 1845; New Orleans *Bee*, December 4, 1844.

51. Adam Huntsman to James K. Polk, September 20, 1844, in Adam Huntsman Papers, Manuscript Division, Tennessee State Library and Archives.

Yet Clay did hold the committed Whig vote. Emphasizing the strength of party loyalty, probably few active Whigs voted for Polk. That outcome, however, does not undermine the importance of Texas. By election time southern Whigs stood in no one place on the Texas issue. The southern Democratic offensive had splintered the party's Texas position, a position that had known disunity since spring. In November, southern Whigs could be found all along the spectrum of Texas opinion. Clay himself had moved to placate unhappy southern Whigs. In short the Polk-Clay contest in the South was not a clear-cut referendum with Texas yes or Texas no as the choices.[52] A southerner voting for Polk was surely voting yes, but a southerner voting for Clay could have rationalized his vote as a yes, a no, or even a maybe.

IV

The election of James K. Polk did not shove Texas from the center of the political stage. Although Polk's victory did not guarantee annexation, it did encourage John Tyler to persist in his efforts to make Texas a part of the United States.[53] With only a few months left in his presidency Tyler wanted to consummate annexation before he left office on March 4, 1845. As he saw it, annexation would be the crowning achievement of his administration as well as a proper reward for his own exertions. To accomplish that goal he knew he had to win the cooperation of the Twenty-eighth Congress which convened for its second session on December 2, 1844. In his annual message sent to the Congress on December 3, Tyler interpreted Polk's election as a mandate for annexation. Accordingly he urged this second session to take the step the first had refused to take— annex Texas. Because the same senators who had so decisively rejected his treaty back in June remained in their seats, Tyler knew he had to plot another course if he hoped to reach his goal of annexation.

52. *Cf.* Sellers, *Polk*, II, 159–61, which minimizes the importance of Texas and maximizes party loyalty. In the South the divisions were not so stark.
53. Merk, *Slavery*, Chap. 6 has the basic story of Tyler's moves; for Tyler's message see Richardson (comp.), *Messages and Papers of the Presidents*, IV, 343–45.

This new route would have to get around the unobtainable two-thirds Senate majority needed to ratify a treaty. Thus Tyler called on Congress to annex by congressional resolution. Such a plan required a yea vote in both the House of Representatives and the Senate, but only a simple majority in each house, not a two-thirds majority.

While the resolution path circled around the two-thirds impediment, it ran directly into a constitutional obstacle. The opponents of Tyler and Texas objected that the Constitution stipulated treaties as the proper instrument for agreements between the United States and any other independent nation. And Texas was clearly a separate country. Rejecting that contention, the administration and its allies claimed that Article IV, Section 3 of the Constitution permitted the Congress to admit new states into the Union. This argument asserted that Texas would be a new state and that condition made annexation by resolution totally legitimate. In spite of the constitutional question the presidential suggestion of annexation by resolution evoked a positive response from many representatives and senators. In December and on into the winter of the new year resolutions were proposed, and debate on annexation dominated the national legislature.

Tyler's determination to press on with annexation insured that southern politicians remained preoccupied with Texas. Happily married to the partner that had rejuvenated them, southern Democrats joyfully joined Tyler's crusade for annexation by resolution. The southern Whigs, on the other hand, found Texas just as troublesome after November as they had during the campaign months. Whigs on both sides of the Texas question identified it as the agent disrupting unity in the state parties. Not all went so far as the Richmond *Whig*, which blamed Texas for rupturing the Virginia party and giving the spring elections of 1845 to the Democrats, but others were deeply concerned about the impact of Texas on state party harmony and success.[54]

54. Richmond *Whig*, May 2, 1845. See also Charles J. Jenkins to John M. Berrien, February 3, 15, 1845, both in Berrien Papers; Thomas W. Thomas to Alexander Stephens, February 21, 1845, in Stephens Papers, Manhattanville College.

Texas continued to act as a powerful centrifugal force intent on pulling apart southern Whiggery. Southern Whigs saw good reason to stand adamantly against Tyler's annexation hopes. Opposition would help preserve party unity, for northern Whigs unanimously opposed annexation. Texas came from the hated Tyler; annexation would reward him. Because Texas had become a Democratic issue, to defeat it meant beating the political enemy. Political motives were not the only ones that influenced southern Whigs in the Texas battle. Tyler's new strategy of annexation by resolution offended the constitutional scruples of men like Virginia's William C. Rives who made a major Senate speech branding annexation by resolution as completely unconstitutional. Other southern Whigs sincerely believed, along with the Richmond *Whig,* that annexation would release forces that "this generation will witness to be productive of the bitterest fruits, social and political, possibly of the most extensive irreparable calamities!" The Raleigh *Register* spoke of "melancholy foreboding" when it contemplated the results of annexation.[55]

On the other hand strong popular sentiment plus a sincere concern felt for southern safety prompted a positive response by southern Whigs to Tyler's new call. On January 14, 1845, the Louisiana legislature, with a Whig majority in both houses, voted overwhelmingly for a resolution favoring annexation. The legislators instructed the governor to forward it to the state's congressional delegation. The Whigs in the Virginia legislature announced that a majority in Virginia favored annexation by any constitutional method. Noting that Virginia action, the Milledgeville *Southern Recorder* expressed the conviction that all in Georgia agreed with the Virginia Whigs. The Tuscaloosa *Independent Monitor* refused to make opposition to annexation a test of Whig loyalty. According to the *Independent Monitor* the southern people spoke for immediate annexation when they voted for Polk. In the *Independent Monitor*'s view, then, any

55. *Congressional Globe,* 28th Cong., 2nd Sess., Appendix, 378–82; Richmond *Whig,* February 25, 1845; Raleigh *Register,* March 7, 1845. See also Willie P. Mangum to Tod R. Caldwell, February 20, 1845, in Shanks (ed.), *Mangum Papers,* IV, 268; A. M. Meid to John M. Berrien, June 13, 1845, in Berrien Papers.

southern Whig in Congress was totally justified in supporting annexation. Finding nothing wrong with annexation by resolution the New Orleans *Bee* indicated satisfaction with the prospect of annexation.[56]

Northern Whigs did not make it easy for their southern colleagues to stand along side them and reject Texas. During 1844 and during the winter of the final debate northern Whigs made a great effort to define Texas as distinctly a slavery issue. According to them the annexation of Texas was a proslavery plot. Thus all who backed annexation supported the proslavery cause, and all who opposed it believed in antislavery or, at the least, antisouthern principles. This syllogism simply reversed the deduction of the southern Democrats. And just as the southern Democratic logic appealed to some southern Whigs, the northern reasoning repelled many of them. Southern Whigs in the Congress saw this sectional attack on the South and slavery firsthand, for northern memorials and resolutions steeped in anti-South and antislavery rhetoric flooded the Congress. Speaking for many southern Whigs, Robert Toombs, a rising star among them, condemned northern Whigs for "foolishly not to say wickedly narrowing it [Texas] down to a single question of pro & anti Slavery." Toombs clearly perceived the danger to southern Whigs from such a strategy; he feared it would be "the reason with many & the excuse with many more of our friends in the South" for deserting the Whig flag.[57]

Faced with such disunity and division back home southern congressional Whigs writhed in the personal and political torment of Texas. While the congressional debate raged through the winter of 1844–1845, the enormous pressure on all southern Whigs focused on those in Congress. The decision would be made in Congress, and the southern Whigs there could not escape being a part of it. Their

56. Winston, "Louisiana and Texas," 103; Milledgeville *Southern Recorder*, February 11, 1845; Tuscaloosa *Independent Monitor*, February 12, 1845; New Orleans *Bee*, February 4, 1845.

57. Merk, *Slavery*, 126–34 has a discussion of the northern Whig attitude; Toombs to John M. Berrien, February 13, 1845, in Berrien Papers.

northern colleagues testified to the extraordinary pressure bearing down upon the southern brethren. The voting pattern of the congressional southern Whigs also records the traumatic effect of Texas. Out of the several annexation resolutions proposed in the House, the one that ultimately passed was introduced by Milton Brown, a Tennessee Whig. When Brown's resolution cleared the House by 120 to 98 on January 25, Brown and eight other southern Whigs voted aye while seven cast nay votes and one did not vote. Of course all the southern Democrats endorsed it. In the Senate the southern Whigs managed a more united front; only two of nine said yes to the annexation resolution that passed the Senate. John Henderson of Mississippi had voted for Tyler's treaty but Henry Johnson of Louisiana changed his stance. Those two votes were critical for the Texas cause because the Senate approved the resolution on February 27 by the extremely narrow margin of 27 to 25. The Senate reversed its earlier stand because northern Democrats toed the party line on Texas and because two southern Whigs broke ranks.[58]

After a year and a half John Tyler had reached his goal. With only hours left in his presidency, Tyler hurried to implement annexation. Although many in Congress, especially northern Democrats, expected the new president, James K. Polk, to act on the resolution, John Tyler was not to be denied. With Calhoun's ardent encouragement he dispatched a messenger to Texas offering annexation under the terms of the resolution. Neither he nor Calhoun feared that Polk would object; after all both Polk and his platform stood squarely on their Texas ground. They assumed correctly; upon taking office Polk did not disrupt the events set in motion by his predecessor.

Finally Texas was over. It had provided John Tyler with the great issue of his administration. It had also galvanized the southern

---

58. Daniel Webster to Franklin Haven, February 2, [1845], in Daniel Webster Papers, Houghton Library, Harvard University and Daniel Webster to Edward Everett, February 26, 1845, in Edward Everett Papers, Massachusetts Historical Society; *House Journal*, 28th Cong., 2nd Sess., 264–65; *Senate Journal*, 28th Cong., 2nd Sess., 220.

Democrats and had given them a presidential election and a renewed sense of their power in their party. In contrast it had smashed the high hopes of southern Whigs, shattered their unity, and endangered their relations with their northern associates. Texas had an even more profound impact: it destroyed the politics of economics. Never again during the life of the second party system would economics or any other topic challenge the supremacy of the politics of slavery.

7 Advent of the Territorial Question

I

THE DEFEAT OF Henry Clay stunned southern Whigs. On the eve of the election the Richmond *Whig* had proclaimed: "If J. K. Polk prevails over Henry Clay, the *WHIG PARTY IS NO MORE!*" By their reaction to Clay's loss southern Whigs turned the dire prediction of the *Whig* into somber reality. While Clay himself spoke of Polk's victory as "so unexpected," his southern followers described a considerably graver situation. Confessing in December, 1844, "that defeat has unmanned us," the Tuscaloosa *Independent Monitor* admitted, "It was a shock from which it will be long before we can recover." The governor of Georgia agreed. In a New Year's letter to John M. Berrien, George W. Crawford made a discouraging assessment: "We are, in Georgia, in a state of bankruptcy as to political feeling—all lost or squandered on the Presidential Election." "Politically, we Whigs are as dead as a skined [*sic*] Coon," moaned a disconsolate Tennessee Whig. As late as the fall of 1846, Willie P. Mangum defined the chief goal of Whiggery as "avoid[ing] a collapse." A Whig editor in Liberty, Mississippi, captured this melancholy in two sad little verses:

> Hark, from the pines a doleful sound,
> Mine ears, attend the cry,
> Ye living Whigs, come view the ground,
> Where all your coons do lie.
>
> Coonies! this Clay will be your bed,
> In spite of all your braggers;
> The old, the wise, the reverend heads,
> Have all got the blind staggers.[1]

---

1. Richmond *Whig*, November 1, 1844; Clay to John M. Berrien, January 14, 1845, and Crawford to Berrien, January 1, 1845, both in Berrien Papers; Tuscaloosa *Independent*

This gloomy outlook plus the divisive effect of Texas upset Whig fortunes in state politics. The state elections held in 1845 and 1846 produced one cheerless result after another for the shaken Whigs, not only in a state like Arkansas, where they had become a permanent minority, but also in those states where they battled Democrats on basically even terms. The Virginia spring elections of 1845 started the unpleasant trend for the Whigs; reversing the outcome of 1844 the Democrats won the day in the Old Dominion. During the summer of 1845 Whig setbacks continued. For the first time since 1839, Tennessee Democrats captured the governor's chair and both houses of the legislature. Democrats in Georgia gained control of the state senate and cut the winning Whig gubernatorial margin by half of the 1843 total, to only 1751 votes. In 1846 Louisiana Democrats held on to the governorship and secured a majority in both houses of the legislature, a first since the birth of Louisiana Whiggery. The Whigs maintained themselves without blemish only in North Carolina, where in 1846 they reelected a governor and retained a legislative majority in the state senate and the state house. The two new states admitted to the Union in 1845, Texas and Florida, added to the woes of the Whigs. The Whigs did not even have an organized party in Texas, whose very existence as a state most of the party had fought. Although Florida had an active Whig organization, the first state elections in 1845 brought a complete Democratic triumph. The Democrats elected the governor and an overwhelming majority in both houses of the legislature, a majority they kept, though slightly diminished, in the 1846 elections.

While caught in these political doldrums, southern Whigs had to

Monitor, December 18, 1844; James Seawell to William A. Graham, January 10, 1845, in J. G. de Roulhac Hamilton and Max R. Williams (eds.), *The Papers of William Alexander Graham* (5 vols.; Raleigh: State Department of Archives and History, 1957–), III, 14–15; Mangum to Paul C. Cameron, November 8, 1846, in Henry Thomas Shanks (ed.), *The Papers of Willie Person Mangum* (5 vols.; Raleigh: State Department of Archives and History, 1950–56), IV, 514; poem quoted in James Elliott Walmsley, "The Presidential Campaign of 1844 in Mississippi," *Publications of the Mississippi Historical Society,* IX (1906), 196–97. Coon became a fairly common appellation for Whigs after the Log Cabin campaign.

confront the war that many of them had predicted, that most of them feared, and that few of them wanted. The antagonism between the United States and Mexico erupted in May, 1846, when at the behest of President Polk, Congress declared war for the first time since 1812. Although many southern Whigs believed President Polk personally responsible for the hostilities, they did not take an open stand against the war. Three basic reasons explain that decision. First, they believed it their patriotic duty to support the military effort during a national crisis. Second, the war was generally popular in the South just as the annexation of Texas had been; to oppose it as a party meant placing Whiggery in opposition to public opinion. Third, southern Whigs remembered the fate of the Federalist party. The Federalists had denounced the War of 1812, and the surge of national pride following that war had helped destroy their party. Whigs did not want history to repeat itself in the 1840s. Southern Whigs came up with no real solution to their dilemma. Without enthusiasm they went along with providing men and money for the American army. They had decided to wait "for a proper occasion" to settle the question of blame. But never did they identify the war as their war.[2]

Not only the outbreak of war but also its probable results troubled southern Whigs. If the United States emerged victorious, and almost everybody expected that outcome, such a victory most probably meant the acquisition of territory previously owned by Mexico. To Whigs the politics of territorial expansion sounded frighteningly like a repeat of the politics of Texas annexation. As they saw it, expansion and slavery would become inextricably intertwined. As a result severe sectional strains would once again plague the Whig party and, at the same time, threaten the South. The fear became reality in August, 1846; when congressmen voted on the Wilmot

2. Milledgeville *Southern Recorder*, August 25, 1846; William B. Campbell to David Campbell, January 16, 1845, in Campbell Papers; George W. Crawford to John M. Berrien, November 28, 1846, in Berrien Papers; Nicholas W. Woodfin to William A. Graham, June 11, 1846, in Hamilton and Williams (eds.), *Graham Papers*, III, 131.

Proviso, which prohibited slavery in any territory gained from Mexico, they divided along sectional lines.[3]

Aware of the difficulties Texas had made for party harmony and hoping to avoid the wrenching experience of a general debate on slavery and expansion, some southern Whigs moved to eliminate the source of potential trouble, Led by Congressman Alexander Stephens and Senator John M. Berrien, both of Georgia, these southern Whigs attempted to place the Congress on record as opposing the annexing of any Mexican territory as a result of the war. That cry echoed from many Whig lips. In proposing no more territory these southern Whigs did not speak against slavery or the rights of the South. Quite the contrary, they insisted that slavery could never be successfully implanted in the barren southwestern desert—thus the new land could not benefit the South. Instead it would endanger the South and slavery by increasing the power of the North and by giving renewed vigor to the cause of abolitionism. According to this rhetoric all southerners truly committed to the protection and salvation of the South must oppose acquiring Mexican territory. This argument convinced neither the Congress nor the southern Democrats. And in all probability it could never have swayed southern public opinion, though such an assertion cannot be proven. No matter, for the continuing success of American arms below the Rio Grande made the Whig position obsolete.[4]

American victories on battlefield after battlefield in Mexico spotlighted the territorial issue and insured that it would dominate political debate in the United States and certainly in the South. In fact by 1847 and 1848 no other issues challenged the supremacy of the territorial question. The national economic issues which had been so

3. William B. Campbell to David Campbell, November 20, 1847, in Campbell Papers; Milledgeville *Southern Recorder*, February 16, 1847; Richmond *Whig*, February 19, 1847; [Thomas L. Clingman (ed.)], *Selections from the Speeches and Writings of Hon. Thomas L. Clingman, of North Carolina, with Additions and Explanatory Notes* (Raleigh: John Nichols, 1877), 197.

4. Arthur Charles Cole, *The Whig Party in the South* (Gloucester, Mass.: Peter Smith, 1962), 119–23.

central in southern politics during the early 1840s did not survive the Texas explosion. Texas shunted them aside, and between 1845 and 1848 they disappeared. On the national level the tariff of 1846 and the Independent or Constitutional Treasury reestablished in that same year represented the last major engagements of the politics of economics. On the Democratic tariff, which lowered the Tariff of 1842, and on the Democratic Independent Treasury, which again made the government its own fiscal agent, southern Whigs and Democrats voted in almost perfect unity on opposite sides—the Democrats for both, the Whigs against both.[5]

Southern politicians recognized that the economic issues had passed from the scene. As early as 1845 Aaron V. Brown, during his successful race for governor of Tennessee, announced that he would not discuss a national bank or any related matter. "All these are now dead and buried questions," Brown declared. However, they were still important in northeastern North Carolina in 1845. When the Whig Asa Biggs fought and won his election to Congress that year, a national bank and the tariff dominated the canvass. But two years later, according to Biggs, they were not discussed at all. In that same year, 1847, congressional candidates in Mississippi from both parties joined in pronouncing the death of financial issues. That view was also held by Zachary Taylor, who had already become a chief topic of conversation among southerners. The New Orleans *Bee*, the Little Rock *Arkansas Gazette*, and the Tuscaloosa *Independent Monitor* all announced that banks and tariffs had expired as issues in southern politics. By 1848 politicians across the South agreed with the dictum of the *Bee*: "Old party issues are worn out and have nearly disappeared."[6]

5. Thomas B. Alexander, *Sectional Stress and Party Strength: A Study of Roll-Call Voting Patterns in the United States House of Representatives* (Nashville: Vanderbilt University Press, 1967), 189, 190, 192, 193.

6. Editors of the Union and American (eds.), *Speeches, Congressional and Political, and Other Writings of ex-Governor Aaron V. Brown of Tennessee* (Nashville: J. S. Marling, 1854– [55]), 185; *Autobiography of Asa Biggs*, ed. R. D. W. Connor (Raleigh: Edwards & Broughton, 1915), 9–11; Taylor to Robert C. Wood, September 27, 1847, in William H.

Likewise the bitter partisan division over financial policy that had characterized state politics in the early 1840s ended. After 1845, Whigs and Democrats from Virginia to Arkansas largely dropped from their political lexicon references to banks, specie payment, repudiation, and similar terms that had been the common political language only a short time before. State financial issues disappeared for many reasons but three seem most important: the general upturn in the southern economy which occurred in the middle of the decade; the political resolution of divisive questions, for example, the final dissolution of the Central Bank of Georgia; the transfer from the political stage of important issues, for example, the new Louisiana Constitution of 1845 prohibited the chartering of any new banks. Although the precise timing of the demise of financial issues varied from state to state, the conclusion reached by the closest student of Mississippi's financial politics holds for the entire South: "Thus, by 1847 banking was no longer the inflammatory issue it had been." [7]

With economic issues no longer providing a platform and with the acquisition of new Mexican territory apparently inescapable, southern Whigs had to come to grips with the territorial question. Failure to do so meant handing the South to the Democrats. As veterans of the politics of slavery and as loyal southerners, they had no difficulty making their basic decision regarding the territories. Southern rights in all newly obtained lands had to be affirmed. Accordingly southern Whigs proclaimed their unalterable opposition to the Wilmot Proviso and all it implied. Although the Congress first dealt with the proviso in August, 1846, widespread southern notice of the proviso and the concurrent condemnation of the effort to exclude slavery from the territories did not commence until 1847. And the Whigs contributed significantly to the rising southern chorus against the proviso. Condemnation of it in the harshest language became

Samson (ed.), *Letters of Zachary Taylor from the Battle-Fields of the Mexican War* (Rochester, N. Y.: Genesee Press, 1908), 134–35; New Orleans *Bee*, March 23, 1848; Tuscaloosa *Independent Monitor*, March 16, 1848; Little Rock *Arkansas Gazette*, June 22, 1848.

7. James Roger Sharp, *The Jacksonians versus the Banks: Politics in the States after the Panic of 1837* (New York & London: Columbia University Press, 1970), 87, 115, 246.

the common rhetoric of Whig editors and speakers. Southern Whigs insisted that all in the South stood resolute against any discriminatory restrictions on slavery in the territories. According to the Whigs any attempt to erect such barriers against slavery would meet implacable southern opposition.[8]

While the southern Whigs struggled with Texas and unpleasant election returns, their Democratic counterparts enjoyed the fruits of victory. Texas had cemented a Democratic unity unknown since the first administration of Andrew Jackson. And as the Whigs suffered through adversity in the state elections of 1845 and 1846, those same elections only increased Democratic joy. The end of state financial issues also made a significant contribution to the political health of the Democrats. The economic and financial problems following the Panic of 1837, and the debate over how to handle them had created considerably more pain for the southern Democrats than for the southern Whigs. From the Conservative defection in Virginia in the late 1830s through the dissension in Arkansas and Mississippi in the early 1840s to the dissident Alabama gubernatorial ticket in 1845, Democrats had fought among themselves over financial matters as well as against the Whigs. After 1845 those divisive economic questions no longer tugged with the same force at Democratic unity.

Texas meant expansion, and the southern Democrats adopted expansion as their own flesh and blood. They looked to expansion to bring political advantage to them as well as glory to the Union and the South. The advent of the Mexican War bothered them not at all; happily they joined behind their president. With southern opinion excited about expansion and enthusiastic about the war that seemed to herald more of it the Democrats seemingly had the Whigs on the political run. Most certainly they had recouped their bleak fortunes of 1843 and early 1844. In a period of little more than a year the South witnessed a political somersault. The Democrats had taken over the political initiative while the Whigs found themselves crouched on the defensive.

8. See p. 240 herein.

The war, however, did not turn out to be the uncomplicated political bonanza the southern Democrats had anticipated. Instead it sparked a double reaction that threatened not only the party's hegemony but even its very existence. First John C. Calhoun refused to heed Polk's call for an offensive war into Mexico. While quite ready to support a defensive stand along the Rio Grande against a Mexican invasion, Calhoun refused to go further without deliberation. Troubled by President Polk's demand for hasty congressional action on the war bill and fearful that Polk was usurping the warmaking power of Congress, Calhoun sat silently in his seat when the Senate voted for war. Calhoun knew that his reaction to the war would be viewed as a hostile act toward the president and the party. But, then, loyalty to either had never been a central feature of his political career. In this instance Calhoun carried with him practically none of his loyalists outside South Carolina. In contrast to their leader most of them shared the general southern exuberance for the war. Although Calhoun alone could not undo Polk's war plans, he could embarrass the party and the administration. In little more than six months Calhoun showed just how embarrassing when he and three of his southern disciples voted with the Whigs to bar from the Senate floor Thomas Ritchie, who had become editor of the major administration newspaper, the Washington *Union*. [9]

The second and far more serious Democratic problem caused by the conflict with Mexico came from the opposite end of the party, from the disciples of Martin Van Buren. On August 8, 1846, an obscure Democratic congressman from Pennsylvania proposed to the House of Representatives an amendment to a bill appropriating two million dollars that President Polk hoped would help him buy peace and territory from Mexico. David Wilmot's proposal, which

9. Charles M. Wiltse, *John C. Calhoun* (3 vols.; Indianapolis and New York: Bobbs-Merrill, 1944–51), III, 282–89, 297–302; Thomas J. Rusk to David Rusk, July 8, 1846, in Rusk Papers; J. W. McClung to James K. Polk, December 22, 1847, in Polk Papers; Edward A. O'Neal to George S. Houston, May 25, 1846, in George S. Houston Papers, William R. Perkins Library, Duke University.

became known as the Wilmot Proviso, declared that slavery could never exist in any territory bought or taken from Mexico. The Wilmot Proviso dramatized the issue, slavery in the territories, that would dominate national politics for the next fifteen years until bullets replaced words. The motivation behind the introduction of the Wilmot Proviso has long interested historians. The two most recent interpretations of the proviso differ on its origins. One sees it as an offensive move: Van Burenites, angry about the defeat of their leader and their loss of influence in Polk's administration, devised the proviso to strike back against the dominant southerners. They wanted to build a North-West coalition that would downgrade the importance of southerners in the party. The other interpretation argues that the Van Burenites were on the defensive, not the offensive. Hard pressed by a growing antislavery sentiment among their constituents, the Van Burenites wanted to return slavery to the place they felt it had occupied under Andrew Jackson and Martin Van Buren—outside the mainstream of the Democratic party. In this scheme Texas and the Mexican War had revolutionized the position of slavery in the party by placing it in the forefront. Thus the adherents of the proviso wanted to undo that revolution.[10]

Southern Democrats, for whom slavery had always been central, had little difficulty in perceiving exactly what the proviso meant for them and their party. In the first place the mere existence of the proviso meant the sectional strains that had plagued the Whigs on Texas now beset the Democrats on expansion, the issue the Democrats themselves had chosen as their own. The proviso also announced to southerners that they had to face the challenge of certain northern Democrats who indicated their unwillingness to follow any longer the southern lead on slavery. That circumstance struck at the very roots of the southern conception of the party. The southern-

10. Chaplain W. Morrison, *Democratic Politics and Sectionalism: The Wilmot Proviso Controversy* (Chapel Hill: University of North Carolina Press, 1967), Chap. 1, argues for the offense while Eric Foner, "The Wilmot Proviso Revisited," *Journal of American History*, LVI (1969), 262–79, makes the defensive case.

ers had always felt that their northern colleagues must toe the southern line on all slavery-related issues. If the proviso challenge were not put down, then southern Democrats knew they faced a bleak future before southern voters. By denouncing the Democrats for associating with those opposing the South and slavery the Whigs would reap a bountiful political crop unless the Democrats excised the proviso from the body of their party.

The two Democratic problems spawned by the war rapidly merged into one. As Chaplain W. Morrison's excellent account shows, the chief topic among southern Democrats in 1847 and 1848 became the proper reaction to the proviso.[11] Obviously no southern Democrat had any intention of allowing it to become party policy, but such a truism provided little help on political tactics. Regular Democrats did not think the introduction of the proviso called for an immediate break with their northern colleagues. Still viewing the party as good, and eager to retain the rewards it offered, they wanted only to squash the proviso. They believed that they could repeat the destruction of Martin Van Buren by flexing their political muscle, by denouncing the proviso and all who stood for it.

But the southern Democrats did not operate in total freedom, for they had to contend with John C. Calhoun. Just as Calhoun had played a major role on Texas, so he would have great influence on the Democratic response to the proviso. Although Calhoun took few with him in his opposition to the war—in fact that course lost him considerable standing among Democrats—the proviso offered him a real opportunity. Because it represented such a direct strike at the South, Calhoun saw it as a vehicle for his politics of confrontation and thought it just might provide the propellant for his dearly held ambition of a southern party. To one of his followers he wrote in the fall of 1847: "I am of the impression that if the South act as it ought, the Wilmot proviso, instead of proving to be the means of successfully assailing us and our peculiar institution, may be made the

11. Morrison, *Democratic Politics*, Chap. 3 and pp. 107–20.

occasion of [our] successfully asserting our equality and rights by enabling us to force the issue on the North." [12] His followers took up the cudgels. The regular Democrats found their Calhounite kinsmen hounding them for a firm and forthright public stand against the proviso. The Calhounites were determined that they, and not the slaves of party, would set the tone of the southern response.

The regular Democrats could not rebuff the Calhounites. Already they felt pressure from the Whigs; everywhere in the South, Whig orators and editors blasted the Democrats for coddling proviso adherents in their party. Also in the state elections of 1847 the Whigs made a strong comeback in the closely contested states. They elected a governor in Tennessee; they won control of both houses in the legislature in Georgia and Florida; they regained control of the state house of representatives in Louisiana. Although these results cannot be explained totally by the proviso, they underscore the pressure on the southern Democrats. Facing this Whig surge, the Democrats did not need a general defection of Calhounites. Thus without a murmur the regulars went down the Calhounite road. From legislatures and state Democratic conventions the Democratic line emerged clear and strong. It had two overriding themes; both would be cardinal tenets of the southern Democrats down to the upheaval of 1860. In February, 1847, the Virginia legislature adopted unanimously a set of resolutions proposed by Lewis Harvie, a Calhounite Democrat. Harvie's resolutions became known as the Platform of the South. They pledged Virginia and Virginia Democrats to "determined resistance" against the proviso "at all hazards and to the last extremity." Four months later the Georgia state Democratic convention, prompted by a friend of Calhoun, proclaimed that Georgia Democrats would support "no candidate for the presidency of the United States who does not unconditionally, clearly, and unequivocally declare his opposition to the principles and provisions

12. Calhoun to Percy Walker, October 26, 1847, quoted *ibid.*, 38.

of the Wilmot Proviso." The actions in Virginia and Georgia were cheered across the South; their impact on party politics was unmistakable. As Professor Morrison has written, "Under the prodding of Calhoun's movement for southern unity, a significant portion of the southern Democracy had made a northern Democratic disavowal of the Wilmot Proviso a *sine qua non* of its continued participation in the national party."[13]

The embrace between the Calhounites and the regular Democrats on the Wilmot Proviso represented considerably more than a marriage of political convenience. In the aftermath of the Wilmot Proviso the two groups stood much closer together than historians have usually admitted.[14] Although the regulars certainly did not accept either Calhoun's basic antipathy toward parties or his strategy of political confrontation, they were southerners who defended their section and its particular social system. That shared background and interest made a powerful mark in the larger political world. Moreover the regular southern Democrats carried as an article of faith the postulate that the national Democratic party must accept not only slavery but also southern control of any political issue related to slavery. For the southerners the other goods inherent in party allegiance came to naught without that special relationship between themselves and the northern Democrats.

President James K. Polk provides an apt illustration of the similarities between the regulars and the Calhounites. Polk was a southerner but he had never been in Calhoun's orbit. On the contrary, he prided himself on his nationalist outlook. In political terms he always emphasized the necessity for holding securely to the northern connection. His devotion to the national Democratic party as a good matched that of Thomas Ritchie. Yet President Polk's

13. Richmond *Enquirer*, February 17, 18, March 9, 1847; Milledgeville *Federal Union*, July 6, 1847; Wilson Lumpkin to Calhoun, August 27, 1847, in Chauncey S. Boucher and Robert P. Brooks (eds.), *Correspondence Addressed to John C. Calhoun, 1837–1849* (Washington: U. S. Government Printing Office, 1930), 398; Morrison, *Democratic Politics*, 51.

14. See, for example, Joel H. Silbey, "The Southern National Democrats, 1845–1861," *Mid-America*, XLVII (1965), 176–90.

attitude toward the proviso bore a striking resemblance to Calhoun's. That conjunction did not arise from political brotherhood, for after Calhoun came out in opposition to the war Polk counted him a political enemy. Still from 1846 to the end of his administration Polk was as implacably opposed to the proviso and the sentiment behind it as was Calhoun.

Polk never accepted the contention of the proviso forces that the expansion of slavery was an evil.[15] Instead he perceived the proviso, not the expansion of slavery, as the sectional evil that threatened the unity of his party and of his country. Polk viewed the relationship between national expansion and slavery much as did his great mentor Andrew Jackson. Adopting the stance Jackson had taken on Texas in 1843 and 1844, Polk insisted that he had no desire to extend slavery per se. He denied that slavery or its expansion had any connection with the aims of the Mexican War. But, as did Jackson, Polk thought the flag protected slavery; the two could not be separated morally or legally because the South was an integral part of the country and the Constitution sanctioned southern slavery. In Polk's view the proviso was un-American; those who pushed for it and for its political arm the Free Soil party Polk condemned as "wicked."

Polk wanted to resolve the territorial dispute in a traditional political manner. He had no patience with the moral absolutes of the proviso men, for he saw no fundamental moral issue at stake. He advocated extending the Missouri Compromise line westward through all the territory won from Mexico even to the Pacific Ocean. When this solution proved to be impossible politically, he indicated his willingness to accept the Clayton Compromise, which proposed to place the slavery question in the hands of the federal judiciary in the territories. Polk did not consider the Clayton plan as a method of camouflaging the imposition of the proviso. Determined to protect the rights of the South and slavery, as he saw them, he assured

15. This analysis of Polk and the proviso is based on Polk's presidential diary; in it he spoke candidly and at length about the proviso. Milo Milton Quaife (ed.), *The Diary of James K. Polk during His Presidency, 1845–1849* (4 vols.; Chicago: A. C. McClurg, 1910), II, 289, 305, III, 501–503, IV, 17–21, 67–78, 254, 366–67.

Calhoun, "I [will] do my duty," in appointing the judges who would rule on the fate of slavery. Polk said his friends "must have a 'generous confidence' that I would do so."

From the day of the proviso's introduction to the end of his term Polk was prepared to veto any territorial bill that included the proviso or even suggested it. In 1848 he accepted the bill organizing Oregon without slavery only after making clear that he did so only because Oregon lay above the old Missouri Compromise line. And he was furious when his statement was not read to the Congress. When he went to the Capitol on the last full day of his presidency to affix the presidential signature on late bills, he carried with him a prepared message vetoing the proviso. A measure with the proviso did not come to him on March 3, 1849, but if it had, Polk was prepared "to do my duty."

Polk's intransigent, even belligerent, opposition to the proviso provides clear evidence of the depth of southern feeling—a feeling that extended from the most ideologically committed to the most politically minded of southerners. In addition Polk's attitude shows once again that the politics of slavery, while providing election gasconade, also and more importantly plumbed the wellspring of southern society.

II

The Wilmot Proviso sparked such a powerful reaction in the South because southerners correctly identified it as a potentially lethal assault on their political power, on their safety, on their honor. The southern response to it replayed the script of Texas annexation on a grander scale—grander for two reasons. The Texas issue concerned only one specific place while the Wilmot Proviso referred to a wide, undefined expanse of land. In addition no partisan differences restrained the full cry of southern outrage at the proviso. Most southern Whigs had never been enthusiastic about Texas, though many of them eventually adopted at least a mild pro-Texas position. With the proviso, however, the Whig crescendo equaled the Democratic.

John C. Calhoun and his followers clearly stated the southern view. To his daughter Calhoun wrote in 1846 that if southerners regarded their safety, "they must defeat it [the proviso], even should the union be rent asunder." As Francis Pickens, a Calhoun associate in South Carolina, saw it, the South simply could not accept the proviso. To do so meant changing the terms of national equality and that, in Pickens' view, the South could not do "without *feeling* our *degradation.*" Pickens had no intention of living in such a condition. Asserting that the South must have equality in the territories, a young Alabama Calhounite declared, "Death is preferable to acknowledged inferiority."[16]

Calhoun and his disciples had no monopoly on such views. Regular Democrats struck at the proviso with identical rhetoric. Senator William R. King of Alabama did not mince words: "We cannot and will not consent to be excluded from a fair participation in all that belongs, or may hereafter be acquired by the Joint efforts of the confederacy." "I deem it to be our duty as a State," newly elected Governor William Trousdale announced to Tennesseeans in 1849, "to proclaim . . . our unalterable purpose of maintaining our rights, at all hazards and to the last extremity." To his old political comrade-in-arms Martin Van Buren, Peter V. Daniel, formerly a leading Virginia Democrat but in 1849 a veteran of almost ten years on the Supreme Court of the United States, expressed amazement at the "arrogant pretension" of the proviso supporters. Never, Daniel warned, would southerners permit their exclusion from the common territory.[17] Although Daniel did not spell out the practical

16. Calhoun to Mrs. Thomas G. Clemson, December 27, 1846, in J. Franklin Jameson (ed.), *Correspondence of John C. Calhoun* (Washington: Government Printing Office, 1900), 716; Pickens to James Buchanan, June 4, 1847, in Buchanan Papers; Jabez L. M. Curry to James H. Joiner, July 19, 1847, in Jabez L. M. Curry Papers, Division of Manuscripts, Library of Congress.

17. King to James Buchanan, June 11, 1847, in Buchanan Papers and to J. W. Womack, March 10, 1849, in William R. King Papers, Southern Historical Collection, University of North Carolina; Robert H. White (ed.), *Messages of the Governors of Tennessee* (8 vols.; Nashville: Tennessee Historical Commission, 1952–72), IV, 303; Daniel to Van Buren, November 19, 1847, in Van Buren Papers.

results of restriction, the forcefulness of his language clearly conveys the depth of his feeling.

Neither Calhoun nor the Democrats outdid the Whigs as opponents of restriction. In 1845 Robert Toombs of Georgia attacked restriction because "Congress has no right to interfere with the social relations of the inhabitants of *any* State"; to Toombs restriction meant that very interference. Two years later Toombs thought that the restriction debate was "fast approaching a crisis" because the South must stand her ground. Two important North Carolina Whigs, Thomas L. Clingman and Willie P. Mangum, contended that the exclusion of slavery from the territories required firm southern action. Advocating an ultimatum on the territorial issue, they were confident of southern unity, for on the question of exclusion all southerners "can have but one destiny." An editorial in the Richmond *Whig* sounded the same call: "We shall indulge in no bluster or bravado on the subject. Of this, however, the North may be assured, that, whenever the South shall be called upon to *act*, it will present an undivided, stern, inflexible front to its fanatical assailants." This determination and steadfastness against restriction infected even frail Alexander Stephens; "My mind is made up," he announced to his brother and alter ego, "I am right for the fight." Summing up the position of fellow Whigs and all southerners, the Milledgeville *Southern Recorder* declared that enactment of the proviso meant dissolution of the Union.[18]

To southerners of both parties as well as to the Calhounites the locking of their expansion door by an antislavery or freesoil majority would mean that relations between the sections had reached a critical mass and the resulting explosion had destroyed the South. De-

18. Toombs to Alexander Stephens, January 24, 1845, in Ulrich B. Phillips (ed.), *The Correspondence of Robert Toombs, Alexander Stephens and Howell Cobb* (Washington: Government Printing Office, 1913), 61–62, and Toombs to John C. Calhoun, April 30, 1847, in Boucher and Brooks (eds.), *Calhoun Correspondence*, 373–74; [Clingman (ed.)], *Clingman Writings*, 232–33; Richmond *Whig*, August 14, 1846, February 19, 1847; Alexander Stephens to Linton Stephens, January 21, 1850, in Stephens Papers, Manhattanville College; Milledgeville *Southern Recorder*, February 16, 1849. See also New Orleans *Bee*, March 4, 1847; Tallahassee *Florida Sentinel*, November 2, 1847; Tuscaloosa *Independent Monitor*, August 31, 1847.

stroyed because congressional passage of the proviso would announce to all that the South had lost control of the slavery issue, hence no longer controlled its own destiny. As southerners saw it, enactment of the proviso presaged a dismal political future for the South. In time would occur more strikes against the South and slavery—and southerners never separated the two—for the new states carved out of the territories closed to slavery could only increase the political might of the anti-South forces. Ultimately slavery itself might be sacrificed to the burgeoning forces overpowering the South. That ultimate catastrophe, should it come, probably lay far in the future, but the possibility became very real to southerners threatened seriously with defeat on a major slave question.

As southerners viewed the Wilmot Proviso, it involved more than a mortal threat to the southern political power that guarded their social system. It also grossly insulted them, as individuals and as a community. For the rest of the nation, acting through the national legislature, to ban slavery from the territories stigmatized southern society as unclean and dishonorable. The proviso made the South the Ishmael of the nation that had to be banished and cut off because of its un-American social system. Southerners who considered themselves and their society honorable and decent would never submit to what they termed outrageous, unprincipled assaults on themselves and their society. Just as individual southerners responded to attacks on their personal honor either with the code duello or with some less punctilious form of violence, the collective South struck back at the proviso and all it connoted by proclaiming that they would never accept the imposition of such a badge of dishonor. To southerners these freesoilers or provisoists became equally as heinous as abolitionists, for both challenged the right of the South to direct its destiny and both desecrated the South's image of itself. Meeting the challenge of the proviso, southerners declared that a Union governed by such principles did not deserve and would not retain the loyalty of the South. General talk of severing the Union in the event of the proviso's passage became commonplace.

Whether or not the vehement insistence by southerners on their right to take slaves into the territories also meant that they wanted or expected slavery to spread into them is a vexed question which has no simple answer. Only two statements can be made with certainty: some southerners did believe that slavery could enter and then thrive in the territories; others thought such an eventuality impossible. How many southerners took the opposing sides of this proposition is unknown and probably unknowable. This issue, however, was not central for southerners during the territorial debate that lasted from the introduction of the proviso through the passage of the Kansas-Nebraska Act in 1854. During those years southerners fought to establish their right to take slaves into the territories or, at the least, to prevent the denial of their right. In those years the concepts of equality, rights, and honor were critical for them. Speaking the mind and heart of every southerner, Calhoun emphasized this point in his Southern Address of 1849: "What then we do insist on, is, not to extend slavery, but that we shall not be prohibited from immigrating with our property, into the Territories of the United States, because we are slaveholders; or, in other words, we shall not on that account be disenfranchised of a privilege possessed by all others, citizens and foreigners, without discrimination as to character, profession, or color. All, whether savage, barbarian, or civilized, may freely enter and remain, we only being excluded."[19]

Between 1846 and 1854 the entire territorial debate was carried on in terms of rights, of whether or not slavery would be allowed to enter the territories. Few southerners spoke about practicality; instead they underscored their theoretical rights. Eventually, of course, the political motive behind southern opposition to the proviso would require new slave states or at least strenuous efforts to obtain them. With their rights secured, southerners could not just sit by and watch while every territory became a free state. Southerners were convinced that would make antislavery pressure unbearable. And when they had the opportunity to create a new slave state,

19. Richard K. Crallé (ed.), *The Works of John C. Calhoun* (6 vols.; New York: D. Appleton, 1854–57), VI, 303.

they seized it. In the late 1850s southerners used all their political power in a futile attempt to make Kansas a slave state.[20] Still, during the controversies of the late 1840s and the early 1850s the central thrust of southern antagonism toward the proviso concerned theoretical rights, not practical expectations.

For party politicians in the South the articulation of the proviso issue created great anguish and, at the same time, offered great opportunity. In 1847 and 1848 neither southern Democrats nor southern Whigs were ready to give up their party allegiances and the connections, rewards, power, and loyalties that went with them—at least not yet. The proviso had not been passed by the Congress nor had it become the platform of either major party. The latter situation furnished the anguish that troubled the southern politicians. The proviso remained absent from the banners of both the Whigs and the Democrats, though strong proviso forces belonged to each. Northern Democrats had given birth to the proviso, and every northern Whig in Congress voted for it. To maintain their parties as powerful agents in southern politics, southern partisans had to prevent the proviso from adorning their banners. For southern Whigs and Democrats alike the crucial test would come in 1848. If the national convention of either party placed a proviso plank in its platform or chose a proviso presidential candidate, then that party and its adherents would be finished in the South. As loyal southerners, politicians would have to reject a political association seemingly bent on ostracizing the South and endangering its future. And practical politics would provide a strong complement to that general ideological motive. The opposition party—be it the Democratic or the Whig—would crucify before southern voters the party formally tied to the Wilmot Proviso. Such a party and its stalwarts could not survive in the politics of slavery.

The political opportunity presented by the proviso to southern Democrats and Whigs matched the anguish they felt. If either party

20. Roy Franklin Nichols, *The Disruption of American Democracy* (New York: MacMillan, 1948), Chaps. 6–9 *passim*.

could convince the southern electoral jury that the other party was allied to a national party committed to the proviso, such a conviction would hurl the condemned party into the political execution chamber. As a result, the South would become the special political preserve of the successful prosecutor. Each party in the South rushed toward that opportunity. In 1847 and 1848 each party struggled mightily to prove that lethal proviso or freesoil connection on the other. Simultaneously, each asserted that it alone had a foolproof way to guarantee southern honor and insure southern safety—the Whigs presented a man, the Democrats a platform.

As southern whigs and southern Democrats struggled for advantage in a political world consumed by the territorial issue, their battle clamped even tighter onto the South the politics of slavery.

III

As they peered into this treacherous political world, southern Whigs saw two different but closely related problems. First they had to come up with a formula to overcome the results of 1844 and their subsequent political depression. Then they had to make the proviso question work for them—and, they hoped, against the Democrats. If they failed to accomplish successfully the latter task, the former would remain with them.

In 1847, when talk about the proviso had reached epidemic proportions in the South, many southern Whigs began to think they had discovered their political magic. American triumphs early in the Mexican War came along the Rio Grande and in northern Mexico. News of the greatest of these victories, the Battle of Buena Vista, got back to the United States in the early spring of 1847. The victorious general in all these engagements was Zachary Taylor. And Taylor's name was on numerous Whig lips. Because of his early successes along the Rio Grande, Taylor became an instant hero. After Buena Vista his heroic status was unassailable. To politicians staring at the dilemma confronting southern Whigs, Taylor presented an enormously attractive image. A professional soldier all his life, Taylor had no involvement with a past that southern Whigs were trying to put behind them. He had no connection with the Clay Whig party, with Clay's economic program, or with the controversy over Texas. Taylor had a perfectly clean political slate, a rare item among potential presidential possibilities. Besides, as a military hero, he came already equipped with wide popularity.

But to southern Whigs, Taylor possessed an even more impressive credential; he was a southern slaveowner. Although Taylor had spent most of his life at various military posts, he called Baton Rouge, Louisiana, home; to that home he returned from Mexico to a hero's welcome in December, 1847. He also owned a cotton plantation in Jefferson County, Mississippi, and more than a hundred slaves. In short, as a potential political leader he embodied something no southern politician had seen since Andrew Jackson—a legitimate military hero who planted cotton and owned slaves. Southern Whigs had never before come close to possessing such a political property. Zachary Taylor seemed a godsend to them. In their visions of political glory Zachary Taylor could become the new Andrew Jackson; he could give them what Jackson had given the Democrats two decades earlier: the domination of southern politics.

While Taylor had devotees in most parts of the country, southerners played a dominant role among his earliest political boosters. In the fall of 1846 three separate groups cast their political nets toward Zachary Taylor.[21] When the second session of the Twenty-ninth Congress opened in December, 1846, a group of young Whig congressmen formed a Taylor club. Led by Alexander Stephens of Georgia, who saw Taylor as a southern champion, these "Young Indians" included Stephens' Georgia colleague Robert Toombs as well as three congressmen from Virginia and one each from Alabama and Florida. One member from Connecticut and one from Illinois, none other than Abraham Lincoln, precluded the club's being

21. Holman Hamilton, *Zachary Taylor: Soldier in the White House* (Indianapolis and New York: Bobbs-Merrill, 1951), 63–65; Joseph G. Rayback, *Free Soil: The Election of 1848* (Lexington: University Press of Kentucky, 1970), 36–38.

pinned as exclusively southern. Even so, the motive of Stephens and the clear majority of southern members gave the group a distinctly southern flavor. As early as September, 1846, John J. Crittenden had begun to view Taylor as the potential savior of Whiggery. Several of Crittenden's associates in Kentucky pushed Taylor's name. Then friends of Taylor in New Orleans, including Alexander C. Bullitt, who were also close to Crittenden, advanced Taylor's claims. Although these last two groups might not have started with the conscious sectional motive that influenced Alexander Stephens, both hailed from slave states and both had an intimate acquaintance with the politics of slavery.

The southern Whig politicians lining up behind Taylor had chosen a man who had stirred up a veritable storm of popular enthusiasm in the South. By the spring of 1847 Whigs, Democrats, and Calhounites alike testified to the Taylor whirlwind. William Gilmore Simms thought the advent of Taylor "stave[d] off the evil day of abolitionism." In a trip through Georgia, Alabama, Mississippi, and Tennessee, one of Calhoun's lieutenants "found but *few* individuals, their number certainly not exceeding one dozen, opposed to Genl. Taylor, for the Presidency." James L. Orr may have exaggerated but not by much. "Everywhere in country & in village there seems to be but one opinion," a Georgia Whig leader informed John M. Berrien, "it is that [Taylor] is the man and the man for the times." An Alabama Democratic stalwart notified President Polk that a Taylor boom had indeed caught fire in the state. Polk heard the same news from his home state; Alfred Balch wrote that he dreaded the forthcoming presidential contest in Tennessee if the Whigs ran Taylor. According to Balch, Taylor's popularity and the belief that he would be the Whig candidate "was one of the chief causes" for the Democratic defeat in the 1847 gubernatorial race. Balch predicted that the presidential battle would repeat 1836 when the Whigs with Hugh White drubbed the Democrats. The Taylor stampede reached into Virginia, where the Whigs clamored for him almost in unison. From Frankfort, Kentucky, John J. Crittenden described the enthusiasm

for Taylor "in this part of the country" as "ardent & almost universal." In Crittenden's opinion the pro-Taylor spirit exceeded anything he had seen during Andrew Jackson's heyday. In truth "the
Taylor fever [was] becoming an epidemic."[22]

Hoping to capture as much of this Taylor sentiment as possible
regardless of its political source, southern Whigs presented their
hero as a nonpartisan hero. They made every effort to picture him as
a man above party, as a man who deserved the loyalty of all. Encouraging Democrats to join the Taylor fold, the Little Rock *Arkansas Gazette* described Taylor as a George Washington-like figure
who steered clear of parties. The New Orleans *Bee* declared that
Taylor did not want to come before voters as a political partisan but
simply as a man of the people. Taylor, "the candidate of the *People*,"
asserted the Raleigh *Register*. Alabama Whigs took care to keep
partisanship out of their campaign for Taylor. The Tallahassee
Florida Sentinel viewed Zachary Taylor as a wise, noble patriot who
had no interest in political partisanship.[23]

Brief assurances that Taylor preferred Whiggery over the Democracy accompanied the effort to place Taylor above party.[24] These
assertions satisfied most southern Whigs; as they viewed the political world, Taylor offered too much to allow the absence of rigorous
party commitments to endanger their hopes. Taylor would be their
candidate, for they dominated his movement. They saw no need to

22. Simms to Benjamin Perry, July 15, 1847, in Mary C. Simms Oliphant *et al.* (eds.), *The
Letters of William Gilmore Simms* (5 vols.; Columbia: University of South Carolina Press,
1952–56), II, 333–34; Orr to Calhoun, August 9, 1847, in Boucher and Brooks (eds.), *Calhoun
Correspondence*, 390; Iverson Harris to Berrien, May 9, 1847, in Berrien Papers; George S.
Houston to Polk, May 18, 1847, and Balch to Polk, September 3, 1847, both in Polk Papers;
Richmond *Whig*, December 17, 22, 1847; Crittenden to Waddy Thompson, May 6, 1847, in
Thompson Papers, South Caroliniana Library, University of South Carolina; W. B. Hodgson
to Thomas Butler King, January 5, 1848, in Thomas Butler King Papers, Southern Historical
Collection, University of North Carolina.

23. Little Rock *Arkansas Gazette*, June 5, August 12, December 9, 1847, January 13,
1848; New Orleans *Bee*, March *passim*, July 27, 1847; Raleigh *Register*, July 9, 21, 1847;
Malcolm C. McMillan, "Taylor's Presidential Campaign in Alabama, 1847–1848," *Alabama
Review*, XIII (1960), 91; Tallahassee *Florida Sentinel*, April 20, 27, 1847.

24. For example see Tallahassee *Florida Sentinel*, May 4, 1847; Raleigh *Register*, July 21,
1847; New Orleans *Bee*, July 22, 1847.

frighten off non-Whigs by trumpeting partisanship. Taylor provided confidence that Whigs could build on their local successes of 1847 and sweep through the South in 1848. Southern Whigs as well as their Democratic counterparts knew that the Wilmot Proviso had become the critical political issue in the South. To meet it with a southern slaveholder seemed a gift proffered by the political gods. Certainly the overwhelming majority of southern Whigs had no intention of refusing it. Moreover with Taylor carrying the Whig flag southern Whigs would not need an antiproviso declaration from the Whig national convention. The nomination of Taylor would provide indisputable evidence that southern Whigs maintained control of the slavery issue in the party. With Taylor as the nominee they had only to prevent any proclamation placing the Whig party on record for the proviso. Thus, as they saw it, Taylor's candidacy would give them the proviso issue in the South and prevent any bitter, disruptive convention fight, a fight that southern Whigs, remembering Texas, knew would severely strain and perhaps dismember the Whig party.

Although the Taylor bandwagon attracted most southern Whigs, a few held back. For these the Taylor men had gone too far with nonpartisanship; besides, for all they knew Taylor might not be a good Whig. They did not stand opposed to Taylor personally; they just wanted him to identify himself more closely with the Whig party. These few unhappy Whigs had little chance of impeding the total capture of southern Whiggery by the Taylor forces. For them to have any substantial impact on the Taylor managers and the Taylor campaign they needed help.[25] In April, 1848, they got that help.

Assistance came from the great leader of ideological Whiggery, Henry Clay. In early April, 1848, Henry Clay announced his candidacy for the Whig presidential nomination. After brooding over the 1844 defeat and the death of his son at Buena Vista, Clay decided to

25. Vicksburg *Weekly Whig*, February 9, 1848; Willie P. Mangum to William A. Graham, January 23, 1848, in Shanks (ed.), *Mangum Papers*, V, 92–93; David Outlaw (North Carolina congressman) to Emily Outlaw, February 11, 1848, in David Outlaw Papers, Southern Historical Collection, University of North Carolina.

try one more time for the prize that had eluded him since 1824. Clay convinced himself that only he could defeat the Democrats; he also strenuously objected to what he called a "once great party descending from its lofty position of principle."[26] With devoted admirers in all parts of the nation including the South, Clay could certainly make a strong run against Taylor or anyone else. For his southern friends he provided a focus for their aversion to the nonpartisanship of the Taylor campaign. No one doubted that Henry Clay was a committed partisan.

Both the rumor in the winter of 1848 that Clay intended to make still another run for the presidency and his actual announcement distressed Taylor's southern supporters. The pro-Taylor press attempted, unsuccessfully as it turned out, to discourage Clay from getting involved. The Taylor camp had two overriding objections to Henry Clay as a candidate. First the Taylor men were confident that Clay could not win. "I entirely agree with you that Mr. Clay cannot possibly be elected," a North Carolina Whig responded to Congressman Daniel M. Barringer. Distressed that Clay was determined to take the presidential plunge once again, a leader among Tennessee Whigs declared, "I shall regard a contest at the next election as worse than useless." Alexander Stephens blurted to his borther Linton that Clay could not possibly win. Admitting that Clay had thousands of admirers, the New Orleans *Bee* still maintained that "Clay lack[ed] that powerful hold upon the affections of the masses, irrespective of party organization."[27]

Important southern Whigs also feared that Clay had leaned too far

26. Several letters from Clay to his close friend Dr. William N. Mercer of New Orleans illuminate Clay's decision; the letters dated December 14, 1847, February 7, March 18, April 14, 1848, are all in the William N. Mercer Papers, Department of Archives, Louisiana State University. Also see Clay to S. S. Prentiss, April 12, 1848, in Clay Papers, Division of Manuscripts, Library of Congress and Clay to James Harlan, August 5, 1848, in Calvin Colton (ed.), *The Works of Henry Clay: Comprising His Life, Correspondence and Speeches* (10 vols.; New York and London: G. P. Putnam's Sons, 1904), V, 571.

27. E. J. Hale to Barringer, January 21, 1848, in Barringer Papers; William B. Campbell to David Campbell, January 23, 1848, in Campbell Papers; Alexander Stephens to Linton Stephens, March 22, 1848, in Stephens Papers, Manhattanville College; New Orleans *Bee*, April 13, 1848. Waddy Thompson to John J. Crittenden, February 9, 1848, in Crittenden Papers; I. S. Locke to Thomas Butler King, May 11, 1848, in Thomas Butler King Papers.

toward the proviso forces. In a widely reported speech he gave at Lexington, Kentucky, in November, 1847, Clay called slavery "a great evil" and denounced the acquisition of any Mexican territory that might allow it to spread. While Clay did not endorse the proviso, his sentiments were certainly not in touch with southern opinion in late 1847. Some southern Whigs thought "they discover[ed] an anxiety on the part of Mr. Clay to conciliate the Wilmot Proviso men." The Tuscaloosa *Independent Monitor* stated simply that no loyal southerner could stand upon the ground occupied by Clay in his Lexington speech. That Clay seemed "prepared to cut loose from the South and rely upon the free states to elect him" troubled John Bell. Tennessee Congressman Meredith P. Gentry was aghast that southerners could work for Clay. In Gentry's mind the "Southern men who cooperated in that opposition [to Taylor's nomination] were practically recreant to the dearest interests of the South and ought never to be pardoned, unless upon the charitable ground that their minds were too narrow to comprehend the issues involved in the struggle." "The truth is [Clay] has sold himself body and soul to the Northern Anti-slavery Whigs," thundered Robert Toombs. Toombs was convinced that "Mr. Clay occupies a position towards the strong anti-slavery men of the North that would make his election the greatest possible danger to the South."[28] With many southern Whigs agreeing with Gentry and Toombs and with all southern Whigs enmeshed in the politics of slavery, a Clay candidacy appeared downright lethal to the health of southern Whiggery. Southern Whigs knew that southern Democrats would annihilate a Whig party running on a platform built from Clay's Lexington speech.

To insure victory and to prevent the Whig party from becoming tied to the proviso the Taylor managers acted quickly to neutralize

28. *Niles' Register*, LXXIII (November 27, 1847), 197–200; Iverson Harris to John M. Berrien, December 15, 1847, in Berrien Papers; Tuscaloosa *Independent Monitor*, November 30, December 30, 1847; Bell to William B. Campbell, April 13, 1848, and Gentry to William B. Campbell, June 18, 1848, both in Campbell Papers; Toombs to James Thomas, April 16, May 1, 1848, both in Phillips (ed.), *Toombs, Stephens, Cobb Correspondence*, 104–105.

Clay's candidacy. Almost as soon as Clay's announcement reached New Orleans, several key Taylor advisors steamed up to Baton Rouge. They carried a draft statement for Taylor's signature, which clearly identified him as a Whig but omitted any references to specific issues or policies. Taylor heard them out, made a few revisions, then signed the statement prepared as a letter to his brother-in-law John S. Allison and dated April 22, 1848. Publicized immediately, the letter included the declaration, "I am a Whig." Although the Allison letter did not endorse any kind of Clay-like Whig party, it satisfied all but the most diehard of Clay's southern followers. In all probability they were hungry to believe that Taylor was one of them, and the morsel provided by the Allison letter satisfied them. One of Taylor's strongest champions certainly thought so. Robert Toombs informed a friend: "It gives universal satisfaction to the Whigs & will probably insure his nomination."[29]

The Taylor men had good reason to mollify the pro-Clay sentiment in the South. However, there was one disadvantage; stepping up the partisan pitch, even slightly, would probably cause defection among Democrats and Calhounites attracted to Taylor. But the advantage inherent in placating the Clay Whigs in the South more than offset that liability. The Taylor managers wanted southern Whiggery united behind Taylor. That unity would give Taylor a big boost at the Whig national convention. Then, too, it would hurt Clay's effort to mount a successful challenge to Taylor by depriving him of his southern support. Also, a statement from Taylor enunciating his Whiggery, even in politically muted tones, made him more attractive to northern Whigs. Absorbing Clay's southern following and currying northern Whig favor increased the chances for a Taylor victory in the national convention. That result would really mean victory for the southern Whigs because it gave them a candidate

---

29. For the story of the Allison letter see Wm. C. C. Claiborne to Henry Clay, April 26, 1848, in Clay Papers, Division of Manuscripts, Library of Congress and Hamilton, *Taylor*, 77–81. Hamilton reprints the letter in full on pp. 79–81. Toombs to [?] Thomas, May 2, 1848, in Robert Toombs Papers, Department of Archives, Louisiana State University.

custommade for the politics of slavery without having to risk smashing the Whig convention and the Whig party on the rocks of the Wilmot Proviso.

As the Whig convention approached, Taylor did seem to have the southern Whig troops marching in close unison behind him. Most major Whig newspapers supported him; even the editor of the Vicksburg *Whig*, who thought Henry Clay the perfect Whig, admitted that anyone who failed to recognize the overwhelming power of Taylor in the South was "far behind the times." Almost every southern Whig congressman and senator was counted in Taylor's column. Taylor's candidacy even sparked the creation of Taylor clubs and a Whig organization in Texas. Whig conventions in several states passed resolutions, often with hardly a dissenting voice, proclaiming Zachary Taylor their choice for president.[30]

Just how successful the Taylor campaign had been in the South became clear when the Whig national convention met in Philadelphia in early June.[31] Southern delegates gave Taylor over one-half of his first ballot total, 62 out of 110 votes. On that first ballot only ten southern delegates, five of them from North Carolina, voted against the general; all ten voted for Henry Clay. Clay's tiny handful of supporters eroded until but three voted for him on the fourth ballot, which nominated Taylor. That Clay polled 97 first-ballot votes demonstrates just how significantly southern solidarity contributed to Taylor's victory.

Southern Whigs had Zachary Taylor, and they got him without having to give up anything on the Wilmot Proviso. An effort to place the convention on record as favoring the proviso failed. This conven-

---

30. Of the nine Whig newspapers I read for the campaign all supported Taylor enthusiastically except for the Vicksburg *Whig*, and even it leaned toward Taylor and admitted that he was the great favorite of southern Whigs. Vicksburg *Weekly Whig*, March 15, 1848; Robert Toombs to James Thomas, April 16, 1848, in Phillips (ed.), *Toombs, Stephens, Cobb Correspondence*, 104; James Love to John J. Crittenden, May 20, 1848, in Crittenden Papers and Randolph Campbell, "The Whig Party of Texas in the Elections of 1848 and 1852," *Southwestern Historical Quarterly*, LXXIII (1969), 19; Richmond *Whig*, February 29, 1848; Milledgeville *Southern Recorder*, May 9, 1848.

31. *Niles' Register*, LXXIV (November 29, December 6, 1848), 349, 354–58.

tion repeated the Harrisburg performance of 1839 and adopted no platform. The southern Whigs were delighted; with Taylor they needed no resolutions.

Although the advent of Zachary Taylor enabled the southern Whigs to avoid a head-on collison with their northern colleagues over the Wilmot Proviso, the proviso itself remained the all-consuming issue for southern Democrats.[32] With no Zachary Taylor and no hope of finding anyone remotely like him, southern Democrats could not substitute a personality for the life-and-death issue embodied in the proviso. Once again their conception of the party compact would be put to the test. In 1847 they made clear their total aversion to the proviso. Yet that negative stance did not immediately provide an alternative. In fact the circumstances accompanying their denunciation of the proviso severely restricted their freedom to resolve the crisis amicably with their northern compatriots.

John C. Calhoun not only influenced the character of the southern Democratic response to the proviso, he also implanted his view of the constitutional relationship between slavery and the territories. Insisting that the territories belonged to all the states in common, Calhoun asserted: "That Congress, as the joint agent and representative of the States of the Union, has no right to make any law, or do any act whatever, that shall directly, or by its effects, make any discrimination between the States of this Union by which any of them shall be deprived of its full and equal right in any territory of the United States, acquired or to be acquired."[33] The fervor of southern rights feeling set off by the proviso and magnified by the debates in legislatures and conventions swayed practically all southern Democratic politicians toward Calhoun's constitutional position. That acceptance precluded their supporting an extension of the Missouri Compromise line through any new territory. The evidence indicates that most of them, some eagerly, some reluctantly, were

32. Once again my treatment of the southern Democrats largely follows Morrison, *Democratic Politics*, esp. Chaps. 5–7 *passim*.
33. *Ibid.*, 34–35.

willing to extend the Missouri line in order to settle the territorial question. And President Polk and many leading northern Democrats like James Buchanan of Pennsylvania favored that solution. But the concept underlying the Missouri Compromise and Calhoun's constitutional arguments could not be reconciled. Having committed themselves to Calhounite constitutionalism, southern Democrats could not embrace the Missouri Compromise strategy. To do so would impale them on the politics of slavery. Without any doubt a shift to the Missouri Compromise approach would bring forth both verbal attacks and defections by the Calhounites, which would result in Democratic division. Then the southern Whigs would level broadsides at them for giving up southern rights. Already saddled with the opprobrium of belonging to the party that gave birth to the proviso, southern Democrats, accepting the obvious restrictions on slavery—no matter how traditional or realistic—inherent in extending the Missouri Compromise line, would have precious little defense against an aroused southern Whiggery brandishing Zachary Taylor. And the southern Democrats knew it.

In their search for a way out of their dilemma southern Democrats had stalwart allies. Although the proviso originated among northern Democrats, most of them believed that the South had some rights in the territories. The northern Democrats were just as committed to territorial expansion as their southern counterparts; they knew that retaining expansion and party unity, not to say sectional harmony, required negating the proviso. At the same time they could not adopt outright Calhoun's position.

The desire of northern Democrats to maintain the national Democratic party spurred them to find a proviso substitute. They knew that most southern Democrats had no interest in Calhoun's idea of a southern party. They were also aware that the southerners were quite willing to back a northerner for president in 1848 provided, of course, he repudiated the proviso.[34] Many northern Democratic

34. Richmond *Enquirer*, March 26, 1847; Cave Johnson to Arthur Crozier, September 10, 1847, in Arthur Crozier Papers, Manuscript Division, Tennessee State Library and Archives;

chieftains were ready to do just that. Those most discussed for 1848—Buchanan, Lewis Cass of Michigan, and Levi Woodbury of New Hampshire—all shunned the proviso and worked actively to convince the southerners that their rights would be in safe hands. Each of the three had friends in the South who carried home messages of friendship. The political battles among southern Democrats in 1847 and 1848 turned on personalities and the ambitions of the southern politicians supporting the various northerners. All southern Democratic politicians recognized the safety of Buchanan, Cass, and Woodbury. And each of those searched for a way around the proviso that would satisfy the South but not alienate the North.

In a public letter appearing on December 30, 1847, and addressed to the Tennessee Democrat A. O. P. Nicholson, Lewis Cass presented to the South and the nation the formula that won Democratic allegiance. Borrowing from an idea first suggested by Vice-President George M. Dallas, Cass proclaimed popular sovereignty as the Democratic plan of salvation for the territories. Declaring the Wilmot Proviso unconstitutional, resting on the supreme Democratic principle that the people ruled, the popular sovereignty doctrine maintained that the settlers in a territory, not the Congress or anyone else, should decide whether or not they wanted slavery in their territory.

Cass made his proposal even more attractive politically by leaving conveniently vague the time frame for the momentous decision on slavery. Although he implied that the settlers could accept or reject slavery during the territorial stage, he said nothing about territorial legislatures and he stipulated the settlers had to follow the basic principles of the Constitution. To northerners who took the implication as the chief thrust, popular sovereignty meant that the first territorial legislature, if it so chose, could ban slavery. To southern-

---

Jefferson Davis to C. J. Searles, September 19, 1847, in Dunbar Rowland (ed.), *Jefferson Davis, Constitutionalist: His Letters, Papers and Speeches* (10 vols.; Jackson: Mississippi Department of Archives and History, 1923), I, 95; Howell Cobb to John C. Holland, May 11, 1848, in Woodbury Papers.

ers who emphasized the constitutional guidelines theme, popular sovereignty meant that a decision on slavery had to await statehood, for territories lacked the sovereignty to decide so fundamental a question as slavery. Cass's formulation of popular sovereignty was inconsistent and vague, but those very characteristics gave it much of its political beauty. Both northern and southern Democrats could read into it or out of it what they wished. And it banished the Wilmot Proviso from the Democratic political dictionary.

The vagueness of popular sovereignty troubled few southern Democrats. As a frustrated Calhoun acknowledged, the regular southern Democrats could use popular sovereignty to perpetuate their party organization and their view that national parties represented the surest way to protect southern interests and guarantee southern safety.[35] As southern Democrats interpreted popular sovereignty, it met every demand: it declared the proviso unconstitutional; it provided that the territories themselves upon achieving statehood would decide for or against slavery, and all southerners accepted the right of a state to determine its own course on slavery; it demonstrated that northern Democrats bowed to the southerners by rejecting the Wilmot Proviso. That popular sovereignty might have a different definition in the North did not distress them. Southerners were content to let northern Democrats electioneer so long as they paid obeisance to the South when required. And southern Democrats were convinced they still had the political muscle to obtain that fealty. For proof they pointed to popular sovereignty.

Southern Democrats scored another party victory in the Democratic national convention which met in Baltimore in late May. When the convention nominated Cass and spurned the proviso, southern Democrats saw their domination of the slavery question reaffirmed by the national party. To be sure, all southerners had not supported Cass, but practically all considered him safe on the slav-

---

35. Calhoun to Henry Conner, December 16, 1847, in Conner Papers and to Franklin H. Elmore, December 22, 1847, in Calhoun Papers, South Caroliniana Library, University of South Carolina.

ery question, the critical item. Thus the adherents of Buchanan and Woodbury had no difficulty in accepting Cass just as the Cass supporters could have easily taken Buchanan or Woodbury if either of them had come out on top. With a safe candidate and with a platform excluding the proviso, southern Democrats were generally satisfied.

When Alabama's William Lowndes Yancey tried to get a more direct condemnation of the proviso, he found few southern supporters. In fact most southern delegates voted against Yancey. To the southern regulars Yancey was treading in Calhoun's path of confrontation. In the manner of Calhoun he demanded a clear, unequivocal, public declaration from the North guaranteeing the southern position on the territories. To the southern regulars this kind of potentially divisive and embarrassing confrontation was unnecessary because they already had what they wanted—northern Democrats, in their view, had played by southern rules. The candidate denied the constitutionality of the proviso and the platform granted the South its rights.

Southerners even got a bonus from the convention. The Van Burenites from New York walked out after the convention refused to accredit them as the only legitimate Democrats in New York. For southerners this action meant that the segment of the party most tainted with the proviso broke the party connection. As a result southerners would have an easier time countering the Whig charge that the Democratic party sustained the originators of the proviso. When disaffected New Yorkers joined with other proviso Democrats and antislavery Whigs to form the Free Soil party in August, southern Democrats had even more cause for rejoicing. Their party was purged of its antisouthern nucleus.

Even though their northern compatriots and their convention did their bidding, southern Democrats did not head for battle against Zachary Taylor with quite the same unity they had enjoyed back in 1844. Although all the regulars lined up behind Cass and the Democratic press began heaping praise upon him, the Calhounites remained aloof. Three different reactions characterized the Calhounite response to the Cass-Taylor contest, though it is impossible to talk precisely about the numbers making the separate responses. Reluctantly and without cheering, probably the largest single group went for Cass. Taylor's identifying himself as a Whig and accepting the Whig nomination turned them away from him; they could not back a card-carrying Whig, even a slaveowning cotton planter. For a few, Taylor's southern identity overrode all objections; they prepared to vote Whig. Still others followed their leader's course; Calhoun, damning both Cass and Taylor as lackeys of party, assumed a neutral position. This Calhounite defection did not, however, undermine the regular Democratic effort. Its fragmentation tempered its impact on the southern Democracy. The dissident Calhounites did not mount an organized campaign against Cass; even those who went for Taylor seem to have done so relatively quietly. They certainly caused no great commotion. As a result, regular southern Democrats did not have to fight Calhounites as well as Whigs.[36]

Although one flank was a bit ragged, southern Democrats were ready for the Whigs and Taylor. With confidence they looked to the campaign.[37] They did not have a slaveowner, but they had a program.

IV

The rhetoric of each party dramatized the election as potentially cataclysmic for the South. Headlines such as "THE CRISIS" and "THE SOUTH IN DANGER" heralded the efforts of southern Democratic editors to convince southern voters that only a Democratic victory could prevent the triumph of an antislavery and antisouthern party.

36. Wiltse, *Calhoun*, III, 318–20, 369–70; Morrison, *Democratic Politics*, 157–60, 166; David L. Yulee to His Wife, June 22, 1848, in Yulee Papers; James H. Hammond to M. C. M. Hammond, September 18, 1848, in Hammond Papers; I. E. Holmes to John M. Clayton, November 13, 1848, in Clayton Papers; R. M. T. Hunter to J. R. Tucker, May 28, 1848, in Tucker Family Papers, Southern Historical Collection, University of North Carolina.
37. Stephen A. Douglas to Lewis Cass, June 13, 1848, in Robert W. Johannsen (ed.), *The Letters of Stephen A. Douglas* (Urbana: University of Illinois Press, 1961), 160–61; in this letter Douglas reported on conversations with Democratic leaders in six states from Louisiana to North Carolina. See also Jackson *Mississippian*, June 2, 1848, and Richmond *Enquirer*, June 2, 1848.

With "the destinies of the South" hanging in the balance southern-ers must not hesitate. They must vote for the party pledged to protect them and their institutions, not for a Whig party that wanted "to violate the rights of the South and [deprive] them of an equal share in the benefits of the Constitution." Likewise southern Whig newspapers foresaw a possible southern *Götterdammerung* on the political horizon. Even before the official beginning of the campaign the Tallahassee *Florida Sentinel* pictured southern institutions facing execution by northern Democrats. "ALARMING," shouted the Vicksburg *Whig* at the prospect of a presidential victory by the proviso party. "With our vital institutions threatened as they are," the Milledgeville *Southern Recorder* called on southerners to save themselves from the hovering vultures masquerading as the Democratic party.[38]

To preserve the South and southern institutions at this critical juncture, southern Democrats presented a platform of two planks—the Nicholson letter, or popular sovereignty, and Lewis Cass's public pledge to veto the Wilmot Proviso if it ever passed Congress. In southern Democratic hands the Nicholson letter with its denunciation of the proviso became a manifesto of southern rights contrasting sharply with Whig silence on that vexed topic. On every count the Nicholson letter guaranteed the honor and safety of the South. Cass's public pledge to veto the proviso, the New Orleans *Louisiana Courier* characterized as a "manly stand in defence [*sic*] of Southern Rights[.]"[39] A Democratic campaigner in Tennessee called Cass's pledge the South's "last anchor," "the last shield of [our] protection and safety." Southern Democratic leaders from regulars like Howell Cobb to those with close Calhounite ties like Dixon Lewis preached to their southern correspondents that Cass stood on

38. New Orleans *Louisiana Courier*, November 6, 1848; Jackson *Mississippian*, August 11, 1848; Milledgeville *Federal Union*, October 17, 1848; Tallahassee *Florida Sentinel*, November 2, 1847; Vicksburg *Tri-Weekly Whig*, November 7, 1848; Milledgeville *Southern Recorder*, July 11, 1848.

39. New Orleans *Louisiana Courier*, June 7, July 14, 1848; Raleigh *Standard*, January 12, June 7, 1848; Tallahassee *Floridian*, June 3, October *passim*, 1848; Richmond *Enquirer*, June 2, 16, August 18, 1848; Milledgeville *Federal Union*, October 3, 1848.

a platform eminently acceptable to the South. As a result of his adopting a platform safe for the South, Cass deserved southern support.[40]

While standing firmly on their platform southern Democrats struck out furiously at the Whigs. Again and again they reminded voters that northern Whigs almost to a man supported the proviso. To prove that case southern Democratic editors published excerpts from northern Whig papers touting the proviso; they pointed out that northern Whigs in Congress consistently voted for the proviso; they reported that northern Whigs presented Zachary Taylor as a man who would never veto the proviso should it reach his presidential desk.[41] Admitting that southern Whigs claimed exactly the opposite, southern Democrats branded the Whigs as practitioners of dishonest politics. "The Northern and Southern sections of the Whig party are playing off the boldest attempt at *fraud* ever made upon the American people," exclaimed the Tallahassee *Floridian*. The Richmond *Enquirer* castigated the "Two Faces" worn by the Taylor campaign. Accordingly the Raleigh *Standard* warned: "LET THE SLAVEHOLDERS OF NORTH CAROLINA [or the South] BEWARE! THEY ARE ABOUT TO BE BETRAYED."[42]

Southern Democrats singled out for special attention the representative of northern Whiggery adorning the Whig ticket alongside Zachary Taylor. "*Mr. Fillmore is unsafe for the South,*" asserted the Milledgeville *Federal Union*. Emphasizing Millard Fillmore's past

40. Editors of the Union and American (eds.), *Aaron Brown Speeches*, 247; Cobb to Hopkins Holsey and Others, June 27, 1848, in R. P. Brooks (ed.), "Howell Cobb Papers," *Georgia Historical Quarterly*, V (1921), 34–37; Lewis to William Lowndes Yancey, June 29, 1848, in William Lowndes Yancey Papers, Alabama Department of Archives and History; William R. King to William Garrett, August 16, 1848, quoted in William Garrett, *Reminiscences of Public Men in Alabama, for Thirty Years with an Appendix* (Atlanta: Plantation, 1872), 680.

41. Raleigh *Standard*, September 6, October 11, November 8, 1848; New Orleans *Louisiana Courier*, September 1, 1848; Tallahassee *Floridian*, July 1, 15, August 19, October 28, 1848; Richmond *Enquirer*, August 18, 29, September 1, 1848; Jackson *Mississippian*, August 11, 1848.

42. Tallahassee *Floridian*, September 16, 1848; Richmond *Enquirer*, September 15, 1848; Raleigh *Standard*, March 29, November 8, 1848.

associations with abolitionists, southern Democrats said southerners ought to have no doubt about his "unsoundness on the question
of Southern rights." As a New York congressman Fillmore had voted
against the southern position on a series of resolutions concerning
abolitionism back in 1838; in that same year he had also affirmed his
opposition to slavery in responding to an inquiry from an antislave
society in his own Erie County, New York. Southern Democratic
editors emblazoned these two episodes on their pages. Discounting
as political claptrap Fillmore's strong campaign statements on the
constitutionality of slavery in the states, the Democratic editors
rightly emphasized that Fillmore said nothing about the proviso.
They asked rhetorically whether or not the South could risk electing
such a man to the vice-presidency. Only betrayers of the South could
join in electing such a man. The Jackson *Mississippian* summed up
the southern Democratic case: "Let every southern man before he
goes to the polls put this solemn question to himself."[43]

Although the southern Democrats hammered away at the antisouthern proclivities of northern Whigs and colored Millard
Fillmore with the abolitionist brush, they hit hardest at Zachary
Taylor himself. They did not challenge the sincerity of Taylor's
southernness; in fact the New Orleans *Louisiana Courier* acknowledged that everyone in Louisiana knew of Taylor's concern for the
safety of both his family and property and of his opposition to all
abolitionist activity. Even so Taylor remained their chief target because he had neither publicly declared himself opposed to the proviso nor pledged himself to veto it. Some southern Democrats,
pointing to the message of northern Whigs, alleged that Taylor had
secretly pledged not to veto it; others denounced him for equivocat-
ing on so critical a matter; still others simply, and correctly, complained that Taylor had taken no public stand against the proviso. All

43. Milledgeville *Federal Union*, June 27, 1848; Richmond *Enquirer*, June 16, 30,
September–October *passim*, 1848; Jackson *Mississippian*, September 19, 1848. Also see
New Orleans *Louisiana Courier*, June 27, 1848; Raleigh *Standard*, July 12, 19, September
13, 1848; Tallahassee *Floridian*, June 24, July 1, 2,, 29, August *passim*, 1848.

three Democratic assaults described Taylor as exhibiting an "awful and ominous silence" on the proviso issue, which marked him as "a man no southerner can support." Southern Democrats then warned voters not to accept on faith that Taylor's southernness insured his soundness on the proviso; unless a public declaration came from Taylor himself, the Democrats insisted, southerners should make no such potentially lethal assumptions. With southerners offered a choice between what they termed a prosouthern platform and no platform the Richmond *Enquirer* put the question that to southern Democrats had but one possible answer: "Can the South hesitate between the two tickets presented them?"[44]

Southern Whigs had their own question for southern voters; speaking for Whigs across the South the Milledgeville *Southern Recorder* asked, "Will the people of Georgia [or the South] vote for a Southern president or a Northern one?" To that paper and to southern Whiggery in general, southerners could answer that question in only one way. In their appeals to voters Whigs talked not about platforms or pledges; instead they staked their future and the South's on a man, Zachary Taylor. Taylor's candidacy and nomination had allowed them to skirt a hazardous showdown with northern Whigs on the proviso. They had no intention of making any changes just because of the Democratic attack. Unquestionably Taylor gave them security on the proviso. Just as unquestionably they counted on his position as a southerner, a cotton planter, and a slaveowner to win the political loyalty of fellow southerners.[45]

"Citizens of the South," cried the Baton Rouge *Gazette*, "Rally to the support of Gen. Zachary Taylor. He is identified with your

44. Editors of the Union and American (eds.), *Aaron Brown Speeches*, 252; Little Rock *Arkansas Banner*, July 25, 1848; Richmond *Enquirer*, June 30, 1848. Also see Milledgeville *Federal Union*, May 30, 1848; New Orleans *Louisiana Courier*, June 30, July 18, September 1, 1848; Raleigh *Standard*, September *passim*, 1848; Little Rock *Arkansas Banner*, August 15, 1848.

45. Milledgeville *Southern Recorder*, October 3, 1848; [Clingman (ed.)], *Clingman Writings*, 227; also sources cited in n. 46 of this chapter.

Although Taylor had not publicly denounced the proviso, southern Whigs assumed that he opposed it and acted on their assumptions—an incorrect one as it turned out. For an analysis of Taylor and the proviso see pp. 273–75 herein.

dearest rights and institutions. In his hands your interest will be safe." John J. Crittenden did not see how any southerner, even Calhoun, could refrain from supporting "a Southern Slave holder" in a contest against a northerner. Appealing for southern votes S. S. Prentiss emphasized that with Zachary Taylor the South had one of her own, loyal to her values and institutions. The Raleigh *Register* thought it ridiculous that any southerner could doubt the complete fidelity of Taylor to the South and all it held dear. As for those doubters, the Democratic spokesmen, the *Register* asked, "Can men go further into absurdity?" In its last issue before the election, the Tuscaloosa *Independent Monitor* underscored the thrust of the southern Whig campaign: "Remember, that the man who is farthest from you in opinion at the South, is NEARER to you than ANY man of EITHER party at the North."[46]

While praising their man southern Whigs condemned the Democrats "for galvanizing the stenchy carcass of that exploded humbug 'NORTHERN MAN WITH SOUTHERN PRINCIPLES' and attempting to palm him off upon the people of the South as sound upon the Wilmot proviso question[.]" Holding up Martin Van Buren as the original northern man with southern principles sponsored by the southern Democrats, the southern Whigs gleefully described the 1848 version of Van Buren. This northerner supposedly loyal to the South now headed the political incarnation of the proviso, the Free Soil party. Whig editors then wanted to know what made Cass any better a risk for the South. That Cass opposed the Wilmot Proviso in his popular sovereignty doctrine impressed them not at all. They noted that Cass had earlier voted for it in the Senate. As the southern Whigs saw it, Cass's shift proved his political opportunism and unreliability. And the South needed loyalty and conviction. Besides, southern Whig editors reminded their readers, southern Democrats had no monopoly on interpreting popular sovereignty. Many north-

46. Baton Rouge *Gazette*, November 4, 1848; Crittenden to Alexander Stephens, September 4, 1848, in Alexander Stephens Papers, Division of Manuscripts, Library of Congress; Vicksburg *Tri-Weekly Whig*, September 2, 1848; Raleigh *Register*, August 2, 1848; Tuscaloosa *Independent Monitor*, November 2, 1848.

ern Democrats defined it as a way to restrict slavery without using the volatile words *Wilmot Proviso*. Such a platform, according to southern Whigs, provided no assurances and no security for South. As for the southern Democrats, they "practiced this fraud upon the Southern people" of attempting to delude them with the treachery of the northern man with southern principles. In fact the election of such a man on such a platform would mean, in the words of the Little Rock *Arkansas Gazette*, "The South is prostrate at the feet of the North."[47]

In their attempt to undermine southern confidence in the Democratic party as protector of southern rights, southern Whigs tried to turn President Polk's signing of the Oregon territorial bill to their advantage. In August, 1848, Polk placed his signature on a measure organizing Oregon without slavery. Polk did so reluctantly and only because Oregon lay above the Missouri Compromise line; in fact he appended to the bill a statement explaining his motives. In agreeing to this bill Polk certainly did not give up his ferocious opposition to the Wilmot Proviso. But even though Calhoun had acquiesced in it, southern Whigs claimed that Polk had deserted the South. As the Whigs told the Polk-Oregon story, it became a striking illustration of the danger Cass and the Democratic party posed to the South. With Polk turning his back on southern interests, southern Whigs asked, "What can we expect from Mr. Cass?"[48]

Expecting so much from Taylor, southern Whigs wanted nothing to jeopardize his election. Thus in July when the Clayton Compromise was proposed to settle the territorial question, a group of southern Whig congressmen led by Alexander Stephens blocked its

47. Tallahassee *Florida Sentinel*, November 2, 1847; Richmond *Whig*, June 30, 1848; Little Rock *Arkansas Gazette*, September 28, 1848. Also see Tuscaloosa *Independent Monitor*, June 15, 29, 1848; Milledgeville *Southern Recorder*, June 6, 27, July 25, 1848; New Orleans *Bee*, June 22, 1848; Richmond *Whig*, October 27, 31, November 2, 7, 1848; Raleigh *Register*, June 7, September–October *passim*, November 1, 1848.

48. Nashville *Republican*, September 6, 1848, quoted in Rayback, *Free Soil*, 241; Little Rock *Arkansas Gazette*, August 31, 1848; Raleigh *Register*, August 23, 1848; S. S. Prentiss to His Brother, August 25, 1848, quoted in *A Memoir of S. S. Prentiss*, ed. His Brother (2 vols.; New York: Charles Scribner, 1856), II, 457.

passage in the House after it had narrowly passed the Senate. Southern Whigs in the Senate and the House divided over the Clayton Compromise, but Stephens and his allies, all avid Taylor men, feared it could hurt Taylor. For one thing the measure, approved by both Calhoun and President Polk, had a strong Democratic identity even though it had some southern Whig support and carried the name of John M. Clayton, Whig senator from Delaware. Also northern Whigs told Stephens that enactment of the Clayton bill would cause problems for Taylor in the North. To safeguard Taylor's election with all it promised for southern Whiggery, Stephens and four of his southern comrades joined with three Whigs from the border slave states, northern Whigs, and freesoil Democrats to defeat the Clayton Compromise. With the Clayton Compromise, as in so many other instances, politics and ideology meshed. Writing to a Georgia friend, Stephens claimed that politics alone did not motivate his opposition. According to Stephens the Clayton proposal, which he called a "Bill of Surrender," took away southern rights in the territories. The Richmond *Whig* defended the Stephens group before southern voters. Denouncing the Clayton Compromise as the product of "trading politicians," the *Whig* preached the southern Whig gospel: "We prefer Old Zack with his sugar and cotton plantations and four hundred negroes to all their compromises." On this particular occasion all southern Whigs did not share the views expressed by the *Whig*, but those sentiments and the action of the Stephens group fit perfectly into the campaign being conducted by southern Whigs.[49]

Southern Whigs insisted that only their party offered the South complete security. Of course the southern Whigs had to contend with Fillmore, a task that presented a certain difficulty. But they

49. Twenty-three of the twenty-four southern Whigs in the House voted; so Stephens and his allies made up just over one-fifth of the southern Whig voting contingent. *Congressional Globe*, 30th Cong., 1st Sess., 1002, 1007; [Clingman (ed.)], *Clingman Writings*, 230; David Outlaw to Emily Outlaw, July 23, 1848, in Outlaw Papers; Stephens to Duncan L. Clinch, October 7, 1848, in Alexander Stephens Papers, William R. Perkins Library, Duke University; Richmond *Whig*, August 4, 1848.

defended him as best they could. Using the same tactics they blasted the Democrats for employing, they displayed Fillmore's statements of abiding belief in the constitutionality of slavery. But their effort for Fillmore was distinctly a sideshow. Their main event was Zachary Taylor. "[Taylor] is essentially at this moment THE MAN OF THE SOUTH," trumpeted the Milledgeville *Southern Recorder*. Taylor as southerner would protect the South. With him there was no need for concern about vice-presidents, certainly no need for platforms or pledges. Every honorable southerner knew that every other honorable southerner stood fast behind southern rights and institutions. And Zachary Taylor was surely an honorable southerner.[50]

The strident sectional rhetoric pouring from both southern Democrats and southern Whigs never ceased; neither party gave in to the other as the champion of the South. Even so, contemporary letters and newspapers give the strong impression, corroborated by the election returns, that the Whigs with their special candidate mounted a more effective crusade than the Democrats. After this blast of sectional gunpowder southern voters trooped to the polls in record numbers with 575,557 casting ballots, 40,000 more than in 1844 and 100,000 more than in the Log Cabin campaign. Zachary Taylor, who won 51 percent of those votes, became the second and the last Whig presidential candidate to win a popular majority in the South. His 51 percent of the vote approached the 53 percent Harrison had claimed back in 1840 and bettered his national showing by four percentage points.

Although Taylor carried only five southern states to Cass's six, which included Calhoun's duchy of South Carolina, Taylor's was the more impressive performance. Cass's total vote exceeded Polk's by less than 1 percent while Taylor bettered Clay's turnout by 14.9

---

50. Robert Toombs to John J. Crittenden, September 27, 1848, in Crittenden Papers; New Orleans *Bee*, July 20, 1848; Little Rock *Arkansas Gazette*, August–September *passim*, 1848; Richmond *Whig*, June 16, September 8, 1848; Tuscaloosa *Independent Monitor*, July 20, 1848; Milledgeville *Southern Recorder*, July 11, 25, 1848.

percent. Of the five states Taylor lost that had a popular election (South Carolina did not), he failed in three of them by the smallest of margins. Losing Alabama by only 691 votes out of 61,659 cast, Taylor came closer to victory there than any other Whig presidential candidate ever did. He came up short in Mississippi by only 792 out of 52,374, and in Virginia a gap of but 1,474 votes out of 92,004 kept him from victory. Thus in three states that had become solidly Democratic in the 1840s, Zachary Taylor laid the foundation for a renewal of Whig vigor. Cass and the Democrats had an easy time only in Arkansas and Texas. In the five states that went for Taylor, he had a relatively close contest only in Georgia. His margins ranged from 51.5 percent there to a high of 57.5 percent in Florida.

Taylor cut into southern Democratic strength and gathered in numbers of new voters. Although it is impossible to be precise about the number of Democratic defections, some southern Whigs expected them and in election postmortems Democrats placed defections and abstentions high on their list of reasons explaining their poor showing. According to those Democratic witnesses, Whig attacks on Cass's safety influenced traditional Democrats either to vote for Taylor or stay home.[51] To supplement Taylor's success with Democrats as well as new voters, southern Whigs repeated their fine showing of 1847 in key state races occurring in the presidential year. In North Carolina they retained the governership, and in Florida they elected a governor and a majority in both houses of the legislature.

With a renewed dedication to the politics of slavery southern Whiggery had rejuvenated itself. To southern Whigs the political darkness of 1844 and 1845 seemed far in the past. Eagerly they embraced the future. With their southern chieftain to lead them in

51. Sam L. Beman to Thomas Butler King, August 13, 1848, in Thomas Butler King Papers and James W. Osborne to William A. Graham, October 11, 1848, in Hamilton and Williams (eds.), *Graham Papers*, III, 246; James F. Cooper to Howell Cobb, November 11, 1848, in Phillips (ed.), *Toombs, Stephens, Cobb Correspondence*, 137; William S. Dickson to George S. Houston, December 17, 1848, in Houston Papers; Raleigh *Standard*, November 15, 1848.

tackling the territorial issue that dominated southern attention, they envisioned a glorious Whig future in the South. Of course for their vision to become reality Zachary Taylor had to act like a good southerner and bring the northern Whigs along with him. The southern Whigs never doubted that he would and could.

8 Parties in Crisis

I

CONVINCED THAT A TAYLOR administration promised them political dominion in the South, southern Whigs wanted to control sectional issues, especially the territorial one, until Zachary Taylor became president. During the short second session of the Thirtieth Congress, which ran from December, 1848, to March 4, 1849, they wanted no action that would embarrass Taylor or sabotage their political prospects in the South. Only with a territorial policy of their own making could southern Whigs claim the political credit and the political rewards they foresaw with certainty. Their determination to preserve the initiative on the territorial issue governed the southern Whig response to John C. Calhoun's new try for southern unity.

Calhoun's move to unite the South during the winter of 1848–1849 stemmed directly from the sectional tension that had gripped the country during most of 1848. While southerners continuously denounced the proviso and filled the election campaign with a cacophony of cries against it, many northerners spoke with equal vehemence for it. The creation of the Free Soil party institutionalized the northern platform demanding imposition of the proviso in the territories. Free Soilers and Whigs, especially, bombarded the northern electorate with strident anti-South and anti-slavery rhetoric. Steamrolling through much of the North this rhetoric helped elect numerous congressmen eager to push their claims in the national legislature.[1]

When the second session of the Thirtieth Congress convened in December, 1848, southerners met together to consider a proper response to what they viewed as dangerous and fanatical outcries

1. Joseph G. Rayback, *Free Soil: The Election of 1848* (Lexington: University Press of Kentucky, 1970), Chaps. 12–13 *passim.*

269

from the North. Southern representatives and senators caucused after the House passed a resolution from a New York Whig instructing the House Committee for the District of Columbia to report a bill outlawing the slave trade in the district. Calhoun saw this genuine southern outrage as the foundation on which he could build the united front he deemed essential for southern safety. To implement his strategy he planned an address listing grievances and calling for a southern convention. This convention would, then, present the South's platform or position or ultimatum to the North. For success Calhoun knew he had to win nonpartisan support. Both Whigs and Democrats had to rally under his banner.[2]

Most southern Whigs in Congress viewed Calhoun's activities with little enthusiasm but much suspicion. While they tended to be just as distressed as Calhoun and the southern Democrats over the new militantly antisouthern stance taken by many northerners, they feared that Calhoun's initiative would undermine their political prospects. If Calhoun obtained the bipartisan support he desired, then southern Whiggery would become merely a tail to the Calhoun or Democratic kite. Accordingly southern Whigs ascribed a purely political motive to the caucus. In their view the Democrats acting in conjunction with Calhoun were trying to reverse the outcome of the presidential election. In the words of Robert Toombs the "perfectly desperate" Calhounite-Democratic combine had mounted "a bold stroke to disorganize the Southern Whigs and either destroy Genl. Taylor in advance or compel him to throw himself in the hands of a large section of the democracy of the South."[3]

Southern Whigs worked to block their political enemies by turning Calhoun's drive for unity into the alley of partisanship. Initially some attended the meetings of the southern caucus; in fact a Kentucky Whig became its first chairman, and Alexander Stephens was

2. Charles M. Wiltse, *John C. Calhoun* (3 vols.; Indianapolis and New York: Bobbs-Merrill, 1944–51), III, 377–88.

3. New Orleans *Bee*, January 5, 1849; Toombs to John J. Crittenden, January 3, 22, 1849, in Ulrich B. Phillips (ed.), *The Correspondence of Robert Toombs, Alexander H. Stephens and Howell Cobb* (Washington: Government Printing Office, 1913), 139, 141.

named to head the committee appointed to prepare an appropriate address. But southern Whigs came not to assist the caucus but "to control and crush it." And for their purposes they succeeded. By arguing that the caucus should adopt no address, by proposing an alternative address, by walking out of the caucus, by refusing to sign the final version of Calhoun's address, they smashed Calhoun's hopes for unity. Complaining that "narrow views & party attachments" foiled the unity that seemed so close, Calhoun testified both to southern Whig motivation and success. "The [Southern] Whigs . . . are opposed to any activity" a saddened Calhoun wrote, "they rely on General Taylor."[4]

Southern Whigs did indeed rely on Zachary Taylor. As Robert Toombs explained to the last session of the caucus he attended: "We did not expect an administration which we had brought into power would do any act or permit any act to be done which it would become necessary for our safety to rebel at." Because of Taylor, southern Whigs feared neither combat with the antislavery forces, even those carrying the colors of the Whig party, nor the reprisals the Democrats would surely level against them for opposing the caucus. "Let us wait," cried the Milledgeville *Southern Recorder*, "and give old Buena Vista a fair trial—defeated partizans [*sic*] to the contrary notwithstanding." Alexander Stephens caught the southern Whig mood exactly when he told John J. Crittenden, we "feel *secure* under General Taylor."[5]

Although southern Whigs felt secure with Taylor and confident about their prosperity under his administration, some of them wanted to eliminate before Taylor's inauguration the territorial issue generated by the Mexican Cession. Agreeing with John J. Critten-

4. Robert Toombs to John J. Crittenden, January 3, 1849, in Phillips (ed.), *Toombs, Stephens, Cobb Correspondence*, 139; Calhoun to Henry Conner, February 2, 1849, in Conner Papers, and Calhoun to James Edward Calhoun, January 17, 1849, in Calhoun Papers, William R. Perkins Library, Duke University.
5. Toombs to John J. Crittenden, January 22, 1849, in Phillips (ed.), *Toombs, Stephens, Cobb Correspondence*, 141; Milledgeville *Southern Recorder*, January 2, 1849; Stephens to Crittenden, January 17, 1849, in Stephens Papers, William R. Perkins Library, Duke University.

den that only the territorial issue posed a threat to the success of
Taylor's presidency, southerners were concerned about northern
Whig support for the proviso. And with good reason, for early during
the congressional session Whig Congressman Caleb Smith of Indiana introduced a bill that organized California and simultaneously
banned slavery in the proposed territory.[6] Southern Whigs could
never accept such a bill. At the same time they wanted no part of
Calhoun's plan, which threatened their political ambitions and
expectations.

Some southern congressional Whigs wanted to bypass the proviso, and the possibility of a bitter intraparty fight, by immediately
creating one state out of the Mexican Cession. By omitting the
territorial stage such an act would preclude any conflict over the
proviso. That this enlarged California would certainly join the Union
as a free state did not bother the proponents of the statehood
strategy. They believed with Robert Toombs that California could
never become slave country. To these men the question of whether
or not California became a slave state or a free state was secondary; in
Toombs's phrase the central issue was "the point of honor."[7] And
since all southerners, including Calhoun, agreed that a state could
make its own decisions on slavery, southern honor would not be
impugned. By giving immediate statehood to California the South
gave up nothing material, and her honor remained unstained. To its
adherents the statehood plan also eliminated all impediments to a
triumphant Taylor administration.

On February 7, 1849, Congressman William B. Preston of
Virginia proposed the California statehood bill to the House. Defending the bill, Preston took care to explain that it did not violate
the honor of the South. Discussing the "great, abiding, solemn ques-

6. Crittenden to John M. Clayton, April 11, 1849, in Clayton Papers; *Congressional Globe*, 30th Cong., 2nd Sess., 71.
7. Toombs to John J. Crittenden, January 22, 1849, in Phillips (ed.), *Toombs, Stephens, Cobb Correspondence*, 141. See also David M. Potter, *The Impending Crisis, 1848–1861* (New York, Evanston, San Francisco, London: Harper & Row, 1976), 91–92, n. 3.

tion of honor that every southern man, who does not stand up to, is recreant to himself and forgetful of his ancestors," Preston thundered, "Now, I yield to no man on these points." Insisting that his measure protected southern honor Preston declared, "I do not, as a southern man, surrender anything to [the North]." Despite Preston's exhortations his effort failed. How many southern Whigs would have joined him will never be known. Before the House voted on Preston's bill, northern congressmen attached an amendment specifically prohibiting slavery in the new state. With it went Preston's case for southern honor. Accordingly the amendment, adopted by the narrow vote of 91 to 87, made it impossible for any southerners, be they Whigs or Democrats, to support Preston's bill. In its final appearance Preston's amended bill received not a single aye vote. In the Senate, John Bell's attempt to gain a hearing for Preston's proposal failed miserably.[8] Although this effort to outflank the proviso came to naught, southern Whigs were not dispirited. They still had Zachary Taylor.

Southern Whigs felt secure prior to Taylor's inauguration because they operated under the same assumptions that had marked their campaign for Taylor. Even though Taylor had said nothing publicly regarding the proviso before, during, or after the campaign, southern Whigs counted on his southernness. In short they believed their own campaign rhetoric. Taylor's private remarks, at least as far as the historical record reveals them, were no more definitive than his public silence. Even so, secondhand assurances and firsthand implications undoubtedly acted to strengthen the conviction of southern Whigs that Taylor believed what they said he believed. In 1847 a Louisiana follower of Calhoun reported that he had absolutely unimpeachable information regarding Taylor and the proviso. James D. B. DeBow declared that his close friend the New Orleans merchant-planter Maunsel White, who was also "[Taylor's] most intimate and particular friend in Louisiana," had assured him that

8. *Congressional Globe*, 30th Cong., 2nd Sess., 319, 477–78, 562, 573, 605–609. For more detail on the Preston Bill see Appendix B herein.

Taylor "[was] a Southern man and [would] of course be opposed to the Wilmot Proviso."[9]

Taylor himself wrote somewhat more circumspectly. Yet what seems circumspection at this date probably seemed less so to southerners caught up in the turmoil of 1847 and 1848. In Mexico and after returning to Louisiana, Taylor, as did southerners on all political sides, lambasted the Wilmot Proviso as a measure "gotten up to array the North against the South." While still in Mexico, Taylor confided to his former son-in-law Jefferson Davis that Congress would probably not admit any slave states from conquered territory. Having said as much Taylor spoke about slavery: "We of the South must throw ourselves on the Constitution & defend our rights under it to the last & when arguments will no longer suffice, we will appeal to the sword, if necessary to do so, I will be the last to yield an inch." During the height of the presidential campaign, Taylor wrote to a Whig elector in Virginia that his "extreme [southern] location . . . [his] own[ing] some one hundred working slaves" should clearly prove his southern orientation. Others received similar declarations.[10] Orthodox southerners needed no more. Given their constitutional position and their equation of freesoil or the proviso with abolition, Taylor's remarks could have but one meaning. It was as if he had stated unequivocally that he opposed the proviso and would protect the South from it.

To southern Whigs Taylor's campaign silence on the proviso became astute politics designed to insure victory and to preclude divulging his specific plans. Approving that course they encouraged Taylor to hold his public tongue between the election and the inau-

9. Taylor to John J. Crittenden, January 3, 1848, in Crittenden Papers; DeBow to Calhoun, December 26, 1847, in Chauncey S. Boucher and Robert P. Brooks (eds.), *Correspondence Addressed to John C. Calhoun, 1837–1849* (Washington: Government Printing Office, 1930), 414.

10. Taylor to Davis, July 27, 1847, April 18, 1848, both in Zachary Taylor Papers, Division of Manuscripts, Library of Congress; Taylor to David Pannill, undated, quoted in Rayback, *Free Soil*, 242. Also see Taylor to Robert C. Wood, September 27, 1847, in William H. Samson (ed.), *Letters of Zachary Taylor from the Battle-Fields of the Mexican War* (Rochester, N.Y.: Genesee Press, 1908), 135.

guration.[11] As their opposition to Calhoun's Southern Address made clear, they remained confident that Taylor still stood with them.

Upon assuming the presidency Zachary Taylor moved forthrightly on the territorial issue, but not in a way that pleased most southern Whigs. Although his inaugural address provided no specific clues to his solution for the most pressing national issue, Taylor evidently had already made up his mind.[12] Three basic assumptions underlay the plan Taylor adopted to deal with slavery and the territories. First, as Michael F. Holt convincingly argues, Taylor was eager to forge a new political coalition. Taylor worked to institutionalize the nonpartisanship of his campaign. He believed the time propitious for the creation of a new party, and he acted on that premise. He wanted to remove slavery from the political stage and construct a national party unencumbered with old issues or old allegiances. Equating his response to the slavery question with patriotism, Taylor called on all patriotic Americans to follow his lead. Second, convinced that slavery could not and should not expand, Taylor wanted to keep it within its 1849 boundaries. His most thorough biographer argues that Taylor's strong nationalist outlook, which grew out of his forty-year military career, and his view of slavery in the territories went hand in hand. Because the furor over expanding slavery was hurting the nation, the cause of all the commotion had to be eliminated. According to Holman Hamilton, Taylor was that rare individual, a southerner deeply committed to slavery but just as sincerely opposed to its extension. Finally, having decided to halt the advance of slavery Taylor had to contend with the Wilmot Proviso. Aware of the intense southern feelings regarding the proviso, Taylor proposed to circumvent it by borrowing Pres-

11. Garrett Duncan to John J. Crittenden, January 15, 1849, in Crittenden Papers.

12. For more on Taylor see Michael F. Holt, *Conflict, Consensus, and the Coming of the Civil War: The Political Crisis of the 1850's* (New York: John Wiley, 1978) and Holman Hamilton, *Zachary Taylor: Soldier in the White House* (Indianapolis and New York: Bobbs-Merrill, 1951), 173–76, 409, Chap. 21. Hamilton reprints Taylor's inaugural on pp. 156–58. Also see Taylor's special message to Congress on the territories in James D. Richardson (comp.), *A Compilation of the Messages and Papers of the Presidents, 1789–1897* (10 vols.; Washington: Government Printing Office, 1896–99), V, 26–30.

ton's statehood proposal. Like Preston he intended to bypass the territorial stage altogether for the Mexican Cession. But, unlike Preston who advocated the creation of one state, Taylor proposed to create two states out of the Mexican Cession and have them immediately admitted to the Union. He looked first to California where the discovery of gold mandated governmental organization of some kind. Before his administration was a month old Taylor acted to implement his plan by dispatching Georgia Congressman Thomas B. King to California. King had instructions to let Californians know that the administration wanted a state constitution adopted, followed by a prompt application for admission to the Union. For New Mexico, Taylor had the same process in mind. If Taylor's strategy succeeded, both California and New Mexico would come in as free states. Slavery was practically nonexistent in each place, and Taylor's plan did away with the territorial phase when slaves could theoretically have been introduced. Taylor's plan shut slavery and the South out of the Cession just as effectively as the Wilmot Proviso.

Southern Whigs were taken aback. Although some of them had been willing to support the statehood approach back in January, few of them were willing to stand on that ground in December. By December the immediate statehood solution to the problem of the Mexican Cession could not be supported as a southern solution. Between January and December of 1849, southern Whigs had been severely buffeted by powerful winds blowing from four different directions: a ringing assault by southern Democrats on the statehood idea; serious reverses in state elections; Taylor's patronage policy; the ascendancy in Taylor's administration of northern Whigs, especially those perceived as unfriendly to the South.

Southern Democrats blasted Taylor's plan as no more than the Wilmot Proviso in different clothes or as the "Executive Proviso." In this view Taylor intended to bypass the territorial stage for California only to make the proviso a *fait accompli*. They claimed that in order to restrict slavery Taylor broke with precedent—a territorial phase had preceded statehood for every new state admitted since 1800 except for Texas, a unique case because it was, or at least claimed to be, an independent nation. According to the southern Democrats, Taylor had turned on his own section and his own people; his plan robbed the South of her just rewards from the Mexican War and mocked her constitutional rights. Taylor confirmed this interpretation in an August speech; to a Pennsylvania audience he affirmed, "The people of the North need have no apprehension of the further extension of slavery."[13]

Southern Democrats emphasized that Taylor's plan meant that southern Whigs had violated their pledges to the South on the most critical question. As the Vicksburg *Whig* acknowledged in October, 1849: "The South cast a large vote for Gen. Taylor, not merely because he had served in the tented field, but principally because she had full confidence in his integrity and in his devotion to those rights which the slaveholding States have been forced to defend." Everyone in the South knew the *Whig* spoke the truth. When Zachary Taylor asserted in his inaugural that sectionalism had played no part in his election campaign, the South Carolinian James H. Hammond blasted the claim as "a gross perversion of fact." Southern Democrats had no intention of letting the voters forget those Whig promises. "In Virginia and the whole South," the Richmond *Enquirer* reminded them, "Gen. Taylor was mainly recommended to go to the death for Southern rights." The Houston *Telegraph* emphasized that southern Whigs had staked all for themselves and the South on their campaign declarations that Taylor would never desert his own section. Southern Democrats told the southern voter and the southern community that southern Whigs were untrustworthy and dishonorable because they had committed the South to a political course that imperiled southern institutions.[14]

13. Tallahassee *Floridian*, May 11, 1850; Taylor's speech quoted in Hamilton, *Taylor*, 225.
14. Vicksburg *Tri-Weekly Whig*, October 11, 1849; Hammond to William Gilmore Simms, March 9, 1849, in Hammond Papers; Richmond *Enquirer*, November 23, 1849; Houston *Telegraph*, December 28, 1848.

Southern Democrats did more than remind southerners of those Whig campaign promises. The Milledgeville *Federal Union* indicted them for "insidiously selling the rights of southern freemen for Northern reputation." In the hands of the southern Democrats, Taylor's California strategy became a "monstrous trick and injustice." The Tallahassee *Floridian* wanted to know whether or not southern Whigs and the president cared a whit for the South. Quoting from a freesoil newspaper praising southern Whigs for opposing Calhoun's Southern Address, the Richmond *Enquirer* drew the obvious political conclusion: "We leave it to Southern Whigs to reconcile to the satisfaction of their constituents, these laudations of a Wilmot Proviso journal with their duty to the South at this moment." Similar accusations echoed across the South.[15]

In addition to bearing the brunt of this rhetorical onslaught southern Whigs had to contend with election reverses. Even in states where they still competed on equal terms with the Democrats, the Whigs fared poorly in all that had major elections in 1849. In Tennessee the Democrats won the governorship and the state senate; and according to a recent student of Tennessee politics the southern issue provided the Democratic margin.[16] Georgia Democrats reelected their governor for the first time in more than a decade and doubled his majority in the process. They also took both houses of the legislature away from the Whigs. Louisiana Whigs managed to hold only the state house while losing both the state senate and the governorship. The congressional elections were equally disheartening; the number of Whigs elected to the House dropped from twenty-four to twenty. As a result Whigs made up only 29 percent of the southern congressional delegation.

Zachary Taylor's patronage policy also troubled the southern Whigs, who detected both unrest at home and menace in the North. The river of political jobs they expected to flow out of the Taylor

15. Milledgeville *Federal Union*, February 13, 1849; Richmond *Enquirer*, November 30, January 26, 1849; Tallahassee *Floridian*, February 4, May 11, 1850. See also New Orleans *Louisiana Courier*, December 28, 1849; Raleigh *Standard*, June 20, July 11, 1849.

16. Paul Herbert Bergeron, "The Jacksonian Party on Trial: Presidential Politics in Tennessee, 1836–1856" (Ph.D. dissertation, Vanderbilt University, 1965), 264–65.

administration came forth with a treacherous current. Not wedded
to the institutional Whig party, Taylor did not think of patronage in a
conventional way. He retained Democrats in key spots; he appointed friends to office with little or no thought about party allegiance or local political considerations; he often disregarded the
efforts of state leaders to obtain federal appointments for their fa-
vorites. Although Taylor undoubtedly hoped that this strategy
would bring new faces and new groups to his standard, his plans
backfired. He often angered local Whig chieftains without increasing his own political strength or that of the party. The activities of
prominent antislavery Whigs like Senator William H. Seward of
New York added to the patronage-inspired woes of the southerners.
They worried that Seward especially and other northern Whigs with
pronounced antislavery views had too much influence over the dis-
pensation of patronage in New York and other northern states. This
combination of antislavery politicians and power over patronage,
complained Robert Toombs, "[would] force the whole Northern
Whig party into the extreme anti-slavery position of Seward, which,
of course, sacked the South."[17]

Toombs's reference to Seward underscored the southern Whig
predicament. Even while hard-pressed on their home front southern Whigs were engaged simultaneously in a more desperate battle
with northern Whigs. Reverses in the South they had known before;
they were an inevitable part of politics. But whether or not an upturn in southern Whig fortunes would ever occur depended upon
the outcome of this second struggle. For southern Whigs the contest
with the northerners involved the quintessence of the party arrangement; they had to set party policy on slavery-related issues.
Without that control they as politicians lay at the mercy of the southern Democrats. Moreover as loyal southerners they could not par-
ticipate in an organization that endangered the South.

According to Robert Toombs, the position of the Taylor adminis-

---

17. Hamilton, *Taylor*, 206–207, 215, 234; Toombs to John J. Crittenden, April 24, 1850,
quoted in Mrs. Chapman Coleman (ed.), *The Life of John J. Crittenden with Selections from
His Correspondence and Speeches* (2 vols.; Philadelphia: J. B. Lippincott, 1871), I, 365.

tration on the territorial question "ha[d] nearly estranged the whole Whig party of the South"; in spite of this dire circumstance, southerners who had done so much to make Zachary Taylor president had little influence on administration policy. Remaining in Kentucky as governor, John J. Crittenden pleaded futilely that Taylor move to mollify southerners and meet at least some of their demands on slavery questions. Toombs, Alexander Stephens, and Whig Congressman Charles W. Conrad from the president's own Louisiana found Taylor deaf to their pleas that he remember their needs. Alexander C. Bullitt and Alfred Burnley who came from New Orleans to edit the administration paper, the Washington *Republic,* grew increasingly disenchanged with the direction of administration policy and their inability to effect changes. Although four slave-state men sat in Taylor's cabinet, John M. Clayton of Delaware, Reverdy Johnson of Maryland, and William B. Preston of Virginia, shared their chief's views on the territorial question. Only William Crawford of Georgia supported the southern Whig position and he had little influence.[18]

The man who grew closest to Taylor was the junior senator from New York, William Henry Seward. Initially interested in patronage, Seward was particularly concerned that he and not his fellow New York Whig Vice-President Fillmore manage the political rewards to be handed out by the new administration. Even before Taylor's inauguration Seward had ingratiated himself with the general's only brother and other members of his family. So naturally Seward became a welcome White House visitor.[19] Seward's status as a family friend, however, did not guarantee that he would become Taylor's

18. Toombs to John J. Crittenden, April 25, 1850, and Crittenden to Orlando Brown, June 7, 1850, both quoted in Coleman (ed.), *Crittenden,* I, 364–65, 373–74; Crittenden to John M. Clayton, April 6, 1850, in Clayton Papers; Thomas L. Clingman to Dr. Ladson A. Mills, October 8, 1852, in [Thomas L. Clingman (ed.)], *Selections from the Speeches and Writings of Hon. Thomas L. Clingman of North Carolina, with Additions and Explanatory Notes* (Raleigh: John Nichols, 1877), 317; Alexander Stephens to John J. Crittenden, May 7, 1850, in Stephens Papers, William R. Perkins Library, Duke University and to Linton Stephens, December 5, 1849, April 4, 1850, in Stephens Papers, Manhattanville College; Iverson Harris to John M. Berrien, December 24, 1849, in Berrien Papers; Hamilton, *Taylor,* 324, 380–81.

19. Hamilton, *Taylor,* 168–70, 298.

political confidant. That relationship developed because Taylor and Seward basically agreed on national policy. Seward certainly supported Taylor's territorial strategy. Zachary Taylor had not been a practicing Whig enmeshed in the politics of slavery. Before the commencement of Taylor presidential talk in 1847 no ties had existed between Taylor and southern Whiggery. Even after he became the candidate of the southern Whigs, they made their own claims for him. Taylor did not join their chorus of southernism. In sum he had no particular fidelity to southern Whigs or to southern Whiggery as an institution. He was headed in a new political direction, and as Holman Hamilton maintains, Taylor's views of the South and the nation were more profoundly influenced by his long army career than by his Louisiana residence.

The general distress felt by most southern Whigs over the course of the Taylor administration was not shared by most northern Whigs. Although the patronage fomented difficulties in the North just as it did in the South, most northern Whigs found Taylor's territorial policy and his looking to northern advisers pleasing indeed. Like their southern brothers northern Whigs had consciously used the sectional issue for their own benefit. In a reverse mirror image of southern Whigs, northern Whigs had constantly denounced northern Democrats for bowing to southern demands.[20] Now that the Taylor administration seemed to be following their precepts they had no intention of giving up what they considered a signal political advantage. The southerners could follow their lead.

Southern Whigs found this attitude fraught with danger. Even before Taylor's election a Georgia Whig had complained to Senator John Berrien, "It seems to me that Northern Whigs exact too much from us, & yield too little themselves." The situation worsened in 1849. North Carolina's Willie P. Mangum and Thomas C. Clingman became increasingly distressed over the strength of antislavery sentiment among northern Whigs and the growing influence of Seward

20. *Ibid.*, 234; Glyndon G. Van Deusen, *William Henry Seward* (New York: Oxford University Press, 1967), 94, 102, 104, 110.

and others sharing his outlook over the Taylor administration. When the Thirty-first Congress assembled, southern Whigs found their northern colleagues in no mood to bend southward. Appalled at the "aggressive . . . spirit of the Northern Whigs," Alexander Stephens in conjunction with other southerners exclaimed, "I [shall] hold no connection with a party that did not disconnect itself from those aggressive abolition movements." Representative Charles Morehead of Kentucky informed Crittenden that the northern Whigs were "blind, absolutely blind to the real dangers" facing southern Whigs. The Raleigh *Register* announced that the South would not support a party bent on destroying the Constitution and dominated by men like Seward, "a hopeless madman." Adopting a militant line the Milledgeville *Southern Recorder* proclaimed that southern Whigs would not remain part of a political organization aiming to destroy the South.[21]

The first direct manifestation of this disaffection came when the House of Representatives elected a speaker. Robert Winthrop, a Massachusetts Whig, had been speaker during the Thirtieth Congress, and he wanted the post again. The Whig caucus in the House selected Winthrop as its candidate, but six southerners from four different states refused to go along. For the first several ballots all six voted against Winthrop, and five of the six voted against him on all sixty-three ballots. Those votes, thrown away mostly on Meredith P. Gentry of Tennessee, deprived Winthrop of victory in the close election. Understandably this defection angered northern Whigs. Six congressmen do not seem like very many, but they accounted for

21. Iverson Harris to Berrien, March 25, 1848, in Berrien Papers; Henry Thomas Shanks (ed.), *The Papers of Willie Person Mangum* (5 vols.; Raleigh: State Department of Archives and History, 1950–56), V, 179, n. 5; [Clingman (ed.),] *Clingman Writings*, 232–33; Stephens to John J. Crittenden, December 17, 1849, in Stephens Papers, William R. Perkins Library, Duke University, and to Linton Stephens, December 2, 1849, in Stephens Papers, Manhattanville College; Morehead to Crittenden, March 31, 1850, quoted in Coleman (ed.), *Crittenden*, I, 363; Raleigh *Register*, April 17, 1850; Milledgeville *Southern Recorder*, December 18, 1849.

more than one-third of the southern Whig ballots cast. Southern voters had elected only twenty Whigs to the Thirty-first Congress, and three of them were not in Washington for the voting.[22]

Zachary Taylor remained impervious to the anger and fear dominating southern Whiggery. When Congress met in December, Taylor informed the lawmakers that he expected California and New Mexico to apply for statehood; he then urged prompt acceptance of the applications. Taylor's message went to a Congress in uproar. In 1849 the sectional tensions and recriminations already permeating the country turned into a raging invective that lacerated the previously exposed nerves of both North and South.[23] Cries on both sides about the Wilmot Proviso, about slavery in the District of Columbia, about the interstate slave trade, about fugitive slaves increased in stridency and bitterness. Angry resolutions and memorials from legislatures and public meetings came forth in ever more powerful torrents. Many new congressmen from each section were products of the furious rhetoric that spoke of disunion, of the end of the republic, of spilling blood. And few returning representatives and senators escaped the acrimonious controversy dominating public debate.

Southern veterans of the congressional scene testified that they had never seen sectional relations so filled with animosity. Alabama's William R. King who had been in Congress or close to it for forty years wrote that a mood of "desperation" predominated among the southern members. Democratic Congressman Frederick P. Stanton of Tennessee talked about southerners making a last ditch stand. "Sectional feeling is stronger than I ever saw it before," witnessed Alexander Stephens. Returning to the Senate after an absence of a half-dozen years, Henry Clay reported "the feeling of

22. *Congressional Globe*, 31st Cong., 1st Sess., 2–66 *passim*. The six were Edward Cabell, Henry Hilliard, Jeremiah Morton, Allen Owen, Alexander Stephens, and Robert Toombs.
23. Richardson (comp.), *Messages and Papers of the Presidents*, V, 18–19; Allan Nevins, *Ordeal of the Union* (2 vols.; New York and London: Charles Scribner's Sons, 1947), I, 219–21.

disunion" and sectional bitterness "is stronger than I hoped or supposed it could be."[24]

In this volatile cauldron Clay moved to dampen the fire.[25] Believing that Taylor's insistence on the admission of a free California and a free New Mexico accompanied by no effort to placate angry southerners might well cause the cauldron to explode, Clay returned to the compromise role he had played in 1820 and 1833. He proposed to quench the sectional conflagration by attempting to mollify all parties. For the North he wanted California in as a free state and an end to the slave trade in the District of Columbia. For the South he advocated organizing the rest of the Mexican Cession in two territories, New Mexico and Utah, with no mention of slavery, and a stringent fugitive slave law that would make the federal government responsible for apprehending and returning bondsmen who had escaped to the free states. He completed his compromise package by providing for a settlement of the contentious Texas–New Mexico boundary question.

Clay's compromise offered southern Whigs a potential political refuge. Because Clay's program contained advantages for the South, it provided positive inducements for hard-pressed southern Whigs. They could not defend Taylor's plan in the South. The southern Democratic offensive against it plus the other troubles plaguing southern Whiggery transformed the president's measure into a lethal political liability. For southern Whigs to tie themselves to Taylor's plan guaranteed annihilation in the politics of slavery. And standing adamantly by his own plan, President Taylor refused to give his blessings to Clay's compromise attempt. Thus the defection from the party and the administration standard that had begun dur-

24. King to James Buchanan, January 13, 1850, and Stanton to James Buchanan, December 20, 1849, both in Buchanan Papers; Stephens to John J. Crittenden, December 17, 1849, in Stephens Papers, William R. Perkins Library, Duke University; Clay to Leslie Combs, December 22, 1849, in Calvin Colton (ed.), *The Private Correspondence of Henry Clay* (New York: A. S. Barnes, 1856), 593.

25. For Clay see Nevins, *Ordeal*, I, 264–85 and Holman Hamilton, *Prologue to Conflict: The Crisis and Compromise of 1850* (Lexington: University of Kentucky Press, 1964), Chap. 3.

ing the election for speaker picked up momentum. The chasm that had opened between northern and southern Whigs over the speakership widened as the southerners rallied to Clay's compromise banner. In the Senate only John Bell of Tennessee "inclined toward Taylor's standard." North Carolina's Mangum and George Badger along with Georgia's William Dawson backed Clay. Berrien of Georgia and Jackson Morton of Florida moved between Clay and the southern Democrats. At the same time almost every northern Whig senator was an implacable foe of compromise; Seward termed it the measure of "the slave power." An identical lineup occurred in the House where almost every southern Whig was for compromise and every northern Whig against. As Robert Toombs reported to a Georgia friend, northern Whig representatives were doing everything in their power to block it.[26]

In the midst of the congressional imbroglio Taylor's erstwhile southern loyalists made a final effort to bring the president back into their orbit. On several occasions during the first half of 1850 southern Whigs trooped from Capitol Hill to the White House to remonstrate with their former hero. During one of these visits an ugly shouting match erupted between Taylor and the Georgians, Toombs and Stephens; the epithets *traitor* and *treason* reverberated through the presidential mansion. Bitterness and enmity had replaced respect and forbearance. By summer the southerners concluded that no hope remained for a reconciliation between them and the president from whom they had expected so much. "The South has no influence with the Cabinet, or with the Administration," the North Carolinian David Outlaw wrote to his wife. "It is in the hands of the North." As far as the southern congressional Whigs were

26. Robert Winthrop to John P. Kennedy, December 4, 1849, in Kennedy Papers; Hamilton, *Taylor*, 285; Seward to Home, June 8, 1850, quoted in Frederick W. Seward, *William H. Seward; an Autobiography from 1801 to 1834. With a Memoir of His Life and Selections from His Letters* (3 vols.; New York: Derby and Miller, 1891), II, 138; Robert Caruthers to Millard Fillmore, August 10, 1850, in Millard Fillmore Papers, Buffalo and Erie County Historical Society; Toombs to Young L. G. Harris, April 20, 1850, in Robert Toombs Papers, Georgia Archives.

concerned, "Genl. Taylor had utterly abandoned the South and her institutions." Among those institutions was the southern Whig party, for Taylor told one southern delegation that he would sacrifice the southern Whigs in order to carry his policy.[27]

This feeling of doom had not yet seeped through to the Whigs back in the states. Although reports of disgust with Taylor's performance were not uncommon, most southern Whig newspapers called on their readers to remain loyal to President Taylor who was still their president and a southerner. At the same time they heaped praise upon Clay's compromise which "truly represent[ed] the wishes of the Southern people"; it became the proper program for southern Whiggery. The editors kept repeating that Taylor would accept the compromise and end the disagreement between the mass of southern Whigs and their president. They considered it inconceivable that Taylor would refuse to accept Clay's compromise.[28] Southern Whigs in Washington knew better.

In the middle of 1850, southern Whig leaders faced the very real prospect that they would have to find their future political home outside the Whig party. Although Clay's compromise provided them a politically defensible platform as well as one they could uphold as southerners, they could not stand upon it as Whigs—not so long as the Whig administration and the northern half of the party opposed it as giving too much to the South. Remaining in such a party would guarantee their political demise in southern politics and threaten their standing in the southern community. Time had seemingly collapsed on these southern Whigs. At the beginning of 1849 they were euphoric; they saw the world of southern politics

27. Hamilton, *Taylor*, 380–82; Harriet A. Weed (ed.), *Life of Thurlow Weed, Including His Autobiography and a Memoir* (2 vols.; Boston: Houghton Mifflin, 1883), II, 176–79; David Outlaw to Emily Outlaw, June 24, 1850, in Outlaw Papers; William McWillie (Mississippi congressman) to His Wife, July 14, 1850, in William McWillie Papers, Mississippi Department of Archives and History; Thomas L. Clingman to Dr. Ladson A. Mills, October 8, 1852, in [Clingman (ed.),] *Clingman Writings*, 317–18.

28. Raleigh *Register*, April 17, May 15, 29, June 12, 19, 1850; New Orleans *Bee*, spring, 1850, *passim*; Richmond *Whig*, March 21, May 17, 31, June 21, 1850; Vicksburg *Weekly Whig*, February 9, 1850; Milledgeville *Southern Recorder*, May 21, 28, June 11, 1850.

lying at their feet. But by mid-1850 those glorious prospects lay in shambles. The president they had chosen to lead them into that political promised land had shattered their dream. While the southern Whigs were preoccupied with the wreckage of their hopes, the southern Democrats prepared for direct action.

II

From late 1848 through 1850 the influence and spirit of John C. Calhoun dominated the actions of the southern Democrats. Accordingly on the fundamental sectional issues confronting the South they advanced considerably beyond the position held by the southern Whigs. Eschewing Clay's compromise—and thereby allowing the Whigs to find a respectable and defensible public posture— southern Democrats in a distinctly Calhounite pose called on the South to declare publicly her demands and then insist that the North guarantee them. As Calhoun formulated plans for his Southern Address, southern legislatures, with Democrats generally in the vanguard, passed resolutions calculating the value of the Union if the North persisted in its iniquitous antislavery and antisouthern course. Led by Calhounites, southern Democrats strove to galvanize the South into an armed ideological camp poised to strike.[29]

Calhoun also spearheaded the southern Democrats in Congress. The congressional movement that resulted in the Southern Address began as a bipartisan movement. But when the southern Whigs pulled out, its new description read southern Democrats only. Southern Democrats went along with Calhoun until they and he finally agreed on the proper form for the Southern Address. When the address was formally adopted in late January, 1849, southern Democrats affixed their signatures in impressive numbers—every southern Democratic senator except the two Texans and more than

29. Avery O. Craven, *The Growth of Southern Nationalism, 1848–1861* (Baton Rouge: Louisiana State University Press, 1953), 52–53; *Niles' Register*, LXXV (January 31, 1849), 73, 94–95; Hopkins Holsey to Howell Cobb, February 24, 1849, in Phillips (ed.), *Toombs, Stephens, Cobb Correspondence*, 154–55; Alexander Stephens to William B. Preston, March 21, 1849, in Alexander Stephens Papers, Robert W. Woodruff Library, Emory University.

two-thirds of the southern Democratic representatives signed. Their commitment to the address provided a legitimate basis for Calhoun's positive evaluation of the importance and effect of his address, even though a few southern Democrats refused to follow his lead.[30]

The dissidents, led by Georgia's Howell Cobb in the House and Thomas J. Rusk and Sam Houston of Texas in the Senate, argued that Calhoun's initiative threatened the Democratic party. Following President Polk, who had favored the movement as a defense of southern rights until the Whig defection, these men condemned Calhoun for endangering the Democratic party. Accusing him of showing base ingratitude to "our only friends at the North," Cobb condemned Calhoun for lumping northern Democrats together with northern Whigs and abolitionists as enemies of the South. Cobb divined Calhoun's purpose as "look[ing] to the dissolution of the democratic party." Concurring, Senator Rusk declared that Calhoun intended "to create a new political organization." Rusk's colleague Sam Houston blasted Calhoun for his "selfish and unholy ambition" that jeopardized the party and the nation. While claiming to defend their party, the South's surest guardian, from the machinations of Calhoun, the Cobbs and the Rusks announced their willingness to face whatever political consequences came their way.[31]

They certainly got their chance. The political difficulties greeting the few southern Democrats who shunned the Southern Address point up the militancy pervading the southern Democrats. Identify-

30. For the signers see Richard K. Crallé (ed.), *The Works of John C. Calhoun* (6 vols.; New York: D. Appleton, 1854–57), VI, 312–13; Calhoun to James H. Hammond, February 14, 1849, and to Mrs. Thomas G. Clemson, January 24, 1849, both in J. Franklin Jameson (ed.), *Correspondence of John C. Calhoun* (Washington: Government Printing Office, 1900), 762.

31. Milo Milton Quaife (ed.), *The Diary of James K. Polk during His Presidency, 1845–1849* (4 vols.; Chicago: A. C. McClurg, 1910), IV, 253, 280–82; Cobb to John B. Lamar, January 16, 24, both in Cobb Papers; Rusk to [?], January 30, 1849, in Rusk Papers; Houston to Henderson Yoakum, January 31, 1849, in Amelia W. Williams and Eugene C. Barker (eds.), *The Writings of Sam Houston, 1813–1863* (8 vols.; Austin: University of Texas Press, 1938–43), V, 71–72.

ing those who signed the address as defenders and upholders of southern honor, southern Democrats indicted the dissenters for deserting the South in "the hour of peril." Warned by friends that Georgia Democrats had targeted him for special attacks, Cobb "hope[d] that I may yet resuscitate my sinking fortunes in Georgia." To save himself from destruction at the hands of his fellows, Cobb assured Georgians that he too preferred "death before dishonor" of the South. He also pressed leading Democrats for statements emphasizing his unswerving loyalty to the South. Although Cobb got the declarations he so desperately wanted, more than half a decade passed before he regained the confidence of the Georgia Democratic party.[32] Thomas J. Rusk found himself besieged with demands to know why he had failed to stand with the South. Defending himself as one totally committed to the South and her constitutional rights Rusk vehemently protested such accusations as "utterly destitute of any foundation in fact." Even so Rusk, who stood second only to Houston as a hero among Texans, had to wait through several postponements before the Texas legislature finally reelected him to the Senate. In Alabama the Calhounites strengthened their hand among Democrats and kept up inexorable pressure upon those who withheld their support from the address. James I. McKay, the only North Carolina Democratic congressman who failed to sign the Southern Address, had to deal with angry constituents talking of turning away from him because he opposed the address. Among advocates and opponents of the address, affirmations of a militant southernism abounded.[33]

32. Herschel V. Johnson to John C. Calhoun, June 28, 1849, in Herschel V. Johnson Papers, William R. Perkins Library, Duke University; Cobb to His Wife, February 8, 1849, in R. P. Brooks (ed.), "Howell Cobb Papers," *Georgia Historical Quarterly,* V (1921), 38; Cobb to John B. Lamar, January 24, 1849, in Cobb Papers; Cobb to James Buchanan, June 2, 17, 1849, in Buchanan Papers; Cobb to James K. Polk, June 2, 1849, in Polk Papers; Cobb to Robert J. Walker, June 2, 1849, in Walker Papers; John B. Lamar to Cobb, May 18, 1849, and Lewis Cass to Cobb, June 19, 1849, both in Cobb-Erwin-Lamar Papers.
33. George D. Phillips to Rusk, April 2, 1849, W. J. Mills to Rusk, January 19, 1850, W. D. Miller to Rusk, August 23, 1850, John H. Moffett to Rusk, August 28, 1850, Rusk to Tod Robinson, September 2, 1849, Rusk to W. J. Mills, February 7, 1850, all in Rusk Papers;

This increasingly strident stand on southern rights carried directly into the Thirty-first Congress. Headlined by threats of disunion sectional rhetoric of the most extreme character dominated the 1849 state campaigns run by southern Democrats. When they reached the halls of Congress, belligerence flashed from their eyes, and talk of secession sprang from their lips. In this angry mood southern Democrats denounced Zachary Taylor's territorial strategy as "utterly worthless and odious," as an open-ended attack upon the South. The possible admission of a free California particularly enraged them. Bypassing the territorial stage in California, which blemished southern honor and precluded any chance for the introduction of slavery, they damned as the enactment of the hated proviso. President Taylor found not a single supporter among the representatives and senators in southern Democratic ranks.[34]

Henry Clay and his compromise fared little better. After all, Clay proposed to admit California as a free state, the same sin committed by Taylor. And in the minds of most southern Democrats, Clay's peace offerings to the South simply did not suffice. Within a month of his final earthly breath Calhoun made a last great call to the South. Dismissing Clay's compromise proposals as superficial bandages, Calhoun told the assembled senators that Clay had glossed over the actual and deep divisions within the country. He proposed no specific solutions, but he did say that the crisis could be safely passed only by congressional adoption of "such measures as will satisfy the States belonging to the southern section that they can remain in the Union consistently with their honor and safety." To Calhoun admission of California would sound the death knell of southern rights. The black pessimism pervading Calhoun's speech clearly

---

George S. Houston to Howell Cobb, June 20, 1849, in Cobb Papers; Henry W. Hilliard to John M. Berrien, May 8, 1849, in Berrien Papers and to Henry S. Foote, May 5, 1849, in Ferdinand J. Dreer Collection of American Statesmen, Historical Society of Pennsylvania; Jno. K. Buie to Edmund DeBerry, April 6, 1849, in Edmund DeBerry Papers, Southern Historical Collection, University of North Carolina.

34. Howell Cobb to William Hope Hull, July 17, 1850, in Phillips (ed.), *Toombs, Stephens, Cobb Correspondence*, 200.

shows he expected no protection of the South from the nation at large. Although few other southern Democrats sounded quite so gloomy, they counterposed thunderous cries for southern rights with ominous declarations of southern intentions if these cries were unheard. In the Senate they called Clay's proposals concessions to the North, not guarantees for the South. Several southern Democrats mounted the podium in the House to excoriate Clay's scheme. Exclaiming that Clay's compromise incorporated "a surrender to the North" of southern rights, southern Democratic newspapers kept pace with their congressional spokesmen. By late spring a few southern Democrats, led by Howell Cobb in the House and Mississippi's Henry S. Foote in the Senate, had come over to Clay's side, but most remained implacably opposed. Few planned to vote for Clay's package; for the salvation of the South as well as their own the southern Demoirats put their faith in a southern convention.[35]

Declaring that the time had come for united resistance to northern aggression, a Mississippi convention meeting in October, 1849, called for a southern convention to assemble in Nashville in June, 1850. Following months of calls to political arms from politicians and legislatures across the South, the Mississippi declaration seemed to herald the fruition of John C. Calhoun's long-cherished dream—a southern convention that would present an ultimatum to the North. Throughout 1849, Calhoun actively lobbied for a convention. Envisioning his Southern Address as a preamble for the general declaration of a southern convention, Calhoun repeatedly urged concerted southern action as the only way to guard southern interests and stave off northern aggression. He was instrumental in the actions of the Mississippians. To his followers in Mississippi he sent encouragement and recommendations. The outcome of the Mississippi con-

---

35. For examples of Democratic speeches see *Congressional Globe*, 31st Cong., 1st Sess., 248–50, 257–61, 336–40, 451–55, and Appendix, 102–105, 157–65, 195–98, 649–55; Tallahassee *Floridian*, February 9, 1850; Jackson *Mississippian*, June 14, 1850; Milledgeville *Federal Union*, January 15, February 5, 1850; Raleigh *Standard*, March 13, May 22, 1850; Richmond *Enquirer*, May 24, 1850; Henry S. Foote to James Buchanan, March 31, 1850, in Buchanan Papers.

vention certainly pleased him. "The course adopted by Mississippi is, in my opinion," he wrote, "the only one that affords any prospect of saving the Union or, if that should fail, of certainly saving ourselves." Exulting he exclaimed, "The whole appears to me excellent."[36]

A major reason for Calhoun's exultation arose from the bipartisanship of the Mississippi convention. Finally his old nemesis of party loyalty had been overcome, for both Democrats and Whigs participated, and a leading Whig, Judge William L. Sharkey, was president. In the fall of 1849 prospects appeared excellent that both parties in the South would heed the Mississippi call. The only visible alternative to the proposed southern convention was Zachary Taylor's plan, anathema to most southerners including Whigs.

Even so, the southern Democrats took the Nashville convention as their own. It seemed like an appropriate forum for their increasingly shrill shouts about the South's need to protect herself. Moreover the Calhounites rejoiced over the convention idea, and the southern Democrats had been responding to the Calhounite baton since the Southern Address. They were not braked by the hope that their president would turn the slavery issue to their advantage—a hope still very much alive among southern Whigs in late 1849. If the southern Democrats could successfully equate the Nashville convention with the safety of the South, they could increase the political pressure on the already burdened southern Whigs. Of course the southern Democrats would have been delighted to have their Whig opponents join their crusade. And to that end they urged southern Whigs to come along.

But when Henry Clay stepped forward with his compromise, the possibility of southern unity evaporated. In embracing Clay's com-

36. For the Mississippi Convention see Wiltse, *Calhoun*, III, 406–408, and Cleo Hearon, "Mississippi and the Compromise of 1850," *Publications of the Mississippi Historical Society*, XIV (1914), 45–68. Calhoun to John H. Means, April 13, 1849, to Andrew Pickens Calhoun, July 24, 1849, to James H. Hammond, December 7, 1849, January 4, 1850, all in Jameson (ed.), *Calhoun Correspondence*, 764–66, 769–70, 775–76, 778–80; Calhoun to David L. Yulee, October 19, 1849, in Yulee Papers.

promise southern Whigs turned against the Nashville convention. They had a political and an ideological motive. Seizing the compromise as a political platform that would stand in the South, they had little interest in heading for Nashville where they would be only a part of the Democratic team. Southern Whigs were also troubled by the obvious delight shown by Calhoun and his coterie. Many feared that Nashville would produce an attempt at nullification or secession. Thus the political possibilities opened by the compromise especially gladdened them.

Instead of following the path broken by Sharkey and anticipated by Calhoun, southern Whigs began dissociating themselves from the proposed convention. In their rhetoric Nashville became a synonym for an uncalled-for radicalism, for nullification, for secession. Disagreeing with the dominant opinion, a minority among southern Whigs thought the convention a good idea or at least that Whigs ought to be represented there. Although precise numbers in each Whig camp are impossible to obtain, the evidence demonstrates that the overwhelming majority of southern Whigs opposed the convention. Even in Mississippi, where Whigs were elected along with Democrats as delegates to Nashville, the party, including Judge Sharkey, began to doubt the efficacy of the convention. To the Vicksburg *Whig* the Nashville convention smelled like a southern Democratic attempt to spark an even deeper sectional crisis or to make a party issue in the South or both.[37]

Fusing southern Democratic partisanship with radicalism or disunion characterized the southern Whig message. This kind of charge was a serious matter, for no major southern group supported disunion in the spring of 1850. Even Calhoun, though despairing, prayed that southern rights could be preserved within the Union. Only the passage of the Wilmot Proviso itself or the total victory of Taylor's plan would change the situation. And the Whig press underscored that nothing so drastic had occurred. The New Orleans

37. Baton Rouge *Gazette*, May 11, 1850; Tallahassee *Floridian*, March 2, 1850; Hearon, "Mississippi," 118–19; Vicksburg *Weekly Whig*, March 6, 1850.

Bee called the convention extreme and unjustified. The Richmond *Whig* saw no need for such a radical move, and the Raleigh *Register* emphasized that the convention would probably harbor nullifiers and secessionists. Discovering the schemes of "crafty politicians" behind the convention, the Helena *Southern Shield* dismissed it as a Democratic trick to subvert the people and the Union.[38]

As a result of the Whig assault on the convention, southern Democrats found themselves in an unpleasant situation. Instead of pressuring their Whig opponents and leading a united South, they found themselves forced to defend both their politics and their convention. Simultaneously they emphatically and truthfully denied that they were disunionists and that the Nashville convention would break up the Union. On the contrary, they insisted that the convention would preserve the Union by uniting the South and forcing the North to recognize southern rights. Continuously southern Democrats tried to shed the partisan cloak placed on the convention by the Whigs. Repeatedly they cried, "This is no party question." Again and again they called for a united southern front, but to no avail.[39]

Whig opposition was not the only problem confronting southern Democrats. By the late winter of 1850 a general apathy toward the convention pervaded the South; the Democrats simply could not recreate the enthusiasm and excitement that had prevailed back in the autumn of 1849. Only in Mississippi and South Carolina did the selection of delegates generate substantial enthusiasm. Elsewhere interest flagged, few voters turned out, and few delegates were chosen.[40] Although such a contention cannot be proved, the advent of Clay's compromise and the widespread support for it among

38. New Orleans *Bee*, April 5, 1850; Richmond *Whig*, January 15, 18, 25, 1850; Raleigh *Register*, January 23, April 17, 1850; Helena (Ark.) *Southern Shield*, March 9, May 11, 1850.

39. New Orleans *Louisiana Courier*, March 12, 19, 1850; Milledgeville *Federal Union*, March 5, April 2, 1850; Richmond *Enquirer*, February 1, March 1, April 26, 1850; Raleigh *Standard*, January 16, 1850. Only the radical secessionists (see just below) hoped for definite disunion moves from the Nashville convention; even the orthodox Calhounites thought in terms of an ultimatum, not secession. James M. Mason to William C. Rives, February 4, 1850, in Rives Papers.

40. Craven, *Southern Nationalism*, 94.

southern Whigs and a few southern Democrats most probably made the national crisis seem less imminent and the need for drastic southern action less immediate. The campaign mounted by southern Whigs to connect the convention with party politics and disunion undoubtedly reinforced the relaxation of southern tension.

Southern Democrats had evidently moved too far too fast for most southerners. Racing along with the momentum of 1849, most of them did not look back to see whether the South followed. Although a few individual exceptions did exist, southern Democrats as a party totally misjudged the impact of Clay's compromise proposal on southerners. Clay's program added a third alternative to the diametric opposites, Taylor's plan and the Nashville convention. With it a possible middle ground appeared. While many southerners had doubts both about the compromise and the willingness of the North to grant the South her rights, their negative reaction to the convention proposal suggests that most southerners wanted to see what happened in Congress before they decided on a course of action.

The Nashville convention did meet on schedule with at least one delegate from every southern state except Louisiana and North Carolina, but it adopted no ultimatums and provided a rickety platform for southern Democrats. Realizing they possessed no mandate for conclusive action, the delegates adopted the policy of wait and see, the path always favored by the procompromise minority among southern Democrats.[41] The convention adopted a series of resolutions affirming southern rights, especially in the territories, and said those rights must be honored by the nation and the national legislature, and finally it reserved the right to judge the adequacy of whatever Congress might do. To insure that the convention would

41. There is no first-rate study of the Nashville convention. The basic source is *Resolutions, Address, and Journal of Proceedings of the Southern Convention . . .* (Nashville: Harvey M. Watterson, 1850); the fullest secondary account is Dallas T. Herndon, "The Nashville Convention of 1850," *Transactions of the Alabama Historical Society,* V (1904), 203–37. Cave Johnson to James Buchanan, January 20, August 14, 1850, both in Buchanan Papers and Pierre Soulé to Charles E. A. Gayarré, May 9, 1850, in Gayarré Papers, Department of Archives, Louisiana State University.

have that chance, the delegates resolved to reconvene after Congress adjourned.

To the true southern radicals this outcome was galling. And the crisis of 1849–1850 did witness the first serious activities of fire-eaters or doctrinaire disunionists or secessionists or political radicals.[42] During these troubled months many loyal party men, especially among the Democrats, did recite disunion litanies, but almost without exception they advocated secession only after the passage of the Wilmot Proviso or some other equally horrendous act. The doctrinaire disunionists were a different breed altogether. They gave loyalty not to parties, not even to Calhoun or his memory, but only to their vision of an independent South. Like Calhoun they believed parties dangerous for southern well-being, but unlike Calhoun they had no attachment to the Union. The committed secessionists were not his legitimate heirs, and they never claimed to be. Although Calhoun had devoted his energies to gaining for the South his conception of its rightful place in the Union, the radicals had no interest in maintaining the Union. While Calhoun had hoped against hope that the Nashville convention would result in protecting southern rights in the Union, the radicals hoped the Nashville convention would be the first step on the march out of the Union.

These radicals dotted the southern landscape in 1850; while no census of their numbers exists, theirs was a small band. With many Calhounites refusing to follow their dictum of secession now the radicals did not enjoy the widespread political influence or respectability possessed by the Calhounites. Neither could they claim a Calhoun among them; no doctrinaire secessionist emerged from among his fellows as a generally recognized and respected leader. State leaders existed, and able ones too, but none became a Calhoun capable of profoundly influencing men and events from one end of the South to the other.

42. A word on terms—the meanings of *secessionist* and *disunionist* are obvious; they describe men who wanted to break up the Union. In the 1850s the terms *radical* and *fire-eater* were often used as synonyms for the other two words. In my text I use the four interchangeably.

In fact in 1850 the radicals exercised substantial political power in only three states—South Carolina, Alabama, and Mississippi.[43] Their stronghold was South Carolina where Calhoun had inculcated a faith in direct action in an entire generation. But Calhoun had hoped that direct action could preserve the Union and he had always believed that he could influence national policy. Those two convictions died with him. Those he left behind in South Carolina inherited neither his devotion to the Union nor his faith that national policy could be shaped to benefit the South. Younger Carolina radicals relished the idea of secession and older ones like Robert Barnwell Rhett had long chafed under Calhoun's tight reins. They hungered to break up the Union. The congregation of radicals in Alabama and Mississippi helped push the Democratic parties of those states toward increasingly militant sectional stands. In Alabama the great orator William Lowndes Yancey spoke for those who had concluded that remaining in the Union was the equivalent of committing suicide. The old Calhounite John A. Quitman, who had become a rabid secessionist, led the radical forces in Mississippi. Elected governor in 1849, Quitman held the highest office of any radical outside South Carolina. All of these men had one common goal—to dissolve the Union as soon as possible.

Standing outside the conventional boundaries, even the Calhounite boundaries, of political behavior the radicals cried continuously for drastic action. According to them the Union was a dagger aimed at the southern heart; to escape the death thrust the South had to

43. The absence of a full study of the fire-eaters forms a shameful gap in southern historiography. Professor William W. Freehling's forthcoming book will undoubtedly fill this void. Although several monographs have recently been published on the secession crisis of 1860–1861, they do not deal with the specific events of 1850–1851 or with the early story of radicalism. By far the best account of the 1850–1851 crisis and the subsequent development of radicalism in the 1850s is the superb study of Alabama by Jonathan Mills Thornton III, "Politics and Power in a Slave Society: Alabama, 1806–1860" (Ph.D. dissertation, Yale University, 1974), Pt. 2 *passim*. For Mississippi and South Carolina see Hearon, "Mississippi," and Philip May Hamer, *The Secession Movement in South Carolina, 1847–1852* (Allentown, Pa.: H. Ray Haas, 1918). Two manuscript collections that are particularly revealing on radical activities in 1850 and 1851 are the Whitemarsh B. Seabrook Papers, Division of Manuscripts, Library of Congress and the J. F. H. Claiborne Papers, Mississippi Department of Archives and History.

leave the Union. Accepting this interpretation of sectional relations, radicals thought waiting on the passage of the Wilmot Proviso or on abolition in the District of Columbia idiotic, because the North had already made its intentions known. Although all radicals embraced immediate secession, they did not all agree on the best way to accomplish it. Some among them urged the secession of any state they could get out of the Union. Others argued that separate state action would be futile; they insisted that cooperation among two or more states was essential for the ultimate success of secession. In 1850 the latter group dominated radical councils.

The incessant drumbeat of their shrill cries caused two different reactions in southern politics. Because numerous radicals maintained at least pro forma ties with the Democrats they tugged the Democratic party leftward especially in Alabama and Mississippi. For a time in 1850 and 1851 it seemed possible that South Carolina would no longer stand alone on her radical pedestal. But the secessionists also offered a convenient target for the orthodox southern politicians. They pictured the radicals as purveyors of doom, as lunatics who called on the South to give up the security of the Union and the Constitution for a leap into the political unknown, into secession. According to the orthodox script, the gloomy portrayals of the radicals missed the mark by a considerable distance. For evidence the orthodox declared that no direct attack on slavery had yet succeeded. And as the results of the events of 1850 and 1851 clearly indicate, few southerners accepted the radical assessment of the southern situation. To be closely connected with the radicals became a liability for a politician or a party. The radicals could flourish only if the South and southern politicians perceived actual danger. Without that perception the radicals would be frustrated—thus their distress at the outcome of the Nashville convention. As long as the compromise remained before the Congress, Rhett, Yancey, Quitman, and their companions could do little more than howl in the political wilderness.

Within the framework of southern politics the result of the convention episode must be termed a Whig victory. The South seemed to be waiting on the outcome of the compromise battle in Congress. And on the compromise, southern Whigs had bet their political future. If it passed the Congress, the political signs in the South indicated they had made a good wager. If, on the other hand, it failed, neither Whig, Democrat, nor radical knew what the future held.

III

As the delegates left Nashville, the fate of Clay's compromise and the future configuration of southern politics remained in doubt. Throughout the spring and early summer of 1850, advocates and foes of the compromise alternately felt despondency and relief as the outlook for the compromise's passage swung back and forth between bright and gloomy. Although the compromise pendulum swayed in the Congress, no movement occurred in the White House. Zachary Taylor remained a steadfast foe of Clay's plan. Because of Taylor's unwavering stand the procompromise forces worked with an added measure of uncertainty. Even if they managed to get the compromise through Congress, a presidential veto could very easily negate all their efforts.[44]

Then in July two momentous events occurred. The first seemed to strengthen the hand of the compromise men. On July 9 Zachary Taylor became the second president to die in office; after a lifetime of surviving frontier hardships and battlefield dangers the old general succumbed in the White House. Taylor spent much of a wickedly hot July 4 outside exercising vigorously and participating in Independence Day activities. Upon returning to the White House he indiscriminately gorged himself with raw fruits or vegetables and cold liquids. Shortly thereafter Taylor was struck with acute gastroenteritis; he lived less than a week. His death seemingly brightened the prospects for the compromise because Millard

44. Hamilton's *Prologue* has the fullest account of the compromise in Congress.

Fillmore's accession placed a friend of compromise in the presidential chair. The advent of Seward had made the vice-president an outsider in the Taylor administration; thus he had gravitated toward the administration's leading congressional opponents, Clay and Daniel Webster. Accordingly Fillmore identified his political future with the compromise. Even so his becoming president did not guarantee its passage.

And three weeks after Taylor's death the Clay compromise crashed in defeat. Clay presented the statehood, territorial, and boundary parts of his program in one great compromise package, called the omnibus by contemporaries. Thus he gave no opportunity to construct temporary coalitions that could possibly pass various sections. The opponents of compromise, chiefly northern Whigs and southern Democrats, had the votes, and on July 31 they wrecked Clay's omnibus. The change at the White House had worked no miracles. Just as Taylor's death brightened the compromise sky, the defeat of the omnibus blackened it.

But the supporters of the compromise refused to give up; the compromise refused to die; phoenixlike it rose from the ashes of the omnibus. This second time new leadership revised legislative strategy and pushed with parliamentary acumen and ferocious energy to pass the compromise. When Henry Clay left for the cool breezes of Newport, Rhode Island, new faces took charge of the compromise forces. Leading this revitalized effort was Stephen A. Douglas, the young Democratic senator from Illinois. Instead of presenting senators and representatives with one bill to accept or reject Douglas divided the omnibus into its component parts and placed separate bills before Congress. Douglas had a strong ally in President Fillmore, who brought the influence of the White House to the aid of the compromisers. Fillmore changed some northern Whig votes from nay to yea, and he obtained some absenteeism on critical prosouthern bills such as the Fugitive Slave Act. With Douglas' masterful performance and Fillmore's assistance the compromise moved steadily through Senate and House. Although strong opposition still came from northern Whigs and southern

Democrats on the parts of the compromise each considered inimical to their section, Douglas' strategy worked. With northern Democrats and southern Whigs forming the consistent voting support each part of the compromise of 1850 passed safely through the Congress. On all bills Fillmore affixed his presidential signature, the last on September 20. Compromise had triumphed in Washington.

The southern reaction to the passage of the compromise—public opinion still spoke of the compromise, though it went through Congress in its individual sections—followed the partisan lines already marked out in congressional debate. Without exception southern Whigs rejoiced; southern Democrats generally registered strong reservations. "I and the Whigs generally," wrote a North Carolina associate to William A. Graham, "have been delighted at the passage of the compromize [sic] bills and the approval of the President." Graham's friend spoke for Whigs everywhere in the South. From Virginia to Arkansas, Whig papers trumpeted the joyful tidings that the compromise had succeeded. To the Whig press the compromise not only solved a national crisis, it also preserved the rights and honor of the South. With the success of the compromise the South had stopped the proviso, had gained congressional admission that Congress should not legislate on slavery in the territories, and had won a strict fugitive slave law. The Richmond *Whig* called for attention to its "sermon" on this definition of the compromise text. Evangelized the *Whig*, "the South finds no fault with the Fugitive Slave law, and none with the territorial Bills, because they contain no interdiction of Slavery." "I thought," William A. Graham phrased it, "we of the South had a new lease for slave property, and it was more secure than it had been for the last quarter of a century." For these blessings southerners had southern Whig congressmen and a Whig president to thank.[45]

45. Richard Hines to Graham, September 16, 1850, Graham to John H. Bryan, June 18, 1851, in J. G. de Roulhac Hamilton and Max R. Williams (eds.), *The Papers of William Alexander Graham* (5 vols.; Raleigh: State Department of Archives and History, 1957-), III, 392, IV, 124; New Orleans *Bee*, September 17, 1850; Helena (Ark.) *Southern Shield*, September 21, 1850; Richmond *Whig*, September 27, 1850, January 31, 1851.

Most southern Democrats interpreted the compromise differently. Pleased when Clay's omnibus failed, they looked with dismay upon the outcome of Douglas' work. The southern Democratic press insisted that the compromise had not settled the slavery question. Even though the bill organizing New Mexico and Utah followed their doctrine of 1848 and even though they cheered the Fugitive Slave Act, they found the compromise lacking. To them the admission of a free California smacked too much of the hated proviso. Claiming that the North had respected neither southern rights nor southern honor, the Democratic press called on southerners not to be deceived. The future of the South remained in jeopardy; only a firm stand against the compromise could protect the South and preserve her honor.[46]

All southern Democrats did not, however, join this anticompromise chorus. A minority among them spoke the Whig language affirming the worth of the compromise; they agreed with the Richmond *Enquirer* which saw it as "New light beam[ing] on us."[47] The very existence of this minority caused trouble for the dominant majority of southern Democrats. A major reason for the impact of the procompromise faction came from the impressive list of party notables leading it. In Virginia the most venerable of all Democratic newspapers the Richmond *Enquirer* broke with the state party chieftains, United States senators Robert M. T. Hunter and James M. Mason, who thought the compromise less than the South needed. Such congressional figures as Thomas J. Rusk and Sam Houston of Texas, Solomon Downs of Louisiana, Henry Foote of Mississippi, Andrew Johnson of Tennessee, and Howell Cobb of Georgia all placed their influence behind the compromise.

Varied motives prompted this minority. In the case of the

46. Jackson *Mississippian*, August 30, 1850; New Orleans *Louisiana Courier*, October 17, 22, 1850; Tallahassee *Floridian*, August 10, November 2, 30, 1850; Raleigh *Standard*, September, 1850, *passim*.

47. Richmond *Enquirer*, September 17, 1850. Of the eight Democratic papers I read for the compromise crisis, only two supported it, the *Enquirer* and the Little Rock *Arkansas Gazette*.

Richmond *Enquirer* the influence of the paper's founder, Thomas Ritchie, was probably decisive. When Ritchie moved from Richmond to Washington back in 1845 to edit the newspaper voice of the Polk administration, he left his two sons, William F. and Thomas, Jr., in charge of the *Enquirer*. After Zachary Taylor replaced James K. Polk, Ritchie continued to run the Washington *Union*. During the crisis of 1850 he believed the Union to be in grave danger; accordingly he made peace with his old enemy Henry Clay and worked for the compromise. Often factional fights within state parties sparked party division over the compromise. In these instances it is extremely difficult to separate political motives from ideological ones. State party concerns certainly influenced Foote, Cobb, and Rusk, but the latter two along with Houston had shown a reluctance to take the advanced position of the southern Democratic majority during the Southern Address episode. The leaders of the anticompromise forces in Tennessee, Senator Hopkins L. Turney and the former governor, Aaron V. Brown, had personal as well as political differences with the close friends, Congressman Andrew Johnson and party stalwart A. O. P. Nicholson, who backed the compromise. In addition Johnson and his east Tennessee constituency had an unshakable commitment to the Union, a commitment that would survive even secession and war. The contest between two titans of Louisiana for domination of the state party clearly affected the Democratic division in that state. Pierre Soulé opposed the compromise but John Slidell did not. More than politics was involved; Slidell did not share the view that the South was in grave danger in 1850, and Senator Downs sincerely believed that the compromise met southern grievances. In Arkansas, party factionalism compounded by the ardent procompromise views of the editor of the major Democratic newspaper, the Little Rock *Arkansas Gazette*, contributed to Democratic division. In Alabama, Georgia, and Mississippi the intraparty squabbles confused party lines. In other states like Louisiana and Tennessee internecine bickering hampered party efforts in state elections. Even though a complex combination of motives governed southern Democratic divisiveness on the compromise, the outcome of that divisiveness was singular and straightforward. [48]

The divergence between the parties and also within the Democratic party pointed to the furor over acceptance of the compromise that dominated southern politics in late 1850 and 1851. This battle had a thunderous impact on party politics. At bottom the fight was chiefly between southern Whigs and southern Democrats just as the congressional contest had been. But the 1850–1851 conflict did not always follow exact party lines; and when it was over, party lines and party loyalties were never the same.

The compromise enabled southern Whigs to reassert themselves in the South. Recognizing that their Democratic opponents had outdistanced southern opinion, southern Whigs rushed to brand them as disunionists, as irresponsible radicals. Because southern Whigs interpreted the compromise as an honorable settlement, even a southern victory, anyone who opposed it fit those categories by definition. Southern Whigs knew they had an issue that could rescue them from the political whirlpool caused by Zachary Taylor. How best to capitalize on it became their central political question.

In three deep-South states, Alabama, Georgia, and Mississippi, Whigs joined with procompromise Democrats and formed new political organizations. In doing so they gave up their old Whig identity for a new one emphasizing the issue raised in the South by the compromise debate. Designating their new political home as the Union or Constitutional Union party the erstwhile enemies underscored their allegiance to the Union protected by the compromise.

48. Charles H. Ambler, *Thomas Ritchie: A Study in Virginia Politics* (Richmond: Bell Book & Stationery, 1913), 280–81; Thomas J. Rusk to David Rusk, April 2, 1850, and to L. D. Evans, November 14, 1850, both in Rusk Papers; Houston *Telegraph,* February 21, 1850; Cave Johnson to James Buchanan, January 20, June 6, October 10, December 13, 1850, November 20, 1853, all in Buchanan Papers; Hopkins L. Turney to Robert Barnwell Rhett, May 1, 1852, in Rhett Papers; Leroy P. Graf *et al.* (eds.), *The Papers of Andrew Johnson* (3 vols.; Knoxville: University of Tennessee Press, 1967–), I, xxiv, 539–40; Slidell to James Buchanan, February 5, 1850, in Buchanan Papers; James Kimmins Greer, "Louisiana Politics, 1845–1861," *Louisiana Historical Quarterly,* XII (1929), 570–89; Little Rock *Arkansas Gazette,* March 15, May 31, July 26, August 30, 1850; see just below for the story in Alabama, Georgia, and Mississippi.

These parties claimed the loyalties of an overwhelming majority of Whigs in each state; additionally a minority faction of Democrats in both Georgia and Mississippi moved into the Union party tent. In Alabama a larger proportion of the Democratic party cooperated with the Unionists. The bulk of the Democrats also dropped old labels. Calling themselves members of a Southern Rights or Democratic State Rights party they deemphasized their Democratic identity and contributed to the new political division stretching from the Savannah to the Mississippi.[49]

For Whigs in these states the Union party stemmed from a political as well as an ideological motive. To be sure unionism provided a fortress for defending the compromise, the political ground the southern Whigs had staked out for themselves. But the Union movement also offered an opportunity for recouping lost or lagging political fortunes. In both Alabama and Mississippi the Whigs had been a distinct minority since the Calhounite-Democratic rapprochement back in the late 1830s. In neither state had the Whigs elected a governor or controlled a legislature during the 1840s, though they did hold a few state offices and did elect an occasional congressman from relatively secure districts. From their "hopeless minority" position, as one Mississippi Whig called it, Whigs in these two states hoped to rejuvenate both the status of their party, albeit under a new banner, and their personal political fortunes. This prospect was a heady tonic for politicians who had been resigned to limited opportunities. Catching this mood Henry W. Hilliard, a three-term congressman from a safe Whig district in central Alabama, rejoiced: "For the first time I am in a majority in my State & believe that I shall reach the [United States] Senate."[50]

The Georgia situation was a bit different. There the Whigs had

49. For detailed accounts of these events consult: for Alabama, Thornton, "Politics and Power," Chap. 4; for Georgia, Richard Harrison Shryock, *Georgia and the Union in 1850* (Durham: Duke University Press, 1926); for Mississippi, Donald M. Rawson, "Party Politics in Mississippi, 1850–1860" (Ph.D. dissertation, Vanderbilt University, 1964), Chap. 3.

50. P. L. Rainwater (ed.), "The Autobiography of Benjamin Grubb Humphreys, August 26, 1808–December 20, 1882," *Mississippi Valley Historical Review*, XXI (1934), 242; Hilliard to Nathaniel Niles, August 13, 1851, in Nathaniel Niles Papers, William R. Perkins Library, Duke University.

remained strong throughout the 1840s; also Georgia had produced two of the leading young spokesmen of southern Whiggery, Alexander Stephens and Robert Toombs. Still, Georgia Whigs had not elected a governor since 1845 and found it increasingly difficult to win a legislative majority. The Democratic sweep of 1849 seemed to portend an even darker future. Besides, Stephens and Toombs had led the rebellion of southern Whigs against Taylor and the northern Whigs. Having already found their old party a less than congenial home, they welcomed the Constitutional Union party. It allowed them to retain power in Georgia without having to embrace their old enemies the Democrats under the despised Democratic banner.

The necessity for the Democratic alliance that insured a majority in each state required a new party. After almost twenty years of partisan political warfare Democrats, even those who were a minority in their own house because they advocated the compromise, had no interest in becoming Whigs—no more than Whigs had in becoming Democrats. They could, however, act with Whigs to promote compromise and political advancement under a new standard displaying the compromise banner. For Howell Cobb, "discarded by most of his party leaders" since his refusal to sign the Southern Address, the Georgia Constitutional Union party allowed him to remain a potent figure in Georgia politics while holding to his pro-compromise position. When United States Senator Henry S. Foote of Mississippi championed the compromise, he found himself an outcast among Democratic chieftains in his state. With the Union party Foote had a future in Mississippi politics; without it he had none. Democrats from northern Alabama tended to support the compromise while those from southern Alabama opposed it. This difference added to a long-term struggle for control of the state party. The compromise furor spurred northern Alabama Democrats into the Union party while their southern counterparts organized the Southern Rights party.[51]

51. Alexander Stephens to John J. Crittenden, November 11, 1850, in Stephens Papers, William R. Perkins Library, Duke University; Hearon, "Mississippi," 149–50; Thornton, "Politics and Power," 249–50.

The great election battle between Unionists and Southern Rightists occurred in 1851. The Union party crusaded for the compromise as an honorable settlement of the outstanding sectional differences. Some Unionists went further; touring Georgia in the summer of 1851, Stephens and Toombs called the compromise a southern document. The Unionists emphasized that it contained a stringent fugitive slave law which proved that the North intended to respect southern rights. While they praised the compromise, the Unionists simultaneously insisted that they would never sacrifice basic southern interests for political gain or any other reason. To reinforce their contention that they would not permit "intolerable oppression" from the North to endanger the South, Unionists buttressed the congressional compromise with the native Georgia Platform, which the Unionists in all three states clasped to their bosom. The Georgia Platform was composed of five resolutions drafted and passed by Georgia Unionists during the state convention of December, 1850.[52]

This Georgia Platform was no milk-toast document. It began with three general resolutions calling the compromise an honorable settlement acceptable to the South. Then the last two resolutions spoke with an emphatic southern accent. Number four proclaimed that Georgia "will and ought to resist," with secession if necessary, any action by Congress directed against slavery in the District of Columbia or in other places within congressional jurisdiction which was "incompatible with the safety, and domestic tranquility, the rights and honor of the slave holding states." That same reaction would follow if Congress refused to admit a slave state, prohibited slavery in either New Mexico or Utah territories, or passed any bill "repealing or materially modifying" the fugitive slave law. After that ringing proclamation the fifth resolution came almost as an anticlimax, though it underscored the importance southerners attached to the fugitive slave law. It declared that the "faithful execution" of that law by "the proper authorities [federal government]" was absolutely

52. During late 1850 and 1851 Unionist newspapers were full of this message; for examples see Vicksburg *Weekly Whig*, November 27, 1850 and Milledgeville *Southern Recorder*, November 5, December 17, 1850, June 17, 1851.

essential for the preservation of the Union. Without any doubt the Georgia Platform bristled with southern weaponry. As a leading Georgia Unionist explained to a northern friend, "While we are good Union Men we are none the less true Southerners." "I believe," Dr. Richard Arnold emphasized, "that [fourth] Resolution, every word of it."[53]

With the compromise to prove that the North had respected southern rights and with the Georgia Platform as a pledge that they would never brook any infringement on those rights, the Unionists had an obviously strong political position. Those who disagreed with the Unionist view of the compromise had precious little room for maneuver; the Georgia Platform usurped it. No matter where the Southern Rights men turned, they found it impossible to avoid the political shroud of disunion fashioned for them by the Unionists. And the Unionists had no intention of letting the Southern Rightists escape their doom. During their tour of Georgia, Stephens and Toombs branded their opponents as disunionists while they praised the compromise. The Vicksburg *Whig* called its Mississippi opponents nullifiers and disunionists. Just enough disunion talk had come from Democratic sources in 1849 and 1850 to give the Unionist argument a kernel of truth.[54]

The Southern Rights men reeled before the powerful political offensive thrown against them. They had to face three exceedingly difficult problems. First they had to contend with the hard evidence indicating the popularity of the compromise in the South. Upon adjournment in June, 1850, the Nashville convention had called for a second session to consider an appropriate southern response to any congressional action. The second session duly convened in Nashville in November, 1850; poorly attended and arousing little interest, it

53. Milledgeville *Federal Union*, December 17, 1850; Arnold to John W. Forney, September 9, 1851, in Richard H. Shryock (ed.), "Letters of Richard D. Arnold, M.D., 1808–1876," *Papers of the Trinity College Historical Society*, Double ser., XVIII–XIX (1929), 56–57. Also see Alexander Stephens to John J. Crittenden, November 11, 1850, in Stephens Papers, William R. Perkins Library, Duke University.

54. This rhetoric was pervasive; for examples see Vicksburg *Weekly Whig*, July 9, 1851; Milledgeville *Southern Recorder*, June 17, 1851; Milledgeville *Federal Union*, October 14, 1851.

was a fiasco. Southerners evidently felt no need to consider their response to the compromise. Then on November 25, 1850, in balloting for delegates to a state convention Georgians voted by 42,000 to 24,000 to accept it. Also, in early 1851 the Virginia Democratic party announced its support.[55] The disunion badge caused a second thorny problem. In late 1850 and 1851 most Southern Rights men did not favor disunion, though they found it exceedingly difficult to shed that label. Finally, they never managed to find their own peculiar niche in the southern ideological sun.

While the Southern Rightists denounced the Unionists as submissionists for accepting the compromise, they never clearly specified where they stood or what they wanted. Calling secession a "dangerous position to occupy," former Congressman Alfred Iverson, a prominent leader in Georgia, announced that he stood for southern rights under the constitution, whatever that meant. Perceiving the difficulty plaguing his opponents, Alexander Stephens told John J. Crittenden that they spoke vaguely about "some sort of resistance under the Constitution." Jefferson Davis underlined the perplexity confronting the Southern Rights men when he reported "great confusion" reigning among them in Mississippi. Denying that he advocated disunion Davis "thought the State should solemnly set the seal of her disapprobation on the source of the measures of 'the compromise.'" To further complicate matters for themselves many Southern Rights men praised the Georgia Platform as a splendid statement of southern principles. Ideological befuddlement and disarray pervaded the entire movement, and the Southern Rights men never effectively repudiated the Unionist charge of disunion, the "disunion humbug" the Jackson *Mississippian* called it. Although the confrontation was not in fact a union-disunion one anywhere, the successful Unionist onslaught made it seem like one.[56]

55. Craven, *Southern Nationalism*, 112; Milledgeville *Federal Union*, December 3, 10, 1850; Richmond *Enquirer*, February 21, 1851.

56. Iverson to John M. Berrien, November 23, 1850, in Berrien Papers; Stephens to Crittenden, October 24, 1850, in Stephens Papers, William R. Perkins Library, Duke University; Davis to David L. Yulee, July 18, 1851, in Yulee Papers and to James A. Pearce, August 22, 1852, in James A. Pearce Papers, Maryland Historical Society; Milledgeville

In such a contest the Southern Rights party had no chance. In his campaign for governor of Georgia, Howell Cobb amassed the largest majority any Georgia gubernatorial candidate had ever received. The Constitutional Union party also won clear majorities in both houses of the legislature. In Mississippi the Unionists carried the day when Henry S. Foote defeated Jefferson Davis for the governorship. Davis, supposedly the most popular man in Mississippi, was a last-minute replacement for the avowed disunionist John A. Quitman but Davis could not overcome the Unionist lead. The Unionists also won control of the state house, though the Southern Rights men captured the senate. Alabama voters did not have an exciting gubernatorial contest but the Unionists won a substantial legislative victory. The congressional elections in all three states also resulted in resounding Union victories.[57]

In the rest of the South the Whigs running as Whigs also made superb showings during the 1850–1851 elections. In Tennessee in 1851 they won back the governorship from the Democrats and carried the legislative elections. They reelected their candidate to Florida's lone congressional seat in 1850, and the Florida legislature during 1850 and 1851 had almost an equal number of Democrats and Whigs. In Louisiana's legislative elections of 1851 the Whigs increased their majority in the state house and took the state senate from the Democrats. Even in Virginia and Arkansas where the Democrats had predominated for a long time, Whigs made their presence felt. Because the Virginia Democratic party had come out in favor of the compromise, acceptance or rejection of it did not become a major partisan issue. But when Virginia held her first popular election for governor in 1851, the Whig candidate won a

---

Federal Union, April 8, June 24, October 14, 1851; Jackson *Mississippian*, November 14, 1851. Also see William L. Yancey to Benjamin C. Yancey, November 7, 1851, in Benjamin C. Yancey Papers, Southern Historical Collection, University of North Carolina.

57. On the Davis-Quitman affair see Reuben Davis, *Recollections of Mississippi and Mississippians* (Boston and New York: Houghton Mifflin, 1889), 315–17, 320; Powhatan Ellis to Margaret Ellis, October 8, 1851, in Munford-Ellis Family Papers. The congressional results were as follows: Alabama, 5 Union, 2 Southern Rights; Georgia, 6 Union, 2 Southern Rights; Mississippi, 3 Union, 1 Southern Rights.

most respectable 47 percent of the vote. In Arkansas the unanimity of Whig legislators insured the passage of legislative resolutions favoring the compromise. Only in North Carolina did the Whigs falter.

But the North Carolina episode had special meaning for southern Whigs. The election of 1850 worked a revolution of sorts in North Carolina politics.[58] In the 1840s North Carolina had been Whiggery's strongest bastion in the South. The Whigs had won all five gubernatorial contests, dominated the congressional delegation, and usually controlled the legislature. Then in 1850 the Democrats elected the governor as well as a majority in both houses of the state legislature. North Carolina Democrats manufactured this striking victory out of two ingredients: utilizing a popular state issue and successfully pinning an antisouthern tag on the Whigs.

The state issue was free suffrage. In 1835 when North Carolinians amended their constitution to democratize elections in the state, a property qualification on voting for members of the state senate was retained. As early as 1848 the Democrats advocated repealing that provision; to dramatize their position they blared the cry of free suffrage. Few Whigs opposed such a constitutional change but they advocated making it in a constitutional convention that would also consider changing the formula for legislative apportionment, which favored the predominantly Democratic eastern part of the state over the more Whiggish western part. The suggestion regarding apportionment opened the gates for the Democrats to rush in with their antisouthern shouts.

The election campaign took place in the summer of 1850 with the election itself occurring on August 1. During these weeks the outcome of the compromise was unknown, and for much of the time the Whigs still wrestled with the unpopularity of Zachary Taylor's territorial plan. The resolutions passed by the Democratic state convention in June emphasized the crisis facing the South and the

58. My discussion of the North Carolina election of 1850 is based on the files of the Raleigh *Register* and the Raleigh *Standard*, especially during June and July of 1850.

unacceptability of Taylor's plan. So when the Whigs talked about a new apportionment formula, the Democrats were primed. The mention of apportionment created an uproar because North Carolina used the federal basis or the three-fifths provision of the federal constitution; in other words slaves were counted in the allocation of state representatives. According to the Democrats tampering with the three-fifths provision in North Carolina threatened southern power and security in the nation. In Democratic rhetoric anybody who disliked the North Carolina system also by definition disliked the federal system, an assault that had special force in the charged atmosphere of mid-1850. Thus indicted, the Whigs categorically denied the Democratic accusation. Without pausing to listen the Democrats constantly sounded the alarm: Whigs opposed democracy and southern safety. That double-barreled political charge felled the Whigs. Victorious, the Democrats credited both barrels for their success.

This North Carolina result dramatizes the importance of the compromise to southern Whigs, because in North Carolina they had no secure southern dam to hold back the antisouthern torrent pouring forth from the Democrats. Accordingly the state elections in 1850 and especially in 1851, which apparently signaled a legitimate Whig upturn in the South, guaranteed the Whigs nothing. The strategy underlying those strong electoral performances placed southern Whigs on extremely treacherous political ground. In the Union party states they had already relinquished their Whig identity; for the moment that decision had all the appearances of a shrewd political move, but no such assurance governed the long-term outlook. The chief problem for the Union party came from the absence of any national connection. It was a local phenomenon, though southern Whigs both inside and outside the Union party states considered the possibility of trying to create a new national party dedicated to the compromise, which for southerners also meant the Georgia Platform.[59] By definition this new party would exclude many northern

59. Robert Toombs to Absalom H. Chappell *et al.*, February 15, 1851, and John H. Lumpkin to Howell Cobb, February 16, 1851, both in Phillips (ed.), *Toombs, Stephens, Cobb*

Whigs who remained steadfastly opposed to the compromise, especially the fugitive slave law which stood at the heart of the Georgia Platform. If this new party did not appear, the Union parties faced a bleak future. Without national allies the promise of the Union party to guarantee that the Congress and the North stood fast by the compromise became a dead letter. Political parties in the South lived and prospered only through their real or supposed ability to protect the South and her institutions. A party confined to Alabama, Georgia, and Mississippi could make no believable claims for protecting anything. In addition such a circumscribed party offered few and limited rewards to ambitious politicians. With the possibility of national victory eliminated, the power and prestige that came to the loyalists of a successful party all but disappeared. On the other hand if the Whigs in the Union coalitions resurrected the Whig party, they risked losing their Democratic allies and any chance of maintaining their dominant position in their states. Thus for the Union party an uncertain long-term future could very easily turn into a hazardous short-term future.

For the southern Whigs outside the Union party states the future was equally uncertain. Almost every southern Whig grapsed the compromise for political security. They reiterated the critical importance of the compromise not only as a platform providing fundamental sectional accord but also as a platform of last resort for them. If anything happened to undo the compromise, especially the repeal of the fugitive slave law, then, according to the Richmond *Whig*, inevitably "the value of the Union will be speedily calculated." The Baton Rouge *Gazette* also clearly enunciated that southern Whigs could not accept any tampering with the compromise. In his inaugural address on October 16, 1851, William B. Campbell, the newly chosen Whig governor of Tennessee, reaffirmed his total commitment to the compromise. He followed that pledge with another: "An interference with [the compromise] will inevitably produce agita-

---

Correspondence, 229–30; Charles Ready to John Bell, January 3, 1851, and Thomas A. R. Nelson to John Bell, January 10, 1851, both in John Bell Papers, Division of Manuscripts, Library of Congress.

tion, mischief and misery." When the Whigs of middle Florida convened in the spring of 1852, their first resolution praised the compromise as a final and just settlement of the sectional dispute. After that praise and in the same resolution these Florida Whigs warned that any attempt to disturb the compromise could only be judged a hostile act. To insure that it remained their strong shield southern Whigs placed their trust and their political future on what William A. Graham called "the fine stand of the President."[60]

Millard Fillmore certainly deserved Graham's accolade. Immediately upon becoming president, Fillmore broke the patterns that had guided Taylor. Just as Fillmore supported the compromise he gave a new direction to his administration. Highlighted by a recasting of Taylor's entire cabinet this new course had a distinctive southern orientation, both in outlook and cast of characters. Fillmore's revamped cabinet waved the compromise banner. Daniel Webster, the leading northern Whig spokesman for the compromise, began his second tour as head of the state department. John J. Crittenden, who had pleaded vainly for Taylor to placate the South, joined the cabinet as attorney general. Charles Conrad, the Louisiana congressman who had begged Taylor to remember his southern friends, became secretary of war. To these stalwarts Fillmore added two more southerners closely identified both with the compromise and with southern Whiggery; William A. Graham of North Carolina went to the navy department, and Alexander H. H. Stuart of Virginia took over the interior department. Thus Fillmore started out down a political road filled with southern signposts.[61]

---

60. Richmond *Whig*, October 18, 1850; Baton Rouge *Gazette*, November 9, 1850; Robert H. White (ed.), *Messages of the Governors of Tennessee* (8 vols.; Nashville: Tennessee Historical Commission, 1952–72), IV, 421; Tallahassee *Florida Sentinel*, June 1, 1852; Graham to John H. Bryan, June 18, 1851, in Hamilton and Williams (eds.), *Graham Papers*, IV, 124.

61. The other two members of Fillmore's cabinet were Thomas Corwin of Ohio in the treasury department and Nathan Hall, the president's former law partner, as postmaster general. For Fillmore on the compromise and the cabinet see Robert J. Rayback, *Millard Fillmore: Biography of a President* (Buffalo: Henry Stewart, 1959), Chap. 13.

Not only did Fillmore help get the compromise through the Congress and surround himself with a procompromise cabinet predominantly southern, he also set out to do what the southern Whigs most wanted—to make the compromise work. In his annual messages to Congress in 1850 and 1851 he described it as the final settlement of sectional differences. He implored the North to honor the bargain struck in the Congress. Fillmore never flinched in his support of the compromise, even the part of it that many northerners, especially northern Whigs, found particularly egregious. Fillmore called for northerners to accept the Fugitive Slave Act, even though cries against it raged through much of the North. In February, 1851, authorities in Boston, acting under the provisions of the fugitive slave law, apprehended one Shadrach and prepared to return him to slavery. Before Shadrach could be removed from the city, however, a small group forcibly liberated him from his captors and cheered by a crowd, whisked him away. Reacting vigorously Fillmore promulgated an executive proclamation denouncing the "sundry lawless persons" who actively participated in the Boston affair as well as the cheering onlookers. Commanding the military to quell promptly any such disturbances in the future, the president also called on all citizens "to rally to the support of the laws of their country." While the administration acted to enforce the unpopular law, speakers and editors, legion in number with Whigs prominent among them, hurled invective at the president and arraigned him for colluding with slave owners.[62]

While northern Whigs heaped obloquy upon Fillmore, southern Whigs lavished praise upon him. After their great disappointment with the southern planter Zachary Taylor southern Whigs, ironically, discovered a champion in the former antislave congressman from Buffalo. Unlike their reaction to Taylor, who had not per-

62. Nevins, *Ordeal*, I, Chap. 12, has an excellent account of the Fillmore-northern opinion-fugitive slave story. For Fillmore's message on the compromise in general and the fugitive slave law in particular see Richardson (comp.), *Messages and Papers of the Presidents,* V, 92–93, 109–10, 137–39.

formed as they promised, they reveled in Fillmore's performance.
As the Vicksburg *Whig* exulted, Fillmore was "fully justifying and
redeeming the pledges made in his behalf, by the whigs of the
south." Although the reorganized cabinet certainly pleased the
southerners, their loudest plaudits came on the fugitive slave question. Fillmore's vigorous insistence that the North obey the fugitive
slave law strengthened the only platform on which southerners could
stand. In short he gave them a platform. They characterized him as a
man "stand[ing] on high ground," a man "wholly untainted with
abolitionism." Evidence that anticompromise northern Whigs like
William Henry Seward were condemning Fillmore only increased
southern joy, a joy, however, pregnant with a potential political
malignancy.[63]

Fillmore did bring new hope to southern Whigs, and he enabled
them to conjoin their state crusades with administration policy. But
he did not reunite the Whig party. Just as Taylor's anticompromise
posture had alienated most southern Whigs, Fillmore's procompromise stance angered the bulk of northern Whiggery. Fillmore's
enforcement of the fugitive slave law, absolutely critical for southern
Whigs, embittered most northern Whigs and blackened his name
among them. As one prominent northern Whig wrote, when
Fillmore signed the fugitive slave bill, he "signed his political
death-warrant."[64] That same bill provided the breath of political life
for southern Whigs.

They recognized that 1852 would be critically important for them.
If they could place their candidate and their party firmly behind the
compromise—if, in other words, they could bring the Whig party
to the position occupied by the Fillmore administration—they
could maintain their party in the South. But if northern opponents of

63. Vicksburg *Weekly Whig*, April 16, 1851; James Graham to William A. Graham, August
10, 1850, and David Outlaw to William A. Graham, April 28, 1851, both in Hamilton and
Williams (eds.), *Graham Papers*, III, 354, and IV, 88; Tallahassee *Florida Sentinel*, July 23,
1850; Richmond *Whig*, July 16, 1850, February 28, 1851; Helena (Ark.) *Southern Shield*,
March 8, 1851; Raleigh *Register*, April 16, November 19, 1851.
    64. Weed (ed.), *Life of Weed*, I, 588.

compromise controlled party deliberations and turned the party into an anticompromise force, the existence of southern Whiggery would be imperiled. Southern Whigs had pledged themselves and the South to the compromise and the Georgia Platform. They could not back away from those pledges and stand with a party committed to repeal the compromise and disregard the platform. As southern men such a stand was unthinkable; as southern politicians such a stand was suicidal.

IV

Southern Democrats did not make the Whig task any easier. The political turmoil of 1850 and 1851 resulted in the complete triumph of the compromise across the South; everywhere the Democrats and the radical disunionists had tried to carry some kind of program for resistance to the compromise, overt or otherwise, they were emphatically put down. They even failed in the citadel of southern radicalism, South Carolina. This outcome angered the committed disunionists like Rhett, Yancey, and Quitman. With scathing pen a "mortified" Quitman likened the Democratic State Rights party of Mississippi to a man who "puts off his principles, as a deserter casts off his uniform." Yancey washed his hands of the "submissionists" dominating the Southern Rights party in Alabama. Without the rancor of the radicals, though not always enthusiastically, most southern Democrats accepted the favorable verdict southerners awarded to the compromise. This acceptance came in many guises, from a formal declaration as in Virginia and Mississippi, to cessations of attacks on it, to statements that the South had agreed to it.[65] No matter the particular vehicle of acceptance and regardless of whether it came with enthusiasm or reluctance, southern Democrats by the end of 1851 had lodged themselves in the compromise

65. For the triumph of the compromise see Craven, *Southern Nationalism*, Chap. 6; Quitman to W. P. Chapman, June 9, 1852, quoted in J. F. H. Claiborne, *Life and Correspondence of John A. Quitman, Major General, U.S.A., and Governor of Mississippi* (2 vols.; New York: Harper & Brothers, 1860), I, 165; Yancey to Benjamin C. Yancey, November 7, 1851, in Benjamin Yancey Papers.

tent. Of course they also embraced the complementary Georgia Platform. The compromise and the platform became Democratic doctrine. Accordingly southern Democrats undermined the alleged *raison d'être* of the Union parties and simultaneously invaded the preserve southern Whigs had claimed for themselves.

The increasingly crowded compromise tent did not account for all the Whig troubles. Whigs in the Union party states had a more immediate concern. With the presidential campaign approaching, Democrats in the Union coalitions became restive. All efforts to make the Union party something more than a local phenomenon were at best stillborn. Because of that failure Union parties had no national connection; it seemed they would be spectators only in the presidential sweepstakes. For most Union Democrats this observer role was an unpalatable prospect.

As a result Democratic fusion began in the Union party states almost in concert with counting the ballots that announced the great Union victory. When the Alabama legislature convened in December, 1851, the Democrats elected as Unionists joined with their Southern Rights comrades to organize that body. "Harmony & [a] studied spirit of conciliation" marked the state Democratic convention that met in January, 1852. By spring, reunion became the watchword among Alabama Democrats. In Mississippi a similar story unfolded. Immediately after the defeat of Jefferson Davis, the Jackson *Mississippian* called for a rapid reunification of Mississippi Democrats in preparation for the upcoming presidential campaign. After a state convention in November, 1851, repudiated secession, no ideological barriers barred the way to Democratic unity. With the new year fresh, Mississippi Democrats eagerly anticipated the presidential contest.[66]

Georgia Democrats followed suit, though they took somewhat longer. Just after Cobb and the Constitutional Union party had

66. Thornton, "Politics and Power," 251; Chas. P. Robinson to John Bragg, January 21, 1852, Herndon L. Henderson to John Bragg, January 15, 1852, Willis Darby to John Bragg, April 18, 1852, all in John Bragg Papers, Southern Historical Collection, University of North Carolina; Jackson *Mississippian*, November 14, 1851; Claiborne, *Quitman*, II, 151.

trounced them, the Southern Rights men furled their defeated banner and unfurled the old Democratic flag. To Georgia and the nation they announced themselves the only true Democrats in Georgia. At the same time they called on all the party faithful to renew their pledge of allegiance to the Democrats, a party controlled of course by former Southern Rights adherents. The Union Democrats rejected those overtures; they were not ready to play follow-the-leader behind their recent opponents. Even so, they soon began plotting their own course towards union with the national Democratic party. In fact the evidence indicates that Cobb, and in all probability Toombs as well, intended such a move all along. Now, however, the Southern Rights men had stolen a march on the Unionists. Still Cobb and his Democratic supporters among the Unionists were anxious to have their Democratic credentials validated. Although the Southern Rights Democrats and the Union Democrats traveled along separate tracks, they had the same destination—a junction with the national Democratic party. Their paths remained separate until the summer of 1852 when for all practical purposes Georgia Democrats again became one.[67]

This Democratic rush toward unity troubled the Unionist Whigs. Even those like Toombs, who probably expected the Union party to end up in the Democratic party and who intended to go along when it happened, balked at the rapidity of the Democratic action and the key role played by the Southern Rightists. Perplexed by the sudden disintegration of what had seemed to be a brilliant political strategy, Union Whigs wandered about the political landscape. Many "struggle[d] . . . to keep up the Union party." Others recognizing the futility of that enterprise contemplated resurrecting the Whig

67. Horace Montgomery, *Cracker Parties* (Baton Rouge: Louisiana State University Press, 1950), Chaps. 3–4; Herschel V. Johnson to Franklin Pierce, July 21, 1852, in Franklin Pierce Papers, New Hampshire Historical Society; Iverson Harris to John M. Berrien, November 19, 1851, in Berrien Papers; Lewis Cass to Howell Cobb, April 25, 1852, in Cobb Papers; Andrew J. Donelson to Howell Cobb, October 22, 1851, Hopkins Holsey to Howell Cobb, February 6, 1852, John H. Lumpkin to Howell Cobb, March 2, 1852, John B. Lamar to Howell Cobb, March 8, 1852, all in Phillips (ed.), *Toombs, Stephens, Cobb Correspondence*, 262–63, 279–80, 287–88.

party and renewing old Whig loyalties. Still others, not wanting to relinquish so quickly the hope, rewards, and power accompanying political dominance, marched behind their Democratic colleagues.[68] While the precise number taking each course is unknown, the outcome of their endeavors is crystal clear. The few clinging to the forlorn Union banner could not keep it flying. By the summer of 1852 the Union movement in each state had died. In its place stood a strengthened, united Democratic party and a weakened, disoriented Whig party.

Although Whigs in the rest of the South had not been plunged so abruptly into the political abyss, they too felt the growing Democratic pressure. Just as the Democrats in the various southern states came back together after dividing, at times bitterly, over the compromise, the national Democratic party began healing old wounds. Recovery in the South was symptomatic of a national occurrence. The congressional session beginning in December, 1851, witnessed a veritable burying of hatchets. Southerners on both sides of the compromise issue, northerners, even the Van Buren defectors of 1848 all passed and shared the pipe of political peace. Recognizing the serious afflictions besetting the Whig party, these Democrats from every direction in the Democratic compass came together in order to win a great victory in 1852 and return a Democratic administration to Washington. This effort to reconcile everybody from Southern Rightists to freesoilers was a gargantuan undertaking. "I do not permit myself to believe," wrote a watchful and disgusted Alexander Stephens, "that it can succeed." But the Democrats were striving mightily to pull themselves together. The desire for the rewards of victory propelled the drive toward unity while the compromise provided a common ideological ground. With southern

68. Thos. E. Irby to John Bragg, December 10, 1851, in Bragg Papers; Alexander Stephens to Howell Cobb, January 26, 1852, in Brooks (ed.), "Cobb Papers," 53–55; Jno. H. Lumpkin to Sim Boyd, May 2, 1852 (a long analysis of the April convention of the Georgia Constitutional Union party), in Georgia Political Leaders Collection, Robert W. Woodruff Library, Emory University; Vicksburg *Whig* and Milledgeville *Southern Recorder*, Winter–Spring, 1852, *passim*.

Democrats' acceptance, it could easily become the message of the national party because it had the warm support of most northern Democrats.[69] Thus southern Democrats would apparently roar into the 1852 campaign armored with national party unity and brandishing a platform and candidate endorsing the compromise. To survive politically an already shaken southern Whiggery would have to match that powerful combination.

69. Stephens to Howell Cobb, December 5, 1851, in Phillips (ed.), *Toombs, Stephens, Cobb Correspondence*, 268, and Stephens to Howell Cobb, December 23, 1851, in Cobb Papers.

9 Victory and Defeat

I

APPROACHING THE 1852 presidential campaign, southern Whigs clung with a desperate tenacity to the moorings which had enabled them to survive the political hurricane of 1850 and 1851—the compromise and Millard Fillmore. They saw the compromise and the president not only as defensible before southern voters but also as indisputable evidence that their opinion still counted in the national Whig party. The recent trauma of the Taylor administration plus the ever present outcry from numerous northern Whigs against the compromise made the southerners acutely aware of the tenuousness of their national political alliance. That their Democratic opponents also laid claim to the compromise reemphasized its criticalness for them. No longer could they shackle the southern Democrats with disunion; the Democrats stood exactly where the Whigs wanted to stand. With southern Democrats glorifying the compromise while a segment of northern Whigs villified it, the compromise became not only a sensible and honorable solution to sectional differences for southern Whigs but also essential for their political survival.

Accordingly the southern Whigs left no doubt about what they expected from the Whig national convention acting for the Whig party. They knew that two of the three Whig national conventions had promulgated no platform. And southern Whigs had been delighted, even eager, to run William Henry Harrison and Zachary Taylor without the baggage of a platform. But southern Whigs saw 1852 in a quite different light. They were convinced that their political salvation required a firm, open commitment to the compromise by the national convention. Because of "the distrust of the Northern Whigs which prevail[ed] at the South," southerners demanded that the convention not only adopt the compromise but also declare it the final solution to the sectional and slavery question. They wanted no room left for northern Whigs to attack the compromise. Addressing his fellow senators in April 1852, Georgia's William C. Dawson dramatized the southern position:

> Hence I avow that I will act with no party which shall endeavor, either directly or indirectly, to open for agitation the questions adjusted by the compromise, even for the purpose of securing votes at the ensuing Presidential election. Nor will I combine to elect any man to the Presidency, whose opinions are not beyond doubt or cavil on the *finality* of the compromise; nor shall I under any circumstances, act with any party that shall not have the firmness publicly to avow their support of the compromise.

Across the South during the spring of 1852, Whig newspapers and Whig state conventions echoed Senator Dawson's ultimatum. In William C. Rives's blunt language the southern Whigs had made defining the compromise as the final solution, "the *sine qua non* of political co-operation in the Presidential election."[1]

Southern Whigs embraced a candidate just as unanimously as they had chosen a platform. The prospect of President Fillmore as the Whig candidate sent a "thrill of gratification" coursing throughout the collective body of southern Whiggery. Without exception Whig state conventions called for his nomination. Cabinet member William A. Graham found his mail filled with letters imploring that Fillmore be nominated. Likewise Whig editors bugled an unending call for Fillmore. This southwide clamor for Fillmore rested on a very practical foundation: Fillmore stood unequivocally behind the compromise; in addition he had given southern Whigs a prominent place in his administration. Fillmore as the nominee of the Whig convention would prove beyond any doubt that southern Whiggery

1. Meredith P. Gentry to William B. Campbell, March 24, 1852, in Campbell Papers; *Congressional Globe*, 32nd Cong., 1st Sess., 1080; Tallahassee *Florida Sentinel*, April 27, 1852; Richmond *Whig*, April 30, 1852; Raleigh *Register*, May 5, 1852; Milledgeville *Southern Recorder*, April 20, 1852; Vicksburg *Weekly Whig*, April 28, May 12, 1852; Rives to James F. Strother, May 5, 1852, in Rives Papers.

and its interests still mattered in the national party. With Fillmore confirmed as party leader, southern Whigs had no doubt that they could compete effectively against the Democrats in the presidential race and maintain the strength of their party organization.[2]

The possible alternatives to Fillmore reinforced the southern commitment to him. Daniel Webster and Winfield Scott were spoken of as possible presidential nominees. Southern Whigs admired Webster for his standing by the compromise; but when he reached for the prize he had coveted for a score of years, he aroused little response in the South. Although southern Whigs considered him a friend and saw him as a symbol of northern willingness to recognize southern rights, most did not think of him as a feasible presidential candidate. For southern Whigs, Webster's past included too many liabilities. The southerners knew that the politics of slavery would destroy Webster and his destruction would undoubtedly endanger their own political health.

While Webster generated no enthusiasm, the possibility of Winfield Scott's winning their party's presidential nomination genuinely frightened the overwhelming majority of southern Whigs. The few who spoke favorably of Scott were scorned by their fellow southerners. At first glance Scott seemed ideal for the southerners. Virginia born and a military hero, he shared the attributes that had made William Henry Harrison and Zachary Taylor so attractive to southern Whigs and southern voters. For the Whigs in 1852, however, Scott's personal characteristics counted for little; they could not separate Scott as an individual from his most avid backers, who terrified them. Southern Whigs correctly identified Scott as the favorite candidate of William H. Seward, hated and feared by southern Whigs since 1850, and the antislavery and an-

2. Helena (Ark.) *Southern Shield*, February 21, 1852; Arthur F. Hopkins to Millard Fillmore, March 8, 1852, William C. Dawson to Millard Fillmore, March 15, 1852, both in Fillmore Papers; James W. Bryan to Graham, March 24, 1852, Arthur F. Hopkins to Graham, April 6, 1852, James W. Osborne to Graham, May 26, 1852, all in J. G. de Roulhac Hamilton and Max R. Williams (eds.), *The Papers of William Alexander Graham* (5 vols.; Raleigh: State Department of Archives and History, 1957–), IV, 265–66, 283–87, 302–304; William B. Campbell to David Campbell, February 15, 1852, in Campbell Papers; Milledgeville *Southern Recorder*, March 2, 1851; New Orleans *Bee*, February 3, 1852.

ticompromise element of northern Whiggery. Seward and those who thought like him made no secret of their preference for Scott. Totally opposed to the compromise, they found both the president and Webster completely unsatisfactory. These northern Whigs wanted a man who had no connection with the compromise, particularly no connection with the enforcement of the Fugitive Slave Act. These men thought Scott the military hero could camouflage divisions within the party and drive the compromise into obscurity.[3]

But southern Whigs wanted no camouflage and no scotching of party unity on the compromise, the current embodiment of the slavery issue. Following that path in 1848 had brought them much too close to total disaster. They repudiated suggestions from the Scott press in the North that southern Whigs let northern Whigs set party policy for 1852. The southerners had too much at stake. The compromise was a life and death matter; without it they faced political extinction. For southern Whigs a Scott candidacy equaled catastrophe because they assumed either repudiation or silence regarding the compromise would accompany his nomination. If Seward and his associates could manage the latter, southern Whigs believed they could surely accomplish the former. And Scott without the compromise, in the words of William A. Graham, "would be ruinous to us at the South." The Whig governor of Tennessee predicted the disbandment of the party in his state should Scott triumph. No southern politicians could take a political course that they themselves had identified as threatening slavery. Thus according to their own testimony, the future of southern Whiggery depended upon the outcome of the national convention scheduled to meet in Baltimore on June 16.[4]

3. Arthur Charles Cole, *The Whig Party in the South* (Gloucester, Mass.: Peter Smith, 1962), 231–32; James W. Osborne to William A. Graham, May 26, 1852, in Hamilton and Williams (eds.), *Graham Papers*, IV, 302–303; Richmond *Whig*, March 19, 1852; John Bell to J. N. Clark, December 27, 1851, in John Bell Papers, Manuscript Division, Tennessee State Library and Archives; Glyndon G. Van Deusen, *William Henry Seward* (New York: Oxford University Press, 1967), 141.

4. Graham to James W. Bryan, March 22, 1852, in Hamilton and Williams (eds.), *Graham Papers*, IV, 263; William B. Campbell to David Campbell, February 15, 1852, in Campbell Papers; New Orleans *Bee*, March 26, 1852; Tallahassee *Florida Sentinel*, April 27, 1852;

The outcome of their national convention surprised the apprehensive southern Whigs; they got their platform, but not their candidate.[5] As the southerners wished, the convention decided to deal with the platform before battling over the presidential nomination. Southerners on the platform committee repeated what all southern Whigs had been insisting upon for months—the convention must assert as the cardinal platform declaration the finality of the compromise. Adopting the southern position the committee presented to the full convention a platform sanctifying the compromise. The convention approved that platform by the one-sided margin of 227 to 66. In this first crucial contest the southern Whigs had won by a surprisingly large majority.

Having settled the platform question, the convention turned to the selection of a presidential nominee. The first ballot demonstrated conclusively southern loyalty to Fillmore; of the 87 southern votes, 86 went for the president.[6] Those votes provided 65 percent of Fillmore's first ballot total of 133 votes. Fillmore led, though he fell just short of the 149 votes required for the nomination. Scott almost matched Fillmore by polling 131 while Webster garnered only 27. In spite of Webster's miserable showing a Fillmore-Webster alliance could clearly carry the convention and the two camps tried to combine their forces, but to no avail. Not surprisingly a substantial number of southerners refused to commit themselves to Webster; for their part the Webster men would not promise to transfer their votes to Fillmore. During this futile effort to construct a workable anti-Scott majority the balloting continued with Scott and Fillmore exchanging the lead. Through the frantic negotiations and the seemingly interminable ballots, the southern delegates

---

Robert Toombs to Howell Cobb, June 10, 1852, in R. P. Brooks (ed.), "Howell Cobb Papers," *Georgia Historical Quarterly*, V (1921), 53–54.

5. For more detail on the Whig convention see Cole, *Whig Party*, 245–57; Robert F. Dalzell, Jr., *Daniel Webster and the Trial of American Nationalism, 1843–1852* (Boston: Houghton, Mifflin, 1973), Chap. 8.

6. The ballot-by-ballot totals by state (with a few exceptions) are in New York *Times*, June 19, 22, 1852, and Philadelphia *Cummings Evening Bulletin*, June 19, 21, 1852.

stood firmly behind Fillmore; never more than a half dozen deserted his column through the fifty-two unsuccessful attempts to select a nominee. Although Scott never managed to disrupt seriously the southern phalanx, the few southern delegates he did capture plus those he picked up in the border slave states and the North edged him closer to the nomination. Finally on the fifty-third ballot he won the prize with 159 votes, only 11 of which came from the southern contingent.

Even so, Scott's nomination occasioned no furor among the southern delegates. This equanimity stemmed directly from their platform triumph, which had given them their *sine qua non,* the compromise as a finality.[7] Also Scott's handful of southern friends assured their fellows that Scott stood squarely on the compromise. They revealed letters from Scott, one written to Senator James C. Jones of Tennessee during the convention, affirming his soundness on the compromise and his complete willingness to support the platform. To the southerners in Baltimore these frank pledges made Scott seem much less of an ogre. With the platform they wanted, with a commitment from the presidential nominee to support it, with a vice-presidential choice of their liking, William A. Graham, most southern delegates announced to the convention their intention of supporting the ticket and the party.

The unity of the southern delegates in Baltimore did not herald a similar unity in the body of southern Whiggery. On the contrary, the outcome of the national convention quite clearly divided southern Whigs. Most of the southern Whig press and an undoubted majority of southern Whig politicians, though precision on this point is impossible, ran up the Whig flag for another encounter with the Democrats. Like the delegates in Baltimore they were enthusiastic over the platform and willing to acquiesce in Scott's nomination. At the

7. Their great enemy Seward certainly did not like the platform; he called it "this wretched platform contrived to defeat General Scott." Seward to [?], June 18, 1852, and to Thurlow Weed, June 25, 1852, both quoted in Frederick W. Seward, *William H. Seward; an Autobiography from 1801 to 1834. With a Memoir of His life and Selections from His Letters* (3 vols.; New York: Derby and Miller, 1891), II, 187–88.

same time, however, a notable minority among the southern Whig leadership refused to join battle in the old manner. Clamoring against the evil influence of freesoilism in the national party and its offspring Winfield Scott, these dissident Whigs hampered the efforts of their brethren to present their party in its finest southern uniform.

For the southern Whig loyalists the platform endorsing the compromise evinced the southern orientation of their party. They waved the platform as a banner of victory before both wavering Whigs and the electorate. "The Platform that has been adopted is very thorough," proclaimed the Richmond *Whig*, "and goes as far as any Southern man has desired." In a public letter affirming his party regularity United States Senator Jackson Morton emphasized to his fellow Florida Whigs that "southern hands" had crafted a platform "acceptable to the South." The Whig state convention in Morton's Florida claimed that the endorsement of the compromise proved the fidelity of northern Whigs to southern Whigs and of all Whigs to the Constitution. Illustrating the loyalist faith in the efficacy and primacy of the compromise plank the New Orleans *Bee* in early July hoisted the precious statement to its masthead. The address promulgated by the Scott convention in Georgia repeated the refrain that the southern victory on the platform guaranteed southern rights in the party. Although the compromise triumph provided a political elixir for southern Whigs, it did not preclude questions about their candidate.[8]

The same loyalists who exulted over the compromise also stood up for Winfield Scott. They admitted that Scott had not been their choice for the nomination; they also admitted that he had been the favorite of Seward and his kindred among the northern Whigs. Having made these admissions, southern Whig spokesmen denied that they turned Scott into an enemy of the South. In their version the

8. Richmond *Whig*, June 22, 1852; Morton, *To the Whigs of Florida* (Washington: n.p., 1852); Tallahassee *Florida Sentinel*, July 20, 1852; New Orleans *Bee*, July 9, 1952; Milledgeville *Southern Recorder*, September 7, 1852.

Sewardites went for Scott, not because he believed in their principles, but because they believed him the most electable Whig. The
southern loyalists also declaimed loudly about Scott's soundness on
the compromise. In their view Scott had committed himself without
qualification to the Whig platform and the compromise, and as an
honorable man he would never violate his word. Praising Scott's
military achievements and personal independence, his southern defenders asserted that a man accustomed to command for nearly half a
century would never allow himself to become the instrument or
pawn of anyone else. Specifically they denied that William Henry
Seward could ever dominate Winfield Scott. "The very proposition
is ridiculous," maintained Jackson Morton, "and carries with it its
own refutation."[9] This defense of Scott sounded very much like the
arguments southern Whigs had made for Zachary Taylor—an independent man who would stand by his principles regardless of the
pressures upon him. But then Taylor, who had been the favorite of
southern Whigs, ended up with unexpected principles, to say the
least. As for Scott, he was not a planter, not a slaveowner, not the
choice of southern Whigs.

Prominent Whigs everywhere in the South responded to those
liabilities, not to the platform or to the loyalties and blandishments
of their colleagues upholding the party. Two complementary
motives prompted this negative reaction. First, according to the
dissidents the spectre that had appeared during the Taylor administration had become reality. The South had lost control of the Whig
party, which meant that the party was no longer a secure vehicle for
political advancement or a bastion for the South. Second, they believed this new situation jeopardized the ability of the South to
control her own destiny. Refusing to support the party, North
Carolina's Thomas L. Clingman spoke directly: "[Scott] was nomi-

9. Tallahassee *Florida Sentinel,* July 13, 1852; Vicksburg *Weekly Whig,* June 30, 1852;
Richmond *Whig,* June 22, July 2, 1852; Raleigh *Register,* June 23, 1852, December 14, 1853;
New Orleans *Bee,* June 24, 1852; John Bell to [?], July 31, 1852, in Bell Papers, Division of
Manuscripts, Library of Congress; Morton, *Florida Whigs.*

330 The South and the Politics of Slavery, 1828–1856

nated by the influence of Seward, Johnston [William F. Johnston, former Whig governor of Pennsylvania], and other antislavery leaders, against the united and determined efforts of the whole South and the Compromise men of the North, and if we [southern Whigs] support him we must expect to constitute a tail to the army of abolitionists in front." Deserting the party ticket a Whig legislator in Georgia explained, "I dislike exceedingly the *influence* which occasioned [Scott's] nomination over Mr. Fillmore and Mr. Webster, and am unwilling to extend that influence in the administration of the Government by him." Alexander Stephens denounced "Scott's *alliance* with the anticompromise party in the North." Stephens and Robert Toombs wired the convention of the Georgia Constitutional Union party not to adopt the Scott standard because of Scott's freesoil friends. Speaking in New Orleans, Louisiana's Whig Senator Judah P. Benjamin announced that he could not speak for his party's candidate against the Democratic candidate, who "has been true to the South." "If the South intends to protect herself in the enjoyment of her constitutional rights," contended Tennessee Congressman Meredith P. Gentry, "she must not *offer Bounties for Anti-Slavery Agitation and Aggression* by supporting a candidate forced upon her by abolition influences." Identical sentiments highlighted a widely circulated letter prepared in Washington by eight Whig congressmen from five different states. According to these eight, freesoil Whigs managed Scott's nomination; thus a Scott victory in the election would bring to power in Washington freesoilers dangerous to "the just and constitutional rights of the Southern states."[10]

10. Clingman to Dr. Ladson A. Mills, October 8, 1852, in [Thomas L. Clingman (ed.)], *Selections from the Speeches and Writings of Hon. Thomas L. Clingman of North Carolina, with Additions and Explanatory Notes* (Raleigh: John Nichols, 1877), 321; Andrew J. Miller to Thomas W. Thomas, October 13, 1852, quoted in Stephen F. Miller, *The Bench and Bar of Georgia: Memoirs and Sketches, With an Appendix, Containing a Court Roll from 1790 to 1857, Etc.* (2 vols.; Philadelphia: J. B. Lippincott, 1858), II, 162; Alexander Stephens to John S. Stephens, July 16, 1852, in Stephens Papers, Manhattanville College; Milledgeville *Southern Recorder*, June 29, 1852; New Orleans *Louisiana Courier*, August 6, 1852; Gentry to William B. Campbell, July n.d., 1852, in Campbell Papers; the letter from the Whig congressmen can be found in the Richmond *Enquirer*, July 9, 1852.

Such outcries against the national ticket and the national party sparked restiveness among the southern Whig faithful. Vice-presidential nominee William A. Graham wrote numerous letters assuring anxious Whigs that Scott would indeed protect southern rights. In Georgia the Whig remnant of the dissolving Constitutional Union party divided between those who heeded the advice of Stephens and Toombs and those who decided to go for Scott. Reports from Alabama and Virginia testified to the rampant dissatisfaction with the Scott candidacy. Claiming that Scott supported freesoil a Whig presidential elector in Texas refused to serve. Much to the delight of the Democrats, Clingman's followers in western North Carolina shared their leader's antipathy toward their old party. Never had such dissension wracked southern Whiggery.[11]

The energy southern Whigs expended during the familial struggle over Scott's nomination and its meaning for Whiggery damaged severely the party's ability to compete against the Democrats. This conflict was not just a battle of words. When tested and successful Whig politicians like Benjamin, Clingman, Stephens, and Toombs warned their constituents that the party had been captured by enemies of the South, they indicted their own party for failing in its primary mission—protecting the South. Staggering from this unprecedented internal challenge to its very legitimacy, a battered southern Whiggery reeled toward collision with southern Democrats.

While centrifugal forces tore at the vitals of southern Whiggery, centripetal forces restored vigor and unity to southern Democrats. Leaving the often bitter divisions over the compromise behind, southern Democrats joined together to renew the old contest against their Whig enemies. Only a fragment of Southern Rights

11. Graham to [?], June 28, 1852, Graham to John Barnett, July 6, 1852, Graham to Samuel F. Patterson, August 25, 1852, Graham to Statesville Committee, September 4, 1852, all in Hamilton and Williams (eds.), *Graham Papers*, IV, 330–31, 340–41, 380–81, 390–91; Milledgeville *Southern Recorder*, July 20, August 24, 1852; F. S. Lyon to John Bragg, July 27, 1852, in Bragg Papers; S. M. Munford to Millard Fillmore, June 24, 1852, in Fillmore Papers; Randolph Campbell, "The Whig Party of Texas in the Elections of 1848 and 1852," *Southwestern Historical Quarterly*, LXXIII (1969), 24; W. W. Holden to Abraham Venable, July 8, 1852, in Venable Papers.

men and radicals remained outside the gathering congregation of southern Democrats. This handful of zealots who continued to insist that the South had to fight the compromise operated outside the party and had practically no impact on party affairs in 1852.

Turning their attention to relations with northern Democrats, southerners found a situation strikingly similar to 1848, and for that matter to the previous twenty years. Northern Democrats clearly wanted to maintain their political connection with their southern partners. They also quite willingly followed the traditional script; no important segment of the northern Democrats tried to override the southern position on the critical sectional question. Southern Democrats had accepted the compromise, though unlike southern Whigs they did not call it the final solution to sectional differences. Still it had become an acceptable measure for the overwhelming majority of southern Democrats. Agreement on the compromise posed no problems for northern Democrats; after all they had provided the most consistent support for the compromise during its congressional journey. Even the northerners, chiefly Van Burenites, who had defected to the Free Soil party back in 1848 returned to their former political home. Like their comrades they too said yes to the compromise.[12]

Among the men eager to wear the presidential ribbon of the reunited Democratic legions none stood against the South or represented a faction feared by southerners. In short no equivalent of William Henry Seward walked among the northern Democrats. That most of the acknowledged presidential candidates were northerners did not bother the southerners; as in 1848 they had no objection to a northerner provided he occupied the essential southern ground—support of the compromise, especially the fugitive slave law, and disavowal of the Wilmot Proviso. Each of the leading contenders, old warhorses like James Buchanan, Lewis Cass, and

12. The fullest account of national party activities including the preconvention maneuvering and the convention itself is still Roy Franklin Nichols, *The Democratic Machine, 1850–1854* (New York: Columbia University Press, 1923), Chaps. 2–9.

William A. Marcy as well as the young warrior Stephen A. Douglas, cultivated southern support and had his southern champions. Although southerners disagreed over which candidate would run strongest in the South, all southern Democrats found all of the aspirants safe enough on southern issues.[13]

The outcome of the Democratic national convention, which met in Baltimore between June 1 and 5, gave the southern Democrats no reason to doubt their power in the party or to reconsider their commitment to it. The convention wrote a platform endorsing the compromise and heaping praise upon the old Democratic shibboleths of states rights and limited government. The choice of a presidential nominee aroused no suspicion among the southerners even though an unexpected name adorned the party banner. In ballot after ballot the strength of the major candidates ebbed and flowed but none found a current strong enough to carry him to victory. When the active candidates proved unable to win the necessary two-thirds majority, the convention turned to a fresh face, a legitimate dark horse. On the forty-ninth ballot Franklin Pierce of New Hampshire became the Democratic nominee for president. Pierce's surprising success created no anxiety in the southern delegations. In fact southern votes materially assisted Pierce's triumph. Southern delegates considered Pierce as safe and secure for the South as any of the contestants he had defeated. On the critical issue of the compromise and the fugitive slave law Pierce certainly stood as resolutely as any of the vanquished hopefuls.[14] Thus with a platform to their liking and a candidate who pleased them southern Democrats had every reason to rejoice over the outcome of their convention.

13. W. W. Holden to Abraham Venable, December 29, 1851, March 26, 1852, both in Venable Papers; Andrew Johnson to A. O. P. Nicholson, December 13, 1851, in Leroy P. Graf *et al.* (eds.), *The Papers of Andrew Johnson* (3 vols.; Knoxville: University of Tennessee Press, 1967–), I, 630; Stephen A. Douglas to Robert M. T. Hunter, May 6, 1851, Douglas to David L. Yulee, six letters in May and June 1852, all in Robert W. Johannsen (ed.), *The Letters of Stephen A. Douglas* (Urbana: University of Illinois Press, 1961), 218, 249–52.

14. Roy Franklin Nichols, *Franklin Pierce: Young Hickory of the Granite Hills* (Rev. ed.; Philadelphia: University of Pennsylvania Press, 1958), 180–81, 201–202.

In the South unanimous delight marked the Democratic reaction. "The Convention could scarcely have pleased us more," crowed the Tallahassee *Floridian*. Echoes of that joyful refrain resounded throughout the South. Accolade upon accolade was bestowed upon Pierce. Southern Democrats who had opposed the compromise thought Pierce a superb selection. Pierre Soulé called him "a man of the greatest merit." Mississippi Congressman Albert G. Brown lavished even more abundant praise on Pierce: "On the question of State Rights, he is as reliable as Calhoun himself; and on the subject of slavery he stands far above *all* suspicion. Of all men living I do not know one who comes nearer up the standard of perfection, than Franklin Pierce." At the same time Democrats who had participated in the Union movement described Pierce as an excellent choice and a guarantor of the constitutional rights of the South. From former president John Tyler to the radicals who maintained nominal ties with the Democrats, the southern chorus cheering Pierce grew louder and louder. As an important South Carolina fire-eater told Pierce, "A nomination so favorable to the South had not been anticipated." Excited and confident southern Democrats proclaimed that they would win in the South by a landslide.[15]

Only in Alabama did the radicals move to thwart Democratic solidarity, but their signal failure underscored the powerful Democratic surge toward unity. A group among the Alabama radicals wanted to run a third party campaign in 1852, though they could not convince all of their radical brethren. Even so the third party faction calling itself the Southern Rights party did nominate a presidential ticket composed of the old Georgia nullifier George M. Troup and the Mississippi secessionist John A. Quitman. From this third-party

15. Tallahassee *Floridian*, June 12, 1852; Soulé to Charles E. A. Gayarré, August 2, 1852, in Gayarré Papers, Department of Archives, Louisiana State University; James Byrne Ranck, *Albert Gallatin Brown: Radical Southern Nationalist* (New York and London: D. Appleton-Century, 1937), 106; John H. Lumpkin to Howell Cobb, June 6, 1852, James Jackson to Howell Cobb, June 8, 1852, both in Ulrich B. Phillips (ed.), *The Correspondence of Robert Toombs, Alexander H. Stephens and Howell Cobb* (Washington: Government Printing Office, 1913), 299–300; Richmond *Enquirer*, June 18, 1852; Milledge Luke Bonham to Pierce, June 7, 1852, in Pierce Papers.

movement regular Democrats in Alabama perceived no threat. Senator Jeremiah Clemens wrote Pierce not to worry about Alabama; according to Clemens the Southern Rights ticket would poll but a tiny vote.[16]

Troup's response to his presidential nomination confirmed the confidence of Clemens, emphasized the futility of the third party, and graphically illustrated the Pierce triumph. In his letter accepting the nomination Troup declared he did so "for the sole purpose of organizing that [Southern Rights] party." As for his own intentions in the upcoming election, Troup informed those who had chosen him to lead them, "I have not expected ever to be able to vote for a Northern man so pure and disinterested as Mr. Pierce." Having such an opportunity Troup said he intended to take advantage of it, and he urged his supporters to do likewise because "you may never have such another opportunity."[17] Troup's leap upon the Pierce bandwagon dramatized the inherent weakness of the third party and for all practical purposes cemented Democratic unity. With their radical flank secured a united, vigorous southern Democracy hurtled into an uneasy, troubled southern Whiggery.

Emphasizing the antecedents of Scott's candidacy southern Democrats bore down on one theme: the Whig party had become the political vehicle of northerners bent on degrading the South and destroying its institutions. Well before the Whig national convention the southern Democratic press had identified Scott as the agent of Seward and his unholy cohorts. Southern Democratic editors asserted that northern Whigs supported Scott in order to run a sectional campaign designed to harass and endanger the South. Having made this claim southern Democrats went on to declare that if

16. Jonathan Mills Thornton III, "Politics and Power in a Slave Society: Alabama, 1806–1860" (Ph.D. dissertation, Yale University, 1974), 344–48; S. D. Moore to John M. Berrien, August 23, 1852, in Berrien Papers; William L. Yancey to Benjamin C. Yancey, September 15, 1852, in Benjamin Yancey Papers; Clemens to Pierce, September 24, 1852, in Pierce Papers. Clemens was right; the Troup-Quitman ticket polled only 5 percent of the vote in Alabama.

17. Troup's letter dated September 27, 1852, is in Edward J. Harden, *The Life of George M. Troup* (Savannah: E. J. Purse, 1859), 530–31.

southern Whigs accepted a Scott nomination, they turned control of their party over to the freesoil segment of northern Whiggery. According to the southern Democrats such an act could only mean that southern Whigs were joining the sworn enemies of the South to pursue a political strategy "look[ing] to practical degradation and disenfranchisement of the Southern States."[18] This southern Democratic stance matched almost exactly the preconvention posture assumed by most southern Whigs.

After Scott actually won the Whig nomination, southern Democrats increased the intensity of their earlier cry. Repeatedly they hammered away on Scott's connections with men like Seward, his fellow New Yorker Horace Greeley, and Thaddeus Stevens of Pennsylvania who, as the southern Democratic script read, had nominated Scott and would surely control his administration. Satisfied that they had established two indisputable facts—first, that Scott represented the Sewards and second, that the Sewards intended irreparable harm to the South—southern Democrats drew their inexorable conclusion. In the words of Aaron Brown the election of Scott "[would] seal the doom of the South."[19]

With such a horrendous possibility confronting the South, southern Democrats implored all southerners, especially Whigs, to stand as southern men. Making this point the Little Rock *Arkansas Gazette* posed a question, "How, we ask, can *southern* men, be they *whigs* or anything else, accept [Scott] as the representative of their principles and sentiments?" In an election eve appeal the Jackson *Mississippian* called on all its readers who "have Southern hearts . . . to awaken them to the importance of using their utmost exertions to prevent the election of Gen. Scott to the Chief Magistracy of the

18. Richmond *Enquirer*, April 11, July 11, 1851, March 12, April 9, 1852; Milledgeville *Federal Union*, February 17, March 16, 1852; New Orleans *Louisiana Courier*, February 14, 1851.

19. This rhetoric pervaded southern Democratic papers. For examples see Milledgeville *Federal Union*, August 17, 1852; Austin *State Gazette*, July 10, 1852; New Orleans *Louisiana Courier*, August 27, 1852; Jackson *Mississippian*, July 2, 1852; Editors of the Union and American (eds.), *Speeches, Congressional and Political, and Other Writings of ex-Governor Aaron V. Brown of Tennessee* (Nashville: J. S. Marling, 1854–[55]), 259.

Republic." Appealing directly to southern honor the Richmond *Enquirer* perfectly summed up the southern Democratic message: "But for a party of Southern men [southern Whigs] to permit their declaration of principles to be derided and spit upon by the [William F.] Johnstons and [Thaddeus] Stevenses of Pennsylvania, and to labor tamely for the promotion of a man whom Johnston and Stevens first brought forward for the public suffrages; is a degree of degradation which the Southern character has never before reached."[20] The force of these powerful entreaties was further magnified, albeit immeasurably, by defecting southern Whigs, who voiced identical views.

Arguing that no self-respecting southerner could vote for Scott and the Whig party, Democrats presented their party and their candidate as stark contrasts to the untrustworthy Whigs. Southern Democrats maintained that their party still protected the South because they dominated in its councils; no Stevenses or Sewards who condemned the South existed among northern Democrats. Even the returning Van Burenites accepted both the compromise and a candidate most pleasing to the South. They pointed out quite correctly that a substantial number of southern votes had gone for Pierce in the Democratic convention. This fact meant that southerners had helped Pierce win while Scott had triumphed in spite of the South. Pierce as a prosouthern man received considerable attention from his southern champions. They praised his clear-cut stand on the compromise and printed speeches and letters attesting to his correctness on slavery and southern rights. They also made gleeful use of northern Whig attacks on Pierce as "the champion of slavery." Thus southern Democrats offered southern voters a distinct choice: danger and dishonor with Whigs or safety and honor with them.[21]

Bombarded by their Democratic foes and beset with internal re-

20. Little Rock *Arkansas Gazette*, August 13, 1852; Jackson *Mississippian*, October 29, 1852; Richmond *Enquirer*, September 7, 1852.
21. In the summer and fall of 1852 all the southern Democratic papers were full of this rhetoric; the quotation is from the Milledgeville *Federal Union*, August 17, 1852.

bellion, southern Whig loyalists tried mightily to counter the Democratic onslaught. Hardpressed and shaken as they were, southern Whigs attempted nothing new in 1852. Assaulting the Democrats and defending both Scott and themselves, they stuck with the time-tested rhetoric of the politics of slavery. Just as the Democrats condemned Scott for freesoil ties, so the Whigs indicted Pierce for the same offense. That the Van Burenites had returned to the Democratic fold provided ammunition for the southern Whig charges. Their newspapers kept listing alleged freesoilers who supported Pierce; usually they named Martin Van Buren and then any number of his confederates, including the infamous David Wilmot. Any man who had such political allies, the southern Whig argument ran, had to harbor antisouthern sentiments. For their case against Pierce, southern Whigs did not rely solely on guilt by association. They played up a Pierce statement expressing a loathing for the fugitive slave law. Answering a question at a New Hampshire meeting in January, 1852, Pierce probably made such a statement, though he insisted he had been quoted out of context. Even so he continuously and emphatically proclaimed that he considered the law constitutional and an essential part of the compromise. Accordingly he backed it fully. These Pierce declarations never made the southern Whig press. Rather Pierce as a foe of the Fugitive Slave Act, friend of Van Burenites, and "NEW HAMPSHIRE YANKEE WHO HATES SLAVERY" filled southern Whig newspapers.[22]

Painting Pierce with antislavery colors did not consume all the energies of southern Whigs. They called on voters to recognize Scott and Whiggery as stalwart guardians of southern interests. For southern Whigs, Scott became the general of the compromise; Scott quotations embracing the compromise pervaded their papers. Comparing Pierce unfavorably with Scott, southern Whig papers often juxtaposed Pierce's utterance against the Fugitive Slave Act

22. Vicksburg *Weekly Whig*, August 11, September 22, October 20, 1852; New Orleans *Bee*, August 24, September 10, 1852; Raleigh *Register*, June 16, July 21, 28, September *passim*, 1852; Richmond *Whig*, July 16, 23, August 27, September 17, 1852. For the Pierce incident see Nichols, *Pierce*, 210–11.

and a Scott declaration of undying support for all of the compromise. As for their party, southern Whigs denied that freesoilers or enemies of the South dominated it. They admitted that the Whig party contained a small number of freesoilers, but they insisted that many more of those ogres wore Democratic stripes. And those few Whig freesoilers posed no serious threat to the South, for General Scott would command a Whig army in which such blackguards would have to march in the rearmost rank.[23]

Even though southern Whig loyalists exerted every effort to equal the performance of southern Democrats, they failed. In view of the disunity plaguing the party they did manage to stir up considerable enthusiasm among the party faithful, especially in Tennessee. Still, a general tenor of defensiveness prevailed among southern Whigs. Southern newspapers and correspondence in 1852 unmistakably show that illusive and unprovable quality, initiative, resting with the southern Democrats. The reality of 1852 hit southern Whigs even before the presidential balloting. In state elections in both North Carolina and Florida the Democrats scored impressive victories. In these two elections the major issues mirrored the national contest.[24] As in 1850 North Carolina Whigs and Democrats battled over free suffrage and legislative apportionment with their debate again getting caught up with national slavery and sectional issues. In Florida, where the Scott nomination hurt Whig unity, talk of southern rights and national party attitudes toward the South dominated the campaign. Democrats in North Carolina reelected their governor by an increased majority and retained control of the state senate, though the Whigs did manage to take the house. The Whigs suffered complete disaster in Florida. For the first time since 1845 the Democrats

23. New Orleans *Bee*, August–October, 1852, *passim;* Richmond *Whig*, June 22, July 2, 1852; Raleigh *Register*, June 23, September–October *passim*, 1852; Vicksburg *Weekly Whig*, August 11, September 8, 15, 1852; Campbell, "Texas Whigs," 25.

24. For the journey of Tennessee Whigs from despondency to enthusiasm see William B. Campbell to David Campbell, June 29, July 29, August 17, 1852, all in Campbell Papers. Raleigh *Standard*, June–August, 1852, *passim;* Raleigh *Register*, June–August, 1852, *passim;* James R. Morrill, "The Presidential Election of 1852: Death Knell of the Whig Party in North Carolina," *North Carolina Historical Review*, XLIV (1967), 354–55, 358; Herbert J. Doherty, Jr., *The Whigs of Florida, 1845–1854* (Gainesville: University of Florida Press, 1959), 54–57.

won the governorship and both houses of the legislature, and with substantial majorities in each case. Additionally they elected the state's lone congressman for the first time ever. These results also influenced the presidential contest in both states. The confidence and pessimism affecting Democrats and Whigs respectively helps explain why the presidential vote in North Carolina and Florida failed to match the vote in the state elections.

The presidential contest resulted in a Democratic landslide. Such a one-sided presidential election had not occurred in the South since 1832. Polling 314,739 votes Pierce carried every southern state save Tennessee and won more popular votes than any previous presidential candidate, either Democratic or Whig. His 56.1 percent of the vote also exceeded the percentage won by anybody since Andrew Jackson, though it was still far below Jackson's astronomical margins. Pierce made this impressive showing despite a decline in the Democratic vote in three states, Alabama, Georgia, and Tennessee, where Pierce won 10,038 fewer votes than Lewis Cass had in 1848. In both Alabama and Georgia the disarray and weakness pervading Whiggery undoubtedly accounted for the smaller Democratic turnout; Democrats realized that Whigs posed no serious threat. However, that explanation does not hold for Tennessee where the Whigs made a supreme effort. Even so, in Tennessee the decrease in the Whig vote was some four times greater than in the Democratic column. In defeat Winfield Scott received only 42.5 percent of the vote, the smallest percentage of any Whig presidential candidate. He won only 238,514 popular votes, 54,335 and 18.6 percent less than Zachary Taylor and fewer than any Whig candidate since Hugh White. Although Scott took Tennessee with 50.7 percent, the Whig percentage declined in every southern state including Tennessee. Aside from Tennessee, the Whigs made a respectable showing only in North Carolina and Louisiana.[25] In none of the old Union party states did Scott even obtain 40 percent of the vote.

25. In Tennessee the Whig total fell by 5,653 votes (8.8 percent) while the Democratic total fell by but 1,327 votes (2.8 percent). The Democratic decline in Alabama (13.8 percent) and Georgia (9.9 percent) was greater, but it paled beside the precipitous decrease in the

This unprecedented southern Whig debacle originated within southern Whiggery itself. The key to the election rested with the tens of thousands of Whigs who refused to vote for Scott. In James M. Mason's graphic words, "In the South, defection in the whig ranks stalked at noon."[26] Simple arithmetic clearly shows, however, that these Whig voters did not transfer their allegiance en masse to the Democrats. Scott's vote fell behind Zachary Taylor's by over 54,000 while Pierce garnered only 32,000 more than Lewis Cass. And new voters, as well as the return of Democrats who had supported Taylor, helped make up the Democratic increase. Obviously more southern Whigs sat out the election than voted for Pierce. But whether a southern Whig voted for Pierce or stayed home, he testified to the influence of the rebellious notables in his own party and to the effectiveness of the southern Democratic rhetoric. The defecting Whigs did believe that the election of Winfield Scott would endanger the South. The returns manifested the existence of a deep dissatisfaction among the rank and file as well as certain leaders of southern Whiggery, a combination that boded ill for the party's future.

II

The southern Whig rout of 1852 continued in 1853. Disaster struck them at every turn. Just before the arrival of the new year, on December 27, 1852, Louisiana held its first election under the Whig-inspired constitution of 1852. Although the Whigs had domi-

---

Whig vote: 50.6 percent in Alabama and 53.8 percent in Georgia (counting the vote for both Scott and the Independent Whig or Webster ticket). The Pierce-Scott percentage totals less than 100 percent for two main reasons. In Georgia an Independent Whig ticket for Daniel Webster won 5,324 votes and the Troup-Quitman ticket won 2,205 votes in Alabama. There were also twelve scattered votes in Texas. While the Whig percentage declined substantially everywhere, the party's popular vote did go up in two states, a tiny increase of 75 in Texas and a sizable increase of 13,467 in Virginia (undoubtedly the result of the liberalized franchise provisions in the Virginia Constitution of 1851). Just to emphasize Whig problems, note the explosion of the Democratic vote in those two states: in Texas up by 3,213, in Virginia up by 27,133. Excluding Tennessee the Whigs obtained over 45 percent of the vote only in two states: North Carolina, 49.5 percent, and Louisiana 48.1 percent.

26. Mason to William C. Rives, November 23, 1852, in Rives Papers. See also New Orleans *Bee*, November 12, 1852, and Thornton, "Politics and Power," 216–18.

nated the constitutional convention,[27] the Democrats swamped them in the elections authorized by the constitution. Convincingly retaining their hold on the governorship the Democrats also took both houses of the legislature away from the Whigs. In Georgia the Constitutional Union majorities of 1851 became Democratic majorities in 1853; supported by Howell Cobb, Herschel Johnson, a leader of the old Georgia Southern Rights party, was elected governor along with a Democratic majority in both legislative chambers. In the other two Union party states, Alabama and Mississippi, the Democrats easily regained the dominant position they had enjoyed before 1851. Even in the only state the Whigs had salvaged from the wreckage of Scott's campaign, the Democrats came out victorious. Tennesseeans in 1853 chose a Democratic governor and a Democratic senate, though they did leave Whigs controlling the house.

Southern politicians vied for eleven governorships, eleven senates, and eleven houses; of those thirty-three the Whigs after 1853 controlled only two, the house in both North Carolina and Tennessee. Elections for representatives to the Thirty-third Congress, which convened in December, 1853, only added to Whig misery. To that Congress southern voters sent sixty-five representatives, but no more than fourteen were Whig, and six of them came from Tennessee alone.[28] This pathetic performance added to the cataclysmic dimensions of Scott's defeat left southern Whigs in the weakest position they had ever known.

In the midst of these seemingly endless southern Whig catastrophes southern Democrats diagnosed their foes as either mortally ill or already dead. Even before the Scott fiasco a prominent Georgia Democrat, an ally of Cobb's who had worked closely with Whigs in the Union movement, observed, "All of the Whigs in this State have lost sight of all alliance with Northern Whiggery." And without that

27. William H. Adams, *The Louisiana Whig Party* (Lafayette: University of Southwestern Louisiana History Series, 1973), 218–22.

28. Because of weakening and breaking party ties it is difficult to be precise about the number of southern Whigs elected to Congress. In my tabulation I gave the Whigs the benefit of every doubt; fourteen is their highest possible number.

alliance no southern Whig party could survive for very long. On the eve of 1853, a year of desolation for southern Whigs, Andrew Johnson told a Tennessee friend, "The whig party is now in fact disbanded." As defeat after defeat piled upon southern Whigs, the Richmond *Enquirer* questioned whether or not the Whig party still existed as a party. The *Enquirer* claimed it could find nothing identifiable as Whig except a few straggling voters. Questions and claims did not enter the calculations of the Tallahassee *Floridian*. On July 2, 1853, the *Floridian* spoke with a blunt finality: "The Whig Party is Dead."[29]

A considerable number of prominent southern Whigs shared that outlook. All of them did not agree with Alexander Stephens who had pronounced, "the Whig party is dead," back in December, 1851, but influential southern Whigs were convinced of their party's dire predicament. They traced its plight to their alliance with northern Whigs insensitive to southern political realities and antipathetic to southern institutions. Despondent over the problems a Scott candidacy posed, the governor of Tennessee blamed the increasing weakness of southern Whiggery directly on the affiliation with northern Whigs like Seward. Peering over the ruins of the Scott calamity Robert Toombs echoed William Campbell's complaint. "We can never have peace & security with Seward[,] Greeley & Co in the ascendant in our National Counshels [*sic*]," he wrote to John J. Crittenden, "& we had better purchase them by the destruction of the Whig party than of the Union." Toombs's views were shared by those who considered him a faithless Whig and bit of a fire-eater. By mid-1853, North Carolina Senator George Badger concluded that an unbridgeable gulf separated the wings of the Whig party. As a result Badger unhesitatingly consigned his party to the political graveyard, though he did so sadly and reluctantly. "So I give up," he confided to his close friend Maryland Senator James A. Pearce. Although the

29. Jno. H. Lumpkin to Sim Boyd, May 2, 1852, in Georgia Political Leaders Collection; Johnson to Sam Milligan, December 28, 1852, in Graf *et al.* (eds.), *Johnson Papers*, II, 102; Richmond *Enquirer*, July 29, 1853; Tallahassee *Floridian*, July 2, 1853.

results of 1852 apparently made Tennessee the flagship of southern Whiggery, Scott's victory there engendered neither optimism nor confidence in Tennessee leaders. Governor Campbell, who refused to run for reelection, felt his party "broken to pieces" while his colleague Senator John Bell, a founder of the southern Whig party, saw "signs of a more decisive breaking up of our party in Tenn. in the next election [1853] than I have seen at any time heretofore." This pessimism weakened the fabric of southern Whiggery. [30]

Even though many chieftains revealed doubts about the political health and the political future of the party, their press still flung the rhetoric of the politics of slavery at southern Democrats. President Pierce's patronage policy became the southern Whig target. Basing his patronage strategy on the Democratic unity of 1852, Pierce awarded federal posts to all who had accepted the platform of 1852 and had supported his candidacy, regardless of their previous actions. [31] This decision meant that Southern Rights men, southern procompromise men, and all northern Democrats, including those who had defected to the Free Soil party in 1848, received Pierce's bounty. That the old freesoilers, particularly the Van Burenites in New York, were rewarded with federal jobs fueled the southern Whig attacks. Throughout 1853, editors kept up an incessant cry; the president's tactics proved the truth of Whig campaign charges that Pierce hobnobbed with enemies of the South. In their reading of events the Pierce administration's "taking Free Soilers to their bosom" could have only one logical meaning: the freesoilers among the northern Democrats, especially Martin Van Buren, had taken control of the Pierce presidency and the Democratic party. According to one editor the situation had gotten so far out of hand that southerners would next see the spectacle of Pierce bestowing his

30. Stephens to Howell Cobb, December 5, 1851, in Phillips (ed.), *Toombs, Stephens, Cobb Correspondence*, 268; Toombs to Crittenden, December 5, 1852, in Crittenden Papers; Badger to Pearce, April 26, June 2, November 7, 1853, all in George Badger Papers, North Carolina Department of Archives and History; William Campbell to David Campbell, February 15, 1852, March 23, 1853, and Bell to William Campbell, February 5, 1853, all in Campbell Papers.
31. For Pierce and the patronage see Nichols, *Pierce*, Chap. 33.

generosity on the notorious Harriet Beecher Stowe, author of *Uncle Tom's Cabin*. Claiming that Pierce's nefarious appointments conclusively demonstrated the freesoil domination of the Democratic party, southern Whigs then pointed to the danger such domination held for all southerners. Southern Democrats had duped their fellow southerners, raged the southern Whig editors, because their assertions that their party protected the South were hollow. Instead of protecting the South the Pierce administration threatened it.[32]

Southern Democrats reacted predictably. They defended their president and their party from the most recent Whig accusations. Even so, a small number of them were distressed about Pierce's king-sized patronage tent. Some old Unionists disliked seeing their former Southern Rights opponents rewarded, and some former Calhounites were unhappy over the Van Burenite appointments. Southern Democrats never denied that Pierce put Van Burenites into office; they never claimed that no former Free Soil party men occupied government jobs. Admitting as much, southern Democrats then asserted and repeated untold numbers of times that all Democrats in 1852 had pledged themselves to the party platform, which guaranteed southern rights. That affirmation, in the words of southern Democrats, superseded whatever went before it and was manifested in Democratic unity behind Pierce. As for President Pierce, southern Democrats proudly proclaimed that the South had no stronger champion; they had no doubt that Pierce "[would] take the strongest and boldest ground possible, in defense of the rights of the South."[33]

32. New Orleans *Bee*, July 12, October 15, November 26, 1853; Vicksburg *Tri-Weekly Whig*, July 16, August 4, 1853; Vicksburg *Weekly Whig*, November 2, December 22, 1853; Milledgeville *Southern Recorder*, summer, 1853, *passim;* Raleigh *Register*, March 1, 1854; Richmond *Whig*, July 8, October 14, 1853.

33. Alexander Stephens to Howell Cobb, March 6, 1853, and P. Clayton to Cobb, May 23, 1853, both in Cobb Papers; Cobb to Thomas DeKalb Harris, January 12, [1853], in Howell Cobb Papers, Georgia Archives; Sam Houston to Washington D. Miller, June 30, 1853, in Amelia W. Williams and Eugene C. Barker (eds.), *The Writings of Sam Houston, 1813–1863* (8 vols.; Austin: University of Texas Press, 1938–43), V, 451; Nichols, *Pierce*, 255; Richmond *Enquirer*, April 29, 1853; Milledgeville *Federal Union*, August 16, 1853; Little Rock *Arkansas Gazette*, August 19, October 14, November 11, 1853.

Powerfully placed southern Democrats in Congress moved to insure that their party and their president stayed on the southern mark. Led by a Senate group including the Virginians Robert M. T. Hunter and James M. Mason along with South Carolina's Andrew P. Butler and David R. Atchison of Missouri the southern Democrats had two primary goals. They feared a growing diffusiveness in the party that could distort its southern orientation.[34] With apprehension, even disfavor, they had watched Pierce hand patronage rewards to Van Burenites. Some of the southerners were skeptical about the Van Burenite loyalty to the Democratic platform, which repudiated the Wilmot Proviso or freesoil in its endorsement of the compromise and popular sovereignty. Because of this doubt these southerners searched for a way to bind more securely the Van Burenites to the platform, to the southern-approved party rules. Success in this endeavor would also accomplish the second goal of the southerners. A renewed commitment by all northern Democrats, but especially the Van Burenites, to the platform of 1852 would dramatically disprove southern Whig charges against the Pierce administration.[35] A new party loyalty test devised by southern Democrats would prove conclusively that Pierce's patronage policy connoted no freesoil leanings in the Democratic party.

Southern senators found what they wanted—a bill proposed by Senator Stephen A. Douglas of Illinois to organize the Nebraska territory.[36] Senator Douglas had not started out linking Nebraska to sectional politics or to the particular needs and desires of the southern Democrats. A western man preoccupied with national growth

34. Roy F. Nichols emphasizes this point in his "The Kansas-Nebraska Act: A Century of Historiography," *Mississippi Valley Historical Review*, XLIII (1956), 201–208.

35. John Bell to R. T. Saunders, April 21, 1854, in "The Hon. John Bell on the Nebraska Bill," *Olympian*, I (1903), 351–52; Howell Cobb to Stephen A. Douglas, February 5, 1854, in Johannsen (ed.), *Douglas Letters*, 300, n. 1; William C. Dawson to Linton Stephens, December 21, 1853, in Stephens Papers, Division of Manuscripts, Library of Congress.

36. The most thorough discussion of both Douglas' role and the congressional history of the bill is Robert W. Johannsen, *Stephen A. Douglas* (New York: Oxford University Press, 1973), 395–400, Chap. 17. See also Gerald W. Wolff, "Party and Section: The Senate and the Kansas-Nebraska Bill," *Civil War History*, XVIII (1972), 293–311.

and expansion, Douglas viewed the organization of Nebraska as a logical, indeed essential, step in the continuing growth of the country. That settlers had pushed to the western borders of Missouri and Iowa, that railroad and telegraph lines were needed to bring California closer to the rest of populated America, these forces, in Douglas' mind, all mandated the official organization of the new territory. A Nebraska bill had passed the House of Representatives in February, 1853, but it failed when Douglas brought it before the Senate just before the Thirty-second Congress expired. Nine months later when the Thirty-third Congress began its first session, Douglas, the chairman of the Senate Committee on Territories, was back with Nebraska.

Southern Democrats grasped the Nebraska bill because it provided a vehicle for a dramatic reaffirmation of the Democratic platform, and, as a corollary, a striking illustration of southern power in the party. Southern Democratic senators wanted the Nebraska bill drawn so that it did not exclude slavery from the Nebraska territory. This task necessitated admitting that the Compromise of 1850 with its territorial doctrine popular sovereignty took precedence over the Missouri Compromise which forbade slavery north of 36 degrees, 30 minutes, except for Missouri: all of the Nebraska Territory lay above the Missouri Compromise line. To southerners, removing the Missouri restriction for popular sovereignty simply restated the Compromise of 1850 and the Democratic platform of 1852. In this instance as in 1848, 1850, and 1852 the southern Democrats viewed popular sovereignty through southern-tinted lenses. To them popular sovereignty had two basic meanings: first, it meant that neither Congress nor a territorial legislature could exclude slavery from a territory during the territorial stage; second, it meant that only a state constitution adopted at the time of statehood could positively disallow slavery.[37] Also if the revised Nebraska bill became an ad-

---

37. Of course, as in the previous instances, most northerners, including Douglas, interpreted it differently. To them it meant that from the earliest settlement a territorial legislature could exclude slavery.

ministration measure, a party measure, the Van Burenites would have to accept it in order to retain their standing in the Democratic party.

The demand of the southern Democrats posed no serious problems for Douglas. More than anything else Douglas wanted to pass a Nebraska bill, and he knew he could never get one through the Senate without southern Democratic support. His unsuccessful bill of March, 1853, which said nothing about popular sovereignty, had obtained the votes of only two slave-state senators, both from Missouri. In order to succeed Douglas would have to unlock southern Democratic votes; adding popular sovereignty to the bill became the key to unlocking those votes. Incorporating popular sovereignty into the Nebraska bill was easy for Douglas. He identified popular sovereignty with the democratic faith he professed, with the West he represented, with the political career he cared most about, his own. In Douglas' mind popular sovereignty was good democratic and Democratic doctrine. The Compromise of 1850 enshrined it; the Democratic platform of 1852 embraced it; the Nebraska bill of 1854 could absorb it. As for popular sovereignty enabling slavery to prosper in Nebraska, Douglas did not believe it could happen. He never considered slavery the primary issue anyway; for him expansion overrode all else. And if placating his southern colleagues with popular sovereignty would get the Nebraska bill through the Senate, Stephen A. Douglas would not hesitate. On January 4, 1854, Douglas reported his Nebraska bill from the territorial committee. Unlike previous Nebraska bills this version employed the language of popular sovereignty: "When admitted as a state or states, the said territory, or any portion of the same, shall be received into the Union, with or without slavery, as their constitutions may prescribe at the time of their admission."

The extent of the southern Democratic influence on Douglas is difficult to measure. They wanted a vehicle; he provided one. He needed their support; they told him what it would cost; he paid their price. But no evidence indicates that he did so reluctantly. That fact should not be surprising, for southerners only asked Douglas to stand by his own doctrine. Now if Douglas had been recalcitrant, the southerners would have undoubtedly moved against him. They had certainly done so with Van Buren in 1844 and would again with Douglas in 1857 and 1858. The most likely interpretation of the Douglas-southern Democratic collaboration in December, 1853, is a simple one; the ambitions of each meshed.[38]

Although popular sovereignty had become an integral part of Douglas' bill, the next logical step had not been taken; the bill did not contain a direct repeal of the Missouri Compromise. Douglas certainly and his southern colleagues apparently were content to rely on indirection to undo the thirty-four-year-old Missouri Compromise. But with southern Democrats and southern Whigs competing for political advantage an indirect approach to an important slavery question had little chance of success. And in fact the Missouri Compromise became the lever southern Whigs used to force themselves into the Nebraska discussion. Senator Archibald Dixon of Kentucky led southern Whigs into the Nebraska fray. Troubled that the language in Douglas' bill jeopardized southern equality in the territories Dixon acted to insure equality; after all the Compromise of 1850 supposedly guaranteed equality in the territories. Accordingly on January 15 Dixon prepared an amendment to the Nebraska bill explicitly declaring the Missouri Compromise inoperative in all territories of the United States. The next day he showed it to Senator James C. Jones of Tennessee and presented it to the Senate.[39]

Southern Whigs had no outside help in mounting this direct strike against the Missouri Compromise. The evidence makes clear that Dixon and other southern congressional Whigs were sincerely concerned about the future of their section and slavery. From this

---

38. This view of Douglas agrees with Johannsen's interpretation whereas Nichols in "Kansas-Nebraska" pictures Douglas buckling under southern pressure.

39. Mrs. Archibald Dixon, *History of Missouri Compromise and Slavery in American Politics. A True History of the Missouri Compromise and Its Repeal, and of African Slavery as a Factor in American Politics* (2nd ed.; Cincinnati: Robert Clarke, 1903), 437–38, 442–43.

perspective Senator Dixon's amendment should be viewed as an attempt to emphasize southern rights and to strengthen the legitimacy of slavery. The few southern Whigs left in the Thirty-third Congress were also southern politicians. They knew that since 1852 southern Democrats had used the slavery issue to weaken seriously their party. For southern Whig politicians the Nebraska bill offered a possible opportunity to recoup some of the ground they had lost since 1852. Southern Democrats had injected popular sovereignty into the Nebraska bill, but they withheld repeal of the Missouri Compromise. Following the classic pattern of the politics of slavery Senator Dixon and his associates rushed to seize repeal for themselves. Then, having openly struck down the restrictive Missouri Compromise, southern Whigs could claim the political prize awarded to alert, ardent protectors of the South. The almost unanimous support among southern Whig senators for Dixon's move testifies both to their prosouthern mood and to the traditionalism of the politics involved. [40]

Southern Democrats could not oppose Dixon's amendment without giving southern Whigs a political victory. At the same time they had no intention of allowing the Whigs to win any advantage from their issue. Besides the Democrats liked the idea of overt repeal; it made the victory of popular sovereignty, of southern rights so much more absolute. In fact, even before Dixon proposed his amendment to the Senate, Democratic Congressman Philip Phillips of Alabama came to an identical conclusion: without a formal repeal of the Missouri Compromise, the Nebraska bill guaranteed the South nothing. Phillips took his doubts to the southern Democratic leadership. Impressed, they conferred with Douglas. Thereupon all concurred

40. For the attitude of southern Whigs consult *ibid.*, 437–38, 442–43, 449, 459, 588–98; [Clingman (ed.)], *Clingman Writings*, 335; Archibald Dixon to John J. Crittenden, February 7, 1854, quoted in Mrs. Chapman Coleman (ed.), *The Life of John J. Crittenden with Selections from His Correspondence and Speeches* (2 vols.; Philadelphia: J. B. Lippincott, 1871), II, 101; Robert Toombs to W. W. Burwell, February 3, 1854, in Phillips (ed.), *Toombs, Stephens, Cobb Correspondence*, 342; John Bell to R. T. Saunders, April 21, 1854, in "Bell on Nebraska," 351–52. (For a discussion of Seward and southern Whig motivation, see Appendix C herein.)

that the Nebraska bill had to remain a Democratic bill and would have to repeal outright the Missouri Compromise. By this time the Dixon amendment was before the Senate. Next the southerners and Douglas wanted to see to the president. Working through Secretary of War Jefferson Davis they got an appointment with Pierce on Sunday afternoon, January 22. Although Pierce had earlier seemed reluctant to countenance repeal, his meeting with Douglas and the southerners changed his mind.[41] Pierce's agreement meant that the bill, which would include a direct repeal, would become an administration measure, a test of Democratic loyalty.

Following the presidential meeting Douglas revised his bill to fit the new provisions. This new version he introduced in the Senate on January 23. As Pierce, Douglas, and the southerners had agreed, this bill declared the Missouri Compromise "inoperative and void"—the southern Whig issue had been preempted. Popular sovereignty, the Democratic doctrine, and Democratic politics prevailed. At this time the bill also took on a second name, for Douglas proposed organizing two territories, Kansas as well as Nebraska. The Kansas-Nebraska bill, a thoroughly Democratic measure, stood before the Senate. Southern Democrats could not help but be pleased.

While southern Democrats in Washington helped forge the Kansas-Nebraska bill, southern Democratic newspapers lauded their goal and their achievement. In December, 1853, both the Jackson *Mississippian* and the Richmond *Enquirer* joined their Washington spokesmen and advocated carrying popular sovereignty to Nebraska. After the turn of the year others followed suit. All of them emphasized that the Compromise of 1850 including popular sovereignty had become Democratic doctrine; all good Democrats had to back legislation implementing the compromise. By definition

41. Henry Barrett Learned, "The Relation of Philip Phillips to the Repeal of the Missouri Compromise in 1854," *Mississippi Valley Historical Review*, VIII (1922), 303–17; on the meeting see Johannsen, *Douglas*, 414–15; Nichols, *Pierce*, 322–23; Jefferson Davis to Mrs. Archibald Dixon, September 27, 1879, quoted in Dixon, *Missouri Compromise*, 457–60.

352   The South and the Politics of Slavery, 1828–1856

When direct repeal of the Missouri Compromise was added to the
bill, the southern Democratic press cheered. As they saw it, that
addition simply formalized Democratic policy. But there was more.
Not only did the Kansas-Nebraska bill provide a measure for Democratic regularity, it also enabled southerners to find out which
northerners genuinely respected southern rights, for it transferred
popular sovereignty from New Mexico and Utah to lands above the
restrictive Missouri line. The southerners warned against hedging
by their northern compatriots. The voting on the Kansas-Nebraska
bill would reveal who stood with the president and the South and
"who [would] give aid and comfort to our enemies." Southern Democrats left no doubt about the penalty for such faithlessness; speaking for its brethren across the South the Tallahassee *Floridian* declared that southern Democrats would "not fellowship" with anyone
who failed to pass the Kansas-Nebraska test. [42]

Equating Kansas-Nebraska with southern rights as well as Democratic orthodoxy, southern Democrats called on all southerners "irrespective of party" to stand up for such a clear manifesto. And the
southern Democrats evinced a particular interest in the stance of
southern Whigs. The Democratic editors gave their opponents no
respite from the open challenges to the southernism of Whiggery
that had swelled unceasingly since 1852. Southern Democrats announced that they expected to have their Whig foes as comrades on
the critical Kansas-Nebraska issue because southern honor and

42. Jackson *Mississippian*, December 30, 1853, February 10, March 17, 24, May 19, 1854;
Richmond *Enquirer*, December 6, 1853, January 24, February 3, 9, 17, 1854; Raleigh *Standard*, February 1, 15, 22, March 15, May 31, 1854; Milledgeville *Federal Union*, February 7,
14, 1854; Tallahassee *Floridian*, January 28, May 13, 1854.

The evidence presented in this and the following paragraphs counters the argument in
Avery Craven's *The Growth of Southern Nationalism, 1848–1861* (Baton Rouge: Louisiana
State University Press, 1953), 196–203 that the South really did not care about Kansas-
Nebraska. The politicians were just as interested as they had been in the Compromise of 1850.
Although public arousal probably did not match the furor over the compromise, it clearly
existed; legislatures even passed resolutions favoring Kansas-Nebraska by lopsided margins.
Milledgeville *Southern Recorder*, February 21, 1854, and Jackson *Mississippian*, March 24,
1854.

equality were at stake. To prevent any southern Whigs from missing the import of the situation or the gravity of this particular challenge southern Democrats spelled it out with unmistakable clarity. As the Richmond *Enquirer* declared, "We certainly have no disposition to cast an unjust imputation on [Southern Whig] patriotism." But, then, claimed the *Enquirer* and others, the past influence of antisouthern northern Whigs on party actions generated doubt. Thus all southerners would have to monitor carefully the Whig reaction to Kansas-Nebraska.[43]

And the southern Whig reaction did differ from the Democratic, at least after a fashion. Shouts of hurrah for Kansas-Nebraska emanated from some southern Whig newspapers. These journals took a special pride in the southern Whig contribution to the measure. In their eyes the direct repeal of the Missouri Compromise, a southern Whig product, provided the capstone of the bill. At the same time other southern Whig papers denounced the Kansas-Nebraska bill as political jobbery. The Raleigh *Register* claimed the entire affair stemmed from Douglas' ambition and demagoguery while the New Orleans *Bee* denied that the South had or should have any interest in Kansas-Nebraska. But neither the *Register* nor the *Bee* led any crusade against the bill. In fact both undermined or negated their opposition to it by simultaneously making perfectly clear that they stood with the South and for the bill, even though they cared little for it. An inclusive terseness marked the *Bee*'s position: "Every Southern Whig will support the measure." In announcing its support of Kansas-Nebraska the Raleigh *Register* paid tribute to the effectiveness of the Democratic challenge and to the power of the politics of slavery, which lay behind the challenge. "Since an issue *has* been or must be joined," the *Register* broadcast, "we see no other alternative left than to carry the measure through." Southern Whigs wanted to leave their Democratic accusers no pretext for finding them less than southern. Answering the Democratic questions

43. See the citations in the previous note; the quotations come from the Little Rock *Arkansas Gazette*, February 3, 1854, and the Richmond *Enquirer*, February 3, 1854.

directly, the Richmond *Whig* declared that no legitimate doubt could exist regarding "the soundness of Southern Whigs upon the questions involving the peculiar institutions of the South."[44]

The congressional voting on Kansas-Nebraska reflected southern opinion, albeit a bit imperfectly. The Kansas-Nebraska Act, which voided the Missouri Compromise and allowed, at least theoretically, the introduction of slavery into the new territories passed the Senate on March 3, 1854 and the House some ten weeks later. In each instance southerners supported it overwhelmingly. When the Senate signified its approval by the one-sided margin of 37 to 14, southern Democrats and southern Whigs voted aye almost in unison. Only one senator from each party, Sam Houston of Texas and John Bell of Tennessee, stood with the minority. In the House the battle was hot and the final vote, 113 to 100, much closer. Southern Democratic representatives maintained the solidarity shown by their senatorial counterparts; only one southern Democratic congressman cast his ballot against the bill. But among southern Whigs the unity of the Senate did not carry over into the lower chamber. Without a doubt southern Whigs made a material contribution to the success of Kansas-Nebraska in the House; seven of them voted for it, and no congressman did more than Alexander Stephens, still in 1854 at least a nominal Whig, who actually shepherded the bill through the House. Yet one-half of the southern Whig representatives voted against the Kansas-Nebraska Act.[45]

Such a deep division on legislation deemed crucial by many southerners, including Whigs, attests to the ongoing disintegration of southern Whiggery. This effect was especially apparent in the strongest Whig state left in the South. The disunity within the Tennessee Whig delegation—in the Senate, Bell voted no while James C. Jones voted yes; Tennessee Whigs in the House also split, four

44. Milledgeville *Southern Recorder*, February 21, 28, 1854; Tallahassee *Florida Sentinel*, July 25, 1854; Richmond *Whig*, January 24, 27, February 21, 24, March 7, 24, 1854; New Orleans *Bee*, February 20, 28, 1854; Raleigh *Register*, February 1, 15, 1854. All six Whig newspapers I read for the Kansas-Nebraska debate supported the bill.
45. *Congressional Globe*, 33rd Cong., 1st Sess., 532, 1254.

against and two for—caused serious repercussions back in Tennessee, which hastened the party's demise there.[46] Though significant, neither the disarray among the congressmen nor the difficulties in Tennessee comprised the most critical problem facing southern Whiggery.

The cancer that had debilitated southern Whiggery since 1850 reappeared during the Kansas-Nebraska struggle. Northern Whigs again balked at following the southern lead on a major sectional issue. This refusal was strikingly revealed in the congressional voting patterns; to a man northern Whigs in both Senate and House cast their ballots against it. This unanimity underscored the intense northern Whig opposition to repealing the Missouri Compromise. Believing that Kansas-Nebraska presented a splendid opportunity to their party, leading northern Whigs wanted to turn their opposition into a general Whig assault on the heinous proposal. They were convinced that Whig unity against the bill would rejuvenate the party and quite possibly bring about a national Whig victory in 1856. These northerners wanted southern assistance. William Henry Seward expressed the 'hope" that southern Whigs would join, even lead, "an opposition to 'the repeal of the Missouri Compromise.'" Others less tarred with Seward's antisouthern reputation shared his feelings. After the bill's passage Robert Winthrop lamented the failure of southern Whigs to strike with their northern comrades against Kansas-Nebraska: "Oh! that the Southern Whigs would have rallied *en masse* against it."[47]

Such a rally as envisioned by Seward and Winthrop was impossible. No southern party expecting to survive could join with northerners to defeat legislation broadly viewed in the South as recognizing southern honor and establishing southern rights. That Seward and other northern Whigs had gained notoriety in the South for their

46. Joseph Howard Parks, *John Bell of Tennessee* (Baton Rouge: Louisiana State University Press, 1950), 300–301.

47. Seward to Thurlow Weed, January 8, 1854, quoted in Seward, *Seward*, II, 217; Winthrop to John Pendleton Kennedy, June n.d., 1854, in Kennedy Papers.

antisouthern and antislave views compounded the impossibility. For individual southern Whigs in Congress who voted against Kansas-Nebraska the consequences were potentially ominous. As John Bell said, "I ran a great risk of losing standing in the South & at home in going against the Nebraska bill." "The peril of my cause," as Bell described it, became very real for southern Whigs who like Bell opposed the bill. The Jackson *Mississippian* withered them: "They stand side by side with Seward, [Salmon P.] Chase, [Charles] Sumner and [Benjamin] Wade, and will go down to posterity with the black mark of treason drawn around their names." A Tennessee Whig congressman who voted yes condemned his fellow southern Whigs who voted nay for "tak[ing] the northern side of the question."[48] And with the northern side composed chiefly of Whigs, southern Whiggery confronted a second impossible situation— maintaining a political alliance with northerners who persisted in taking vigorous antisouthern positions on critical sectional issues.

Southern Democrats tried to make the Whig burden even heavier. Jubilant over the passage of the Kansas-Nebraska Act, southern Democrats were enthusiastic over the unity in their ranks and over the support given the bill by northern Democrats. The unity of 1852, not the disunity of 1850–1851, marked the Democratic response to Kansas-Nebraska, and the southerners still controlled party policy on slavery-related questions. Among major southern Democratic leaders, only Sam Houston stood firm against the bill, though a few others had doubts about its benefits for the South. Houston's fate dramatized the ardent Kansas-Nebraska sentiment pervading the southern Democracy. Even though Houston was the greatest hero of Texas, a Texas Democratic convention unanimously adopted a resolution disapproving Houston's vote and praising the positive vote given by Senator Thomas J. Rusk and the state's

48. Bell to William B. Campbell, August 10, 1854, in Campbell Papers; Jackson *Mississippian*, March 17, 1854; Felix Zollicoffer to John [?], June 21, 1854, in Correspondence by Author, Felix Zollicoffer, Tennessee Historical Society. Southern Whig congressmen who voted against the bill claimed they were the ones upholding the true interests of the South. Sion H. Rogers to William A. Graham, May 25, 1854, in Hamilton and Williams (eds.), *Graham Papers*, IV, 515–16.

two congressmen. This difference drove Houston out of the Texas Democratic party. The powerful support given the bill by northern Democrats also delighted southerners. They awarded special praise to President Pierce and to Senator Douglas as statesmen determined to protect the just rights of the South. In the southern Democratic press northern Democratic senators and representatives who lined up with their southern brethren became stalwarts of the South who deserved the warm appreciation of all good southerners.[49]

While congratulating themselves on the fine showing of the entire Democratic party, southern Democrats carefully pointed out that the Whig performance had been quite different. Southern Democratic newspapers kept up the refrain: the bill passed without the support of a single northern Whig, or, in a different version, northern Whigs voted in droves against Kansas-Nebraska. Adding another verse they published numerous extracts from northern Whig papers blasting Kansas-Nebraska as a southern plot against the nation. Then the southern Democratic editors asked how could Whigs, who called themselves southerners, hold a common political allegiance with men who denounced the South's legitimate rights. To the Tallahassee *Floridian* the combination of anti-Nebraska votes and editorials could only mean that northern Whigs intended to direct "a general war upon the South." Not all southern Democrats got quite so exercised, but all thought such votes and editorials should disturb every southerner. As the Raleigh *Standard* concluded, they "present[ed] food for grave reflection."[50]

Southern Whigs acknowledged the gravity of their party situation. Without exception southern Whig newspapers admitted that

49. George W. Jones (Democratic congressman from Tennessee) to Howell Cobb, February 16, 1854, in Brooks (ed.), "Cobb Papers," VI (1922), 149–50; Ernest William Winkler (ed.), *Platforms of Political Parties in Texas* (Austin: University of Texas Press, 1916), 66; Francis R. Lubbock, *Six Decades in Texas: The Memoirs of Francis R. Lubbock, Confederate Governor of Texas*, ed. C. W. Raines (Austin and New York: Pemberton Press, 1968), 201–202; Richmond *Enquirer*, February 9, 1854; Jackson *Mississippian*, March 17, May 19, 1854; Milledgeville *Federal Union*, February 14, May 30, 1854; *Raleigh Standard*, March 15, 1854.

50. Jackson *Mississippian*, May 19, June 2, 1854; Milledgeville *Federal Union*, May 30, 1854; Tallahassee *Floridian*, February 18, March 11, May 13, 1854; Raleigh *Standard*, March 15, May 31, 1854.

the attitude of northern Whigs greatly distressed them. The Richmond *Whig* was deeply troubled by "the impulses of a wild fanaticism" that seemed to have infected all northern Whigs, even the old Fillmore men. Agitated by the solid northern Whig vote against Kansas-Nebraska, the Tallahassee *Florida Sentinel* reported, "the Whigs of Florida have already *waived* their party affinaties [sic] and allegiance with Northern Whigs until they shall give unmistakable evidence of repentence." The Milledgeville *Southern Recorder* found northern Whig opposition to Kansas-Nebraska ominous because it indicated that they had repudiated the Compromise of 1850 and the Whig platform of 1852. In so doing northerners treated the South as inferior, and there the *Southern Recorder* drew the line: "We will have no party association that will not admit and treat us as *equals.*"[51]

The word equality embodied for the southern proponents of the bill what Kansas-Nebraska guaranteed to the South and southern institutions. After successfully guiding the bill through the House, Alexander Stephens exulted: "So the Missouri Restriction will be taken off—Hurrah for the Compromise of 1850—Is not this glory enough for one day." According to South Carolina Congressman James L. Orr, Kansas-Nebraska made slavery and southern rights stronger than they had been "at any preceding time." Virginia's Robert M. T. Hunter had no doubt that the bill he helped shape represented a great victory for the South and slavery. Southern honor untarnished, this theme pervades such sentiments. A Georgia Democratic congressman said it this way: Kansas-Nebraska redeemed the South because it removed "the Stigma placed upon her by Missourie [sic] restriction."[52]

51. Richmond *Whig*, February 10, 24, June 10, 1854; Tallahassee *Florida Sentinel*, June 20, July 4, 1854; Milledgeville *Southern Recorder*, March 14, 1854.

52. Stephens to Thomas W. Thomas, May 23, 1854, in Stephens Papers, Division of Manuscripts, Library of Congress; Orr to Benjamin F. Perry, March 6, 1854, in Perry Papers; Hunter to George Booker, May 14, 1856, in George Booker Papers, William R. Perkins Library, Duke University; William B. W. Dent to Herschel Johnson, June 13, 1854, in Johnson Papers.

The question of whether slavery would actually exist in the new territory was distinctly secondary to most of those who fought for the bill. Some of the Democratic Senate chieftains did believe that pro-slavery forces in Missouri would lead a successful march into Kansas. For most southerners, however, the conviction that Kansas-Nebraska signified a renewed legitimacy of southern rights was victory enough.[53]

III

In the six months after the passage of the Kansas-Nebraska Act the southern Whig party disintegrated as an organized political force. While still grappling with the ultimate political meaning of Kansas-Nebraska, southern Whigs were smashed once again by southern voters. North Carolina and Florida, two states in which Whigs had maintained their organization and morale, held major elections in the late summer and early fall of 1854. In Florida the Democrats swept the Whigs aside by winning the governor's race and domination of the legislature just as they had done in 1852. North Carolina Whigs not only lost the governorship and the state senate for the third consecutive time, they also relinquished control of the state house to the triumphant Democrats. Extending the almost unbroken string of southern Whig election reverses since 1852, these two defeats further demoralized southern Whiggery. Calling the Whig loss in North Carolina a "great disaster," the Raleigh *Register* described the party as "floored, routed, battered, bruised and whipped." Although the *Register* tried to keep up a positive front, its list of past participles accurately reflected the condition of Whiggery across the South as well as in North Carolina.

53. Andrew P. Butler to William Elliott, February 5, 1854, in Elliott-Gonzales Papers, Southern Historical Collection, University of North Carolina; David R. Atchison to Robert M. T. Hunter, March 4, 1855, in Charles Henry Ambler (ed.), *Correspondence of Robert M. T. Hunter, 1826–1876* (Washington: Government Printing Office, 1918), 160–61; David R. Atchison to Jefferson Davis, September 24, 1854, in Jefferson Davis Papers, William R. Perkins Library, Duke University; Felix Zollicoffer to John [?], June 21, 1854, Zollicoffer Correspondence; Richmond *Enquirer*, May 26, 1854; Richmond *Whig*, February 14, 1854.

In other southern states no prominent elections dramatized the continuing Whig decline, but everywhere southern Whiggery was folding its tent. After North Carolina and Florida the southern Whig party ran no more major statewide campaigns; fewer and fewer politicians displaying the Whig badge appealed to the southern electorate. Although Whig sentiments lingered and individual Whigs clung to past loyalties, by the end of 1854 the Whig party had vanished from the southern political scene.[54]

Endless electoral disasters were only symptoms, not the basic reason, for southern Whiggery's terminal illness. Death was caused by the stiffening antisouthern stance of northern Whiggery, a rigidness the southern Whigs proved unable to relax. In 1850 the northern Whigs opposed the compromise; in 1852 they kept up that opposition and refused to accept Millard Fillmore; in 1854 they denounced the Kansas-Nebraska Act. A growing segment of southern Whig leadership and increasing numbers of southern Whig voters perceived that northern Whigs in both word and deed endangered the South and her institutions. This perception destroyed the legitimacy of the Whig party.

Because of the adamant stand of northern Whigs on critical slavery-related questions the southerners concluded they could no longer remain politically allied with their former comrades. Ideological and political motives governed their thinking. It was unthinkable for loyal southerners to embrace acknowledged enemies of the South; it was political suicide for southern politicians to keep waving the stained flag of the Whig party. This decision made the party useless, even dangerous, for no such party could provide substantial political rewards for its adherents; nor could it be defended as a protector of southern interests. The impossibility of presenting the party as a southern guardian plus the weakening commitment of the

54. Raleigh *Register*, August 23, 1854. All the state studies agree on this timing. See, for example, Adams, *Louisiana Whigs*, 262–64, 267; Gene Wells Boyett, "The Whigs of Arkansas, 1836–1856" (Ph.D. dissertation, Louisiana State University, 1972), 385–87; Paul Murray, *The Whig Party of Georgia, 1825–1853* (Chapel Hill: University of North Carolina Press, 1948), 171.

party faithful led to an avalanche of defeats at the ballot box as southern Whig voters withdrew their support. Some went over to the Democrats; many others simply stayed home on election day. Either way they sent the same message—the Whig party was no longer acceptable to them.

In the aftermath of Kansas-Nebraska, southern Whigs knew that their party was finished. Coming on top of 1850 and 1852, Kansas-Nebraska demonstrated that northern Whigs had no intention of helping their southern colleagues keep pace with southern Democrats as champions of the South. It also made clear to southern Whigs that southern rights and honor, as understood in the South, were empty concepts to northern Whigs. In fact northern Whigs looked for political gain by attacking Kansas-Nebraska as a proslavery plot.[55]

Facing what they deemed an intransigent northern Whiggery, the southerners, with a powerful unanimity, declared their independence. Finding rampant among northern Whigs both opposition to Kansas-Nebraska and an "undying hatred to slavery as it exists in the Southern States of the Union," the Richmond *Whig*, confident that it spoke for "the entire Southern Whig party," dissolved the party with the cry "We love the South more." Writing to long-time friend Andrew Johnson, a Mississippi Whig noted that the two men had always differed politically, "yet from the present aspect of the political horizen [*sic*], I do not see how we can long remain Separated[.] I can never again act with the Whig party of the North, unless they come to us of the South, and I have no hope of that." For the Tallahassee *Florida Sentinel* the strident antislavery strictures that accompanied northern Whig opposition to Kansas-Nebraska made it "out of the question for us to unite as a party any longer." Looking at the same combination the South Carolinian George Bryan asked, "But can we of the South maintain brotherly relations

55. William Henry Seward to [?], February 16, 1854, and to Home, February 19, 1854, both quoted in Seward, *Seward*, II, 219, 222; Allan Nevins, *Ordeal of the Union* (2 vols.; New York and London: Charles Scribner's Sons, 1947), II, 316–22.

with men whose power is based upon sectional agitation against *our section*?" Bryan answered his own question negatively. In sum, southern Whigs who had always demanded that northern Whigs stand on a southern platform, or at least not on an antisouthern one, had no intention of reversing roles. The New Orleans *Bee* captured the essence of the predicament: "The Southern Whig cannot stand on a Northern platform." In truth, as John Bell had feared, Kansas-Nebraska "put an extinguisher upon the Whig party."[56]

It was fitting for the politics of slavery to preside over the demise of southern Whiggery. Twenty years earlier southern Whiggery had begun its political life with the lusty cry of "the South endangered" on its lips. Southern Whiggery had helped spawn the politics of slavery. The party and the politics had nurtured each other, but the creation turned out to be immensely more powerful than the creator. A party could survive in the South only within the framework of the politics of slavery. Primarily it had to be able to defend itself as a shield of the South before southern voters. For southern Whigs this requirement meant that northern Whigs had to march under southern colors on critical slavery-related issues. When northern Whiggery said no and began actually assaulting the southern position, then southern Whigs found themselves totally vincible. With the southern Democrats constantly hounding them, they recognized their plight and the mortal weakness of their party. Thus, Frankensteinlike the politics of slavery devoured the southern Whig party.

IV

The death of southern Whiggery did not extinguish the politics of slavery. Southern Whigs did not rush en masse into the Democratic party. Although the party was gone, most Whigs had no desire to

56. Richmond *Whig*, September 26, 1854; Orlando Davis to Johnson, July 20, 1854, in Graf *et al.* (eds.), *Johnson Papers*, II, 240; Tallahassee *Florida Sentinel*, June 20, 1854; Bryan to John Pendleton Kennedy, August 23, 1854, in Kennedy Papers; New Orleans *Bee*, December 22, 1854; Bell to R. T. Saunders, April 21, 1854, in "Bell on Nebraska," 352.

become instant Democrats. The old party loyalties and enmities ran deep, forged through twenty years, five presidential races, and innumerable local contests. Hundreds of politicians and thousands of voters yearned for a new political home, a new party that would honor southern rights as well as offer them sustenance and reward. They could leap to a new party, but they could not leap out of the politics of slavery.

Seemingly most southern Whigs soon had their wish fulfilled. As the Whig party disintegrated, the Know-Nothing or American party spread across the South. In 1854 and 1855, the Know-Nothing organizations replaced Whig with such rapidity that the new party appeared practically full blown. Overwhelming evidence testifies that the partyless Whigs greeted the new party enthusiastically and in impressive numbers flocked to its standard. Its initial growth was astounding, for in 1855 the party mounted campaigns against the Democrats in every southern state. The infusion of many old Whigs who brought along their organization and their newspapers made this impressive performance possible.[57]

The Know-Nothing party arose out of nativist sentiments. Although nativism or opposition to foreigners had existed in the United States and the South throughout the nineteenth century, it assumed this powerful political manifestation only in the early 1850s. Originating in the Northeast the Know-Nothing party institutionalized the antagonism many native Americans felt toward the huge influx of immigrants, chiefly Irish, that poured into the eastern seaboard cities during the late 1840s and early 1850s. To the

57. Both Know-Nothing and American refer to the same party, though Know-Nothing was the most widely used designation in the South. I use Know-Nothing exclusively.

For a detailed account of the growth see W. Darrell Overdyke, *The Know-Nothing Party in the South* (Baton Rouge: Louisiana State University Press, 1950), Chaps. 4–7. Contemporary evidence of the excitement caused by the new party is in Jno. H. Lumpkin to Howell Cobb, May 4, 1855, in Cobb Papers; H. L. Clay to C. C. Clay, Sr., September 19, 1855, in Clement C. Clay Papers, William R. Perkins Library, Duke University; Manuscript Autobiography by Herschel Johnson (p. 81), in Johnson Papers; William B. Campbell to David Campbell, January 4, 1855, in Campbell Papers; letter fragment dated Lincolnton, N.C., April 5, 1855, in William A. Hoke Papers, Southern Historical Collection, University of North Carolina; all six Whig newspapers that I read for 1854 and 1855 endorsed Know-Nothingism.

nativists these immigrants imperiled the stability and the sanctity of the American polity because they did not and probably could not understand American values. According to the nativists the immigrants also undermined the American political system because collusion between unscrupulous political bosses and the ignorant immigrants corrupted the purity of the ballot box. That most of the newcomers professed the Roman Catholic faith added religious bias to nativist thinking. Claiming that Roman Catholics gave allegiance to the Pope, not to the Constitution of the United States, nativists identified the immigrants as threats to American liberty. Thus the political nativism expressed by the Know-Nothing party became anti-Catholic as well as antiforeign. Secrecy, including clandestine meetings and esoteric ritual—thus the name Know-Nothing— added to their rhetoric heightened the nativist appeal to working class men who believed their jobs and status threatened by the immigrants. Recently two new suggestions have been made to help explain the party's early popularity. First, Know-Nothings insisted their party represented something new in politics, a claim that appealed to many who condemned the existing party structure for their plight. And, second, many working-class Americans had suffered from momentous social and economic changes caused by the completion of trunkline railroads connecting the Midwest and the Atlantic coast.[58]

The ideology of the Know-Nothings never mattered so much for southern adherents as it did for the northerners.[59] Although the southerners did accept, some wholeheartedly and vociferously indeed, the basic tenets of the party, orthodox Know-Nothing doctrine was distinctly secondary in importance to most southern Know-Nothings. The forces generating Know-Nothing strength in the North either did not exist in the South or were considerably less

58. Good accounts of the general background of the party are in Overdyke, *Know-Nothing Party,* Chaps. 1, 3; Nevins, *Ordeal,* II, 323–28; Michael F. Holt, "The Politics of Impatience: The Origins of Know-Nothingism," *Journal of American History,* LX (1973), 309–31.
59. Overdyke, *Know-Nothing Party, passim,* esp. Chap. 12.

consequential. Although some southerners were distressed about the scale of immigration and fearful of Roman Catholic influence, the absence of large-scale immigration or a significant Roman Catholic population, except in Louisiana, made that two-sided issue much less pressing in the South. And political realities mitigated the influence of ideology even in Louisiana; there the heavily Roman Catholic sugar-planting areas, which had been Whig strongholds, became centers of Know-Nothing activity. Moreover in the early 1850s no trunkline railroads with their resulting economic and social impact were built in the South.

The Know-Nothing party prospered in the South only as a replacement for Whiggery. Southern Whigs embraced the new party because it provided a political base outside the Democratic party. Southern Know-Nothings hoped the northern wing of the party would be controlled by conservatives who would make it a bastion against anti-Nebraska and freesoil sentiment. But the Know-Nothing party was not just the Whig party reincarnated. Although most Whigs went over, and they certainly dominated the new party, all did not. In addition an unknown, but undoubtedly small, number of Democrats, who in all probability would not have joined the Whig forces, came into the Know-Nothing camp.[60] Even though it was not exactly southern Whiggery in a different suit, southern Know-Nothings had the same opponents, the southern Democrats.

Southern Democrats who had just obliterated southern Whiggery wasted no time in attacking this new challenger. They denounced the secrecy, the antiforeignism, and the anti-Catholicism associated with the Know-Nothings.[61] In southern Democratic rhetoric such practices and beliefs undercut the basic premises and promises of

60. Boyett, "Whigs of Arkansas," 390–97; William Garrett, *Reminiscences of Public Men in Alabama, for Thirty Years with an Appendix* (Atlanta: Plantation, 1872), 616; Parks, *Bell*, 303, 311–12; Donald M. Rawson, "Party Politics in Mississippi, 1850–1860" (Ph.D. dissertation, Vanderbilt University, 1964), 167–69.

61. For examples see Editors of the Union and American (eds.), *Aaron Brown Speeches*, 608; Little Rock *Arkansas Gazette*, August 25, 1854; Richmond *Enquirer*, July 14, 1854; Raleigh *Standard*, September 27, 1854, May 30, 1855; Jefferson Davis to James Buchanan, July 23, 1855, in Buchanan Papers.

America. According to southern Democrats a party espousing such ideas was a blight on the country and on the South. Although southern Democrats did make forays on this front, they aimed their heavy artillery toward another. They well knew what counted in southern politics. As soon as the Know-Nothing party reared its head in the South, southern Democrats bombarded it with the same ammunition that had destroyed the southern Whigs.

"KNOW-NOTHINGISM IS ABOLITIONISM," screamed the Raleigh *Standard.* This cry set the tone for the treatment southern Democrats gave their new competitor. Speaking in Gallatin, Tennessee, in July, 1855, Aaron V. Brown derogated the party for its northern antecedents, where it "had no element to compose it but Whigs and Abolitionists." If the Know-Nothing party succeeded, Brown declared, it "can bring nothing but disaster upon the Southern States." The Milledgeville *Federal Union* condemned the Know-Nothings for "divid[ing] their blanket with the foul mouthed abolitionists of the North." All southerners, shouted the *Federal Union,* "must know that the Know-Nothings are a division of the great Abolition army."[62]

Southern Democratic editors did more than shrill charges against the party. Just as in their attacks on southern Whiggery they deluged their readers with evidence designed to prove what they termed the "stern and terrible reality" of "the intimate and easy relationship" between northern Know-Nothings, freesoilers, and abolitionists. They printed copious extracts from northern journals claiming allegiance equally to the Know-Nothings and freesoil. Stories of self-confessed and alleged freesoil, antisouthern politicians supported and elected by northern Know-Nothings filled the columns of southern Democratic newspapers.[63]

62. Raleigh *Standard,* January 24, 1855; Editors of the Union and American (eds.), *Aaron Brown Speeches,* 623; Milledgeville *Federal Union,* October 31, December 19, 1854.
63. Richmond *Enquirer,* December 1, 1854, January 19, February 22, 1855; New Orleans *Louisiana Courier,* November 10, 26, December 6, 20, 1854; Raleigh *Standard,* January 24, June 13, 1855; Jackson *Mississippian,* November 15, 1854, February 28, April 11, September 26, October 24, 1855; Milledgeville *Federal Union,* October 31, November 7, December 19, 1854.

Because "the 'Know-Nothing' skies ha[d] become overcast with shadows of abolitionism," southern Democrats called on all southerners to join the crusade to preserve the South and its institutions. Crying that in the North, Know-Nothing meant abolition, the Jackson *Mississippian* exhorted southerners, "In the name of all that is sacred, is not that terrible monster [abolitionism] increasing in power and strength fast enough, without receiving aid from those it is intended to ruin." The Richmond *Enquirer* placed the burden of protecting or endangering the South directly on southerners leaning toward the Know-Nothing party: "Patriots of Virginia [or the South], would you invite aggression on the rights of the South and multiply the forces of Abolitionists beyond all possibility of resistance? Then assist in consolidating the power of Know-Nothingism." The *Enquirer* asserted that southerners faced a simple question, "WILL THE SOUTH BOW TO THE YOKE?" Southern Democrats knew that southerners could give only one answer to that question. They also knew that the question and its answers had ultimately doomed southern Whiggery; they hoped an identical fate would befall southern Know-Nothings.[64]

Southern Know-Nothings knew exactly what their Democratic opponents were about. In the words of the New Orleans *Bee* the southern Democrats were using the slavery issue as "the battering ram." Sam Houston, who had come to the Know-Nothing party after he and the Texas Democracy broke over Kansas-Nebraska, made the same point with a different image. In a public letter to Texas Know-Nothings, Houston proclaimed that southern Democrats brought up the specter of abolition in order to "strangle the American [Know-Nothing] feeling." And southern Know-Nothings had no doubts about the efficacy of the Democratic strategy; after all, as Whigs most of them had been eyewitnesses to its potency. In fact, according to its most recent student, the party reacted to the Demo-

64. Rev. C. C. Jones to Charles C. Jones, Jr., June 11, 1855, in Robert Manson Myers (ed.), *Children of Pride: A True Story of Georgia and the Civil War* (New Haven and London: Yale University Press, 1972), 148; Jackson *Mississippian*, November 15, 1854; Richmond *Enquirer*, January 19, 1855.

cratic onslaught in the traditional southern manner. While touting its own abilities to defend slavery and southern interests, it condemned the southern Democrats as untrustworthy defenders of those interests.[65] Regardless of the public stance taken by southern Know-Nothings, their leaders and those friendly to the party recognized that survival in the South required their northern adherents to stand on ground defensible in the South. In 1855 that ground included accepting the Fugitive Slave Act, the Kansas-Nebraska Act, and popular sovereignty in the territories. Although southern Know-Nothing newspapers claimed that northern Know-Nothings would occupy such ground, the politicians had serious doubts. In 1855 and 1856 the party's national conventions, the meetings of the national council in Know-Nothing terminology, confirmed the politicians' fears. In 1855 southerners got a slavery plank to their liking, but in doing so antagonized many northerners. Then in 1856 northerners managed to defeat the southern plank.[66] These contests over a slavery plank or resolution proved that northern and southern Know-Nothings could not unite on a slavery platform that could succeed in the politics of slavery.

Constantly battered by the incessant southern Democratic barrage on the slavery question and unable to forge a satisfactory northern link, the Know-Nothing party had a short, unhappy life in southern politics. From the Potomac to the Rio Grande the state elections of 1855 turned into a Know-Nothing nightmare. The Democrats won all seven gubernatorial contests and top-heavy legislative majorities in every state except Tennessee. There a Whig–Know-

65. New Orleans *Bee*, December 22, 1854; Williams and Barker (eds.), *Houston Writings*, VI, 195. Michael Marius Carriere, Jr., "The Know Nothing Movement in Louisiana" (Ph.D. dissertation, Louisiana State University, 1977), esp. 116–22, 169–74, 195–99.
66. Tallahassee *Florida Sentinel*, February–April, 1855, *passim*; Raleigh *Register*, June 6, 1855; Helena (Ark.) *Southern Shield*, June 23, 1855; William C. Rives to William M. Burwell, March 19, 1855, in Rives Papers; T. Butler King to William M. Burwell, November 8, 1855, in William M. Burwell Papers (Personal Papers Miscellaneous), Division of Manuscripts, Library of Congress; David Campbell to William B. Campbell, June 6, 1855, and Milton Haynes to William B. Campbell, January 19, 1856, both in Campbell Papers; Kenneth Rayner to Daniel Ullman, June 2, 1856, in Daniel Ullman Papers, New York Historical Society; Overdyke, *Know-Nothing Party*, 127–36, covers the conventions.

Nothing coalition held a paper-thin majority in both houses. This depressing showing presaged the outcome of the 1856 presidential election when the Know-Nothing party ran its only presidential candidate. Even though Millard Fillmore, the old friend of southern Whigs, carried the Know-Nothing banner, the party fared poorly in the South. Winning 58 percent of the popular vote and carrying every state, the Democrat James Buchanan drubbed Fillmore. After the trouncing the party took in the presidential race, it disappeared from the southern political scene. Although a Know-Nothing party did hang on in a few isolated pockets like the city of New Orleans,[67] never again did it mount a serious challenge to the southern Democratic party. The Know-Nothing party in the South had been like a meteor—initially a bright flame, then rapidly burning out. The party simply could not survive a plunge into the politics of slavery.

67. Leon Cyprian Soulé, *The Know-Nothing Party in New Orleans: A Reappraisal* (Baton Rouge: Louisiana State University Press, 1961).

Epilogue
Toward 1860

THE RAPID COLLAPSE of the southern Know-Nothings following the demise of southern Whiggery produced a dramatic change in
the topography of southern politics. No new party promptly stepped
forward to grasp the anti-Democratic banner, though there was no
lack of potential recruits. Between 1856 and 1860 various groups
composed chiefly of former Whigs and Know-Nothings challenged
Democrats in local campaigns across the South. The vote for the
Constitutional Union party in the 1860 presidential election provides a measure of the Southwide strength of the anti-Democrats.
The ticket headed by John Bell of Tennessee polled 344,765 votes in
the southern states, or 40 percent of the total, which clearly shows
the potential opposition to southern Democrats. The absence of
local issues certainly did not preclude the formation of another
party. Division among southerners occurred in many areas including taxation and public education, but probably the most pressing
issue in the mid-1850s concerned state aid to railroads.[1] But neither
the availability of party voters nor the conspicuousness of local issues
could nurture a successful political party in the South.

To prosper in the South a political party had to present itself as a
champion of southern honor and a protector of southern interests.
For southerners slavery in its various manifestations dominated all
other public questions between 1830 and 1860. Thus any political
party that hoped to flourish in the South had to convince southerners

1. Arthur C. Cole, *The Whig Party in the South* (Gloucester, Mass.: Peter Smith, 1962),
326–41; the best account of local issues in the South during the 1850s is Jonathan Mills
Thornton III, "Politics and Power in a Slave Society: Alabama, 1806–1860" (Ph.D. dissertation, Yale University, 1974), Chap. 5.

that it could protect slavery.[2] For southerners protecting slavery meant considerably more than merely defending their peculiar institution. Protection meant guaranteeing control over their own destiny, a destiny inextricably caught up in slavery. Loss of control meant jeopardizing their freedom and independence, and southerners knew better than anyone else that loss of freedom and independence led to slavery, to a status of abject dependency and subordination. For southerners their institution of slavery was also inseparably intertwined with their sense of honor and equality. Because southerners believed the institution of slavery honorable and viewed it as an American as well as a southern institution, they demanded that the national government recognize its legitimacy. Although the southern definition of legitimacy was not a constant—for example, in the 1830s it specified no abolition publications in the mails; in the 1850s it specified no Wilmot Proviso—the demand that the national government accept the southern definition was constant.

Dual motives underlay this demand. First, only the national government could take decisive action against slavery, and from the beginnings of the abolition movement through the Kansas-Nebraska Act the national government had made the significant decisions regarding slavery. Southerners perceived a simple logic in this situation: if the national government accepted the southern determination of legitimacy, it would never act against the South. Second, the national government represented the nation as a whole; for it to adopt the southern position on slavery would confirm the South's own image of its peculiar institution, of itself, and of its Americanism. Obversely, for the national government to reject the southern-defined legitimacy would affront southern honor and deny southern equality. Only a national party could give this broad protection within the nation because such protection required an effective voice and influential presence in the national government.

2. Even the Constitutional Union party did not violate this law. John V. Mering, "The Slave-State Constitutional Unionists and the Politics of Consensus," *Journal of Southern History*, XLIII (1977), 395–410.

Parties also assumed this role in the South because the party men assigned it. Since the time of Andrew Jackson they had defended the existence of political parties as knights pledged to uphold southern rights. On this point no differences separated southern Democrats and southern Whigs. Only John C. Calhoun before 1850 and the fire-eaters after 1850 opposed this view. Through 1856 neither of them managed to shake seriously the faith of either the party men or the southern voters in the protectiveness of the parties. Of course parties also provided office and power for the faithful, and southern politicians hungered for both just like politicians outside the South. Coming from one section, and a minority one at that, southern politicians could expect to attain national power only by operating through national parties. As southern politicians reached for political power, they assured southern voters that a desire to protect the South, not any lust for power and the prerequisites of office, prompted their efforts. For most politicians the two goals of gaining power and protecting the South meshed into one. Thus southern politicians could reap substantial political rewards while engaged in the noblest of tasks, protecting the South and her institutions.

Although most southern politicians saw a national party as essential for defending the South in the nation and as necessary for attaining great political rewards, they knew that a national party had to play by southern rules. On critical questions involving slavery the northern wing of any national party had to occupy southern ground, or at least not occupy antisouthern ground. Because the national political arrangement had to be defended in the South, southern politicians could not escape a continuous rendering of accounts before southern voters. And on that rendering depended the personal political fortunes of southern party men. The early Jackson party claimed a special relationship to the South; challenging that claim and asserting that they offered the South even more security, southern Whigs created a place for themselves in southern politics. Out of that initial contest between Democrats and Whigs came the rules that governed southern politics for the life of the Democratic-

Whig conflict, and beyond. The constant battle for southern votes required the never-ending blaring of the slavery issue in its many forms, for nothing else so aroused southern voters. As a result, the politics of slavery became the politics of the South. Every other issue, every other concern was either ephemeral or secondary. Southern sectional politics defined and molded national parties and national politics. Ironically, then, national parties fostered and nourished sectional politics in the South.[3]

Southern Democrats won in the mid-1850s because only they held to the traditional success formula in southern politics. Before the voters they could defend their party as a southern fortress; they could truthfully say that northern Democrats followed their dictates on slavery. Challenged by southern Democrats to do likewise, southern Whigs and southern Know-Nothings could not respond effectively. Their northern wing had disregarded the southern script. As loyal southerners, Whigs and Know-Nothings could not remain in an antisouthern party. To ambitious southern politicians such a party also became a liability, a vehicle of political defeat instead of political victory; accordingly, many old leaders defected and few ambitious younger men were attracted. Neither group had bright prospects in any future party because no southern-oriented northern connection remained. As northerners rapidly built their own sectional party, southern Democrats had a lock on those northerners still willing to play the party game according to southern rules.

After 1856 southern Democrats apparently stood as the undisputed masters of southern politics. They had seemingly recaptured the dominance they had enjoyed during the heyday of Andrew Jackson. But they had not suppressed all challengers. In the late 1850s southern Democrats had to contend with a growing legion of fire-eaters. These radicals, who had been relatively quiet since 1851, grew noisy once again. The creation and growth of the Repub-

3. For a suggestion of the importance of this point see David M. Potter, *The Impending Crisis, 1848–1861* (New York, Evanston, San Francisco, London: Harper & Row, 1976), 28.

lican party, the furor over bleeding Kansas, John Brown's raid, all fueled fire-eater rhetoric. Opposing the very concept of party, the fire-eaters attacked southern Democrats for their strategy for protecting the South as well as for specific failures resulting from the strategy. The fire-eaters found hollow the southern Democratic insistence that the umbrella of the Democratic party protected the South within the Union. In contrast the fire-eaters maintained that the South could fulfill her destiny only outside the Union. In the southern political arena the fire-eaters pressed the Democrats to demonstrate the efficacy of their southernness just as the Democrats had pressed the Whigs and the Know-Nothings. Dedicated to guarding the interests of the South, accustomed to holding power and controlling the northern wing of their party, assaulted by the fire-eaters, the Democrats could not take lightly either rebellion against their rule in their own party or a loss of power in Washington. They were totally bound to the politics of slavery. And Kansas, Charleston, and Abraham Lincoln were just beyond the horizon.

Appendix A

JOHN C. CALHOUN AND THE PAKENHAM LETTERS

Calhoun's motives for making such assertive statements have caused considerable controversy among historians. His major biographer Charles Wiltse argued (*Calhoun*, III, 167–71) that Calhoun thought he was writing private letters which would never be published. Charles Sellers convincingly refutes Wiltse's contention and, in turn, maintains that Calhoun dramatized the Texas-slavery connection in order to wound Van Buren (*Polk*, II, 58–59 and n. 58). Without making a major case Merk in his *Slavery*, 57–59, 68–69, implies that Calhoun's letters were a part of the Tyler administration propaganda barrage on Texas. In a recent essay review of Merk's *Slavery* and *Fruits*, Sydney Nathans posits that Calhoun, troubled about southern divisiveness on Texas, wanted to alarm and excite the South. Nathans also suggests that Calhoun wanted to provoke a British counterattack to his strong proslavery stance, a counterattack that Calhoun hoped would lead to a patriotic surge to save Texas from a perfidious Great Britain. "The Southern Connection: Slaveholders and Antebellum Expansion," *Reviews in American History*, I (1973), 394.

In my view Sellers and Nathans especially have valid points which are part of my story; to them, however, I would add still another. As I contended, the Pakenham correspondence offered Calhoun an opportunity to declare unequivocally the intimacy between slavery and the nation. By doing so he could hope to force the North to accept his conception both of the relationship between slavery and the Union and of southern rights. In conclusion it seems to me that Calhoun had multiple motives that are impossible to rank order. Surely he thought he was aiding the administration campaign for annexation. Without any doubt he wanted to hurt Van Buren in any

way possible. Certainly he desired to rouse the South. If that required arranging a national revulsion against Great Britain, so be it.
And to get a national commitment to his view of slavery's place in the
nation would cap his effort. In sum Calhoun acted completely in
character.

Appendix B

SOUTHERN WHIGS AND THE PRESTON BILL

It is impossible to be precise about the number of southern Whigs favoring Preston's bill. In the letter cited in Chapter 8, n. 7, Toombs asserted that they were "nearly unanimous" in their support, but there is no way to test his assertion. The only House vote on the Preston bill, before its final defeat, came on the antislavery amendment; and neither the *House Journal* nor the *Congressional Globe* has a roll call. Even so, the 87 votes against the amendment probably included every southern Whig and southern Democrat who cast a ballot, because exactly 87 congressmen, including all southerners voting, said nay when later on the same day the House passed a California territorial bill with an antislavery section.

Bell had none of his fellow southern Whigs backing him. When the Senate buried his proposal by 39 to 4, only one other southerner, the Louisiana Democrat Solomon Downs, voted with him, and the other southern Whigs voted against him or did not vote. Why Bell had no southern Whig allies is difficult to explain in view of Toombs's claim, unless Toombs was referring only to House members or was exaggerating. Bell's proposal and Preston's bill had the same goal, though there were slight differences (chiefly Bell specified the Rio del Norte as the eastern boundary of California— thus excluding eastern New Mexico, an area claimed by Texas—and Preston included all of the Cession). Bell was not fighting a battle already lost, because the Senate voted on his proposal on February 21, six days before Preston's bill was torpedoed in the House by the antislavery amendment. I have no evidence that satisfactorily explains the behavior of southern Whig senators. Of them, only Senator John M. Berrien spoke against Bell. Basing his objections on constitutional grounds, Berrien declared that Congress could not create a state; that action had to come from the citizens of the state itself (*Congressional Globe*, 30th Cong., 2nd Sess., Appendix, 253–55, 279–81). Undoubtedly Berrien also had other motives. In Georgia his southernness had been questioned concerning Texas; moreover there was political animosity between him and the younger men Toombs and Stephens. (See C. B. Strong to Berrien, April 25, 1845, J. S. Peterson to Berrien, September 17, 1845, Iverson Harris to Berrien, August 17, December 24, 1849, Berrien to Charles Jenkins, December 10, 1849, all in Berrien Papers). In sum, the Senate action pointed in only one direction; all southern Whigs did not back Preston's scheme.

Appendix C

SEWARD, SOUTHERN WHIGS, AND KANSAS-NEBRASKA

The argument has been made, especially by Nichols in his "Kansas-Nebraska," 205, that Seward instigated Dixon and the southern Whigs to go for outright repeal. Seward's motive was his desire to turn northern opinion against the Democratic party. There are two problems with this interpretation. First, southern Whigs needed no outside force to push them toward repeal; as participants in the politics of slavery it was the logical thing for them to do. Second, the evidence for Seward as Machiavelli is slim indeed, though Seward did lay claim to the role. At the time southern Whigs made no mention of Seward's role, and later Dixon specifically denied that Seward had one (Dixon, *Missouri Compromise*, 588–98). Although Dixon's denial came after the fact, Seward's story that he originated the idea also came some years after 1854. Seward's most thorough biographer found that some, though not conclusive, evidence did exist to support Seward's claim, but referring to this specific case he also said, "[Seward] was not at all averse to magnifying the importance of his acts." (Van Deusen, *Seward*, 150, 587, n. 3.) At the time Seward himself testified that the southern Whigs were consumed with slavery; he wrote home that they "wanted to talk about slavery all the time." He also reported that Senators Dixon and Jones told him that his opposition to slavery was "ruining great prospects" for the Whig party. (Seward to Home, December 24, 1853, quoted in Seward, *Seward*, II, 213.)

Bibliography

BECAUSE THIS BOOK was written chiefly from primary sources, the bibliography contains only primary sources and only those actually cited in my notes. I have certainly benefited from the labors of many previous historians, though only those who have edited collections of primary materials appear here. In my notes I have tried to indicate my indebtedness to the historians who have written helpful articles and books.

MANUSCRIPT COLLECTIONS

Alabama Department of Archives and History, Montgomery.
    Hall, Bolling. Papers.
    Perry, Benjamin F. Papers.
    Yancey, William Lowndes. Papers.

Buffalo and Erie County Historical Society, Buffalo, N.Y.
    Fillmore, Millard. Papers.

Robert Muldrow Cooper Library, Clemson University, Clemson, S.C.
    Crallé, Richard K. Papers.

Divsion of Manuscripts, Library of Congress, Washington, D.C.
    Bell, John. Papers.
    Biddle, Nicholas. Papers.
    Blair Family. Papers.
    Burwell, William M. Papers (Personal Papers Miscellaneous).
    Campbell, George W. Papers.
    Clay, Henry. Papers.
    Clayton, John M. Papers.
    Conner, Henry W. Papers (photostats).
    Corwin, Thomas. Papers.
    Crallé, Richard K. Papers.
    Crittenden, John J. Papers.
    Curry, Jabez L. M. Papers.
    Donelson, Andrew Jackson. Papers.
    Elmore, Franklin H. Papers.
    Floyd, John. Papers.
    Green, Duff. Papers.

Hammond, James H. Papers.
Harrison, Burton. Papers.
Harrison, William Henry. Papers.
Jackson, Andrew. Papers.
Legaré, Hugh S. Papers (Personal Papers Miscellaneous).
Polk, James K. Papers.
Polk Family of North Carolina. Papers.
Preston, William C. Papers.
Ritchie, Thomas. Papers.
Rives, William C. Papers.
Seabrook, Whitemarsh B. Papers.
Stephens, Alexander. Papers.
Stevenson, Andrew. Papers.
Taylor, Zachary. Papers.
Thompson, Waddy. Papers.
Tyler, John. Papers.
Van Buren, Martin. Papers.
White, Hugh. Papers.
Woodbury, Levi. Papers.

William R. Perkins Library, Duke University, Durham, N.C.
Booker, George. Papers.
Brown, Bedford. Papers.
Burt, Armistead. Papers.
Campbell, David. Papers.
Clay, Clement C. Papers.
Clay, Henry. Papers.
Davis, Jefferson. Papers.
Harden, Edward. Papers.
Houston, George S. Papers.
Johnson, Herschel V. Papers.
McDowell, James. Papers.
Munford-Ellis Family. Papers.
Niles, Nathaniel. Papers.
Rutherfoord, John. Papers.
Stephens, Alexander. Papers.
Turner, Jesse. Papers.

Robert W. Woodruff Library, Emory University, Atlanta, Ga.
Fort, Tomlinson. Papers.

Georgia Political Leaders. Collection.
Stephens, Alexander. Papers.

P. K. Yonge Library, University of Florida, Gainesville.
Yulee, David L. Papers.

Georgia Archives, Atlanta.
Cobb, Howell. Papers.
Toombs, Robert. Papers.

Ilah Dunlap Little Memorial Library, University of Georgia, Athens.
Baber-Blackshear. Papers.
Cobb, Howell. Papers.
Cobb-Erwin-Lamar. Papers.
Lumpkin, Joseph H. Papers.

Houghton Library, Harvard University, Cambridge, Mass.
Dearbon, Frederick M. Collection.
Webster, Daniel. Papers.

Department of Archives, Louisiana State University, Baton Rouge.
Butler, Thomas. Papers.
Gayarré, Charles E. A. Papers.
Hamilton, William S. Papers (George M. Lester Collection).
Mangum, Willie P. Papers.
Mercer, William N. Papers.
Quitman, John A. Papers.
Toombs, Robert. Papers.

Manhattanville College, Purchase, N.Y.
Stephens, Alexander. Papers.

Maryland Historical Society, Baltimore.
Pearce, James A. Papers.
Taney, Roger B. Papers.
Wirt, William. Papers.

Mississippi Department of Archives and History, Jackson.
Claiborne, J. F. H. Papers.
McWillie, William. Papers.
Poindexter, George. Papers.

New Hampshire Historical Society, Concord.
Pierce, Franklin. Papers.

New York Historical Society, New York City.
    Polk, James K. Papers.
    Ullman, Daniel. Papers.
    Verplanck, Gulian C. Papers.
    Walker, Robert J. Papers.

New York Public Library, New York City.
    Barbour, James. Papers.
    Jackson, Andrew-William B. Lewis. Correspondence.

North Carolina Department of Archives and History, Raleigh.
    Badger, George. Papers.
    Reid, David S. Papers.

Southern Historical Collection, University of North Carolina, Chapel Hill.
    Barringer, Daniel M. Papers.
    Berrien, John M. Papers.
    Bragg, John. Papers.
    DeBerry, Edmund. Papers.
    Dromgoole, Edward. Papers.
    Edwards, Weldon. Papers.
    Elliott-Gonzales. Papers.
    Elmore, Franklin H. Papers.
    Garnett-Wise. Papers.
    Gaston, William. Papers.
    Green, Duff. Papers.
    Grundy, Felix. Papers.
    Hoke, William A. Papers.
    King, Thomas Butler. Papers.
    King, William R. Papers.
    Lesesne, Joseph. Papers.
    Niles, Jason. Diary.
    Outlaw, David. Papers.
    Rhett, Robert Barnwell. Papers.
    Tucker Family. Papers.
    Venable, Abraham. Papers.
    Yancey, Benjamin C. Papers.

Historical Society of Pennsylvania, Philadelphia.
    Buchanan, James. Papers.
    Dreer, Ferdinand J. Collection of the Letters of American Statesmen.

Gratz, Simon. Collection of Administration Papers.
Poinsett, Joel R. Letters (Henry D. Gilpin Collection).
Poinsett, Joel R. Papers.

George Peabody Department, Enoch Pratt Free Library, Baltimore, Md.
Kennedy, John Pendleton. Papers.

Firestone Library, Princeton University, Princeton, N.J.
Blair-Lee. Papers.

South Caroliniana Library, University of South Carolina, Columbia.
Butler, Pierce. Papers.
Legaré, Hugh S. Papers.
Petigru, James L. Papers.
Pickens, Francis W. Papers.
Thompson, Waddy. Papers.
Williams-Chesnut-Manning. Papers.

Tennessee Historical Society, Nashville.
Donelson, Andrew Jackson. Papers.
Heiss, John P. Papers.
Overton-Claybrook. Papers.
Zollicoffer, Felix. Correspondence by Author.

Manuscript Division, Tennessee State Library and Archives, Nashville.
Bell, John. Papers.
Cole, Whitefoord. Collection.
Crozier, Arthur. Papers.
Grundy, Felix. Papers.
Horn, Stanley. Collection.
Huntsman, Adam. Papers.
Nicholson, A. O. P. Papers.

Eugene C. Barker Texas History Center, University of Texas, Austin.
Rusk, Thomas J. Papers.

Howard-Tilton Memorial Library, Tulane University, New Orleans, La.
Gayarré, Charles E. A. Papers.
Slidell, John. Letter.

Alderman Library, University of Virginia, Charlottesville.
Hunter, Robert M. T. Papers.

Special Papers Projects

The projects created to publish the papers of John C. Calhoun, Henry Clay, and Daniel Webster have gathered massive amounts of manuscript material. In each citation from documents collected by these projects (I visited the Calhoun and Clay projects and used the microfilm edition put out by the Webster project), I cited the original source of a document, though I actually used a photocopy provided to the individual project.

John C. Calhoun Project, University of South Carolina, Columbia.
    Calhoun, John C. Papers (Robert Muldrow Cooper Library, Clemson University).
    Calhoun, John C. Papers (William R. Perkins Library, Duke University).
    Calhoun, John C. Papers (Division of Manuscripts, Library of Congress).
    Calhoun, John C. Papers (South Caroliniana Library, University of South Carolina).
    Conner, Henry. Papers (Charleston Library Society, Charleston, S.C.)
    Galloway-Maxey-Markoe. Papers (Division of Manuscripts, Library of Congress).
    Leigh, Benjamin W. Papers (Alderman Library, University of Virginia).
Henry Clay Project, University of Kentucky, Lexington.
    Clay, Henry. Papers (Indiana University, Bloomington).
    Leigh, Benjamin W. Papers (Alderman Library, University of Virginia).
    Porter, Peter B. Papers (Buffalo Historical Society, Buffalo, N.Y.).
    Reeves. Collection (William L. Clements Library, University of Michigan, Ann Arbor).
Daniel Webster Project, Dartmouth College, Hanover, N.H.
    Everett, Edward, Papers (Massachusetts Historical Society, Boston).
    Webster, Daniel. Papers (Division of Manuscripts, Library of Congress).

NEWSPAPERS

General
    Niles' Register.

Democratic

    Austin *State Gazette*.
    Houston *Telegraph*.
    Jackson *Mississippian*.
    Little Rock *Arkansas Banner*.
    Little Rock *Arkansas Gazette* (Democratic 1836–42, 1850–56).
    Milledgeville *Federal Union*.
    New Orleans *Bee* (Democratic 1832–38).
    New Orleans *Louisiana Courier*.
    Raleigh *Standard*.
    Richmond *Enquirer*.
    Tallahassee *Floridian*.

Whig

    Baton Rouge *Gazette*.
    Helena (Ark.) *Southern Shield*.
    Little Rock *Arkansas Advocate*.
    Little Rock *Arkansas Gazette* (Whig 1843–49).
    Milledgeville *Southern Recorder*.
    New Orleans *Bee* (Whig 1839–56).
    Raleigh *Register*.
    Richmond *Whig*.
    Tallahassee *Florida Sentinel*.
    Tuscaloosa *Independent Monitor*.
    Vicksburg *Whig*.

The following were used for supplementary purposes in specific instances.

    DeBow's Review.
    Milledgeville *Georgia Journal*.
    Natchez *Courier*.
    Natchez *Free Trader*.
    Natchez *Natchez*.
    New York *Times*.
    Philadelphia *Cummings Evening Bulletin*.
    Tribune Almanac.
    Vicksburg *Advocate & Register*.
    Woodville (Miss.) *Republican*.

OFFICIAL PUBLICATIONS

Resolutions, Address, and Journal of Proceedings of the Southern Convention. Held at Nashville, Tennessee, June 3d to 12th, Inclusive, in the Year 1850. Nashville: Harvey M. Watterson, 1850.

Richardson, James D., comp. *A Compilation of the Messages and Papers of the Presidents, 1789–1897.* 10 vols.; Washington, D.C.: Government Printing Office, 1896–99.

State Papers on Nullification: Including the Public Acts of the Convention of the People of South Carolina, Assembled at Columbia, November 9, 1832 and March 11, 1833; the Proclamation of the President of the United States, and the Proceedings of the Several State Legislatures Which Have Acted on the Subject. Boston: Dutton and Wentworth, 1834.

Thorpe, Francis Newton, ed. *The Federal and State Constitutions, Colonial Charters, and Other Organic Laws of the States, Territories, and Colonies Now or Heretofore Forming the United States of America.* 7 vols.; Washington D.C.: Government Printing Office, 1909.

United States Congress:
Congressional Globe.
House Journal.
Register of Debates.
Senate Documents.
Senate Journal.

White, Robert H., ed. *Messages of the Governors of Tennessee, 1796–1907.* 8 vols.; Nashville: Tennessee Historical Commission, 1952–72.

Winkler, Ernest William, ed. *Platforms of Political Parties in Texas.* Austin: University of Texas Press, 1916.

CONTEMPORARY ACCOUNTS, INCLUDING TRAVEL ACCOUNTS

Andrews, E. A. *Slavery and the Domestic Slave-Trade in the United States.* Boston: Light & Stearns, 1836.

Bremer, Fredrika. *The Homes of the New World: Impressions of America.* 2 vols.; New York: Harper & Brothers, 1854.

Buckingham, J. S. *The Slave States of America.* 2 vols.; London and Paris: Fisher, Son, n.d. [ca. 1842].

Claiborne, J. F. H. "A Trip through the Piney Woods." *Publications of the Mississippi Historical Society,* IX (1906), 487–538.

Grund, Francis J. *The Americans, in Their Moral, Social, and Political Relations.* Boston: Marsh, Capen and Lyon, 1837.

Hundley, D. R. *Social Relations in Our Southern States.* New York: Henry B. Price, 1860.

Jennings, Dudley S. *Nine Years of Democratic Rule in Mississippi Being Notes Upon the Political History of the State, from the Beginning of the Year 1838, to the Present Time.* Jackson: Thomas Palmer, 1847.

Kemble, Frances Anne. *Journal of a Residence on a Georgia Plantation in 1838–1839.* New York: Harper & Brothers, 1863.

Longstreet, Augustus Baldwin. *Georgia Scenes, Characters, Incidents, & C.* Augusta: S. R. Sentinel Office, 1835.

Lyell, Charles. *A Second Visit to the United States of North America.* 2 vols.; New York: Harper & Brothers, 1849.

Mackay, Alexander. *The Western World; or, Travels in the United States in 1846–47: Exhibiting Them in Their Latest Development, Social, Political, and Industrial; Including a Chapter on California.* 2 vols.; Philadelphia: Lea & Blanchard, 1849.

Miller, Stephen F. *The Bench and Bar of Georgia: Memoirs and Sketches. With an Appendix, Containing a Court Roll from 1790 to 1857, Etc.* 2 vols. Philadelphia: J. B. Lippincott, 1858.

Morton, Jackson. *To the Whigs of Florida.* Washington: n.p., 1852.

[Munford, William, comp.]. *A Collection of Plays and Poems, by the Late Col. Robert Munford of Mecklenburg County, in the State of Virginia.* Petersburg: William Prentis, 1798.

Olmsted, Frederick Law. *A Journey in the Back Country.* New York: Mason Brothers, 1860.

―――. *A Journey in the Seaboard Slave States, with Remarks on Their Economy.* New York: Dix & Edwards, 1856.

[Poinsett, Joel R.]. *Letter of the Hon. J. R. Poinsett to His Fellow-Citizens of Charleston.* Washington: n.p., 1840.

Pulszky, Francis and Theresa. *White, Red, Black: Sketches of American Society in the United States during the Visit of Their Guests.* 2 vols.; New York: Redfield, 1853.

[Ritchie, Thomas]. "An Address to the Democrats of Virginia, 1840." *John P. Branch Historical Papers of Randolph-Macon College,* III (1911), 263–70.

Royall, Anne Newport. *Letters from Alabama, 1817–1822.* Edited by Lucille Griffith. University, Ala.: University of Alabama Press, 1969.

Thomson, William. *A Tradesman's Travels, in the United States and Canada, in the Years 1840, 41 & 42.* Edinburgh: Oliver & Boyd, 1842.

Tocqueville, Alexis de. *Democracy in America.* Edited by Phillips Bradley. 2 vols.; New York: Vintage, 1954.

[Walker, Robert J.]. *The South in Danger.* Washington, D.C.: n.p., 1844.

AUTOBIOGRAPHIES, DIARIES, MEMOIRS

Adams, John Quincy. *Memoirs of John Quincy Adams.* Edited by Charles Francis Adams. 12 vols.; Philadelphia: J. B. Lippincott, 1874–77.

Ambler, Charles H., ed. "Diary of John Floyd." *John P. Branch Historical Papers of Randolph-Macon College,* V (1918), 119–233.

Benton, Thomas Hart. *Thirty Years' View; or, a History of the Working of the American Government for Thirty Years, from 1820 to 1850.* 2 vols.; New York and London: D. Appleton, 1854.

Biggs, Asa. *Autobiography of Asa Biggs.* Edited by R. D. W. Connor. Raleigh, N.C.: Edwards & Broughton, 1915.

[Crockett, Davy]. *Davy Crockett's Own Story: As Written by Himself.* New York: Citadel, 1955.

Davis, Reuben. *Recollections of Mississippi and Mississippians.* Boston and New York: Houghton Mifflin, 1889.

Douglas, Thomas. *Autobiography of Thomas Douglas, Late Judge of the Supreme Court of Florida.* New York: Calkins & Stiles, 1856.

Garrett, William. *Reminiscences of Public Men in Alabama, for Thirty Years, with an Appendix.* Atlanta: Plantation, 1872.

Gilmer, George R. *Sketches of Some of the First Settlers of Upper Georgia, of the Cherokees, and the Author.* Americus, Ga.: Americus Book, 1926.

Green, Duff. *Facts and Suggestions, Biographical, Historical, Financial and Political, Addressed to the People of the United States.* New York: Richardson & Co., 1866.

Guild, Joseph C. *Old Times in Tennessee with Historical, Personal, and Political Scraps and Sketches.* Nashville: Tavel, Eastman & Howell, 1878.

Harris, Wiley P. "Autobiography of Wiley P. Harris." Edited by Dunbar Rowland. *Courts, Judges, and Lawyers of Mississippi, 1789–1835.* Jackson: Hederman Bros., 1935, 270–329.

Lubbock, Francis R. *Six Decades in Texas: The Memoirs of Francis R. Lubbock, Confederate Governor of Texas.* Edited by C. W. Raines. Austin and New York: Pemberton, 1968.

A Memoir of S. S. Prentiss. Edited by His Brother. 2 vols.; New York: Charles Scribner, 1856.

Quaife, Milo Milton, ed. *The Diary of James K. Polk During His Presidency, 1845–1849.* 4 vols.; Chicago: A. C. McClurg, 1910.

Rainwater, P. L., ed. "The Autobiography of Benjamin Grubb Humphreys, August 26, 1808–December 20, 1882." *Mississippi Valley Historical Review*, XXI (1934), 231–55.

Scott, Nancy N., ed. *A Memoir of Hugh Lawson White, Judge of the Supreme Court of Tennessee, Member of the Senate of the United States, Etc. Etc. With Selections from His Speeches and Correspondence*. Philadelphia: J. B. Lippincott, 1856.

Seward, Frederick W. *William H. Seward; an Autobiography from 1801 to 1834. With a Memoir of His Life and Selections from His Letters*. 3 vols.; New York: Derby and Miller, 1891.

Sioussat, St. George L., ed. "Diaries of S. H. Laughlin, of Tennessee, 1840, 1843." *Tennessee Historical Magazine*, II (1916), 43–85.

Van Buren, Martin. *The Autobiography of Martin Van Buren*. Edited by John C. Fitzpatrick, Washington, D.C.: Government Printing Office, 1920.

Weed, Harriet A., ed. *Life of Thurlow Weed, Including His Autobiography and a Memoir*. 2 vols.; Boston: Houghton Mifflin, 1883.

Wise, Henry A. *Seven Decades of the Union*. Philadelphia: J. B. Lippincott, 1872.

Wise, John S. *The End of an Era*. Boston and New York: Houghton Mifflin, 1900.

PUBLISHED COLLECTIONS OF CORRESPONDENCE AND SPEECHES

Ambler, Charles H., ed. *Correspondence of Robert M. T. Hunter, 1826–1876*. Washington, D.C.: Government Printing Office, 1918.

Barbee, David Rankin, ed. "A Sheaf of Old Letters." *Tyler's Quarterly Historical and Genealogical Magazine*, XXXII (1950), 77–102.

Bassett, John Spencer, ed. *Correspondence of Andrew Jackson*. 7 vols.; Washington, D.C.: Carnegie Institution of Washington, 1926–35.

"The Hon. John Bell on the Nebraska Bill." *Olympian*, I (1903), 351–52.

Boucher, Chauncey S., and Robert P. Brooks, eds. *Correspondence Addressed to John C. Calhoun, 1837–1849*. Washington, D.C.: Government Printing Office, 1930.

Brooks, R. P., ed. "Howell Cobb Papers." *Georgia Historical Quarterly*, V (1921), 50–61, 29–52, 35–55, 43–64 and VI (1922), 35–84, 147–73, 233–64.

[Clingman, Thomas L., ed.]. *Selections from the Speeches and Writings of Hon. Thomas L. Clingman of North Carolina, with Additions and Explanatory Notes*. Raleigh, N.C.: John Nichols, 1877.

Cluskey, M. W., ed. *Speeches, Messages, and Other Writings of the Hon.*

Albert G. Brown, a Senator in Congress from the State of Mississippi. Philadelphia: Jas. B. Smith, 1859.

Coleman, Mrs. Chapman, ed. *The Life of John J. Crittenden, with Selections from His Correspondence and Speeches.* 2 vols.; Philadelphia: J. B. Lippincott, 1871.

Colton, Calvin, ed. *The Private Correspondence of Henry Clay.* New York: A. S. Barnes, 1856.

———, ed. *The Works of Henry Clay: Comprising His Life, Correspondence and Speeches.* 10 vols.; New York and London: G. P. Putnam's Sons, 1904.

Crallé, Richard K., ed. *The Works of John C. Calhoun.* 6 vols.; New York: D. Appleton, 1854–57.

Editors of the Union and American, eds. *Speeches, Congressional and Political, and Other Writings of ex-Governor Aaron V. Brown of Tennessee.* Nashville: J. S. Marling, 1854–[55].

Graf, Leroy P., *et al.*, eds. *The Papers of Andrew Johnson.* 3 vols.; Knoxville: University of Tennessee Press, 1967–.

Gulick, Charles Adams, Jr., *et al.*, eds. *The Papers of Mirabeau Buonaparte Lamar.* 6 vols.; Austin: A. C. Baldwin & Sons and Von-Boeckmann-Jones, 1921–27.

Hall, John, ed. *Forty Years' Familiar Letters of James W. Alexander, D.D., Constituting, with Notes, a Memoir of His Life.* 2 vols.; New York and London: Charles Scribner and Sampson Low, Son, 1860.

Hamilton, J. G. de Roulhac, ed. *The Papers of Thomas Ruffin.* 4 vols.; Raleigh, N.C.: Edwards & Broughton, 1918–20.

——— and Max R. Williams, eds. *The Papers of William Alexander Graham.* 5 vols.; Raleigh, N.C.: State Department of Archives and History, 1957–.

[Hammond, James H.]. *Selections from the Letters and Speeches of the Hon. James H. Hammond of South Carolina.* New York: John F. Trow, 1866.

Hoogenboom, Ari and Herbert Ershkowitz, eds. "Levi Woodbury's 'Intimate Memoranda' of the Jackson Administration." *Pennsylvania Magazine of History and Biography,* XCII (1968), 507–15.

Jameson, J. Franklin, ed. *Correspondence of John C. Calhoun.* Washington, D.C.: Government Printing Office, 1900.

Johannsen, Robert W., ed. *The Letters of Stephen A. Douglas.* Urbana: University of Illinois Press, 1961.

Writings of Hugh Swinton Legaré. . . . Edited by His Sister, 2 vols.; Charleston: Burges & James, 1846.

McGrane, Reginald C., ed. *The Correspondence of Nicholas Biddle, Dealing with National Affairs, 1807–1844.* Boston and New York: Houghton Mifflin, 1919.

Monroe, Haskell M., Jr. and James T. McIntosh, eds. *The Papers of Jefferson Davis.* 2 vols.; Baton Rouge: Louisiana State University Press, 1971–.

Myers, Robert Manson, ed. *Children of Pride: A True Story of Georgia and the Civil War.* New Haven and London: Yale University Press, 1972.

Oliphant, Mary C. Simms, *et al.*, eds. *The Letters of William Gilmore Simms.* 5 vols.; Columbia: University of South Carolina Press, 1952–56.

"Original Letters." *William and Mary Quarterly*, lst Ser., XX (1911), 1–10.

Phillips, Ulrich B., ed. *The Correspondence of Robert Toombs, Alexander H. Stephens and Howell Cobb.* Washington, D.C.: Government Printing Office, 1913.

"Three Letters from Thomas Ritchie to Howell Cobb." *John P. Branch Historical Papers of Randolph-Macon College*, III (1912), 354–57.

"Unpublished Letters of Thomas Ritchie." *John P. Branch Historical Papers of Randolph-Macon College*, III (1911), 199–252.

Rowland, Dunbar, ed. *Jefferson Davis, Constitutionalist: His Letters, Papers and Speeches.* 10 vols.; Jackson: Mississippi Department of Archives and History, 1923.

Samson, William H., ed. *Letters of Zachary Taylor from the Battle-Fields of the Mexican War.* Rochester: Genesee Press, 1908.

Shanks, Henry Thomas, ed. *The Papers of Willie Person Mangum.* 5 vols.; Raleigh, N.C.: State Department of Archives and History, 1950–56.

Shryock, Richard H., ed. "Letters of Richard D. Arnold, M.D., 1808–1876." *Papers of Trinity College Historical Society*, Double Ser., XVIII–XIX (1929), 5–171.

Sioussat, St. George L., ed. "Letters of James K. Polk to Cave Johnson, 1833–1848." *Tennessee Historical Magazine*, I (1915), 209–56.

Stoney, Samuel Gaillard, ed. "The Poinsett-Campbell Correspondence." *South Carolina Historical and Genealogical Magazine*, XLII (1941), 31–52, 122–36, 149–68, and XLIII (1942), 27–34.

"Correspondence of Judge Tucker." *William and Mary Quarterly*, 1st Ser., XII (1903), 84–95.

Tyler, Lyon G. *The Letters and Times of the Tylers.* 3 vols.; Richmond and
    Williamsburg: Whittet & Shepperson, 1884–85, 1896.
"Virginia and Texas, 1844." *John P. Branch Historical Papers of
    Randolph-Macon College,* IV (1913), 116–37.
Weaver, Herbert, *et al.,* eds. *The Correspondence of James K. Polk.* 3
    vols.; Nashville: Vanderbilt University Press, 1969–.
Williams, Amelia W. and Eugene C. Barker, eds. *The Writings of Sam
    Houston, 1813–1863.* 8 vols.; Austin: University of Texas Press,
    1938–43.

Index

Abolition: use of, 58–59; southern reaction to, 59–64; relationship with free soil, 64–65

Adams, John Quincy: policies of, 6, 7, 8, 16, 55; in election of 1828, p. 11; analysis of southern politics, 65; mentioned, 14, 49, 56, 94, 193

Alabama letters, 216–17, 218

Allison letter, 251

American party. See Know-Nothing party

Andrews, E. A., 62

Anti-Mason party, 15

Arnold, Richard, 60, 308

Atchison, David, 346

Badger, George, 285, 343

Balch, Alfred, 84, 194, 240

Bank of the United States: Old Republican opposition to, 49–50; congressional voting on, 50; withdrawal of deposits from, 50–52; in election of 1836, pp. 78, 82, 89; mentioned, 22, 44, 57, 163. See also Banking; Economic issues

Banking: as national issue, 78, 82, 89, 132–33, 155–57, 162, 229; as state issue, 157–62, 230. See also Bank of the United States; Economic issues

Barbour movement: analysis of, 17–22; mentioned, 43, 54, 58, 144

Barbour, Philip P., 17–22, 91

Barringer, Daniel M., 249

Barrow, Alexander, 212

Bell, John: founder of Whig party, 56; in election of 1836, pp. 78, 83; wary of Clay, 250; and Preston bill, 273, 377; in 1850 crisis, 285; on Whig decline, 344, 362; and Kansas-Nebraska Act, 354, 356; as presidential candidate, 370

Benjamin, Judah P., 330, 331

Benton, Thomas Hart, 46, 203

Berrien, John M.: opposition to Jackson party, 14; founder of Whig party, 56; and political use of slavery, 68; supports Harrison, 127–28; opposed to territorial expansion, 228; in 1850 crisis, 285; and Pre-

ston Bill, 377–78; mentioned, 225, 246, 281

Biggs, Asa, 229

Blair, Frank, 47, 87, 130, 193

Borland, Solon, 60

Branch, John, 14, 19–20, 56

Bremer, Fredrika, 62

Brown, Aaron V.: and Texas, 190, 192; on economic issues, 229; in 1850 crisis, 303; in election of 1852, p. 336; attacks Know-Nothings, 366

Brown, Albert G.: congressional race in 1849, pp. 1–4; on southern honor, 70; and Texas, 196; in election of 1852, p. 334

Brown, Bedford, 116, 145, 167

Brown, Milton, 223

Bryan, George, 121, 361

Buchanan, James, 254, 255, 257, 332, 369

Buckingham, James S., 63, 66

Buena Vista, Battle of, 244, 248

Bullitt, Alexander C.: and political use of slavery, 135; and Texas, 207; supports Taylor, 246; and Taylor administration, 280

Butler, Andrew P., 346

Butler, Frances Kemble, 125

Calhoun, John C.: and early Jackson party, 7, 9; and Jackson, 12–14; in election of 1832, p. 43; in nullification crisis, 44, 46, 48–49; in election of 1836, p. 79; and Independent Treasury, 103, 117; returns to Democratic party, 103, 119, 147; influence in South of, 103–18 passim; views of party, 104–18 passim, 171–73, 372; impact on parties, 112–18; abolition resolutions of, 112, 122; Polk, 118, 205–206; and Mexican War, 118, 232, 237; presidential campaign in 1844, pp. 169–75 passim, 180–81; and Tyler, 179–81, 184–88; and Texas, 184–89, 191–92, 223; and Pakenham letters, 191–92, 375–76; and Wilmot Proviso, 234–36, 239; territorial position of, 242, 253, 265, 272; and popular sovereignty, 256; in crisis of 1849–

395